TRAVEL IN THE BYZANTINE WORLD

Society for the Promotion of Byzantine Studies

Publications
10

TRAVEL IN THE BYZANTINE WORLD

Papers from the Thirty-fourth Spring Symposium
of Byzantine Studies, Birmingham, April 2000

edited by
Ruth Macrides

Copyright © 2002 by the Society for the Promotion of Byzantine Studies, Hon. Secretary, James Crow, Dept of Archaeology, The University, Newcastle-upon-Tyne NE1 7RU

All rights reserved. No part of this publication may be reproduced, stored in a retrieval system, or transmitted in any form or by any means, electronic, mechanical, photocopying, recording, or otherwise without the prior permission of the publisher.

Published by Variorum for the Society for the Promotion of Byzantine Studies

Ashgate Publishing Limited	Ashgate Publishing Company
Gower House, Croft Road	131 Main Street
Aldershot, Hants	Burlington
GU11 3HR	VT 05401–5600
England	USA

Ashgate website: http://www.ashgate.com

British Library Cataloguing in Publication Data
Travel in the Byzantine world. – (Publications for the
    Society for the Promotion of Byzantine studies)
    1. Travel, Medieval–Congresses 2. Byzantine Empire–
    Civilization–Congresses 3. Byzantine Empire–Description
    and travel–Congresses
    I. Macrides, R.J. II. Society for the Promotion of Byzantine
    Studies
    914. 9' 5' 042

Library of Congress Control Number: 2001099935

ISBN 0 7546 0788 7

This volume is printed on acid free paper.

Printed and bound in Great Britain by MPG Books Ltd, Bodmin, Cornwall

SOCIETY FOR THE PROMOTION OF BYZANTINE STUDIES – PUBLICATION 10

Contents

Editor's Preface   vii
List of Abbreviations   ix
List of Figures and Tables   xi

Introduction

1.	M. McCormick	Byzantium on the move: imagining a communications history	3

Section I: Going there — the technicalities of travel

2.	J. H. Pryor	Types of ships and their performance capabilities	33
3.	P. Gautier Dalché	Portulans and the Byzantine world	59
4.	K. Belke	Roads and travel in Macedonia and Thrace in the middle and late Byzantine period	73
5.	A. McCabe	Horses and horse-doctors on the road	91
6.	D. Ch. Stathakopoulos	Travelling with the plague	99

Section II: Getting around — the purposes of travel

7.	J. Koder	Maritime trade and the food supply for Constantinople in the middle ages	109
8.	N. Günsenin	Medieval trade in the Sea of Marmara: the evidence of shipwrecks	125
9.	F. van Doorninck, jr	The Byzantine ship at Serçe Limanı: an example of small-scale maritime commerce with Fatimid Syria in the early eleventh century	137
10.	A. Kuelzer	Byzantine and early post-Byzantine pilgrimage to the Holy Land and to Mount Sinai	149

Section III: Being there

11.	K. Ciggaar	Bilingual word lists and phrase lists: for teaching or for travelling?	165
12.	A. Berger	Sightseeing in Constantinople: Arab travellers, c. 900-1300	179
13.	R. Macrides	Constantinople: the crusaders' gaze	193
14.	M. Angold	The decline of Byzantium seen through the eyes of western travellers	213

Section IV: Going over it — representations of travel and space

15.	L. Brubaker	The conquest of space	235
16.	M. E. Mullett	In peril on the sea: travel genres and the unexpected	259

Index   285

Editor's Preface

The contributions to this book derive from papers presented to the 34th Spring Symposium of Byzantine Studies, on 'Travel in the Byzantine World', held in Birmingham, 1-4 April 2000. Symposiasts from three continents travelled in a spring of wintry conditions to see the customary miracle of the blooming daffodils and to discuss a subject which has recently been attracting greater interest but has never been treated as a whole for Byzantium.

Interest in individual travellers has often been expressed and the symposium was no exception in this respect. Three papers were concerned with travellers to Constantinople. But the papers covered also technical aspects, the ways and means of travelling, with sea travel dominating this discussion. A heated debate arose concerning the number of amphoras a *dromon* could hold and how much water a ship would have to carry for the needs of its crew. Or was it wine? Purposes of travel, especially trade and pilgrimage, were examined. Attitudes to travel as reflected in images and in texts constituted another area of investigation. The examination of several shipwrecks and the lively descriptions of the perils of travel in letters, romances, and hagiography left no room for imagining that travel was enjoyable for the Byzantines except, that is, when they were recollecting and recording the experience, 'going over it'. This volume preserves the thematic structure of the symposium and, it is hoped, recaptures the occasion both for those who were there and for those who were not.

The publication of these papers owes a great deal to those who made the symposium possible: Bryer, for his muse-like inspiration and generous sharing of vast experience; the postgraduates of the Centre for Byzantine, Ottoman and Modern Greek Studies who devoted themselves from morning until night to make things run smoothly; the symposiasts for their essential participation and for their warm expression of appreciation; the sponsors, the many charitable trusts, foundations, and individuals — The British Academy, The British Institute of Archaeology at Ankara, The Hellenic Foundation, The A. G. Leventis Foundation, The Seven Pillars of Wisdom Trust, Mr. R. K. Swan and Swan Hellenic, Ashgate Publishing. Their generous and enthusiastic support enabled our speakers to travel, our map to be scrutinised, our refreshments at stopping-off places to flow.

Thanks are due also to Elizabeth Jeffreys, the editor of the series, for advice and encouragement, Angus Stewart who magically transformed these papers into camera-ready copy and to Ece Turnator for preparing the index.

Ruth Macrides
Birmingham, November 2001

List of Abbreviations

AASS	Acta Sanctorum
ACO	Acta Conciliorum Oecumenicorum
AJA	American Journal of Archaeology
AnBoll	Analecta Bollandiana
BAR	British Archaeological Reports
BBA	Berliner Byzantinische Arbeiten
BBOM	Birmingham Byzantine and Ottoman Monographs
BBTT	Belfast Byzantine Texts and Translations
BCH	Bulletin de Correspondance Hellénique
BF	Byzantinische Forschungen
BHG	Biblioteca Hagiographica Graeca
BMGS	Byzantine and Modern Greek Studies
BSl	Byzantinoslavica
Byz	Byzantina
BZ	Byzantinische Zeitschrift
CahArch	Cahiers Archéologiques
CCCont Med	Corpus Christianorum Continuatio Mediaevalis
CCSL	Corpus Christianorum Series Latina
CFHB	Corpus Fontium Historiae Byzantinae
DOP	Dumbarton Oaks Papers
GRBS	Greek, Roman and Byzantine Studies
Hell	Ἑλληνικά
INA	Institute of Nautical Archaeology
JÖB	Jahrbuch der Österreichischen Byzantinistik
JRSt	Journal of Roman Studies
LexMA	Lexikon des Mittelalters
LThK	Lexikon für Theologie und Kirche
MGH	Monumenta Germaniae Historica
OCP	Orientalia Christiana Periodica
ODB	Oxford Dictionary of Byzantium
PG	Patrologia Graeca
PL	Patrologia Latina
PLP	Prosopographisches Lexikon der Palaiologenzeit
PO	Patrologia Orientalis

PPS	Pravoslavnyj Palestinskij Sbornik (St. Petersburg, 1883-1913)
RAC	Reallexikon für Antike und Christentum
RE	Paulys Realencyclopädie der classischen Altertumswissenschaft
REB	Revue des Études Byzantines
REG	Revue des Études Grecques
RSBN	Rivista di Studi Bizantini e Neoellenici
SC	Sources Chrétiennes
PSPBS	Publications for the Society for the Promotion of Byzantine Studies
StT	Studi e Testi
Theoph.	Theophanes, *Chronographia*, ed. C. de Boor, 2 vols. (Leipzig, 1883-1885)
TIB	Tabula Imperii Byzantini
TM	Travaux et Mémoires
WBS	Wiener Byzantinistische Studien
ZDPV	Zeitschrift des deutschen Palästinavereins
ZPE	Zeitschrift für Papyrologie und Epigraphik

List of Figures and Tables

Figures

1.1	Communications microzones and local ceramic distribution: Byzantine Galilee and Judaea	15
2.1	Longitudinal section of a tenth-century bireme dromon	39
2.2	Oarage system of a tenth-century bireme dromon	42
2.3	Tenth-century bireme dromon heeling under sail to ten degrees	44
2.4	Oars of a tenth-century bireme dromon drawn in the middle of the return stroke at 67° to the centre line	52
2.5	Stowage of barrels or amphorae	56
4.1	Map of the Balkan peninsula showing the main roads and cities mentioned (adapted from John V.A. Fine, jr., *The Early Medieval Balkans*. Ann Arbor, 1983, map 3 and 4)	75
5.1	A horse suffering from exhaustion (*Parisinus graecus* 2244, f. f. 3v)	93
8.1	Map showing the sites mentioned in the text	126
8.2	Discoveries to date around the Marmara Islands	130
15.1	Madaba, mosaic map	250
15.2	*Christian Topography*, the journey of Saul from Jerusalem to Damascus (Sinai. gr. 1186, f. 126v)	251
15.3	Madaba, mosaic detail: Jerusalem	251
15.4	Madaba, mosaic detail: Nile delta	252
15.5	Umm al-Rasas, Church of the Lions, mosaic detail: Kastron Mefaa	253
15.6	Umm al-Rasas, St. Stephen, mosaic detail: Kastron Mefaa	253
15.7	Umm al-Rasas, St. Stephen, mosaic detail: Jerusalem	254
15.8	Damascus, Great Mosque, mosaic detail: Barada landscape	254
15.9	*Christian topography*: the world in the shape of the ark of the covenant (Sinai. gr. 1186, f. 69r)	255

15.10 Vienna Genesis: Rebecca and Eliezer (Vienna, Nationalbibliothek, cod. theol. gr. 31, pict. 13)   256
15.11 Paris Gregory: scenes from the life of Joseph (Paris. gr. 510, f. 69v)   256
15.12 Paris Gregory: detail, parable of the Good Samaritan (Paris. gr. 510, f. 143v)   257
15.13 Paris Gregory: detail, Gregory leaving his family (Paris. gr. 510, f. 452r)   257

Tables

1.1 Byzantine travellers: known birthplaces compared with residences   24

2.1 Durations and speeds of voyages of Porphyrios of Gaza according to Mark the Deacon   36
2.2 Some reported voyages of ancient and medieval galleys and galley fleets with generally favourable prevailing winds   48

Introduction

1. Byzantium on the move: imagining a communications history

M. McCormick

In memory of Nikos Oikonomides, friend and teacher

Among Europe's medieval civilisations, Byzantium poses most pressingly the historical problem of travel and communications. For a thousand years, Byzantium succeeded at the daunting challenge of integrating politically, economically and culturally lands and peoples that today comprise some dozen independent states. The processes that led to that success were static and kinetic. Static integration did not require physical movement, though movement might well foster it: shared religion, élite language and cultural values (that is costume or cuisine, as well as literature or sacred art) helped weave together the disparate peoples. Even in a remote province, for instance, precedence in state dignities defined who went first to receive communion every Sunday.[1]

But this symposium concerned the kinetic processes of integration, which required travel and transport. A centralised state and its supercity lent transport exceptional administrative and economic urgency.[2]

---

[1] On these two types of integration: M. McCormick, 'The imperial edge: Italo-Byzantine identity, movement and integration, A.D. 650-950', in H. Ahrweiler and A. E. Laiou, eds., *Studies on the Internal Diaspora of the Byzantine Empire* (Washington, D.C., 1998), 17-52, here 18; for Sunday services, McCormick, 'The imperial edge', 45-52.

[2] I. Ševčenko's essay on the mental and other relations of capital and provinces remains fundamental: 'Constantinople viewed from the eastern provinces in the middle Byzantine period', reprinted in Ševčenko, *Ideology, Letters and Culture in the Byzantine World* (London, 1982), no. VI; for inter-provincial communications, see McCormick, 'The imperial edge', (as in n. 1), 41-42.

From *Travel in the Byzantine World*, ed. Ruth Macrides. Copyright © 2002 by the Society for the Promotion of Byzantine Studies. Published by Ashgate Publishing Ltd, Gower House, Croft Road, Aldershot, Hampshire, GU11 3HR, Great Britain.

How did Byzantium capitalise on the communications systems that arose from the interplay of myriad historical actors and factors — bureaucracies, producer and consumer regions, shipping lanes, and so on? Byzantinists have been interested in the theme at least since Philippson in the 1930s, and that interest continues today in books and dissertations, as well as in the *Tabula imperii byzantini*.[3] But more remains to be done. Where should we look for the communications world of Byzantium? And what might we find, now and down the road? First, however, a word on some basic concepts, for they shape how we look and, therefore, what we might find.

Scholars speak, traditionally, of transport — the movement of things, especially goods — and of travel, the movement of people. It is good to be clear what exactly we mean when we use some critical terms that recur regularly. 'Routes' for instance, might refer to a particular way of getting from point A to point B, narrowly defined as, for instance, a road system and its local variants. When, for convenience's sake, we segregate segments of a route by mode of transport — overland vs. sea or river legs of a journey — we must remember that such segmentation is merely an analytical convenience: most routes incorporated multiple modes of transport. For instance, the Via Egnatia linked the Adriatic port of Dyrrachion with the Aegean one of Thessalonike and, ultimately, Constantinople. West of Dyrrachion, and from Thessalonike or Maroneia eastward, travellers could take ships.[4] One's goal was not to walk on the Egnatian Way or ride aboard a ship, but to get to the capital from Bari, using whatever infrastructures were most attractive at a particular time, for a particular stretch of route. 'Corridors' refers more broadly to the constellation of roughly parallel routes across the same regions, for example, the different routes that cross the Balkans over the some 300 km swath from the Via Egnatia to the Gulf of Corinth. 'Infrastructure' means physical structures: roads, as well as bridges, ports, and the like. But it should include groups and institutions that fostered travel: the

---

[3] See esp. A. Philippson, *Das Byzantinische Reich als geographische Erscheinung* (Leiden, 1939); G. Makris, *Studien zur spätbyzantinischen Schiffahrt* (Genoa, 1988); E. Malamut, *Sur la route des saints byzantins* (Paris, 1993); I. Ch. Dimitroukas, *Reisen und Verkehr im Byzantinischen Reich vom Anfang des 6. Jhr. bis zur Mitte des 11. Jhr.* (Athens, 1997); the various chapters in *TIB*, devoted to 'Die Verkehrsverbindungen', etc., e.g., P. Soustal, *TIB* 1 (Vienna, 1976), 90-104 and J. Koder *et al.*, *TIB* 10 (Vienna, 1998), 99-108; as well as the bibliography cited below.

[4] Land, sea, and mixed travel are well attested along this corridor in the ninth century: see e.g. *Ignatios Diakonos und die Vita des hl. Gregorios Dekapolites* (BHG 711), ed. G. Makris (Stuttgart, 1997), 52.1-29, 112-114; 53.1-2, 116; 77.1-2, 140; *Liber pontificalis*, ed. L. Duchesne and C. Vogel, 2 (1886-1957; repr., Paris, 1981), 180.1-7.

constellation of men, beasts, obligations, and resources that constituted the imperial post, for example, or the human expertise it took to build and maintain ships.

Not all trips are created equal. Another indispensable conceptual clarification classifies differing types of movements by travel ranges. In my own research at least three different ambits stand out clearly. 'Long-distance' travel surpasses 500 km: for example, movements between Constantinople and the frontier, or further. In terms of the time units medieval people themselves preferred for describing longer trips, this means, roughly, more than 10 days' or two weeks' travel.[5] An 'intermediate' travel range encompasses regional and inter-regional trips, between about 100 and 500 km. The third ambit comprises micromovements covering less than a hundred km, and implying travel times lasting between a few hours and a few days. The three ranges of movements are often interconnected. Even so, each may obey its own rules and rhythms, and one must not confuse their potentially divergent patterns. At sea, the long-distance *dromon* speeding urgent news from the centre to the commander of Byzantine Bari will have quickly left behind the small ships whose frequent short hops linked the quarters of the capital and its hinterland, just as it will have swept past trading vessels working along the Aegean coast. On land, a donkey's effective load drops once it walks more than 15 km.[6]

Another, broader category is 'communications': quite simply, *all* forms of the movements of people — whether individuals or groups — and things — whether ships, relics, letters, information, or even diseases. Envisioning the problem more broadly as one of communications invites us to supplement our limited source base by casting a wider net for Byzantium on the move. This in fact expands the evidence we can bring to bear on the underlying economic, social, and even mental structures which shaped the Byzantines' world.

One example will illustrate how this concept can help address seemingly intractable problems. Since Henri Pirenne, historians have argued about Mediterranean merchants and long-distance shipping in the eighth and ninth century. A comprehensive review of the Latin and Greek evidence turns up more long-distance merchant voyages than were previously known, but not so many as to revolutionise the debate: 22 voyages, involving 18 specifically documented merchants. Nearly a quarter (5; 23%) of these traders had business connections or a home base

---

[5] M. McCormick, *Origins of the European Economy. Communications and Commerce, A.D. 300-900* (Cambridge, 2001), chap. 16 (hereafter McCormick, *Origins*).

[6] See below, n. 42.

in the Byzantine empire; another third came from the Byzantine protectorate of Venice (7; 37%).[7] With Pirenne, some historians have argued that so few merchant trips are mentioned because so few occurred. Others maintain that the same evidence shows just the opposite. For them, these merchant voyages are but the visible tip of a huge iceberg of merchant travellers that have gone unrecorded. With so little evidence to go on, stalemate set in, and debate has continued inconclusively. The way out of the stalemate proved to be simple in conception, if not in execution. By turning to the whole universe of communications, and tracking down and plotting over time and space *all* voyages in the Mediterranean including those implied by the movements of, for instance, objects or news, by expanding our net to encompass the broader phenomenon of communications, it proved possible to discern hitherto invisible instances of movement. And these neglected communications occur in such numbers — 410 to be exact — that it suddenly became possible to speak of rhythms and volumes of communications, of the ship movements implied by the travels across the sea of pilgrims, diplomats, mercenaries, and exiles. These movements were not always those of commercial vessels, though often they were that. But they supplied a general context of shipping movements, routes, and infrastructures. That general context showed that the 22 explicitly commercial voyages were in fact typical of a much larger, unobserved universe of shipping. In a word, this new method made possible the deduction that communications — and commerce — between western Europe and the eastern Mediterranean surged dramatically in the final decades of the eighth century.

If the study of communications can shed light on a controversy as intractable as that of Mediterranean trade in the early middle ages, surely it can contribute to discovering Byzantium on the move. Explicit descriptions of sea voyages are the place to start. Theodore Stoudites, for one, has left an exquisitely detailed account of his spring trip from Asia Minor to Thessalonike in 797.[8] But it is not enough simply to

---

[7] See in general, my *Origins*, chap. 9; for the total, Table 14.1. Business connections with, or within, the Byzantine empire: an Egyptian ship sailing between Naples and the Aegean in 723, McCormick, *Origins*, R (= 'Register of Communications') 109; R186, Byzantine slavers operating off the Lombard coast and trading with the Arabs; R417, merchant ships setting out from Ephesos; R523, Basil, a small-time merchant and Palestinian monk, sailed back and forth between Rome and Constantinople at least once because of business; R729, a merchant sailing between Rome and Demetrias. Venetians: R147; R230 and 233; R321; R406; R408; R428.

[8] *Theodori Studitae Epistulae*, ed. G. Fatouros, CFHB, 31.1 (Berlin, 1992), *ep*. 3, 13.68-15.105; for place-names and dates, Fatouros, *Epistulae*, pp. 143*-146*; further discussion, McCormick, *Origins*, chap. 16; and, for the routes, J. Lefort, 'Les communications entre

tabulate what he explicitly records. We must use modern navigational aids, charts, and ship guides like the Royal Navy's *Mediterranean Pilot* to force Theodore's and others' descriptions of sea voyages to yield their full testimony in the light of local sailing conditions.[9] Even less fully recorded ship movements can prove precious, if they are analysed in the same way, and viewed in the light of a larger database of ship movements. Liudprand of Cremona's story of sailing along the west coast of Greece, for example, appears perspicacious when analysed with the *Mediterranean Pilot* in hand.[10] Byzantine, western and Arab sources preserve much such partial evidence which begs for study with new eyes.[11]

Even so, the usual narrative sources will not suffice. One type of less conventional source in particular boasts abundant travellers: it describes ships' courses, their crews, even sailing speeds or dates. Yet historians of communications have almost entirely ignored these travellers, except when they have used them inadvertently. These travellers occur in Byzantine historical fiction.

We have been allergic to fiction. The reason is itself historical, since most fiction is masquerading as hagiography of an earlier era. Ihor Ševčenko and others have given us a start in retrieving the hundreds, perhaps thousands of pages of hagiographical romances from the dustbin of historical research.[12] Quite unlike the erotic romances of

---

Constantinople et Bithynie', in C. Mango and G. Dagron, eds., *Constantinople and its Hinterland*, (Aldershot, 1995), 207-218.

[9] Following John Pryor's example; see e.g. his 'The voyages of Saewulf', in *Peregrinationes tres: Saewulf, John of Würzburg, Theodericus*, ed. R.B.C. Huygens, CCCont Med 139 (Turnhout, 1994), 35-57; see also Pryor, 'Types of ships and their performance capabilities', in this volume. For Byzantinists, the most relevant navigational guides are Great Britain, Admiralty, *Black Sea Pilot*, 12th edn. (n. pl., 1990), *Mediterranean Pilot*, 10th edn. (Taunton, 1978-88), and Great Britain, Air Ministry, Meteorological Office, *Weather in the Mediterranean*, 2nd edn. (London, 1962); among regional guides, I have also found helpful H. M. Denham, *The Aegean. A Sea-Guide to its Coasts and Islands*, 5th edn. (Southampton, 1983).

[10] Liudprand of Cremona, *Legatio*, 58-65, ed. J. Becker, *MGH Scriptores rerum Germanicarum* (1915), 207.8-212.26; McCormick, *Origins*, chap. 16.

[11] Two good collections of material are P. Koukoules, Βυζαντινῶν βίος καὶ πολιτισμός IV (Athens, 1951), 318-341 and V (Athens, 1952), 344-386, and A. Kazhdan et al., *Dumbarton Oaks Hagiography Database of the Eighth, Ninth and Tenth Centuries* (Washington, D.C., 1999), now on line and free (http://www.doaks.org/Hagio.html), as well as the many travels mentioned in Dimitroukas, *Reisen und Verkehr* (as in n. 3).

[12] I. Ševčenko, 'Religious missions seen from Byzantium', *Harvard Ukrainian Studies* 12-13 (1988-1989), 7-27, here 20-23, made a powerful case for using fictional missions to illuminate real ones. Scholars of Byzantine Italy have been quick to seize this new opportunity, e.g.: A. A. Longo, 'Siracusa e Taormina nell'agiografia italogreca', *RSBN* n.s. 27 (1990 [1991]), 33-54 and C. J. Stallman, 'The past in hagiographic texts: S. Marcian of

the twelfth century, these historical novels abound in travel and geographical information.[13] The most outrageous are set in the remote, apostolic past. Forced to invent the background of their heroes' movements, pious forgers usually looked no further than the realities of their own time. The very anachronisms that proved their undoing in the eyes of earlier scholars are precisely what make these historical novels so precious for us. Do we laugh to learn that a ninth-century Apulian imagined that Venice existed in Roman times to send ships to apostolic Alexandria?[14] When the laughter subsides, we recognise that inadvertently, the way Byzantine fiction imagined antiquity preserves precious truths about the age in which it was written. Naturally, we must be careful to separate reality from fantasy. Yet even flights of fancy follow what is imaginable. Thus the ninth-century magic ship that flew St. Leo of Catania to Constantinople in one day, passed over Reggio, Crotone and Otranto, an itinerary that Byzantium's real, water-bound ships might have followed.[15] Similarly, a supposed late antique hagiographer who, in fact, was probably writing in Rome around 800, wraps fourth- and seventh-century personalities around a late sixth-century Sicilian. The author probably came from the region of Agrigento and wished to bolster the veneration of his home town

---

Syracuse', in G. Clarke, ed., *Reading the Past in Late Antiquity* (Singapore, 1990), 347-365; M. F. Auzépy, 'L'analyse littéraire et l'historien: l'exemple des vies de saints iconoclastes', *BSl* 53 (1992), 57-67; McCormick, 'The imperial edge', 36-37, and, on the general problem of Sicilian hagiography, G. Philippart, 'L'hagiographie sicilienne dans le cadre de l'hagiographie de l'Occident', in R. Barcellona and S. Pricoco, eds., *La Sicilia nella tarda antichità e nell'alto medioevo. Religione e società* (n. pl., 1999), 167-204, esp. 200-201, n. 165-166.

[13] F. Meunier, 'Le voyage imaginaire dans le roman byzantin du XIIème siècle', *Byz.* 68 (1998), 72-90, observes that the romances either sharply circumscribe the ample geographic horizons of their ancient models or leave reality completely behind and invent an imaginary geography. See also M. Mullett, 'In peril on the sea: travel genres and the unexpected', in this volume.

[14] *Vita Leucii* (*Bibliotheca hagiographica latina* nos. 4894, 4894b), ed. *Bibliotheca casinensis*, 3 (Monte Cassino, 1877), 'Florilegium', 358-365, here 363. F. Lanzoni, *Le diocesi d'Italia dalle origini al principio del secolo VII (an. 604)*, 2nd edn., StT 35, 1 (Vatican City, 1927), 306-308, dated it to the eighth-tenth centuries, since Brindisi is not depicted as subordinate to Rome. In fact, it must be post-828, since it mentions (p. 363) the translation of the relics of St. Mark to Venice. The work is preserved in a late eleventh-century manuscript, Monte Cassino, Archivio della Badia, ms. 146; E. A. Lowe and V. Brown, *The Beneventan Script*, 2nd edn. 2 (Rome, 1980), 72.

[15] *Vita Leonis Cataniae* (*BHG* 981), 9, ed. A. A. Longo, 'La Vita di S. Leone vescovo di Catania', *RSBN* n.s. 26 (1989 [1990]), 3-98, here 89.1-90.6, and 12, 93.1-17. For its composition c. 813-40, *ibid.*, p. 54; cf. on this text M. F. Auzépy, 'L'analyse littéraire et l'historien' (as in n. 12), 62-67 and A. A. Longo, 'A proposito di un articolo recente sull'agiografia iconoclasta', *RSBN* n.s. 29 (1993), 3-17.

saint.[16] He lards his novel with details of the hero's imaginary voyages: sailing dates and durations, routes, etc. Analysis of his data in the light of real movements shows that they usually conform to the prevailing patterns of Byzantine communications around 800.[17] In short, we must not fear to turn to fiction in order to establish fact.

More light comes from those indirect indicators which so fascinated the late and lamented Alexander Kazhdan, and which have begun to yield a kind of psychology of travel among the Byzantine elite.[18] For once Byzantine rhetoric helps rather than hinders the historian. The vocabulary and metaphors littérateurs used *for* travel point to the mental associations that travel carried with it in the Byzantine mind. Symptomatically, for instance, the classical Greek verb *skyllein*, 'to trouble', 'bother' etc., is used to mean 'to come' in the ninth century.[19] The metaphors *of* travel are also precious. 'Ship' for example, meant different things in the Byzantine mind. The 'ship of state' is a famously positive metaphor and it also did duty for the church.[20] But there was something sinister about ships: their dark shapes slicing through the water made ninth-century men think of snakes, and snakes evoked ships.[21] A literary flourish confirms that night sailing was familiar in tenth-century Byzantine waters. Unless they had seen helmsmen steering by the stars, how would listeners have made sense of a biographer's metaphor, that St. Theodore was 'a bright star ... guiding the steering of that spiritual ship of the brethren', that is, the

---

[16] Leontius of St. Sabas, *Vita Gregorii Agrigenti* (BHG 707), ed. A. Berger, *Leontios presbyteros von Rom, Das Leben des heiligen Gregorios von Agrigent*, Berliner BBA 60 (Berlin, 1995), 26-28 and 49-50; he shows great familiarity with both Rome and Agrigento.

[17] See Berger, *Das Leben des heiligen Gregorios von Agrigent*, intro. pp. 51-52 on Italian and African ship movements; cf. for further examples, McCormick, *Origins*, e.g. ch. 22 n. 40 or ch. 25 n. 68.

[18] A. Kazhdan and G. Constable, *People and Power in Byzantium* (Washington, D.C., 1982), 162-178; attitudes toward the sea introduce Kazhdan's analysis of the literary values and attitudes of Niketas Choniates and Nikephoros Gregoras: Kazhdan and S. Franklin, *Studies on Byzantine Literature of the Eleventh and Twelfth Centuries* (Cambridge, 1984), 263-278; and, esp., C. Galatariotou, 'Travel and perception in Byzantium', *DOP* 47 (1993), 221-241; cf. Mullett, 'In peril on the sea: travel genres and the unexpected', in this volume.

[19] Thus, e.g., *Vita Davidis, Symeonis, et Georgii* (BHG 494), 8, ed. [J. Van den Gheyn], 'Acta graeca Ss. Davidis, Symeonis et Georgii', *AnBoll* 18 (1899), 209-259, here 218.8.

[20] See in general H. Rahner, *Symbole der Kirche. Die Ekklesiologie der Väter* (Salzburg, 1964), 304-405 and 432-503; for, e.g., the ship of state in Niketas Choniates, Kazhdan and Franklin, *Studies on Byzantine Literature*, 265.

[21] The Greek word *chelandion*, which designates a new type of Byzantine warship, probably derives from words for 'water-snake' or 'eel': H. Kahane and R. Kahane, 'Abendland und Byzanz: Sprache', *Reallexikon der Byzantinistik* 1 (Amsterdam, 1970-1976), 345-640, here 412-413; a snake sliding into the water evoked a ship: Sabas, *Vita S. Ioannicii* (BHG 935), *AASS* Nov. 2.1.361A.

monastery of Stoudiou?[22] And the sea's terrifying power comes through loud and clear in Byzantine blessings for travellers, or the vows relieved sailors scratched into the rocks of an Aegean cove.[23]

The search for Byzantium on the move must not stop at the explicit descriptions of travel, real or imagined, and literary conceits. The great number of communications that lie implicit in the sources offer precious proxy data on travels. At the very least, they create a deeper context for analysing explicit accounts of trips. Indeed, the aggregate implicit evidence itself sometimes uncovers new patterns. For example, there is no complete description of a trip from Constantinople to the early medieval west. Yet assembling the totality of trips and scattered details — date of departure or arrival, intermediary stages in the voyage, etc. — that emerge from the prosopography of all travellers, evinces changing patterns over time and space. Whether or not the sources tell us exactly how they travelled, the picture of where individuals travelled, and when, allows one to deduce the infrastructure of travel that they used. This method of analysing the 410 movements mentioned earlier plots how Byzantium's routes to the west changed between 750 and 850. It discloses not only the nature and course of a route but its history, for routes — no less than empires or estates — changed, grew and declined.

This sort of study should consider large series of dated administrative documents. Patriarchal registers conceal powerful data on communications networks and their ebb and flow over the years and the seasons, especially if we can imagine new ways to question them.[24]

---

[22] *Vita Nicolai Studitae* (*BHG* 1365), *PG* 105.869B; the phrase conceivably echoes Ignatios the Deacon's prologue to his *Vita Nicephori patriarchae* (*BHG* 1335), ed. C. De Boor, *Nicephori archiepiscopi Constantinopolitani opuscula historica* (Leipzig, 1880), 139.18-19. On the *Life* and its date, A. Kazhdan, *ODB* 2.1471.

[23] E.g. ΕΥΧΟΛΟΓΙΟΝ *sive rituale Graecorum*, ed. J. Goar (Venice, 1730; repr. Graz, 1960), 636-637, a prayer for a storm at sea, according to which the human disorder (*ataxia*) of sin precipitates the disorder of nature; 680-1, a *panagia* ritual for a departing traveller; 685, a blessing for the departure of a patriarch. Cf. the early medieval *L'eucologio Barberini gr. 336*, eds. S. Parenti and E. Velkovska, Bibliotheca *Ephemerides liturgicae*, Subsidia, 80 (Rome, 1995), 203 (patriarchal blessing for a *dromon*), and 213 (for travellers). G. Kiourtzian, *Recueil des inscriptions grecques chrétiennes des Cyclades*, TM Monographies 12 (Paris, 2000), 135-200, has just published an important group of graffiti, mostly by early Byzantine sailors, from the island of Syros; I am grateful to him for sharing the proofs of this work with me.

[24] See below for one example. The modern registers are the place to start: for the pope, P. Jaffé, S. Loewenfeld *et al.*, *Regesta pontificum Romanorum ab condita ecclesia ad annum post Chr. n. MCXCVIII* (Leipzig, 2nd edn., 1885-1888), hereafter JL; for the patriarchs, V. Grumel and J. Darrouzès, *Les régestes des actes du patriarcat de Constantinople*, 2nd edn. (Paris, 1972-), particularly the rich series of the 14th century, ed. H. Hunger, O. Kresten, *et al.*, *Das Register des Patriarchats von Konstantinopel*, CFHB 19.1- (Vienna, 1981-). Note,

Letter collections are nearly as valuable if, like those of Photios or Theodore Stoudites, they allow us to localise a fair number of addressees. Of course, one must take into account the principles by which the letters were selected for the collection. Even so, examining the letters as a whole raises some interesting questions. Thus the places to which Photios sent 66 (out of 298) of his letters are clear. In his case, the addressees' social status influenced the letters selected for inclusion. No one will be surprised to learn that Constantinople looms large in his epistolary geography, as it does in practically every other facet of Byzantine life. But it is still important to recognise that the single largest share of surviving letters Photios sent to one town went from Constantinople to Constantinople (13 of 66, i.e. 20%). The proportion only climbs if one includes other addressees in the capital region. A substantial contingent also went to western Europe (13); a slightly larger group (16 of 66; 24%) travelled to the Arab world. Among western addressees, one is surprised to meet Venetian prelates. In the ninth century, the Venetian church was scarcely home to the sort of leading figures with whom one would expect a patriarch to correspond. Rather, their presence among Photios' correspondents probably reflects 'spill-over' from the newly burgeoning Venetian shipping centres, which had resuscitated an Adriatic corridor of communications around 775.[25] Venice had become a hub through which communications directed to disparate places like Rome or France might now transit; the swelling streams of ships fostered increased Byzantine communications with church centres in the Veneto.

Coins and seals provide wonderful proxy data for the movements of human beings. We know where most Byzantine coins were minted. Knowing where they were found is a step towards tracing their travel. It is only a first step because, barring unusual circumstances, coins will not often have travelled directly to their place of deposit. Yet sometimes hoards can indicate the ports — and therefore the route — through which a purse full of money travelled on the way to its final resting place. Thus, copper coins from a shipwreck off the French coast indicate that, late in Heraclius' reign, this doomed Byzantine merchant mariner sailed from Constantinople and stopped in Sicily, on its way to the Visigothic port of Narbonne.[26] A Roman case study has

---

however, that the seasonal datings of Grumel, as well as of F. Dölger, *Regesten der Kaiserurkunden des oströmischen Reiches* (Munich, Berlin, 1924-1965), are often mere guesses based on assumptions about travelling seasons.

[25] McCormick, *Origins*, chap. 18.
[26] C. Morrisson, 'Les monnaies byzantines', in Y. Solier, ed., *Les épaves de Gruissan*, Archaeonautica, 3 (Paris, 1981), 35-52.

shown how a large series even of stray coins can supply new information about the routes and tempo of communications.[27]

About 50,000 lead seals survive from the imperial administration. When we know their place of deposit, we can map the flow of command.[28] Localised seals are particularly precious because the documents to which they were once attached are less likely than coins to have made multiple movements. Each seal find stands for the movement of a messenger who once transmitted the instructions of empire; as their numbers grow, they may suggest changing flows over time.

For the era before the seals become loquacious, ceramic distribution is revealing. Long-distance shipments of fine tableware and a few distinctive amphoras first captured scholars' attention;[29] they multiply a hundredfold the instances of well-mapped transport, as identified production sites and chronology improve every year.[30] Whether they travelled for trade or piggybacked on taxes, the distribution patterns of fineware such as African red slip dishes depict Byzantine Africa's changing long-distance communications; Phocaean ware is starting to do the same for Asia Minor. The Gaza amphoras that transported the powerful Palestinian wine savoured from Marseille to Constantinople are taking their place next to them.[31]

---

[27] F. Berger, *Untersuchungen zu römerzeitlichen Münzfunden in Nordwestdeutschland*, Studien zu Fundmünzen der Antike, 9 (Berlin, 1992). For a sketch of broad patterns of Constantinopolitan coin circulation, see C. Morrisson, 'La diffusion de la monnaie de Constantinople: routes commerciales ou routes politiques?' in *Constantinople and its Hinterland* (as in n. 8), 77-89.

[28] J. C. Cheynet and C. Morrisson, 'Lieux de trouvaille et circulation des sceaux', in N. Oikonomides, ed., *Studies in Byzantine Sigillography*, 2 (Washington, D.C., 1990), 105-136.

[29] See e.g., recently, C. Panella, 'Merci e scambi nel Mediterraneo tardoantico', in A. Schiavone, ed., *Storia di Roma*, 3.2 (Turin, 1993), 613-697; P. Reynolds, *Trade in the Western Mediterranean, AD 400-700: The Ceramic Evidence*, BAR International Series 604 (Oxford, 1995), as well as the many important contributions in *Ceramica in Italia: VI-VII secolo*, ed. L. Saguì, Biblioteca di Archeologia medievale, 14 (Florence, 1998).

[30] Some key studies of late Roman production sites are M. Mackensen, *Die spätantiken Sigillata- und Lampentöpfereien von El Mahrine (Nordtunisien)*, Münchner Beiträge zur Vor- und Frühgeschichte, 50 (Munich, 1993); J. Y. Empereur and M. Picon, 'Les régions de production d'amphores impériales en Méditerranée orientale', in *Amphores romaines et histoire économique. Dix ans de recherche*, Collection de l'École française de Rome, 114 (Rome, 1989), 223-248; B. Johnson and L. Stager, 'Ashkelon: wine emporium of the Holy Land', in S. Gitin, ed., *Recent Excavations in Israel* (Boston, 1995), 95-109.

[31] E.g. the articles cited above, in n. 29-30; Marseilles: M. Bonifay and D. Piéri, 'Amphores du Ve au VIIe s. à Marseille: nouvelles données sur la typologie et le contenu', *Journal of Roman Archaeology* 8 (1995), 94-117; at Constantinople: J. W. Hayes, *Excavations at Saraçhane in Istanbul*, 2, *The Pottery* (Princeton, 1992), 64-65: Gaza amphoras are the second most common type in contexts from the construction of St. Polyeuktos, i.e. A.D. 524-527.

Around 700 these particular wares peter out of the archaeological record, but that does not mean the middle Byzantinist can neglect this kind of evidence.

Archaeology and fictional travellers illustrate how a multi-pronged approach juxtaposes evidence of independent origins to clarify communications infrastructures. A Greek passion preserved in eleventh-century manuscripts tells the wild tale of St. Nikon of Naples. This pagan soldier was converted by his mother's entreaties and Christ's help in fighting barbarians who were threatening 'Roman' Naples. He sailed off to seek spiritual guidance in Constantinople.[32] En route, St. Nikon put in at Chios, where he decided to 'get close' to God. A vision instructed him to board the first ship he met and go wherever it was heading. That first ship was going to Mt. Ganos (modern Gaziköy), on the western shore of the Sea of Marmara. Why there? Around 900, an Arab description of the main shipping route between the Aegean and the Black Sea says nothing about Ganos.[33] Because the Mount attracted monks in the tenth or eleventh century, I was inclined to reckon its mention merely as a fantastic detail which threw more light on the geography of spirituality than on patterns of middle Byzantine shipping. Then I met Nergis Günsenin's discovery of a large-scale amphora production centre at Mt. Ganos. Those containers (Günsenin I) transported the wine produced in this zone which Turkish vintners still favour today. Dr Günsenin has already uncovered seven shipwrecks off the site: they are still carrying their wine containers; one held a cargo estimated at 20,000 amphoras.[34] Moreover, laboratory analysis has detected some Ganos amphoras aboard the eleventh-century shipwreck at Serçe Limanı — on the southern stretch of the coastal route that runs past Chios.[35] Suddenly, archaeology revealed that real life inspired

---

[32] (*BHG* 1360), *AASS* Mart. 3 (1865). *15B-*18E; two southern Italian 11th-C. MSS survive: McCormick, 'The imperial edge', 37, n. 39; he supposedly was martyred and buried at Taormina, which was probably the cult centre.

[33] Ibn Khurradadhbih, tr. M. J. De Goeje, *Ibn Khordâdbeh, Kitâb al-masâlik wa'l-mamâlik* (Leiden, 1889), 76.

[34] N. Günsenin, 'Le vin de Ganos: les amphores et la mer', in M. Balard *et al..*, *EYΨYXIA. Mélanges offerts à Hélène Ahrweiler* 1 (Paris, 1998), 281-287; N. Günsenin, 'Ganos, centre de production d'amphores à l'époque byzantine', *Anatolia antiqua* 2 (1993), 193-201; P. Armstrong and N. Günsenin, 'Glazed pottery production at Ganos', *Anatolia antiqua*, 3 (1995), 179-201. See also N. Günsenin, 'Medieval trade in the sea of Marmara: the evidence of shipwrecks', in this volume.

[35] N. Günsenin and H. Hatcher, 'Analyses chimiques comparatives des amphores de Ganos, de l'île de Marmara et de l'épave de Serçe Limanı', *Anatolia antiqua* 5 (1997), 249-260. For the wreck at Serçe Limanı see F. van Doorninck, 'The Byzantine ship at Serçe Limanı: an example of small-scale maritime commerce with Fatimid Syria in the early eleventh century' in this volume.

this detail of Nikon's fictitious voyage: a flourishing wine trade centred on the mountain explains that no middle Byzantine eyebrow went up at the implied banality of ships bound for Mt. Ganos. What is more, if the fictitious life were invented in Byzantine Italy, as the saint's cult centre and the manuscripts might suggest, this particular port of call on the Sea of Marmara was well known at the western edge of the Byzantine communications world. As ongoing research clarifies the changing reach of the Ganos amphoras, from the Black Sea to Chios and beyond, we may also begin to observe rising and falling ship movements connecting to this particular port. One could push the problem further, in terms of economics and communications networks. Are we not witnessing here the rise of one of the new sources of supply scholars have hypothesised for the Byzantine capital, after the Arab triumph cut off the old ones?[36] Archaeology and hagiography join hands to recover a once lost shipping pattern, and underscore that ceramics have a part to play in the communications history of middle Byzantium.

So far, I have emphasised macrozones and long-distance communications. Archaeologists are now detecting regional and sub-regional microsystems of communications. One recent study shows how early Byzantine ceramics were manufactured, probably in the Judaean countryside, and marketed at Jerusalem. In Justinian's time, these eight Judaean wares replaced locally the imports of Africa and Asia Minor, and then developed through the Persian invasion, Heraclius' reconquest, and the Islamic triumph.[37] Their geography delineates distribution microzones of differing densities, and appears to follow the Roman roads in the region.[38] The Judaean hill country defines the main diffusion area, which looks like a distinct economic region. To the north the products rarely went beyond the lower Galilee; to the south a few reach Nessana. They do not much penetrate the nearby coastal areas.

Three microzones stand out. A first, dense distribution falls well within a radius of 15 km from Jerusalem (see fig. 1.1). On foot, this implies distances of two to three hours from the central point, at the usual walking speed of some three English miles (4.8 km) per hour. The next, lighter density spreads over a 40 km radius, i.e. some eight hours'

---

[36] The present chronology of the amphoras suggests that the development of this alternative source of wine for the capital did not immediately follow the Arab conquest. For that chronology, see Günsenin, 'Le vin de Ganos', 284; Hayes, *Excavations at Saraçhane* (as in n. 31), 73 (type 54).

[37] J. Magness, *Jerusalem Ceramic Chronology, circa 200-800 CE* (Sheffield, 1993).

[38] Magness, *Jerusalem*, figs. 5-12 and discussion; roads: 179.

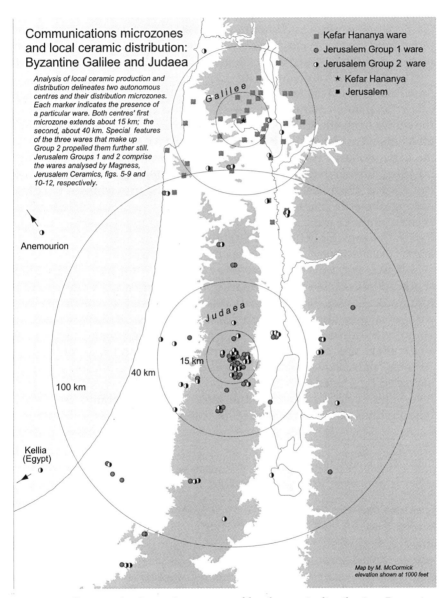

Figure 1.1 Communications microzones and local ceramic distribution: Byzantine Galilee and Judaea

walk from the market. The last, sparse zone reaches about 100 km to the north or south, i.e. 20 hours of travel. This translates into about three days' distance and probably signals a different type of diffusion from that of the first two microzones.

Three of the four wares (fig 1.1: my Jerusalem Group 2) which travelled furthest have special characteristics which sustained their exceptional movement. The large candlestick lamps were pilgrim souvenirs from the Christian shrines of Jerusalem: local and regional travellers were always the backbone of pilgrimage, as a Greek source of the early Abbasid period reminds us.[39] A local fineware presumably travelled further because of its higher quality, and therefore higher value. The third item consists of casseroles with wishbone handles. Among domestic coarse ware, cooking vessels tend to circulate further, even in times of economic contraction: such ceramics typically handle the heat of cooking better, and so could command a superior price that might justify higher transport costs than other vessels.[40]

A few wares travelled a few days' distance. But most sold within about 12 km of the probable market centre. In economic terms, this communications pattern suggests diffusion through a weekly market, with a catchment area defined by a few hours' walk.[41] Given the ubiquity of donkeys in the Judaean hills, this microzone's limits may well reflect the comparative economics of transport, since Roman customs' data shows that under 15 km, a donkey's burden could be increased by a third.[42]

As the curtain closed on the late antique economy, few other microregions enjoyed the special wealth that allowed Byzantine

---

[39] *Ibid.*, 166-177; Leontius, *Vita Stephani thaumaturgi* (BHG 1670), 133, *AASS* Iul. 3 (1868), 557D-E, which describes how the author's paternal aunt and her maidservant habitually came from 'her own city' (138, 559D) to Jerusalem to celebrate Easter and then continued on pilgrimage to Sinai, before returning home via the Holy City. Since Leontius came from Damascus (*ibid.*, 116, 550A), it is likely that was his aunt's home as well. For recent bibliography on this Life, see A. Kazhdan with L. F. Sherry and C. Angelidi, *A History of Byzantine Literature (650-850)* (Athens, 1999), 171-172.

[40] The Talmudic descriptions of the cooking ware of Kefar Ḥananya discussed hereafter emphasise precisely its special thermal qualities: *Mishna Shabbat* 16.5 and *Bavli Shabbat* 120b as cited and translated by D. Adan-Bayewitz, *Common Pottery in Roman Galilee: a Study of Local Trade* (Ramat-Gan, 1993), 39. The reason for the six or seven outliers of the ovoid lamps with large filling holes (Magness, *Jerusalem Ceramic*, fig. 9) is less clear.

[41] L. De Ligt, *Fairs and Markets in the Roman Empire* (Amsterdam, 1993), 15, defines the catchment area of local periodic markets as under 50 km. This may encourage the suspicion that donkey loads (see next note) were a critical factor.

[42] W. Habermann, 'Statistische Datenanalyse an den Zolldokumenten des Arsinoites aus römischer Zeit, II.', *Münstersche Beiträge zur antiken Handelsgeschichte* 9.1 (1990), 50-94, here 62-65.

Judaea to produce local finewares when foreign imports slackened. Hence the tool of choice for detecting most microzones will be the coarse wares of kitchen and hearth, whose histories are still in their infancy. Here again the early Byzantine period leads the way in a neighbouring region, Byzantine Galilee, 100 km to the north of the Judaean microeconomy. Neutron activation analysis (which allows definitive identification of a vessel's clay), excavation and historical sources have uncovered the production centre, distribution radius and chronology of a particular cooking ware, even as the laboratory excluded its nearest competitors and imitators. The deposit sites sketch an economic and communications microregion in which one rural craft village, Kefar Ḥananya, supplied other villages and cities up to 50 km away. The same basic structure that occurs in Judaea recurs here: two microzones of differentiated density of diffusion separate at about 15 km from the production site. Some pots crossed the Jordan river, although another very similar ware successfully competed against the Ḥananya vessels on the far side of the river. Administrative geography may also have helped define these potters' economic horizons.[43]

I know of no place within the middle Byzantine empire where the coarseware allows a similar microregional investigation. But recent advances give hope in Byzantine Italy, Thasos and Cyprus.[44] In Italy, future ceramic results could be laid next to patterns derived from archaeology, coins and seals, prosopography, and the good archival records.[45] Perhaps the richly documented agrarian hinterland of Mount Athos might some day yield similiar materials? Here, comparison

---

[43] This Adan-Bayewitz (*Common Pottery*, 215) rejects, although he admits it might explain the sharp difference in the proportion of Kefar Ḥananya ware at Tel Anafa and 8 km away, at Tel Dan, since the boundary between the late Roman provinces of Phoenicia and Palestina II ran somewhere nearby. Administrative geography seems to have influenced Roman pottery diffusion: D. Gabler, 'Die Unterschiede im Keramikimport der Rhein- und Donauprovinzen', *Münstersche Beiträge zur antiken Handelsgeschichte* 4.1 (1985), 3-29.

[44] See e.g. H. Patterson and D. Whitehouse, 'The medieval domestic pottery', in F. D'Andria and D. Whitehouse, eds., *Excavations at Otranto* 2 (Lecce, 1992), 87-195; the discovery of a coarseware production complex from the seventh-eighth centuries at Otranto should be the first step toward mapping local microzones: P. Arthur and H. Patterson, 'Local pottery in southern Puglia in the sixth and seventh centuries', in *Ceramica in Italia* (as in n. 29), 511-530; for recent publications on Thasos, Pergamon and Cyprus, see P. Yannopoulos, 'Ceramica byzantina', *Byz* 68 (1998), 246-249.

[45] J. M. Martin and G. Noyé, 'Guerre, fortifications et habitats en Italie méridionale du Ve au Xe siècle', in *Castrum 3: Guerre, fortification et habitat dans le monde méditerranéen au moyen âge*, Collection de l'École française de Rome 105 (n. pl., 1988), 225-236.

with the early medieval west may be instructive, since there are signs that western pottery distribution overlaps with estate structures.[46]

These objects invite scrutiny today. Tomorrow, new things will help detect communications patterns. Study of building materials has already begun.[47] Glass is just entering the debate.[48] For Byzantium's last centuries, western paper may hold real promise. Until now, watermarks, the manufacturer's trademarks preserved on medieval paper, have interested only codicologists intent on dating manuscripts. But why not look beyond palaeography, and ask how, when, and which Italian paper makers penetrated the Byzantine and post-Byzantine market, and what this says about the circulation of goods? The carefully documented watermarks of the manuscripts preserved at the Athonite monastery of Dionysiou spring to mind.[49] Similar light might come from the wood used in Byzantine buildings. The Byzantines sometimes went far to get lumber. Since some trees grow only in certain places, we might recover movements of timber down the torrents and through the channels of Byzantium's transport systems. Western archaeologists are already using macroscopic study of different wood types to this end. Some of Pompeii's wood, for instance, came all the way from the Alps, while silver fir used at the Carolingian trading centre of Dorestad, near Utrecht, had floated far down the Rhine.[50] Of

---

[46] U. Gross, 'Beobachtungen zur Verbreitung frühmittelalterlicher Keramikgruppen in Südwestdeutschland', *Archäologische Informationen* 10 (1987), 194-202, here 197 and 199-200 with Abb. 3 and 5, respectively.

[47] J. P. Sodini, 'Le commerce des marbres à l'époque protobyzantine', in *Hommes et richesses dans l'empire byzantin*, 1 (Paris, 1989), 163-192; N. Herz and M. Waelkens, eds., *Classical Marble: Geochemistry, Technology, Trade* (Dordrecht, 1988).

[48] For provenance and scientific analysis, see J. Henderson, 'Ancient vitreous materials', in P. J. McGovern *et al.*, 'Science in archaeology: a review', *AJA* 99.1 (1995), 79-142, here 117-121; for a survey of Byzantine glass, J. Henderson and M. Mundell Mango, 'Glass at medieval Constantinople. Preliminary scientific evidence', in *Constantinople and its Hinterland* (as in n. 8), 333-356.

[49] See R. W. Allison, 'Archive of watermarks and papers in Greek manuscripts', http://abacus.bates.edu:80/Faculty/wmarchive/INTRO_images.html.

[50] Distant movements of wood are recorded in, e.g. Alexandrian requests for large wood beams from Pope Gregory I: *Registrum*, e.g. 10, 21, ed. D. Norberg, CCSL, 140-140A (1982), 855.117-123; Calabrian beams for Byzantine Rome: McCormick, *Origins*, R45 and 90; in 971, the Venetians agreed to John Tzimiskes' demand that they cease shipping large timbers 'ad naves faciendum' to the Arabs: *Urkunden zur älteren Handels- und Staatsgeschichte der Republik Venedig*, eds. G. L. F. Tafel and G. M. Thomas (Vienna, 1856), 27. Western examples: W. A. Casparie and J. E. J. Swarts, 'Wood from Dorestad, Hoogstraat I', in W. A. Van Es and W. J. H. Verwers, eds., *Excavations at Dorestad*, 1, Nederlandse Oudheden, 9 (Amersfoort, 1980), 262-285 and, from Roman Pompeii (as well as annual updates): 'Aegean dendrochronology project' at http://www.gs.cornell.edu/dendro/97news/97adplet.html. For an overview in printed format, see P. I. Kuniholm, 'Dendrochronology',

course, trees have DNA, and this emerging kind of physical evidence may extend the testimony of such Byzantine wood as turns up.

DNA beckons even Byzantinists. We ignore molecular biologists' interest in Byzantium at our own peril.[51] The cost of DNA analysis is dropping, though still steep, and the problems of contamination real. It is nonetheless certain that ancient DNA reveals genealogical links among centuries-old human remains, including ancient and medieval populations.[52] So far, however, most work has targeted prehistoric migrations of European or Amerindian populations, and the distance which separates them from our African ancestors.[53] But migrations and population transfers also constitute an essential chapter in the history of Byzantine communications. The first soundings around Europe are indicating some extraordinary genetic stories over the centuries. To cite just one new case: two years ago, scientists uncovered a strong genetic correlation of the present-day population of north-east Derbyshire — but not of those of the rest of the East Midlands — with modern-day Danes. The geographic distribution of those English individuals overlaps, almost exactly, with the density of Old Norse place-names.

---

in McGovern, 'Science in archaeology' (as in n. 48), 99-102. For the archaeological problems and promise, see L. Chabal, L. Fabre *et al.*, 'L'anthracologie', in C. Bourquin-Mignot, J. E. Brochier, *et al.*, *La botanique* (Paris, 1999), 43-104, and C. Bourquin-Mignot and F. Guibal, 'La dendrologie', *ibid.*, 138-156.

[51] See e.g. McCormick, 'The imperial edge', 24, n. 18.

[52] See in general S. Audic and E. Béraud-Colomb, 'Ancient DNA is thirteen years old', *Nature Biotechnology* 15 (1997), 855-858. A German research team has demonstrated genetic connections among the individuals buried in an aristocratic family tomb from 1546 to 1749: J. Gerstenberger, S. Hummel, *et al.*, 'Reconstruction of a historical genealogy by means of STR analysis and Y-Haplotyping of ancient DNA', *European Journal of Human Genetics* 7.4 (1999), 469-477. DNA from an individual believed to be Charlemagne's Saxon nemesis, Widukind, invites comparison with genealogical identifications proposed from the written evidence: S. Hummel, T. Schultes *et al.*, 'Ancient DNA profiling by Megaplex amplications', *Electrophoresis* (1999), 20, 1717-1721, in conjunction with K. Schmid, *Gebetsgedanken und adliges Selbstverständnis im Mittelalter* (Sigmaringen, 1983), 59-105. A similar study is planned for a group of Pompeians who died together: M. Cipollaro, G. Di Bernardo *et al.*, 'Ancient DNA in human bone remains from Pompeii archaeological site', *Biochemical and Biophysical Research Communications* 247 (1998), 901-904. DNA identification of a parent-children relationship has been reported from a Merovingian group burial: S. Hummel and B. Herrmann, Verwandtschaftsfeststellung durch aDNA-Analyse', *Anthropologischer Anzeiger* 55 (1997), 217-223.

[53] For an overview from one of the leaders of this new area of investigation, L. L. Cavalli-Sforza, 'Genetic and cultural diversity in Europe', *Journal of Anthropological Research* 53 (1997), 383-404.

1000 years after the fact, molecular biology detects the Viking settlement in this microregion.[54]

Do we dare to hope that part of the molecular record still lives in the peoples of the lands that once answered the emperor's command, and that as the advances of modern medicine begin to follow economic development into those regions, some part of that living record may be seized and recorded? There is no reason that biology should be less revealing of Thrace or Bithynia than of Britain. Already, modern Italian epidemiology of the genetic blood disorder beta-thalassemia suggests that, on a molecular level, Italo-Byzantines may have enjoyed a superior resistance to malaria, compared with other inhabitants of their peninsula. In other words, ecology may have conspired with genetics and disease to establish a lethal communications barrier between Byzantine and non-Byzantine Italy, the genetic traces of which persist in the blood of twentieth-century Italians.[55] Chances are growing that we will be able to discover some traces of this — and of other lost patterns — in the palaeopathological and genetic material still hidden in Byzantine skeletal remains.[56]

Finally, we know well that Byzantine ships were not immune to strange pathogens. The spread of contagious diseases is therefore vital for studying Byzantium on the move. The bubonic plague, its mechanisms of transmission and their implications for communications systems are fairly well understood today. We know that the first, Justinianic contagion was borne by Byzantine rats which crossed long Mediterranean distances only aboard ships. We have patchy records of the great two-hundred year cycle of epidemics triggered by the plague of 541, and good written evidence for the spread of the Black Death in fourteenth- and fifteenth-century Byzantium.[57] That advancing

---

[54] S. S. Mastana and R. J. Sokol, 'Genetic variation in the East Midlands', *Annals of Human Biology* 25.1 (1998), 43-68.

[55] McCormick, 'The imperial edge', 24-31. While that study was in press, a report confirmed, on the molecular level, a case of β-thalassemia in an Ottoman-era skeleton displaying the lesions associated with that diagnosis by palaeopathologists: D. Filon, M. Faerman *et al.*, 'Sequence analysis reveals a β-thalassaemia mutation in the DNA of skeletal remains from the archaeological site of Akhziv, Israel', *Nature Genetics* 9 (1995), 365-368.

[56] For the evidence hitherto available from hard tissue and its limitations, see M. D. Grmek, *Diseases in the Ancient Greek World*, tr. M. and L. Muellner (Baltimore, 1989), 47-86; C. Roberts and K. Manchester, *The Archaeology of Disease*, 2nd edn. (Ithaca, 1997), 9-10; for recent breakthroughs of molecular archaeology, see previous note, and below.

[57] The raw materials for the Black Death at Byzantium are assembled by M. H. Congourdeau, 'Pour une étude de la Peste noire à Byzance', in *ΕΥΨΥΧΙΑ* (as in n. 34), 1, 149-163; for more on the Justinianic plague, McCormick, 'Bateaux de vie, bateaux de mort', in *Morfologie sociali e culturali in Europa fra tarda antichità e alto medioevo*, Settimane di studi del Centro italiano di studi sull'alto medioevo, 45 (Spoleto, 1998), 35-122, here 48-65, and

epidemic depicts the late medieval maritime communications system with striking precision. The more sporadic data on the Justinianic plague, on the other hand, affords only occasional glimpses of the earlier Byzantine communications world.[58] The details of the outbreak of 743, for instance, prove that direct shipping traffic between Constantinople and the Arab Levant was at that moment at a standstill.[59]

A new breakthrough, conceivably, will revolutionise the study of both bubonic pandemics, and therefore of Byzantine communications systems. In 1998, a French team published the first molecular traces of the medieval bubonic infection: DNA of the plague bacillus, *Yersinia pestis*, extracted from the teeth of sixteenth-century plague victims. The same techniques will probably work for human remains, not only from the first wave of the Black Death in 1347-48, but also for those of the great Byzantine plague of the sixth to eighth centuries. The implications are breathtaking: it should become possible to map with unexpected precision exactly *where* the Byzantine plague hit between 541 and 748, and where *it did not*. The regions which were still 'plugged into' Mediterranean shipping and communications networks should emerge with undreamed of clarity. But molecular biology suggests an even more dizzying perspective. As an infectious disease works its way through a population, its DNA undergoes minor mutations. By identifying and classifying each occurrence's specific mutations as they accumulate, molecular geneticists are increasingly able to track the course of an infection over space and time.[60] If ancient DNA were to become available in quantities and qualities that allow such phylogenetic study, it might establish not only the relative chronology of individuals' deaths between 541 and 748, but also the

---

E. Kislinger and D. Stathakopoulos, 'Pest und Perserkriege bei Prokop. Chronologische Überlegungen zum Geschehen 540-545', *Byz* 69 (1999), 76-98 and D. Ch. Stathakopoulos, 'Travelling with the plague', in this volume.

[58] For the Justinianic plague, see J. N. Biraben and J. Le Goff, 'The plague in the early middle ages', in R. Forster and O. Ranum, eds., *Biology of Man in History*, trans. E. Forster and P. M. Ranum (Baltimore, 1975), 48-80 and L. I. Conrad, 'The plague in the early medieval Near East', Diss., Princeton University, 1981 [Ann Arbor, University Microfilms International 1996]. Data on the conditions of transmission in the pioneering work of J. N. Biraben, *Les hommes et la peste* (Paris, 1976), must be revised to take into account more recent medical investigation: see e.g., O. J. Benedictow, *Plague in the Late Medieval Nordic Countries. Epidemiological Studies* (Oslo, 1992), 227-264; cf. 126-146.

[59] McCormick, *Origins*, chap. 17.

[60] M. Drancourt et al., 'Detection of 400-year-old *Yersinia pestis* DNA in human dental pulp: an approach to the diagnosis of ancient septicemia', *Proceedings of the National Academy of Sciences of the United States of America* 95.21 (1998), 12637-12640. I owe a pleasant debt to my colleague, Prof. Markus Meister, for illuminating me about phylogenetic analysis.

routes and sequence of the transmission of the pathogen. In a word, it might retrace the movements of ships which, a millennium and a half ago, sailed into the oblivion their infection carried with them.

Pipe dreams from someone who has lived too close to two of the great centres of molecular discovery over the last two decades? Maybe. But we are barely a generation removed from the great breakthrough of Watson and Crick; only in the last four years has the controversy dissipated among microbiologists over whether it is even possible to obtain uncontaminated ancient DNA; and it is hard for biologists to keep abreast of the daily discoveries stemming from the great race to map the human genome, much less for us historians.

There is another kind of human remains with which scholars are more familiar, if not more comfortable. They too may bear witness to ancient movements and they too can be dated and localised with some accuracy. I know of no adequate study of whatever relic hoards have survived the shipwreck of time in Byzantium. But such treasures have come to light from the shrines of the early medieval west: tiny bundles of bones, pebbles, or shreds of textiles which claim, implicitly or explicitly, to come from Ephesos, from Sinai, from Jerusalem, Euchaita and Aya Thekla. As their script and language attest, the labels which identify them were often written at the moment they reached the shrines of France — as far back as the seventh century.[61] What similar treasures may survive among the holy relics of Mt Athos, Patmos, or in the ecumenical patriarchate?[62] Impending publication of a hoard preserved in the papal shrine of the Sancta sanctorum is particularly exciting. The pope who crowned Charlemagne constructed a cedar cabinet for relics; 100-year old photographs show that it holds bundles labelled in Greek majuscules, and also in Syriac.[63] Another study will argue that the relics deposited in the treasury of the French cathedral of Sens between the seventh and the ninth centuries, echo from afar the

---

[61] McCormick, *Origins*, chap. 10.

[62] O. Meinardus, 'A study of the relics of saints of the Greek Orthodox church', *Oriens christianus* 54 (1970), 130-278, published an inventory of 3,602 relics preserved in eastern monasteries. He supplies no details on the authentics which presumably accompany at least some of these relics. For Byzantine reliquaries (and relics as well as authentics) which migrated to France, largely in connection with the Fourth Crusade, see the first fruits from J. Durand's important and on-going inventory project, e.g. 'A propos des reliques du monastère du Prodrome de Pétra à Constantinople', *CahArch* 46 (1998), 151-167.

[63] See for now P. Lauer, *Le trésor du Sancta sanctorum*, Académie des inscriptions et belles-lettres, Monuments et mémoires, 15.1-2 (Paris, 1906) and H. Grisar, *Il sancta sanctorum ed il suo tesoro sacro* (Rome, 1907). I am grateful to Profs. Jean Vezin and Hartmut Atsma for alerting me to Dr Bruno Galland's impending publication of this collection, in the Vatican series *Studi e testi*.

decline of the shrines (and cities) of Byzantine Asia Minor. Recently discovered relics from a royal nunnery near Paris, on the other hand, point to eighth-century connections with Constantinople and the Black Sea.[64]

So there is evidence aplenty for Byzantine communications, and that evidence invites new questions, and new solutions to old ones. Two concrete examples will conclude this invitation to explore Byzantine communications. The first concerns the role of geographic mobility in the life, and life-style of the Byzantine elite. What was the usual geographic range of an elite individual's movements in the ninth century? Did it change in the tenth or eleventh centuries? Where did that geographic mobility take them? And what does it tell about the tenor of Byzantine society and civilisation? My own work has studied the life movements of 234 Byzantine travellers to the west between 700 and 900 A.D. for whom we have some geographic data beyond the fact of their travel. It was surprising, for instance, to discover that a significant fraction of these middle Byzantine voyagers to western Europe also travelled in the Arab world (12%; 28).[65] In nearly half the cases, it was possible to identify a main place of residence prior to their journey (46%; 93 of 234 with geographic data), as the table shows. We even know birthplaces in more than a tenth of the cases (12%; 28 of 234).

---

[64] McCormick, *Origins*, chap. 10.
[65] McCormick, *Origins*, chap. 8.

Places*	Birthplace		Residence	
	n	%	%	n

Italy
    Sicily 9
    Rome 1
    Reggio (Calabria) 1
	11	39	26	24

Asia Minor (1 each)
    Amneia
    Amorion area
    Kyzikos
    Eirenopolis in Isauria
    Synada
	5	18	19	18

Europe
    Greece 4
        Athens   1
        Thessalonike   2
        'Graecia'   1
    'Moesia' (i.e. the lower Danube) 1
    Dalmatia 1
	6	21	9	8

Constantinople	4	14	44	41
Georgia Kaxeti 1	2	7	0	0

Caliphate (1 each)
    Jerusalem
    Alexandria
	0	0	2	2

Totals	28	100	100	93

Table 1.1 Byzantine travellers: known birthplaces compared with residences

*Numbers in this column specify birthplaces.

Eastern travellers to non-Byzantine Europe frequently resided in Byzantine Italy: unsurprisingly, proximity bred travel, and the nearest region supplied a good many travellers. From another angle, Italian *birthplace* — and subsequent migration to another region of the Byzantine empire — correlates strongly with travel to the west. Analysis of the movements of a couple of hundred travellers suggests therefore that Italian immigrants either constituted a large share of the Byzantine elite in these generations, or they were

---

[66] For more on this table, see McCormick, *Origins*, chap.8.

disproportionately disposed to travel back to the west and the borders of their native region.[67]

The same data fills out the picture of imperial efforts to repopulate the shrunken capital mentioned briefly by Nikephoros and Theophanes. Comparing the travellers whose residence is known with those whose birthplace is recorded shows that the proportion of Constantinopolitan residents is almost three times (44%) the size of the proportion of native Constantinopolitans (14%).[68] Because this sample of travellers is particularly heavy with governmental types (52; 72% of 72 total travellers of known birthplace, residence or both, who departed from the Byzantine empire) it illustrates nicely the centripetal power of Constantinople for the empire's administrative elite.[69] But more than a quarter of the travellers were *not* associated with the government, so that the pattern of inward immigration to Constantinople holds for them too. This sample of 234 Byzantines on the move indicates that the influx of aspiring members of the elite to Constantinople was already powerful in the eighth and ninth centuries.

Our final example concerns a turning point in the empire's early history. The migrations of Slavs and Bulgars blocked the old overland corridors that had linked Constantinople, since its founding, to western Europe. The consequences were incalculable for the empire's subsequent development, and that of Europe. What better statement of the early Byzantine importance of the Balkan corridor, and its most celebrated road, the Via Egnatia, than the fact that this road ended at the Golden Gate of Constantinople? In terms of political control, the Balkans offered crucial arteries for armies marching west and messengers speeding east; when they closed, only seaborne communications remained.[70] Then the well-known Mediterranean suspension of sea

---

[67] Only three of the 57 envoys were certainly of Italian birth, and one of them did not represent the government. This is insufficient to prove that the imperial government made a practice of selecting envoys with special regional backgrounds: McCormick, *Origins*, chap. 8.

[68] In fact, it is even greater than first appears, since a good number of the residents of Asia Minor included in this table resided in the greater capital region of Constantinople: see McCormick, *Origins*, chap. 8.

[69] A. P. Kazhdan and M. McCormick, 'The social world of the Byzantine court', in H. Maguire, ed., *Byzantine Court Culture from 829 to 1204* (Washington, D.C., 1997), 167-197, here 171, for some anecdotal evidence.

[70] On the speed and safety of travel across the Balkans, D. Claude, *Der Handel im westlichen Mittelmeer während des Frühmittelalters*, Abhandlungen der Akademie der Wissenschaften in Göttingen, philologisch-historische Klasse, 3rd series, 144 (Göttingen, 1985), 149-150. See also K. Belke, 'Roads and travel in Macedonia and Thrace in the middle and late Byzantine period', in this volume.

travel during the winter months from October or November through February practically cut off the empire's western provinces for nearly a third of the year. To grasp the importance of the land communications with the rest of Europe, we need only recall the revolutions — including the First Crusade — precipitated when those land corridors reopened in the eleventh century. Surely the progressive loss of Byzantine Italy was, in part, connected with the annual interruption of relations with the capital, which left the provincial authorities on their own for months at a time. No one has tried to study how the movement of people along these various routes ebbed and flowed in antiquity, nor even to determine when exactly long-distance travel on them ceased. But it did end.

A first guess based on recorded individuals' movements would be that the various Balkan routes went out of regular use at different times between c. 550 and 650. Disruption probably began in the north and affected the southernmost route last, since the migrations moved that way, and the Corinth route mostly avoided contested land masses. As early as 552, even an army marching to Italy along the famous 'Heerstrasse' was temporarily blocked at Philippopolis by marauding 'Huns'.[71] Sixth-century travellers between Italy and Constantinople may have preferred the southernmost routes; whether for speed or security is unclear. Legations travelled overland on the Via Egnatia.[72] Other travellers used the even more southerly route through Corinth.[73] As late as the winter of 591, Gregory the Great's nuncio to Constantinople travelled east that way.[74] The fact that he set out in February coheres with what is explicitly recorded, that, from Corinth, the envoy took a land route across Greece. During the seventh century, however, archaeology suggests that Slavic colonisation of the Balkans

---

[71] Proc., *BG* VIII.21.21, ed. J. Haury and G. Wirth, 2 (Leipzig, 1962-1964), 602.25-603.9.

[72] *Collectio avellana*, 167, 3, ed. O. Günther, *Corpus scriptorum ecclesiasticorum latinorum* 35.2 (1895-1898), 618.16-18, where Aulona, Scampae and Lignidus (=Lychnidus) reveal the route; on the road to Italy, Peter the Patrician had met Italian envoys heading for Constantinople; he stopped in Aulona to await new instructions: Proc., *BG*, I. 4. 20-1; 2.23.8-14.

[73] Thus Gregory I, *Dialogi*, 3, 2, 1, ed. A. de Vogüé, *Grégoire le Grand, Dialogues*, SC 251, 260, 265 (Paris, 1978-80), 2.266.1-12, about the trip of Pope John I (523-526), where the detail about changing horses shows that the pope continued overland toward Constantinople; and, *ibid.*, 3, 3, 4, 1-4, 2.270.1-272.36, for the trip of Datius, bishop of Milan, sometime between 538 and 550 (cf. *ibid.*, 270-272n.1 on the date). A Merovingian envoy to Constantinople c. 533/47, also used this route, since he was delivered of a kidney stone when his ship put in at Patras: Gregory of Tours, *Liber in gloria martyrum*, 30, ed. B. Krusch, *MGH Scriptores rerum merovingicarum* 1.2 (repr., Hanover, 1969), 56.32-57.15.

[74] Gregory, *Registrum*, 1, 26 (JL 1095), CCL 140.34.14-35.28; cf. 1, 24 (JL 1092), *ibid.*, 22-32.

ended imperial control and interrupted travel on the Via Egnatia. The same developments, apparently, also disrupted normal communications through Corinth.[75] But the archaeology is not without controversy, nor is its chronology precise and secure.

If we reformulate the problem in terms of the *seasonal* pattern of communications, a vital clue emerges from the aggregate papal correspondence with the Byzantine empire and points east. Between 515 and 880, in addition to a few imperial letters, 140 papal letters survive which were sent eastward and which are dated down to the month. Although the letters usually make no reference to how they were transmitted, we know the season of their sending. Letters sent in June or July could have gone by land or by sea, in the fine Mediterranean summer. But letters sent from Rome between November and February will not normally have travelled by water. With few exceptions, Mediterranean shipping came to a standstill during the dangerous winter weather.

Letters nonetheless travelled east in every month except January. Before 650 and after 865, letters regularly left Rome in November and February, and one was even sent east in December. But, between 650 and the late 860s, *no* papal letters went east in the winter months.[76] Like most surviving imperial letters, other normal communications observe this same pattern.[77] Papal letters dated to winter months resume in

---

[75] For a still valuable overview of the Balkan migrations, P. Lemerle, 'Invasions et migrations dans les Balkans depuis la fin de l'époque romaine jusqu'au VIIIe siècle', *Revue historique* 201 (1954), 265-308. For an effort to map the invasions and settlement of the Balkans, see V. Popović, 'Les témoins archéologiques des invasions avaro-slaves dans l'Illyricum byzantin', *Mélanges de l'École française de Rome. Antiquité* 87 (1975), 445-504; V. Popović, 'La descente des Kotrigours, des Slaves et des Avars vers la Mer Égée: le témoignage de l'archéologie', *Comptes rendus. Académie des inscriptions et belles-lettres* (1978), 596-648, and 'Aux origines de la slavisation des Balkans', *ibid.*, 1980, 230-257, with the criticism of D. M. Metcalf, 'Avar and Slav invasions into the Balkan peninsula (c. 575-625)', *Journal of Roman Archaeology* 4 (1991), 140-148.

[76] Fourteen dated or datable papal letters went east toward the Balkans or the Levant between 650 and 865: JL 2080-2081, 2090-2092, 2109-2110, 2448, 2682-2683, 2690-2692, 2796; in addition, Pope Martin I's transfer to Constantinople began on 18 June 653: McCormick, *Origins*, R19; the exception of nos. 2090-2092 is only apparent: *Origins*, chap. 3.

[77] Two letters of Constantine IV to Rome dated 13 and 23 December 681 constitute a seeming exception: ed. R. Riedinger, *ACO*, 2nd ser. 2.2.894.26 and 867.10, respectively. However, they were not sent immediately; rather they accompanied the acts of the Third Ecumenical Council (*ibid.*, xxiii; 871.8-9), which almost certainly travelled by sea. With the papal legates, they arrived at Rome only at the height of the sailing season, that is in July of 682, as their recipient records. He then develops a metaphor which reinforces the likelihood that they arrived by ship: their arrival triggered the relief that one feels when entering a calm port after an emotional storm: *ibid.*, 871.3-14; cf. the Greek tr. 870.3-13. Justinian II's letter dated 17 February 687 (*ibid.*, 887.19) is a more likely exception; however,

866, just as winter imperial letters begin again in December of 867. This is no fluke, for the sudden resumption of overland travel between Byzantium and the West is explicitly documented in the year 866.[78] In other words, the aggregate seasonal patterns of papal correspondence provide a context for interpreting the scattered data of other Byzantine communications with the early medieval West: the late antique dyad of land and sea routes expired around 650, and regular land communications resumed only in 866. Overland travel and communications then surged for some thirty years, until the wars with Bulgaria and the arrival of the Magyars again disrupted them.

If, studied in this way, communications can illuminate immigration into the capital and overland travel to the West in the most obscure periods of the Byzantine millennium, then we may begin to imagine what they may deliver in the better documented later centuries. Travel accounts, prosopographies, sunken ships, seals, coins, relics, and, soon, ancient and modern molecules, all await investigation from new perspectives. In its variety, the repertory of evidence offers a compelling beauty. Historians may fear that individuals' trips are too few to justify conclusions about an empire's patterns of communications. They may entertain similar concerns for each sort of evidence. But the seals, the pottery, the shipwrecks, the DNA, the relics, each comes to us under circumstances which owe nothing to those which have preserved the rare written records. The conditions of preservation of each may, to some extent, distort the picture that it presents. But when laid next to one another, each set *is independent*. Where their testimony coincides, it can do so only because each independently emerged from the same reality. Of this the mutually reinforcing amphoras, shipwrecks and fictional trip of St. Nikon provided a fine illustration. When these different kinds of evidence converge, we begin to discern infrastructures and patterns of communications which have lain hidden these many centuries. Dare we hope to hear again, in their rise and fall, the heartbeat of an economy long since dead? In any case, people and things under way over Byzantium's time and space have

---

even in this case, the document could easily have been delivered in view of a March sailing, such as are in fact attested in this period: McCormick, *Origins*, chap. 15. Between about 650 and 750, only two trips hint at a land leg over any part of Greece in any season. But even these hints are uncertain and, in any case, arose in highly exceptional circumstances: McCormick, *Origins*, chap. 3. D. Obolensky, 'The Balkans in the ninth century: barrier or bridge?' *BF* 13 (1988), 47-66, here 51, suspects that tenuous links may have continued between c. 600 and 750 because eastern Illyricum still fell under papal jurisdiction, but he adduces no specific evidence. Even for him the Balkans became a barrier no later than c. 750-780.

[78] McCormick, *Origins*, chap. 19.

much to tell us about the economy, society, and the movements of ideas and arts. Their patterns lead to the structures and infrastructures that underpinned so much of what is distinctive of Byzantine civilisation, if we have but patience and wit enough to think where and how to look.

Section I
Going there — the technicalities of travel

2. Types of ships and their performance capabilities[*]

J. H. Pryor

Sailing ships

At the end of his *Histories*, Theophylaktos Simokattes (late 6th century-post 641) recounted a story of a calligrapher in Alexandria who saw in a vision the statues of the emperor Maurice and his family coming alive and creeping down from their pedestals in Constantinople.[1] Nine days later a messenger bringing news of the murder of Maurice by Phokas on 23 November 602 reached Alexandria. Supposedly, a ship covered the minimum distance of around 1030 miles from Constantinople to Alexandria, at the onset of winter, in 8-8.5 days, an average speed of around 4.4 knots if sailing around the clock. But no one in their right mind would try to sail the Dardanelles or the east coast of the Aegean by night in winter. They would obviously have to do so from Rhodes to Alexandria, but that is only about 450 miles. For the rest, at that time of the year they would have a maximum of around ten hours of daylight. The actual average speed under way would therefore have had to have been an incredible 6.5 knots.

Theophylaktos's story was a 'miraculous narrative' as he wrote, and no doubt he intended his audience to recognise it for what it was. At the beginning of the seventh century no ship could reach Alexandria from Constantinople at the end of November in nine days, not even the fastest imperial *dromon*. To put the story in perspective, in 1798 Nelson

---

[*] Much of this paper is founded on research conducted for a forthcoming book by John Pryor and Elizabeth Jeffreys: *The Byzantine navy: evolution of the ships and their capabilities* The author acknowledges the publisher's permission to re-use material presented here.

[1] *Theophylacti Simocattae historiae*, ed. P. Wirth (Stuttgart, 1972), VIII.13.7-14 (pp. 309-311). The story was later repeated by Theophanes the Confessor (c. 760-817): Theoph. (A.M. 6095), p. 291.

From *Travel in the Byzantine World*, ed. Ruth Macrides. Copyright © 2002 by the Society for the Promotion of Byzantine Studies. Published by Ashgate Publishing Ltd, Gower House, Croft Road, Aldershot, Hampshire, GU11 3HR, Great Britain.

sailed from Syracuse in pursuit of Napoleon at top speed in midsummer on 25 July with the best ships that Lord St. Vincent had been able to give him. He reached Alexandria via Korone on 1 August in 7-7.5 days: 1000 miles at an average speed of around 5.0 knots. We are asked by Theophylaktos to believe that a seventh-century ship could outperform what was the finest squadron in the British Mediterranean fleet in 1798.

According to Pliny the Elder, the senator Valerius Marianus (or Marinus) reached Alexandria from Pozzuoli in summer on the ninth day (in 8-8.5 days) 'with a very gentle breeze (... *lenissumo flatu*)': 1200 miles at an average speed of 5.25 knots, even if the shortest high-seas route was taken. Two imperial prefects of Egypt, Galerius (Gaius Galerius, prefect under Tiberius) and Balbillus (Claudius Balbillus, prefect in 55 A.D.) did even better. They made Alexandria from the straits of Messina in 6-6.5 and 5-5.5 days respectively: 1000 miles at 5.8 and 9.15 knots respectively.[2] To put this in perspective again, Cutty Sark reached Sydney from London in 1885 in 78 days: 15,000 miles at an average speed of around 7.25 knots. Pliny asks us to believe that Roman ships could match or better the performance of one of the fastest nineteenth-century clipper ships ever built, even though the latter's average speed was greatly increased because she drove for days through the Roaring Forties at up to 15 knots.

One must be careful about accepting such data, as has been done so often. Historians are too credulous of narrative sources. Pliny's purpose in recounting such voyage times was to show what a 'marvel' (*miraculum* was his word) was the flax plant, used to make linen for sails.

We actually know precious little about Byzantine sailing ships. We do have the evidence of the seventh-century Yassi Ada ship,[3] and we have a good reconstruction of its hull. However, since we have no idea of its sail plan, it is impossible to make any conjectures about its performance. We do not even know whether it had only one mast, since no mast step was found. How well would such a ship with an overall length of 20.52 m and a beam of around 5 m perform with only a single mast and sail? It would probably have tended to luff up into the wind badly when tacking. Can we even be confident that it had lateen

---

[2] Plin., *HN*, XIX.1.3; trans. H. Rackham, Pliny, *Natural History*, 10 vols (London, 1938-62), vol. 5, pp. 420-422.

[3] G. F. Bass and F. H. van Doorninck, Jr., eds., *Yassi Ada volume I: a seventh-century Byzantine shipwreck* (College Station, 1982).

rather than square sails? It probably did, but the sixth-seventh-century evidence on that issue is ambiguous.

After that we have little until the Serçe Limanı ship of c. 1025, another small coaster of around 15.36 m overall length and 5.12 m beam, which may or may not have been Byzantine built. She was smaller and stubbier and flatter in the floor than the seventh-century Yassı Ada ship.[4] We do now have the ship found near Bozburun on the mainland opposite Rhodes which is tentatively dated to the late ninth or early tenth centuries. Certain things are known about it; for example, that there is no evidence of mortise-and-tenon edge joining of planks, that it was probably built frame first, and that there was driven caulking between the planks. All of this is important but there is as yet no reconstruction, and no mast step or indication of the location of a mast has been found.[5]

Illustrations of ships exist in three manuscripts, the Khludov Psalter (Moscow, Historical Museum, MS. 129 D, fol. 88r), dated to 843-47, the Paris, Bibliothèque Nationale manuscript of the Sermons of Gregory of Nazianzus (MS. Gr. 510, esp. fol. 367v) of c. 879-82, and its contemporary the *Sacra Parallela* attributed to St. John of Damascus (Paris, Bibliothèque Nationale, MS. Gr. 923, fol. 207). The third depicts ships with two masts.[6] But apart from these, we have only a very few and very arguable literary sources.

Can we know anything about the performance characteristics of such small coasting vessels of the empire? Much has been made of evidence from the late Roman empire, including such sources as Mark the Deacon's *Life of Porphyrios of Gaza* (composed after 420); however, such polemical sources should be distrusted.

---

[4] J. R. Steffy, 'The reconstruction of the eleventh-century Serçe Liman vessel: a preliminary report', *International Journal of Nautical Archaeology and Underwater Exploration* 11 (1982), 13-34. A monumental report on the ship is currently in press with Texas A. & M. University Press under the editorship of F. van Doorninck, jr. See also the chapter by F. van Doorninck, jr. in this volume.

[5] F. M. Hocker, 'The Byzantine shipwreck at Bozburun, Turkey: the 1997 field season', *INA Quarterly* 25.2 (1998), 12-17 and Hocker, 'Bozborun Byzantine shipwreck excavation: the final campaign 1998', *INA Quarterly* 25.4 (1998), 3-13. The timber for the ship was felled in 874 A.D. (personal communication from Dr F. Hocker).

[6] Reproduced in V. Schepkina, *Miniaturi Khludovskoe Psaltiri* [*Miniatures of the Khludov Psalter*] (Moscow, 1977), no. 88 (no page nos.); K. Weitzmann, *Byzantine book illumination and ivories* (London, 1980), chap. IV, fig. 1; K. Weitzmann, *The miniatures of the Sacra Parallela: Parisinus Graecus 923* (Princeton, 1979), fig. 203 (pl. LIII).

Reference: Date of voyage:	From: To: Distance:	Prevailing Winds:	Duration: Average speed in knots
§ 6 (p. 6): ante 392	Askalon: Thessalonike: 1180 miles/1900 km	adverse ('a happy crossing')	13 days: 3.30 knots
§ 6 (p. 6): ante 392:	Thessalonike: Askalon: 1180 miles/1900 km	favourable:	12 days: 3.60 knots
§ 26 (p. 23): 398:	Gaza: Constantinople: 1230 miles/1980 km	adverse:	20 days: 2.20 knots
§ 27 (p. 23): 398:	Constantinople: Gaza: 1230 miles/1980 km	favourable:	10 days: 4.45 knots
§ 34 (p. 29): 23 Sept. - 2 Oct. 400	Caesarea (Palestine): Rhodes: 570 miles/920 km	adverse ('a good voyage'):	10 days: 2.05 knots
§ 37 (p. 31): October 400:	Rhodes: Constantinople: 580 miles/935 km	adverse:	10 days: 2.10 knots
§§ 54-5 (p. 45): 18-22 April 402:	Constantinople: Rhodes 580 miles/935 km	favourable:	5 days: 4.20 knots
§§ 56-7 (pp. 45-47): 22-28 April 402:	Rhodes: Gaza: 650 miles/1045 km	favourable (but hit by storm):	6.5 days: 3.60 knots

Table 2.1 Durations and speeds of voyages of Porphyrios of Gaza according to Mark the Deacon[7]

These records of voyage durations by Mark the Deacon are extremely unlikely to have been those of voyages actually made by Porphyrios of Gaza. They are much more likely to represent what his biographer considered to be normal durations of voyages between such destinations. And, for the most part, they sound as though he was reckoning only what could normally be achieved when under sail at sea, discounting lay-overs by night. They read as though they are about two-thirds to double what could reasonably be expected if taking into account lay-overs by night. An average of around four knots for voyages before the prevailing winds of summer, and of a half of that for voyages against prevailing winds, is too high, given that most of these voyages

---

[7] Mark the Deacon, 'Βίος τοῦ ἁγίου Πορφυρίου ἐπισκόπου Γάζης', in H. Grégoire and M.-A. Kugener, eds., *Marc le Diacre: Vie de Porphyre, évêque de Gaza* (Paris, 1930).

involved coastal navigation and no one would run along the coast of Asia Minor by night except in the most dire circumstances. The reported voyage from Askalon to Thessalonike in 13 days would have been impossible, except in the most extraordinarily favourable weather conditions.

The pilgrim Saewulf almost certainly travelled on a Byzantine coaster from Chalkis to Jaffa on his pilgrimage in 1102. One could wish that he was more generous with his chronology; however, he did write that Patara was a day's voyage from Rhodes. The distance is around 58 miles and although the current was adverse it was slight and his ship was driven into Patara by evening by a storm. In midsummer there should have been around 14 hours of daylight, so the boat made around 3.6 knots: good sailing. Against this, leaving Cape Chelidonia the crossing of a mere 145 miles to Paphos took three days, a slow passage at only around 2.0 knots, even counting only the daylight hours on the first and third days.

Saewulf's return voyage is a real eye-opener. He reached Rhodes on 22 June 1103 but there decided with some companions to leave the ship on which they had come from Jaffa and to take what was almost certainly another Byzantine coaster to go north to Constantinople. He was then held up at Strobilos by contrary winds for many days. At Chios he changed ships again, most probably because his companions gave up the attempt to reach Constantinople against the prevailing winds but he decided to persevere. He was not to reach Rhaidestos until 29 September. His narrative breaks off at Herakleia but after all his perseverance in the face of adverse winds, one can only hope that he did eventually reach Constantinople to pray in Hagia Sophia. Three months for the 500 miles by an extreme coastal route from Rhodes to Rhaidestos at an average speed of less than 0.2 knots shows just how dependent such small craft were on the wind. Against the prevailing *meltemi* they simply could not proceed and had to wait it out.[8]

Performance capabilities were governed by two factors above all others. The first was speed and upwind sailing capability. But the second was 'fuel', fresh water supplies. The amount of water carried determined how long a ship could stay at sea. Aboard the seventh-century Yassı Ada wreck there was found a single, large, globular *pithos* which had no handles, unlike all the other amphorae, and was obviously set in place somewhere aboard ship.[9] It was almost certainly

---

[8] See J. H. Pryor, 'The voyages of Saewulf', in R. B. C. Huygens, ed., *Peregrinationes tres: Saewulf, John of Würzburg, Theodericus*, CCCont Med 139 (Turnhout, 1994), 35-57.
[9] Bass and van Doorninck, eds., *Yassı Ada volume I* (as in n. 3), 186-187.

the container for the ship's water. It had a height of 71 centimetres and a maximum diameter of 58.5 centimetres. Unfortunately no estimate of its capacity was ever made and it has since been allowed to disintegrate. Nevertheless, its capacity was obviously limited. This ship was a small merchant coaster and whether it carried passengers is unclear. Perhaps such ships could carry more than one such water *pithos* if carrying passengers. But whether or not they could, running out of water was a common occurrence, as is suggested by two tales included in the *Spiritual Meadow* of John Moschos († 619 or 634). In the first, an anchorite named Theodore, bound by ship for Constantinople, turned sea water into fresh when supplies ran out. In the second, a pious *naukleros*, master of a ship bound for Constantinople, prayed for rain for four days to relieve the distress of crew and passengers who had foolishly exhausted their water supplies. He was rewarded by a shower which was confined to the area of the ship, whose course the cloud followed.[10] The author made no mention of oars for these ships and surely intended them to be understood to have been sailing ships. The tales of their running out of water indicates that they carried limited supplies of it, did not even try to stay at sea for extended periods, and had very limited ranges. Normal voyaging patterns almost certainly involved coastal runs and inter-island hops of no more than a few days, putting into beaches and ports for supplies, water, and overnight lay-overs whenever possible. According to Mark the Deacon, when Porphyrios of Gaza was returning from Constantinople to Gaza in April 402 and the ship made port at Rhodes, its *naukleros* refused a request from his passengers for time to visit the anchorite Prokopios because the wind was favourable. The ship sailed for Gaza after spending only enough time in port to take water on board.[11]

---

[10] John Moschos, *Pratum spirituale*, §§173-174, PG 87.3, 2843-3116, here 3041C-3044A; John Moschos, *The Spiritual Meadow (Pratum Spirituale)*, trans. J. Wortley (Kalamazoo, 1992), §§173-174 (pp. 142-143).

[11] Mark the Deacon, *Vie de Porphyre* (as in n. 7), §55 (p. 45).

Galleys: dromons *and* chelandia

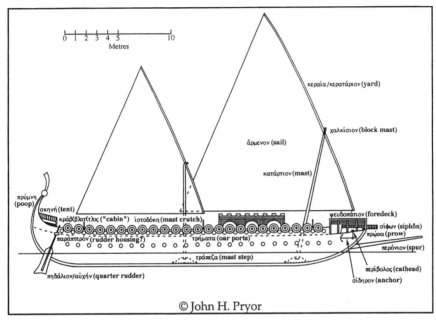

Figure 2.1 Longitudinal section of a tenth-century bireme dromon

We either know or can deduce some essential facts about tenth-century war galleys, δρόμωνες (hereafter *dromons*), and χελάνδια (*chelandia*), as they were known at the time, from which some hypotheses about their construction and performance capabilities can be reached.[12] This, in spite of the fact that their reconstruction has been bedevilled by the unsatisfactory edition by Alphone Dain of the texts in the manuscript Milan, Ambrosiana Library MS. B 119-sup. [gr. 139] and especially by the fact that maritime historians have not realised that the treatise *Naval warfare, commissioned by the Patrikios and Parakoimomenos Basil* was not a shipwright's manual but rather a juvenile exercise in philology.[13]

There were both larger bireme *dromons* and also smaller ones, called γαλέαι (*galeai*) by Leo VI; however, virtually nothing can be deduced about the latter. According to Leo VI, and also Nikephoros Ouranos,

---

[12] The following section is based on dozens of pages of research and argument in J. Pryor and E. Jeffreys, *The Byzantine navy* (forthcoming).

[13] Published by A. Dain as Ναυμαχικὰ Συνταχθέντα παρὰ Βασιλείου πατρικίου καὶ παρακοιμωμένου, in *Naumachica partim adhuc inedita* (Paris, 1943), 57-68 (hereafter Dain, *Naumachica*).

the standard bireme *dromon* had two banks of 25 oarsmen per side, one below deck and one above it, for a total of 100 oarsmen. This is a figure supported in its parameters by that of either 108 or 110 crew for a standard *ousia* or ship's complement, excluding officers and marines, as detailed by the problematical inventories for the Cretan expeditions of 911 and 949 later inserted into the treatise *De cerimoniis*. This treatise is traditionally ascribed to Constantine VII but was actually compiled in its final form under the auspices of Basil the *Parakoimomenos* during the reign of Nikephoros II Phokas.[14]

Because one bank of oarsmen was below deck, both banks would have to have been fully seated and they could not have used the stand-and-sit stroke of later western galleys. That means that the standard 'room' for an oarsman, the *interscalmium*, the distance between any two tholes, cannot have been much more than a metre. It is impossible for a fully seated man, without a moveable seat such as is used in modern rowing shells, to pull the handle of an oar through more than a metre or so. *Olympias II*, if she is ever built, will have *interscalmia* equivalent to two archaic cubits or 0.98 metres.[15]

Assuming that the oarsmen of the upper and lower banks were staggered on average by half an *interscalmium*, a metre each for the twenty-five *interscalmia* makes 25.5 metres and one must then allow for prow and poop to the extremities of the stem and stern. On thirteenth-century western galleys this increased the total length by around 22.5%,[16] which would give a bireme *dromon* an overall length of

---

[14] Leo VI, *The Naval Warfare of the Emperor Leo* (Ναυμαχικὰ Λέοντος Βασιλέως), in Dain, *Naumachica*, §8, pp. 19-33. This treatise was in fact Constitution XIX of the *Taktika* written by, or compiled under the auspices of, the emperor Leo VI (886-912), which is dated to 905-906. Some time later, in the compilation of the manuscript Milan, Biblioteca Ambrosiana, MS. B 119-sup. [Gr. 139] the text of the entire *Taktika* was included in the manuscript at folios 186r-322r, with the exception of Constitution XIX, which was excerpted, included at folios 323r-331v, and followed by other materials on naval warfare. Cf. Nikephoros Ouranos, Περὶ θαλασσομαχίας, in Dain, *Naumachica*, §7, pp. 69-88; Constantine VII Porphyrogennetos, *De cerimoniis*, II§44-45, ed. I. Reiske, 2 vols (Bonn, 1829), I, 651-678, here 664-665; for a new edition of these sections, with translation and commentary, see J. F. Haldon, 'Theory and practice in tenth-century military administration', *TM* 13 (2000), 203-352.

[15] *Olympias* is the reconstruction of a classical Greek *trieres* built under the auspices of the Trireme Trust in 1987. See J. S. Morrison, J. F. Coates, and N. B. Rankov, *The Athenian trireme: the history and reconstruction of an ancient Greek warship*, 2nd edn. (Cambridge, 2000). On the revision of the length of *interscalmia* to 0.98 metres, see pp. 239, 245-246, 268-269. For the *interscalmia* see figure 2.5 below.

[16] See J. H. Pryor, 'From dromon to *galea*: Mediterranean bireme galleys AD 500-1300', in J. Morrison, ed., *The age of the galley: Mediterranean oared vessels since pre-classical times* (London, 1995), 101-116; here 110-114.

approximately 31.25 metres, or at least somewhere between 31 and 32 metres. This is as accurate an estimate of its length as is possible and seems quite reasonable.

As for the beam amidships, the ratio of maximum beam at the *parexeiresiai* amidships to overall length from stempost to stern of *Olympias II* would be approximately 1:6.65. That at the hull proper would be approximately 1:8.21, whereas that of thirteenth-century Sicilian galleys was 1:8.57. However, *triereis* with *parexeiresiai* had a completely different oarage system to medieval western galleys, whose outrigger began to curve outboard only above deck. Given the lack of any empirical data for *dromons*, it is necessary to make a choice. Either the hull began to flare outboard upwards from the lower oarports in a manner parallel to, but not the same as, *triereis* with *parexeiresiai*, or it did not and *dromons* were straight-hulled.

All of the problems resulting from the intermeshing oar blades and associated factors in *Olympias* have led to the conclusion that the hull and oarage designs should be modified to ensure that in any future *Olympias II* the oar blades would not intermesh.[17] We believe that for similar reasons Byzantine *dromons* would also have had hull and oarage systems which avoided having the blades of the oars of the two banks intermeshing. This could in fact be achieved by a quite moderate flaring of the upper hull above the lower oarports. As a result the beam of the ships at the deck would be increased from approximately 3.80 metres to 4.46 metres. The flare on either side would only be around 33 centimetres, hardly a matter of great importance.

There is little or nothing in the iconography to support this interpretation, but there is nothing to contradict it either. The only probable representations of *dromons* are those in the *Roman Vergil*, *Ilias Ambrosiana*, *Sacra Parallela*, and the Panteleemon manuscript of the Sermons of Gregory of Nazianzus.[18] None may be said to show

---

[17] Morrison, Coates and Rankov, *The Athenian trireme* (as in n. 15), 272.

[18] *Roman Vergil*: Rome, Biblioteca Apostolica Vaticana, MS. Vat. Lat. 3867, fol. 77r, late fifth century, reproduced in E. Rosenthal, *The Illuminations of the Vergilius Romanus (Cod. Vat. Lat. 3867): a stylistic and iconographical analysis* (Zürich, 1972), plate VIII (p. 52). *Ilias Ambrosiana*: Milan, Biblioteca Ambrosiana, Cod. Ambros. F 205 Inf., esp. miniatures I, III, V, VIII, XI, XXXII, XXXVIII, XLIV, XXXXVI early sixth century, reproduced in R. B. Bandinelli, *Hellenistic-Byzantine miniatures of the Iliad (Ilias Ambrosiana)* (Olten, 1955), Figures 31, 39, 96, 104, 116, 135, 167, 214, colour plates II & III, and esp. min. XXVII (fig. 190). *Sacra Parallela*: Paris, Bibliothèque Nationale, MS. Gr. 923, fol. 207r, third quarter of ninth century, reproduced in Weitzmann, *Miniatures of the Sacra Parallela* (as in n. 6), fig. 203 (plate LIII). Panteleemon Sermons of Gregory of Nazianzus: Mount Athos, Panteleemon, Cod. 6, fol. 138r, twelfth century, reproduced in S. M. Pelekanides, *et al.*, Οἱ Θησαυροὶ τοῦ Ἁγίου Ὄρους 2 (Athens, 1975), fig. 307, p. 182.

clearly a flaring in the upper hull, although the first three do show a separate 'band' at the top of the hull with oar ports in it. It is not inconceivable that the artists intended to depict a bank of oars rowed from above deck where the hull had been flared out. That being said, none of them showed two banks of oars.

Olympias, of course, does not have a full deck; therefore, it is not possible to calculate a depth in hold from floor to deck for her. However, that of the thirteenth-century galleys of the kingdom of Sicily, similar to *dromons* in that they were also fully decked, was 2.04 metres; by comparison, that of the smaller *dromons* was probably around 1.75-1.85 metres.[19]

Dromons almost certainly used oars of different lengths for the two banks of oars above and below deck.

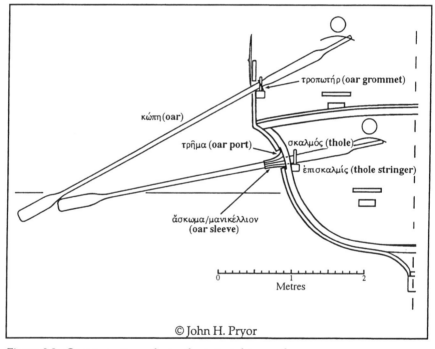

Figure 2.2 Oarage system of a tenth-century bireme dromon

With the lower oars 4.66 metres long (the same as those of *Olympias II*) rowed at 11° to the water when the blades were submerged, the upper

---

[19] See J. H. Pryor, 'The galleys of Charles I of Anjou, king of Sicily: ca.1269-84', *Studies in Medieval and Renaissance History*, 14 [old series, 24] (1993), 33-103, here 45.

oars would need to be 5.178 metres long when rowed at 28° to the water so that the strokes of the upper and lower oarsmen would be the same in horizontal plane, which was the important thing.

Dromons were small ships. They were designed for one purpose only: to pack the biggest punch possible in battle. It is important to bear in mind that in ship design everything was a compromise. One thing could be achieved only at the expense of another. Human comfort, stowage capacity, and seaworthiness had to be sacrificed if one wanted to build a warship which would develop maximum power from the oars for short-term speed in battle, which would have maximum manoeuvrability, carry maximum crews for battle, and also have sufficient sturdiness to withstand attack. And this was what battle *dromons* had to be able to be capable of. Much of what Leo VI wrote about naval warfare in Constitution XIX of his *Taktika* is of doubtful practicality; however, he was surely right when he wrote that:

> The construction of the *dromons* should be neither too heavy, or they will be sluggish when under way, nor built too lightly, or they will be weak and unsound and quickly broken up by the waves and the attacks of the opposition. Let the *dromon* have suitable workmanship so that it is not too sluggish when under way and remains sturdy and unbroken when in a gale or struck by the enemy.[20]

Almost certainly standard bireme *dromons* had two masts and two masts only. There is no evidence for three masts that stands up to scrutiny and if they only had one mast, such ships would almost certainly luff up into the wind if they tried to tack.

The performance capabilities of such ships were controlled by four factors: their ability to tack into the wind, their inability to survive in heavy seas, the speed that their crews could sustain under oars over time, and their stowage capacity for provisions, especially for fresh water.

Any war galley such as a *dromon* could, of course, make way either under sail or under oars. In light conditions it might be possible to use both oars and sails, but that would have been difficult and was unusual.[21] However, galleys were simply not designed to be sailed and

---

[20] Leo VI, Ναυμαχικὰ Λέοντος Βασιλέως, in Dain, *Naumachica*, §4, pp. 19-33.

[21] The sea trials of *Olympias* have shown that both oars and sails may be used together but only in light breezes from astern or on the quarter. Obviously oars could not be used when a ship was heeling under sail with a wind from abeam. See J. Coates and J. Morrison, 'The sea trials of the reconstructed Athenian trireme *Olympias*: a reply to Lucien Basch',

throughout history they were always notoriously poor sailers. Their lack of deep keels meant that they made excessive leeway when beating into the wind.

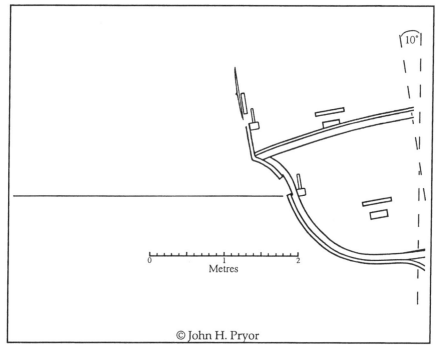

Figure 2.3 Tenth-century bireme dromon heeling under sail to ten degrees

Their shallow draft and low freeboard meant that they could not heel under sail very much. Their narrow beam and low depth in hold meant that their hulls did not have the structural strength to carry a large press of sail. Their extreme lengths:beam ratio and lateen sails meant that they carried pronounced weather helm, constantly griping, the bows coming up into the wind.[22] Their poor upwind performance under

---

Mariner's Mirror 79 (1993), 131-41, here 139; J. Coates, S. K. Platis, and J. T. Shaw, *The trireme trials 1988: report on the Anglo-Hellenic sea trials of Olympias* (Oxford, 1990), 39; Morrison, Coates and Rankov, *The Athenian trireme* (as in n. 7), 258-259.

[22] J. H. Pryor, *Geography, technology, and war: studies in the maritime history of the Mediterranean, 649-1571* (Cambridge, 1988), 71-73; M. A. Bragadin, 'Le navi, loro strutture e attrezzature nell'alto medioevo', in *La navigazione mediterranea nell'alto medioevo* (Settimane di studio del Centro Italiano di studi sull'alto medioevo, XXV), 2 vols. (Spoleto, 1978), I, 389-407; here 393-394; J. F. Guilmartin, *Gunpowder and galleys: changing technology and*

sail is nothing to be wondered at for they were not designed for this. And *dromons* may have been even worse sailers than later medieval western galleys because, with oarsmen below deck, there would have been nowhere to stow ballast and without ballast any ship heeling under sail would be extremely unstable. Moreover, a heel under sail of a mere ten degrees or so would put the under edges of the lower oar ports at the flat water line and at that point it is highly debatable whether the oar sleeves would have prevented water from flooding in, even if they were tied off tight. That being said, with a favourable light breeze from astern, say around Beaufort scale 3 (7-10 knots with large wavelets up to 2 ft or 61 centimetres), a *dromon* could no doubt bowl along quite nicely. In fine conditions a *dromon* might make a voyage such as that from Constantinople to Rhodes in as little as 8-10 days or to Paphos in Cyprus in 10-12 days.[23]

Before the prevailing North-to-East light winds of summer, such a *dromon* sailing from Constantinople at dawn, around 5.00 a.m., on a fine summer's day in July, might well drive across the Sea of Marmara on a West-South-West course with the wind only two to six points on the starboard stern quarter and even make Rhaidestos, 80 miles away, by evening around 8.00 p.m. at an average speed of around 4.6 knots.[24] Herakleia, around 65 miles from Constantinople, would have been even more reachable at an average speed of around 3.8 knots. Prokonnesos

---

Mediterranean warfare at sea in the sixteenth century (Cambridge, 1974), 205-206.

[23] Beaufort Scale: a scale for wind and sea conditions developed by the British Rear Admiral Sir Francis Beaufort (1774-1857). What follows takes the scale up to Force 7 only.

Force on Beaufort Scale	Knots	Description	Height of sea in feet (and metres)	Deep sea criteria
0	0-1	Calm	—	Flat calm, mirror smooth
1	1-3	Light airs	0.25 (0.075)	Small wavelets, no crests
2	4-6	Light breeze	0.5 (0.15)	Small wavelets, crests glassy but not breaking
3	7-10	Light breeze	2.0 (0.61)	Large wavelets, crests beginning to break
4	11-16	Moderate breeze	3.5 (1.07)	Small waves, becoming longer, crests breaking frequently
5	17-21	Fresh breeze	6 (1.83)	Moderate waves, longer, breaking crests
6	22-27	Strong breeze	9.5 (2.90)	Large waves forming, crests breaking more frequently
7	28-33	Strong wind	13.5 (4.11)	Large waves, streaky foam

[24] In July at Istanbul the wind prevails from the North to East around 70% of the time and calms represent another 12%. The mean wind speed is only 11 knots. Winds from the West to South occur less than 3% of the time. See Great Britain, Admiralty, *Black Sea Pilot*, 11th edn. (London, 1969), 72.

was only around 30 miles South-South-West of Herakleia, an easy run, and Abydos 70 miles from Prokonnesos. Even the 95 miles from Rhaidestos to Abydos would not have been impossible with the assistance of the current through the Dardanelles.[25] The run from Abydos to Tenedos was only around 30 miles. Heading south into the Aegean with the wind prevailing strongly from the north,[26] a *dromon* would reach Rhodes from Constantinople in 8-10 days with daylight passages of around 80 miles to Mytilene, 70 miles to Chios, about the same to Samos, and perhaps two days with a stopover somewhere among the scattered islets of the Sporades for the 100 miles to Kos, and then a final day's sail of around 80 miles to Rhodes.[27] The 250 miles from Rhodes to Paphos ought to have been coverable before the prevailing West to North winds in three days with a first-night lay-over somewhere around Patara or Finike.[28]

Nicholas Mouzalon wrote that he was virtually ordered to the archbishopric of Cyprus by Alexios I Komnenos in 1107 and it is tempting to think that he may have been provided with an imperial *dromon* for the voyage. In similar circumstances St. Symeon of Mytilene had been provided with one by the Empress Theodora when he was appointed to the bishopric of Mytilene.[29] Unfortunately, but predictably, Mouzalon simply used the generic for a ship, *ploion*, when he wrote that he made Cyprus from Constantinople in 10 days.[30] The

---

[25] A run from Rhaidestos to Abydos would have been almost directly South-West. At Çannakale near Byzantine Abydos, the wind in July prevails from the North to East 88% of the time at an average of 10.5 knots. See Great Britain, Admiralty, *Black Sea Pilot*, 71.

[26] In July in the Aegean the wind prevails strongly from the North to East-North-East in the northern sector, swinging to the North-West to North-North-East in the central Aegean and then to the West-North-West to North-West in the South approaching Rhodes. The strength is commonly in the order of Beaufort scale 1-4, 0-16 knots, in the North, strengthening to 3-5, 7-21 knots, in the central Aegean and to 4-5, 11-21 knots, in the South towards Rhodes. See Great Britain, Admiralty, *Mediterranean Pilot*, IV, 9th edn. (London, 1968), fig. 6.

[27] At Rhodes in July the wind averages 76.5% from West to North at an average speed of 18 knots, driving any ship straight into it from Kos. Great Britain, Admiralty, *Mediterranean Pilot*, IV, 33.

[28] At Paphos the wind in July prevails from the West to North around 66% of the time at a mean wind speed of a gentle 6 knots. See Great Britain, Admiralty, *Mediterranean Pilot*, V, 6th edn. (London, 1976), 29.

[29] See C. de Smedt, *et al.*, 'Acta Graeca SS. Davidis, Symeonis et Georgii Mitylenae in insula Lesbo', *AnBoll* 18 (1899), 209-259; here 253: '... καὶ δρόμωνος ἐπιβάντες βασιλικοῦ...'.

[30] S. Doanidou,"Ἡ παραίτησις Νικολάου τοῦ Μουζάλωνος ἀπὸ τῆς ἀρχιεπισκοπῆς Κύπρου. Ἀνέκδοτον ἀπολογητικὸν ποίημα', *Hell* 7 (1934), 109-150; here 119 (hereafter Doanidou,"Ἡ παραίτησις Νικολάου τοῦ Μουζάλωνος').

future patriarch was, however, making a point when he wrote that he made the voyage in the best possible anticipated time because his ship had excellent sailors and the Holy Spirit filled its sails. We do not know at what time of the year he made the voyage, but assuming that it was spring or summer with around 14 hours daylight, the voyage was made at an average of around 5.25 knots, which would certainly be at the upper level of expectations, but not impossible. Did his mention of excellent sailors point to an imperial *dromon*?

The scenario would be very different if the wind rose to Beaufort scale 4-5 (16-17 knots). That would raise waves of around 4.75 feet, 1.45 metres. All galleys at all times were designed to cut through the water rather than to ride with the waves and such a wind, which is just a 'moderate' to 'fresh' breeze on the Beaufort scale, nothing out of the ordinary, would send waves washing over the deck of any *dromon*. Even if the wind were astern, she would still be forced to run for the coast. If the wind were ahead, it would be worse because that would mean that the ship was attempting to beat to windward and therefore would be heeling over, probably with one gunwale continuously underwater. And, in the Aegean in summer the *meltemi* can rise to a very strong wind even up to Beaufort scale 7 (28-33 knots), particularly in the channels between the islands, raising short steep seas and generating strong currents.[31] Even modern yachts can be forced to take shelter. Scale seven winds can raise seas up to 13.5 feet (4.115 metres) and no *dromon* would stand a chance of continuing its voyage in such conditions. The *meltemi* becomes strongest from July through to September and from noon through to evening, so the optimum time for a voyage from Constantinople to Rhodes would be spring, from April to June, and in the mornings.

The speed that oared ships of all kinds could maintain under oars is a matter of considerable scholarly debate. Different scholars have directed their attention to different periods and various types of oared ships and have produced results which are very difficult to reconcile.

What one would like, of course, is reliable historical data for voyages made by *dromons* in pressing circumstances in conditions which would suggest that the voyages were made under oars in calm conditions or at worst against light breezes. However, little data can be derived from the Byzantine sources. For the most part we are compelled to have recourse to data from the sources for classical antiquity and the western middle ages.

---

[31] See H. M. Denham, *The Aegean: a sea-guide to its coast and islands*, 5th edn. (London, 1983), pp. xxv-xxvi.

Sources:[32]	AW =	*The African War*
	App =	Appian, *The Civil Wars*
	Bc =	*Breve chronicon de rebus siculis*
	C =	Caffaro, *De liberatione civitatum Orientis liber*
	D =	S. Doanidou, "Ἡ παραίτησις Νικολάου τοῦ Μουζάλωνος'
	H =	Herodotos, *Histories*
	IP =	*Itinerarium peregrinorum*
	L =	Livy, *From the foundation of the city*
	Lu =	Lucan, *The Civil War*
	NM =	Niketas Magistros, 'The life of Theoktiste'
	Po =	Polybios, *The Histories*
	Proc =	Procopius, *The Vandal War*
	Theoph =	Theophanes the Confessor, *Chronographia*
	Xh =	Xenophon, *Hellenika*

Source: Date of voyage:	Fleet: Commander: Composition:	From: To: Approximate distance: Voyage objective: Degree of haste:	Current: Oars or sails: Time taken: Approx. average speed:
H, VIII.66: 480 B.C.:	Persian: Not stated: Not stated:	Euripos: Phaleron: 115 miles/185 km: Invasion force: Moderate:	Generally favourable: Prob. sails then oars: 3 days: 1.39 knots:
Xh, II.1.30: 405 B.C.:	Milesian: Theopompos: Single ship:	Aigos potamoi (opp. Lampsakos): Lakedaimon: 420 miles: Report of victory: High:	Neutral: Probably both: After the battle to the third day, c. 42-54 hours: 6.75-8.6 knots:

Table 2.2 Some reported voyages of ancient and medieval galleys and galley fleets with generally favourable prevailing winds

[32] *The African war*, in A. G. Way, trans., *Caesar: Alexandrian, African and Spanish wars* (London, 1955); Appian, *The Civil Wars*, in H. White, trans., *Appian's Roman history*, 4 vols;. vols. 3-4 (London, 1913); *Breve chronicon de rebus siculis a Roberti Guiscardi temporibus inde ad annum 1250, ...*, in J.-L.-A. Huillard Bréholles, *Historia diplomatica Friderici secundi*, 6 vols. (Paris, 1852-61), vol. 1, part 2, 887-908; Caffaro, *De liberatione civitatum Orientis liber*, in Caffaro, *Annali genovesi di Caffaro e de' suoi continuatori dal MXCIX al MCCXCIII*, eds. L. T. Belgrano and C. Imperiale, 5 vols., Fonti per la Storia d'Italia (Rome and Genoa, 1890-1929), vol. 1, 95-124; S. Doanidou, "Ἡ παραίτησις Νικολάου τοῦ Μουζάλωνος' (as in n. 30), 109-150; Herodotos, *Histories*, in A. D. Godley, trans. *Herodotus*, 4 vols (London, 1920-25); *Itinerarium peregrinorum et gesta regis Ricardi*, ed. W. Stubbs, in *Chronicles and memorials of the reign of Richard I*, vol. 1 (Rolls series, 38.1) (London, 1864); Livy, *From the foundation of the city*, in B. O. Foster, *et al.*, trans. *Livy*, 14 vols (London, 1919-59); Lucan, *The Civil War*, in J. D. Duff, trans., *Lucan* (London, 1928); Niketas Magistros, 'The life of our blessed mother Theoktiste of Lesbos who practiced asceticism and died on the island named Paros', in

TYPES OF SHIPS

Po, V.110.5: 216 B.C.:	Macedonian: Philip V: 100 *lemboi*:	Saso (Sazan) island: Kephallenia: 190 miles/305 km: Fleeing Romans: Highest:	Slightly adverse: Probably both: 'On the second day' (1- 1.5 days): 4.6-6.9 knots:

L, XXVI.19.11,
42.6:
209 B.C.:
	Roman:
	Publius
	  Cornelius Scipio Jr.:
	30 quinqiremes:
		Mouth of the Ebro:
		Cartagena:
		295 miles/475 km:
		Coasting, accompanying
		  land forces:
		Low:
			Slightly favourable:
			Probably both:
			'On the seventh day'
			(6-6.5 days):
			1.65–1.8 knots:

L, XXIX.27.6-8:
204 B.C.:
	Roman:
	Publius
	  Cornelius Scipio Jr.:
	50 quadriremes and
	  quinquiremes, 400
	  transports:
		Lilybaion (Marsala):
		Cape Bon:
		90 miles/145 km:
		Invasion:
		Moderate:
			Neutral:
			Sails:
			1 day (24 hours):
			3.25 knots:

L, XLV.41.3:
167 B.C.:
	Roman:
	Lucius Aemilius
	  Paulus:
	Not stated:
		Brindisi:
		Corfu:
		140 miles/225 km:
		Opening campaign:
		Moderate:
			Slightly adverse:
			Probably both:
			9 Roman hours (10.5
			  hours):
			11.6 knots (impossible):

App, II.89: 48 B.C.:	Roman: Julius Caesar: Unknown number of triremes:	Rhodes: Alexandria: 350 miles/563 km: Opening campaign: Moderate:	Neutral: Sails: Three days: 4.2 knots:

AW, 2:
47 B.C.:
	Roman:
	Julius Caesar:
	'a fast ship and a
	  few warships':
		Aponiana (Favignana):
		Africa:
		95 miles/155 km:
		Opening campaign:
		Moderate:
			Neutral:
			Sails:
			'After the fourth day'
			  (3-3.5 days):
			1.0-1.15 knots
			  (exceedingly slow):

Lucan, IX. 1004-5: 48 B.C.:	Roman: Caesar: Not stated:	Troy: Alexandria: 750 miles/1210 km: Opening campaign: Moderate:	Neutral: Probably sails: 7 days: 3.9 knots:

AASS Nov., 4 (Brussels, 1925), 224-233, trans. A. C. Hero, in A.-M. Talbot, ed., *Holy women of Byzantium: ten saints' lives in English translation* (Washington, 1996), 95-116; Polybios, *The Histories*, in W. R. Paton, trans., *Polybius: the histories*, 6 vols (London, 1922-27); Procopius of Caesarea, *The Vandal War*, in *History of the Wars*, in *Procopius*, 7 vols., trans. H. B. Dewing (London, 1914-40), vol. 2 (1916); Theophanes the Confessor, *Chronographia*, ed. C. de Boor, 2 vols. (Leipzig, 1883); Xenophon, *Hellenika*, in C. L. Brownson, trans., *Xenophon*, 7 vols., I-II (London, 1918-21).

Theoph. A.M.: 6026: 533:	Byzantine: Belisarios: Not stated, but included 90-92 *dromons*:	Kaukana (nr Cape Scalambri, Sicily): Caputvada (Ras Kaboudia, Tunisia) [via Malta]: 250 miles/400 km: Invasion force: Moderate:	Neutral: Probably sails: 'On the third day' (2-2.5 days): 3.6-4.5 knots:
Proc, III.25.21: 534:	Vandal: Tzazon: Unspecified νῆες:	Cagliari: African coast: 130 miles/210 km: Responding to news of Vandal defeat: Highest:	Neutral: Probably sails: 'On the third day' (2-2.5 days): 1.9-2.35 knots:
NM, §13: 910:	Byzantine: Niketas Magistros: Probably a single *dromon*:	Naxos: Crete: 120 miles/195 km: Part of invasion force: Moderate:	Neutral: Probably sails: 'On the second day' (1-1.5 days): 2.9-4.35 knots:
D, p. 119: 1107:	Byzantine: Not known: Possibly an imperial *dromon*:	Constantinople: Cyprus: 850 miles/1370 km: To take up archbishopric: Moderate:	Slightly adverse: Sails: 10 days: 3.1 knots:
C, p. 102: 1097:	Genoese: Not known: 12 *galeae* and a *sandanum*:	Genoa: Port St Simeon (Süveydiye): 2200 miles/3540 km: First Crusade: High:	Neutral: Probably mainly sails: Approx. 4 months from mid July to around 20 Nov.: Approx. 0.65 knots:
IP, II, 26-31: 1191:	English: Richard Coeur de Lion: Some Mediterranean *galeae*:	Messina: Limassol: 1350 miles/2175 km: On crusade: High:	Neutral: Probably mainly sails: 21 days at sea (20-20.5 days): 2.4 knots:
IP, II, 26-28: 1191:	French: Philip II: Some Mediterranean *galeae*:	Messina: Acre: 1550 miles/2495 km: On crusade: High:	Neutral: Probably mainly sails: On the 22nd day (21-21.5 days): 2.65 knots:
Bc, p. 898: 1228:	Sicilian: Frederick II: 40 *galeae*:	Brindisi: Limassol: 1200 miles/1930 km: On crusade: High:	Neutral: Probably mainly sails: On the 24th day (23-23.5 days): 1.85-1.89 knots:
Average			**3.5 knots**

The evidence of the various sources varies enormously and few of the reports are verifiable, except for the voyages of the crusader fleets.

Invariably the reports have some literary, didactic, or polemical purpose and cannot be read as 'Shipping Notices'. In many cases they probably represented what their authors thought ought to have been possible rather than what actually happened. Longer voyages also obviously incorporated time spent in ports of call and even shorter ones sometimes incorporated lay-overs by night. Nevertheless there is perhaps sufficient consistency in the data to suggest that in favourable conditions fleets could maintain around 3-4 knots while at sea.

The narrator of the *Life of St Theoktiste of Lesbos*, Niketas Magistros, was told on Paros by a hermit called Symeon that from Paros he would sail to Naxos, lie there in harbour for one day, sail for Crete on the second day and reach it on the third.[33] Since at the time Niketas was accompanying the expedition of Himerios to Crete in 910, he was probably on a war galley, a *dromon*, and the voyage predictions read like a reflection of what could normally be accomplished by a *dromon* sailing before the prevailing northerlies of summer south to Crete. Naxos to Chandax (Iraklion) in Crete, via Ios and Thera is only around 120 miles; easy sailing before the prevailing northerlies of summer in, say, 30 hours at an average speed of around 3.5 knots.

It is usually assumed that galleys used their oars when the winds were adverse and they could not use their sails. This is no doubt true. However, when discussing the use of oars against adverse winds, the serious limitations created by waves is an issue which is invariably overlooked. All winds raise waves. The optimum position for a seated man pulling an oar is to have the handle just below the level of his shoulders when his arms are fully extended to begin the stroke. At the end of the stroke he must lower his hands to lift the blade clear of the water for the return. But the distance between the shoulders and the top of the legs of a seated man is only around 40 centimetres. The implication is that the lower oars of a *dromon*, or indeed of any galley with similarly geared oars, simply could not be raised more than around 80 centimetres above the flat calm waterline.

---

[33] *AASS* Nov., 4 (Brussels, 1925), §13, 224-33; trans. Hero (as in n. 32), 95-116, here 107-108.

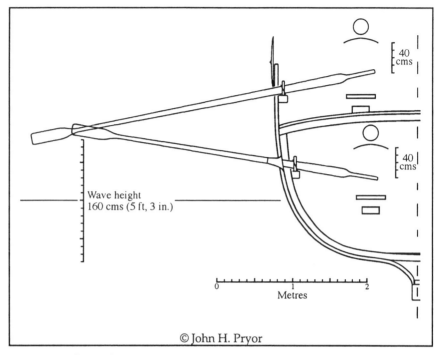

Figure 2.4 Oars of a tenth-century bireme dromon drawn in the middle of the return stroke at 67° to the centre line

That would mean that in any waves above 1.60 metres (5 feet, 3 inches) the lower oars could not have been used because the oarsmen could not achieve a return stroke. Winds of Beaufort scale 4, 'moderate breezes' of 11-16 knots, will begin raising waves of that height towards the top of the range. In anything more than a moderate breeze the lower oars of a *dromon* could not be used and it is very debateable whether the upper oars alone would permit her to make any headway at all against a 16 knot breeze.

Supplies of fresh water were vitally important because it was the 'fuel' which drove any galley. Unless a galley could use its sails, it would come to a stop within hours if its water supplies ran out; dehydration would quickly enfeeble the oarsmen.

Estimates of the amount of water crews required have been revised upwards dramatically over the past decade or so. During sea trials of the reconstructed Greek trireme *Olympias*, it has been found that oarsmen need a litre per hour, just for drinking, to prevent dehydration.[34] More would have been needed for the soupy stew of salt meat and legumes that was the staple diet of medieval crews.

Around eight litres per day for galley crews is increasingly supported by a range of evidence from antiquity to the seventeenth century.[35] If we consider the standard *ousia* of 108 men of a Byzantine *dromon* or *chelandion*, the water requirement can confidently be expected to have been a minimum of 108 × 8 = 864 litres per day. Increasing that to at least 1,000 litres or one tonne of water per ship per day when officers and marines are also taken into account would surely be reasonable. And this would be to discount supernumeraries, *dromons* with two *ousiai* as crews, and the various higher figures for crews reported for the ships of the Cretan expeditions.[36] One tonne of water per day would have been an absolute bare minimum.

By the tenth century it is probable that Byzantine fleets were using both barrels and amphorae as water containers. One inventory for the Cretan expedition of 949 specified five κάδοι (*kadoi*) per *dromon* and *kados* was a word used commonly since antiquity for a ship-board water amphora.[37] The *kadoi* depicted on the *Cista Ficoronica* of c. 300 B.C., in a representation of Jason and the Argonauts watering at the spring of the Bebrycians, are estimated to have weighed around 18 kg for a capacity of 27 litres.[38] Five *kadoi* such as those of the *Cista Ficoronica*

---

[34] B. Rankov, 'Reconstructing the past: the operation of the trireme reconstruction *Olympias* in the light of historical sources', *Mariner's Mirror* 80 (1994), 131-146, here 138; S. Platis, 'The Greek crew trials with Olympias in 1988', in Τρόπις III/*Tropis III: 3rd International symposium on ship construction in antiquity, Athens 1989. Proceedings* (Athens, 1995), 335-345, here 340; Morrison, Coates, and Rankov, *The Athenian trireme*, 238.

[35] Earlier estimates of water requirements, as low as four pints (2.25 litres) per day, are now regarded as hopelessly inadequate. See A. W. Sleeswyk and F. Meijer, 'The water supply of the Argo and other oared ships', *Mariner's Mirror* 84 (1998), 131-138, here 133-135; J. Dotson, 'Economics and logistics of galley warfare', in Morrison, ed., *The age of the galley* (as in n. 16), 217-223; Pryor, *Geography, technology, and war* (as in n. 22), 75-85; Idem, 'From dromon to *galea*' (as in n. 16), 114; Idem, 'The geographical conditions of galley navigation in the Mediterranean', in Morrison, ed., *The age of the galley* (as in n. 16), 206-216, here 210.

[36] The figures for the two expeditions of 911 and 949 and for various types of ships vary considerably: *chelandia pamphyla* of 120 or 150 men, *chelandia ousiaka* of 108 and 110 men, *chelandia* and *dromons* of 220 men, *dromons* of 200 or 220 men. Crews were tailored to suit circumstances and expedition objectives and in many cases the ships obviously carried supernumeraries either as landing assault troops or to provide two 'watches' to keep the galleys moving around the clock if necessary.

[37] Constantine VII, *De cerimoniis*, ed. Reiske, I, 671; also Haldon, 'Theory and practice in tenth-century military administration' (as in n. 14), 227.

[38] Sleeswyk and Meijer, 'The water supply of the Argo and other oared ships' (as in n. 36), 133. The '*Cista Ficoronica*' is a bronze water urn from Palestrina (Praeneste), south-east of Rome, dated to the second half of the fourth century B.C. and of Greco-Etruscan workmanship. It was acquired by the antiquarian Francesco Ficoroni in 1738. It is now in

would contain only around 135-150 litres of water and therefore they cannot have been the main storage receptacles of *dromons* for water. The inventories did not specify barrels or any other items which might have been. However, a letter from the Cairo Geniza dated to the mid-eleventh century mentioned buckets which contained 'half a Byzantine barrel'. This is the first known reference to barrels in Byzantium but the reference makes it clear that, by that period, it was well known that the Byzantines used barrels.[39] How long they had been doing so is unknown.

Amphorae were less efficient as water containers and also much heavier as containers in relation to their contents. Their dry weight to capacity ratio was around 1:1.5. Barrels are much more efficient than this. Traditional oak wine barrels weigh between 50 and 65 kg for 225 litres capacity. Their dry weight to capacity ratio is around 1:3.5-4.5.

On bireme *dromons* both the storage of water and also its weight must have been a problem. Thirteenth-century Sicilian galleys, the earliest for which we have construction details, had only around 50 cm freeboard amidships and a tonne of water would sink them by a centimetre or so.[40] No more than a quarter or so of their 40 tonnes of deadweight tonnage could have been used for water because of the weight of the food, armaments, equipment, spare gear and myriad other essentials required. It is extremely improbable that the smaller 25-tonne Byzantine *dromons* could have carried much more than around five tonnes of water. Later evidence from Genoa suggests that the larger war galleys of the fourteenth and fifteenth centuries could carry between 4 and 8 tonnes of water,[41] but they had no oarsmen rowing in the hold.

With two files of oarsmen rowing below deck, where could water have been stored? A 245 litre (54 gallon) capacity oak cask has a maximum diameter at its pitch of 28 inches (71 centimetres), a head diameter of 23 inches (58.5 centimetres), a height of 36.5 inches (92.5

---

the Villa Giulia museum of Etruscan antiquities in Rome, Inv. no. 24787. See T. Dohrn, *Die Ficoronische Ciste in der Villa Giulia in Rom* (Berlin, 1972).

[39] S. D. Goitein, *A Mediterranean society: the Jewish communities of the Arab world as portrayed in the documents of the Cairo Geniza. Vol. I: economic foundations* (Berkeley and Los Angeles, 1967), 321. The letter is in the Taylor-Schechter collection of Cambridge University Library, MS. TS 12.241. It is written in Judaeo-Arabic, medieval Arabic written in Hebrew script. The relevant lines are recto 6-7, transliterated as follows: '... n'ml fy 'l'nbb' b'lnwb' kmsyin dlw w'ldlw 'ldy ystq' bh nṣf bty' rwmy' ...', translated as '... we laboured at bailing by turns of fifty buckets and each bucket holds half a Byzantine barrel ...'. Here the Arabic *dlw* meant a 'bucket', *bty'* a 'barrel', and *rwmy'* 'Roman' or 'Byzantine'.

[40] Pryor, 'From dromon to galea', 112-113.

[41] Pryor, *Geography, technology, and war*, 77-79.

centimetres), and would occupy a cylindrical space of around 370 litres.[42] The only place in the hold of a bireme *dromon* where casks such as these could have been stowed would have been on the floor down the centre-line of the ship. However, that space would surely have had to have been reserved for the long spare gear that had to be carried: rudders, oars, yards, even masts.[43] Such gear could obviously not have been carried above deck on a warship.

In the case of galleys such as classical *triereis* and Byzantine *dromons* we are forced to conclude that each oarsmen carried his own water supply in a *kados* or a small barrel.

---

[42] K. Kilby, *The Cooper and his trade* (Fresno, 1971), 61.
[43] Leo VI, Ναυμαχικὰ Λέοντος Βασιλέως, §5, in Dain, *Naumachica*, 19-20.

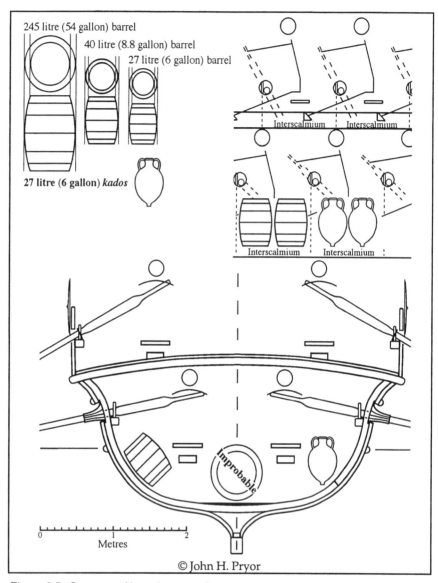

Figure 2.5 Stowage of barrels or amphorae

It is tempting to associate an optimum size for a small portable barrel with that of the size of the Genoese *quartarolo* (39.75 litres) or the Neapolitan *barile* (43.625 litres). Barrels much bigger than 40 litres (8.8 gallons) would be too heavy and large to be handled by a single man. Forty litres is also about double the size of a normal bucket;

buckets containing more than that and weighing over 20 kilograms become extremely difficult to manoeuvre. Forty litres would weigh 40 kg (88 lb); this together with around 10 kg for the weight of the barrel makes 50 kg (110 lb), and the barrel would measure approximately 14 inches (35.5 cm) across the head, 17.75 inches (44.5 cm) at the pitch [circumference of 55 inches (140 cm)], and 21 inches (54.5 cm) high.[44] A man could not get his arms around anything much bigger than that to lift it.

It would be just possible to stow two 27-litre *kadoi* or two 40-litre barrels alongside the thwarts of the oarsmen of the lower bank between them and the hull, two for each oarsman. Half of the barrels or *kadoi* may well have been stowed similarly above deck for the oarsmen of the upper bank but obviously they could not have stayed there during battle and there must have been room to stow them below if necessary. Or were they jettisoned before battle?

After reflection, the only logical conclusion to the problem of the water supply of *dromons*, a supply which then governed their cruising range, is that they could stow away around 100 40-litre barrels weighing around 5 tonnes when full or around 100 27-litre amphorae weighing around 4.5 tonnes. This would give a *dromon* a minimum range under oars in summer, using one tonne of water per day, of three days. With an average speed in favourable conditions of around 3.5 knots and an average of around 14 hours of daylight during summer campaigning seasons, three days' water supply would give Byzantine fleets a range of no more than 170 miles under oars. All things were variable, of course. Conditions made all the difference, as did the use of sails when possible, cool weather, and human endurance, strength, and skill. Fleets could also proceed by night if out to sea away from coasts and islands, or if the skies were clear and the moon was full, or even if the need was great. But in normal circumstances, Byzantine fleets would not have ranged much more than around 170 miles without watering. When packed to the gunwales with supernumeraries, as they were for the assaults on Crete, that figure would have to be lowered dramatically.

It is no wonder that Syrianos Magistros, followed by Nikephoros Ouranos, recommended that not only the *strategoi* but also each and every ship in a fleet should have aboard seamen familiar with the coasts and where fresh water could be obtained. As Nikephoros wrote:

> It is appropriate for a *strategos* to have with him men who have accurate knowledge and experience of the sea in which he is sailing,

---

[44] Kilby, *The Cooper and his trade*, 61.

which winds cause it to swell and which blow from the land. They should know both the hidden rocks in the sea, and the places which have no depth, and the land along which one sails and the islands adjacent to it, the harbours and the distance such harbours are the one from the other. They should know both the countries and the water supplies;[45] for many have perished from lack of experience of the sea and the regions, since winds frequently blow and scatter the ships to one region and another. And it is appropriate that not only the *strategos* should have men with this knowledge we have discussed but also each and every ship should have someone knowing these things to advise well when appropriate.[46]

---

[45] Nikephoros Ouranos and Syrianos Magistros almost certainly meant 'fresh water' by ὕδατα (*hydata*). The knowledge required was of where to obtain precious fresh water, rather than knowledge of the 'waters'; i.e., the seas.

[46] Nikephoros Ouranos, §119.1.1-3, in Dain, *Naumachica*, 93 (checked by us against the manuscript, Oxford, Bodleian Library, MS. Baroccianus Graecus 131):

Ἁρμόζει τὸν στρατηγὸν ἔχειν μεθ' ἑαυτοῦ τοὺς γινώσκοντας ἀκριβῶς τὴν πεῖραν τῆς θαλάσσης εἰς ἣν πλέει, τὸ ποῖοι ἄνεμοι κυμαίνουσιν αὐτὴν καὶ τὸ ποῖοι φυσῶσιν ἀπὸ τῆς γῆς· ἵνα δὲ γινώσκωσι καὶ τὰς κρυπτομένας πέτρας εἰς τὴν θάλασσαν καὶ τοὺς τόπους τοὺς μὴ ἔχοντας βάθος καὶ τὴν παραπλεομένην γῆν καὶ τὰς παρακειμένας αὐτῇ νήσους, τοὺς λιμένας καὶ τὸ πόσον ἀπέχουσι οἱ τοιοῦτοι λιμένες εἷς ἀπὸ τοῦ ἄλλου· ἵνα δὲ γινώσκωσι καὶ τὰ χωρία καὶ τὰ ὕδατα· πολλοὶ γὰρ ἐκ τοῦ ἔχειν ἀπειρίαν τῆς θαλάσσης καὶ τῶν τόπων ἀπώλοντο, ἐπειδὴ φυσῶσι πολλάκις ἄνεμοι καὶ σκορπίζουσι τὰ πλοῖα εἰς ἄλλον καὶ ἄλλον τόπον. Καὶ ἁρμόζει ἵνα μὴ μόνον ὁ στρατηγὸς ἔχῃ τοὺς γινώσκοντας ὅπερ εἴπαμεν, ἀλλὰ καὶ ἐν ἕκαστον πλοῖον ἵνα ἔχῃ τὸν ταῦτα γινώσκοντα, πρὸς τὸ βουλεύεσθαι καλῶς τὸ συμφέρον.

Cf. Syrianos Magistros, Ναυμαχίαι Συριανοῦ Μαγίστρου, §5.1-3 in Dain, *Naumachica*, 45-46.

3. Portulans and the Byzantine world

P. Gautier Dalché

The common understanding of the term 'portulan' is 'maritime chart'. This definition is incorrect. In the middle ages and long after, 'portulan' always designated books with nautical instructions today called 'pilot books', but never maps. It is only in the last century that scholars have assimilated the map and the book, creating the bizarre expression 'portulan chart' (in French 'carte-portulan'); they have been relying on the assumed similarity between the nature and usage of the two tools, a relation which has never been proved.[1] The text-portulans have not usually been considered documents of great importance, and thus have not been studied in any depth. For this reason, their origin and their cultural significance are still virtually unknown.

Among the avenues that could be explored, those that concern historical geography undoubtedly occupy an important place.[2]

---

[1] Among many others, I quote two authors supporting, without any discussion, the same thesis, although separated by half a century: 'A second kind of chart ... was the *portolano* or harbor-finding chart, originally designed to accompany the early coast pilots (peripli)': L. A. Brown, *The Story of Maps* (Boston, 1949), 113; 'The pilot books complemented the charts': J. E. D. Williams, *From Sails to Satellites. The Origin and Developments of Navigational Science* (Oxford, 1994), 28; for this author, the *Conpasso de navegare*, the first portulan, is a 'Latin translation'; see *infra*, p. 61. In a similar way, O. A. W. Dilke, thinking that 'portulan' means both text and map, and that *periploi* are true sailing directions, notes that the ancient *periploi* 'continued to lack accompanying maps': 'Cartography in the Byzantine Empire', in J. B. Harley, D. Woodward, eds., *The History of Cartography*, I: *Cartography in Prehistoric, Ancient and Medieval Europe and the Mediterranean* (Chicago and London, 1987), 259-260.

[2] Scholars have seldom made use of portulans for historical geography. For the contribution of portulans to our knowledge of littoral and insular regions in the Byzantine world see, e.g., J. Ferluga, 'Les îles dalmates dans l'empire byzantin', in F. Thiriet, ed., *Les îles de l'empire byzantin. Symposion Byzantinon. Colloque international des historiens de Byzance, Strasbourg, 25-29 septembre 1973, BF* 5 (1977), 35-71; A. Pertusi, 'Le isole Maltesi

From *Travel in the Byzantine World*, ed. Ruth Macrides. Copyright © 2002 by the Society for the Promotion of Byzantine Studies. Published by Ashgate Publishing Ltd, Gower House, Croft Road, Aldershot, Hampshire, GU11 3HR, Great Britain.

However, I have preferred to treat medieval portulans in a different fashion, first by examining the different problems raised by this type of document (excluding the Atlantic descriptions), and then by showing how contemporary geographers or authors of travel literature used the portulans to gain knowledge of the regions they described, especially the Greco-Byzantine world.

General characteristics

There is only one general work on the portulans, written by the historian of geography, Konrad Kretschmer.[3] Published almost a century ago, the work betrays its time by its desire to explain the origins of the genre. But its great merit lies in its provision of a number of texts edited for the first time, and a detailed study of the manuscripts, together with a toponymic index. We had to wait nearly half a century for a more thorough study, namely the publication of the oldest known portulan, the *Conpasso de navegare* by B. R. Motzo, with a general introduction concerning the problems of the portulans, principally their relation to maritime charts.[4] More recently, in 1987, another version of the *Conpasso* was published.[5] Since then certain Venetian portulans transcribed in nautical manuals in the fifteenth century have been published, but their particular characteristics have barely been noticed amidst the varied material contained in those manuals.[6] Many texts are thus available, but we still lack an in-depth study of medieval portulans, based on a modern methodology that integrates and goes beyond technical history, reaching into the domain of cultural history.

---

dall'epoca bizantina al periodo normanno e svevo (secc. VI-XIII) e descrizioni di esse dal sec. XII al sec. XVI', *BF* 5 (1977), 253-306; A. Laronde and Ph. Rigaud, 'Le coste libiche secondo un portolano del secolo XIII', in A. Mastino, ed., *L'Africa romana. Atti del IX Convegno di studio (Nuoro, 13-15 dic. 1991)* (Sassari, 1992); Anna Avraméa, 'Les côtes de l'Asie mineure d'après un texte pisan de la seconde moitié du XIIe siècle', in S. Lampakis, ed., *Byzantine Asia Minor (6th-12th cent.)* Institute for Byzantine Research, International Symposium 6 (Athens, 1998), 285-295.

[3] K. Kretschmer, *Die italienischen Portolane des Mittelalters* (Berlin, 1909).

[4] B. R. Motzo, *Il Compasso da navegare, opera italiana della metà del secolo XIII* (Cagliari, 1947), hereafter *Compasso*. The more recent and far better edition of M. Angelotti unfortunately remains unpublished: *Un duecentesco Compasso da navegare* (Tesi di laurea, Università degli studi di Pisa, Facoltà di Lettere e Filosofia, 1984-85).

[5] A. Terrosu Asole, *Il portolano di Grazia Pauli, opera italiana del secolo XIV trascritta a cura di Bacchisio R. Motzo* (Cagliari, 1987).

[6] G. Bonfiglio Dosio, ed., *Ragioni antique spettanti all'arte del mare et fabriche de vasselli*, Fonti per la storia di Venezia, sez. V. Fondi vari (Venice, 1987); A. Conterio, ed., *Pietro di Versi Raxion de' marineri. Taccuino nautico del XV secolo*, Fonti per la storia di Venezia, sez. V. Fondi vari (Venice, 1991).

Let us consider, then, the earliest preserved portulan, the *Conpasso de navegare*, for which our oldest surviving manuscript dates from the end of the thirteenth century. Written in a vernacular Italian that incorporates dialectal forms of varied origins, it describes the coasts of the Mediterranean starting from Cape Saint-Vincent and the area around the Strait of Gibraltar. It then enumerates the crossings, called *pileggi* (from *pelagion*?), between opposite points from coast to coast (continental and island coasts). It describes the perimeter of the large islands and ends with the coast of the Black Sea. The assembled information is of interest to the sailor: reefs, sea depths and salient features of ports. But the two essential elements are the distance, expressed in miles, between two neighbouring points on the coast or between the two extremities of a *pileggio*, and the direction of the coast or of the *pileggio*, according to a rose with 8 or 16 winds.

Here are the regions that the *Conpasso* details, starting from Cape Malea. An introductory sentence, as is common, makes the transition from the preceding passage: 'And from cape Malea, by sea with the land in view, to Constantinople'.[7] Thereafter, we can distinguish several groupings identified by rubrics. The Balkan coast is described up to Bocca d'Avedo (= Abydos, in other words, the Dardanelles) and Constantinople. Then comes the *scala de Romania*, in other words, the Aegean islands, in two parts: from Melos to Rhodes, then from Santorini to Cape Sounion. This passage describing the Archipelago is framed by two sentences that set it off: 'Here is explained what the ladders of Romania are, namely the islands of the Archipelago' and 'The aforesaid islands that I have mentioned are called the islands of the Archipelago.'[8] The text then follows the coasts of Asia Minor to the gulf of Alexandretta. At the end of the portulan, the Black Sea is described in two sections, western and eastern: 'From here, one will speak of the great sea of Romania and, first of all, of the western part'; 'Here is treated the eastern part'.[9] In that grouping, as elsewhere, the authors of the portulans are interested almost exclusively with the line of contact between land and sea. The forms of the coast are often very carefully analysed, for example: 'This cape is high and black, and becomes thinner to the north.'[10] The landmarks are sometimes noted, for

---

[7] 'E de Mallea Sancto Angelo, per estarea de ver terra ferma, ver Costantinopoli': *Compasso*, 38.

[8] 'Qua se contene quale sono la Scala de Romania, zoè a ssavere l'isole de l'Aczo pelago'; 'Le predicte isole ch'io ammentovai se clama isole de l'Aczo pelago da levante': *Compasso*, 48, 56.

[9] 'Ecqui ennanti parlarà e devizarà de lo Mare Maiore de Romania. En primaramente de ra parte de ponente'; 'Qua devisa de la parte da levante': *Compasso*, 129, 131.

[10] 'Lo dicto capo è alto e negro e vai assoctillianno da ver la tramontana': *Compasso*, 49.

example: 'And facing the port (of Braco), there is an island on which there is a church.'[11] The different sorts of reefs, visible or invisible, and the depths are differentiated with a precise vocabulary. Finally, the ports, natural or artificial, are mentioned.[12] To give an idea of the detailed precision that characterises the descriptive procedure, notably in the approaches to the ports, here is the example of the port on the island of Marmara:

> Facing the said point, there is another island called Marmara, five miles to the north; and it is ten miles long, and it has a port on the north side. The approach to the port is thus: at the end of the west part of the said island, there is a small island, and from that small island, go toward the levant, and you will find an eroded (?) cape, and pass around this cape by the west, and go between the islands by the south, and that is where the port is.[13]

This kind of description can be surprising for the modern reader. To take another example, for the *Conpasso* the form of Constantinople is not a triangle, in contrast to a commonplace repeated by western travellers.[14] The city has, indeed, three *facze*; but these are its three sides that are bordered by the sea: one oriented east-west (it ends with Cape Mangana), the other from the north-west to the south-east (this is the side that ends with the Blachernai), and the last, from the Golden Gate, runs between the east and north-east.[15] The continental side is thus not mentioned.

Portulans survive in two dozen manuscripts that date for the most part from the fifteenth century. They are sometimes parts of compilations and collections of texts and diagrams treating maritime matters, such as the size of sails, maritime regulations, *computus* or astronomy, but also things less closely linked with nautical techniques, such as very elementary arithmetic. Others are self-standing; these are true compositions where we feel the presence of a personality who organises the material, with transitional phrases and rubrics. They are

---

[11] 'E sopre lo porto à una isola en que stai una chiegia': *Compasso*, 46.

[12] The highly varied vocabulary is thoroughly studied by A. Terrosu Asole, *Il portolano di Grazia Pauli* (as in n. 5), xvii-xxviii.

[13] 'Sopre la dicta punta à una altra isola, che à nome Marmora, da tramontana v millara, et è longa x millara, et à porto da tramontana. La conoscenza de lo porto si è cotale: en capo de la dicta isola da ponente à una isolecta, e de la dita isolecta va per levante, e trovarete uno capo muczo, e larga quello capo da ponente, e va entro per meczo dì, e là è lo porto': *Compasso*, 46.

[14] J. P. A. van der Vin, *Travellers to Greece and Constantinople. Ancient Monuments and Old Traditions in Medieval Travellers' Tales*, 2 vols. (Istanbul, 1980), I, 250.

[15] *Compasso*, 45.

consciously written to present an ordered image of the space they are covering. Considering the particular characteristics of the surviving manuscripts, it is just possible that the portulans that were actually used on board ship have all disappeared.

The surviving manuscripts are distinguishable according to the region where they were copied: they are either Tuscan or Venetian. The absence of Genoese or Catalan manuscripts is strange. But we know that such books must have existed: for example, in 1323, the king of Aragon paid 25 sous in the money of Barcelona for a *libre de navegar*.[16] As for Greek portulans, we know of none before the sixteenth century, and they are all copied from Italian portulans.[17] The texts sometimes alleged by some scholars to be portulans are not navigational tools;[18] they are in fact administrative or literary elaborations, lacking the basic characteristics of the portulans, namely the directions and the information about the ports.

The portulans are not collections of unchanging precepts. Their compilers, on the contrary, never cease to develop and rework the available texts, with their errors, dialectic variants, extracts and additions that correspond to their own interests, corrections and rewritings. More than any other type of practical or technical text, the portulan excludes the notion of normalisation. For example, in the oldest manuscript of the *Conpasso de navegare*, the description of the coasts of the Black Sea has probably been added because the person for whom the book was made wanted to have a description of the entire zone of activity of international commerce. In a Venetian nautical

---

[16] 'Item un altre libre appellat Libre sobre la carta de navegar en cathala scrit en paper de Xativa ab cubertes de pergamins senars lo qual comença "Del cap de sent Vicens" e faneix "carta de vent"': J. Massó-Torrentes, 'Inventari dels bens mobles del rey Martí d'Aragó', *Revue hispanique*, 12 (1905), 418, n. 26. Rather unfortunately, this manuscript has become a 'book published in Játiva' in the secondhand work by R. Cerezo Martínez, *La cartografía náutica española en los siglos XIV, XV y XVI* (Madrid, 1994), 10.

[17] A. Delatte, *Les portulans grecs* I (Liège and Paris, 1947) Bibliothèque de la Faculté de philosophie et lettres de Liège, CVII; II (Brussels, 1958) Académie de Belgique, Mémoires, LIII; N. Svoronos, 'Portulans grecs', in *REG* 62 (1949), 237-240; H. Bibicou, 'Sources byzantines pour servir à l'histoire maritime', in M. Mollat, ed., *Les sources de l'histoire maritime en Europe, du Moyen Age au XVIIIe siècle. Actes du quatrième colloque international d'histoire maritime* (Paris, 1962), 131-135.

[18] H. Ahrweiler is wrong in calling the statiodromika (*sic*) 'portulans de l'époque byzantine'. The examples cited are all maritime itineraries in hagiographical texts: *Byzance et la mer. La marine de guerre, la politique et les institutions maritimes de Byzance aux VIIe-XVe siècles* (Paris, 1966), 164. Likewise, the section of the *De cerimoniis* studied by G. Huxley is not a genuine portulan but rather a *stadiodromikon* with only the number of miles between places on the way from Constantinople to Crete: 'A Porphyrogenitan portulan', in *GRBS*, 17 (1976), 295-300.

manual of the fifteenth century, one finds an extract entitled: 'Portulan from Venice to Cape Malea, and further on into Armenia, to Cyprus, passing by the Barbery coast and the ports beyond and within the Archipelago, and in the Black Sea.'[19] For these reasons, we need editions of each manuscript before we try to sort out in detail the different interests, conceptions and representations reflected by the variants, even the smallest, which are an essential characteristic of the genre.

Genesis and construction

The genesis of the portulans is obscured by a series of questions for which answers are not always evident. The first concerns the relation they may have had with the *periploi* (or maritime itineraries) of antiquity.[20] Despite the fact that some scholars are prone to think that they are true portulans,[21] the *periploi* are quite different. For the most part they are works of erudition, or travel guides intended for the educated, not sailing directions for sailors. They contain historical and mythological information, as well as other details unrelated to navigation. Those that may have been used (and the conditional tense is imperative) by ancient sailors are extremely rare. Only one, the *Stadiasmos of the Great Sea*, supposed to date from the third century B.C. and preserved in a tenth-century manuscript, resembles the portulans in enumerating the sections of the coasts and in giving the distances between ports or capes; but there are almost no directions. It may be that Greek portulans did exist but, in that case, the *periploi* are not representative of their exact nature and content.[22] There is no

---

[19] 'Portolan da Veniexia fin capo Maleo e fuora in Armenia in Cipro lorando per la Barbaria e per le schalle de fuora et in Arzipiellego e dentro del Mar Maior': G. Bonfiglio Dosio, ed., *Ragioni antique* (as in n. 6), 28.

[20] They are collected by C. Müller, *Geographi Graeci minores*, 2 vols. (Paris, 1855-61). The nature and the tradition of these texts are re-examined by D. Marcotte in his most valuable introduction to *Géographes grecs*, Coll. des Universités de France, I (Paris, 2000).

[21] The title of the work of A. Peretti is clear in this respect: *Il periplo di Scilace. Studio sul primo portolano del Mediterraneo* (Pisa, 1979), but the reasons alleged are not convincing; see P. Counillon, Λίμην ἔρημος, in P. Arnaud, P. Counillon, eds., *Geographia historica* (Bordeaux and Nice, 1998), 55-67.

[22] The link between the *periploi* and the medieval or modern sailing directions is usually not questioned. D. W. Waters affirms, without any discussion, that the origins of medieval sailing directions 'can be traced back, though the links are at times tenuous, to the peripli of classical times': *The Rutters of the Sea. The Sailing Directions of Pierre Garcie. A study of the first English and French sailing directions* (New Haven and London, 1967), 7-8. L. Albuquerque is even more precise, yet without scrutinising that thesis. For him, the medieval portulans are direct heirs of ancient *periploi*, corrected and completed: *A náutica e*

question of a continuous line of transmission of these mariners' tools from ancient to medieval times: in many regions of the Mediterranean, the ancient place-names, Greek or Latin, disappeared or were transformed in such a way that it is impossible to think in terms of a progressive improvement of ancient *periploi*.[23] In these conditions, and until someone proves differently, we must consider the portulans a medieval creation.

According to B. R. Motzo, the same person was responsible both for the creation of the first complete portulan of the Mediterranean and the first maritime chart. That double innovation would have taken place in the mid-thirteenth century. The unknown author would have assembled partial portulans, corresponding to small sections of the coasts or to particular basins of the Mediterranean; this would have caused the disappearance of earlier material. Again according to this theory, it is only the use of the compass that would have allowed one to determine the directions in the *Conpasso de navegare*. Finally, these new operations would have taken place in the alleged 'school of mathematics' of Leonardo Fibonacci and his student Campano da Novara.

This construction has the merit of being systematic; unfortunately, there are no facts to back it up. Let us examine each element briefly.

First of all, we know that partial portulans always existed, both before and after the achievement of the *Conpasso de navegare*. From the middle of the twelfth century, and up until the beginning of the thirteenth, there appear in the north of Europe accounts of the crusades that tell of voyages by sea to the lands held by the infidel. As these texts sometimes interrupt the story in order to give nautical information, we can suppose that their authors used sources of information such as the portulan. What is more, the *Conpasso* is not the first portulan of the whole Mediterranean. Two earlier works describe the coasts of the Mediterranean. The first, entitled *De viis maris*, which is in the process of being published, is of English origin and dates from the end of the twelfth century. It presents the ports from York to Egypt; it goes even further to the east and refers briefly to the monsoon. Another text, written in Pisa at the end of the twelfth century or at the beginning of

---

a ciência em Portugal. Notas sobre as navegações (Lisbon, 1989), 46. More recently, P. Janni, 'Cartography et art nautique dans le monde ancien', in P. Arnaud, P. Counillon, eds., *Geographia historica* (Bordeaux and Nice, 1998), 41.

[23] Roman maritime itineraries existed, like the *Antonine Itinerary*; they were administrative or military tools, not sailing directions. Generally speaking, coastal descriptions are very rare in the Latin literature, unlike the Greek: R. Güngerich, *Die Küstenbeschreibung in der grieschischen Literatur*, 2nd edn. (Münster, 1975), n. 60.

the thirteenth, the *Liber de existencia riveriarum et forma maris nostri Mediterranei*, describes the coasts of the Mediterranean and the Black Sea using not only a maritime chart, but also what the author calls the *gradientes nautarum*, which is translated exactly by the word 'portulan'. There are many common traits between this text and the accounts of the crusade that I just mentioned, namely the presence of *pileggi*. The *Liber* adds a method of definition of the orientations which is very close to that of the surviving portulans of a later date.[24] From all these facts one can conclude that the portulans existed already in the twelfth century, perhaps in a less sophisticated form, but this last point is in no way certain.

Furthermore, there is no exact correspondence between the maritime chart and the portulan. Forty per cent of the names present on the maritime chart which is considered to be the oldest, the so-called Pisan chart, are absent in the *Conpasso*; and, when one tries to draw the Mediterranean using only the indications of direction and distance recorded in the *Conpasso*, the result is lacking in cartographic precision and exactitude.[25] Moreover, the toponyms are quite different.[26]

Lastly, the use of the compass to determine direction is not entirely obvious. The large majority of directions in the *Conpasso* are defined with reference to the eight winds alone. The more perfected instruments that allow one to note precise bearings do not appear before the fourteenth century. It is thus probable that the directions brought together in the medieval portulans were determined without great precision; and moreover, for the same journey, they vary somewhat from manuscript to manuscript. The idea that a mathematician was behind a systematic creation that appeared in the mid-thirteenth century seems to me to be a modern illusion.[27] As a genre, the portulans are the result of the formalisation of the age-old empirical experience of the men of the sea, a formalisation that must have begun in the Italian cities at the same time that international commerce was developing, from the eleventh century onwards. This cautious conclusion helps eliminate two unproven hypotheses: that of the single genius, working in the circle of the most celebrated mathematicians of the thirteenth

---

[24] P. Gautier Dalché, *Carte marine et portulan au XIIe siècle. Le «Liber de existencia riueriarum et forma maris nostri Mediterranei» (Pise, circa 1200)* (Rome, 1995).

[25] See J. T. Lanman, *On the origin of the portolan chart* (Chicago, 1987), plates 1 and 2.

[26] S. Conti, 'Portolano e carta nautica. Confronte toponomastico', in *Imago et mensura mundi. Atti del IX Congresso Internazionale di storia della cartografia*, I (Rome, 1985), 55-60.

[27] E.g. E. G. R. Taylor, 'The oldest Mediterranean pilot', *Journal of Navigation* 4 (1951), 81-85; *The Haven-finding art* (London, 1956); 'Mathematics and the navigator in the thirteenth century', *Journal of Navigation* 13 (1960), 1-12; E. G. R. Taylor and M. W. Richey, *The Geometrical Seaman* (London, 1962).

century, and that of a sudden and unexplained technical leap forward that would have occurred at the same time.

The contribution of portulans to our knowledge of the Byzantine world

The answer to the question what exactly do portulans contribute to our knowledge of the Byzantine world depends above all on the way in which they were used. The situation, however, is contradictory and does not allow for a simple response. Certainly a ship captain, or a pilot, could have owned a portulan. Portulans are addressed directly and explicitly to men of the sea, as is indicated by a wealth of expressions such as 'enter into such and such a port', 'go in such and such a direction', 'beware of such and such a danger'. But the vast majority of surviving manuscripts are, if not deluxe books, at least very large books with decorated letters, which seem to lack the necessary simplicity of books intended for daily use.[28] The portulans themselves are often accompanied by other texts that have nothing to do with navigation in the strict sense, such as customs' tariffs or rudimentary problems in arithmetic and geometry. One can thus suppose that these texts, once they had been assembled into these books, were destined for more than simple nautical usage. In my opinion, they must have had a double function: a symbolic function, in that they represented the theatre of action of the entire *gente di mare* of the commercial cities; and a practical function, in that they allowed the preparation of commercial voyages by means of a synthetic and, at the same time, detailed view of the spaces that would be covered.

It would be excessively fastidious, and indeed impossible, to list and identify here all the ports of the Balkans, Asia Minor and the islands of the Archipelago mentioned in the portulans. I prefer, therefore, to approach the question from another direction. Since the portulans, as much as any technical instrument, reflect the culture of the men of the sea, it would be interesting to see if, and how, these texts have been used by medieval authors of geographical descriptions and travel narratives.

The chronicles of the crusades of the twelfth and thirteenth centuries have left traces of the use of portulans. Thus, in both his *Chronica* and the *Gesta regis Ricardi* attributed to him, the Englishman

---

[28] See, for example, the portulan (end of the fifteenth or beginning of the sixteenth century), kept in the Biblioteca civica of Bergamo, with large rubricated filigreed initials, and one very fine drawing of Venice and the lagune, partly painted in watercolour, on f. 30v: reproduction in M. L. Gatti Perer, M. Marubbi, eds., *Tesori miniati. Codici e incunaboli dei fondi antichi di Bergamo e Brescia* (n.p., 1995), 247.

Roger of Howden offers an account of the Third Crusade which systematically uses sailing directions on two occasions, in recounting the voyage of the English fleet from London to Messina, and in evoking the maritime itinerary of the return of Philip Augustus, in part *per costeram Rumaniae*. The king goes from Alexandretta to Rhodes, following the coast of Asia Minor, then crosses the Archipelago to Cape Malea and ends his maritime voyage at Corfu. This return trip is framed within two nautical indications: the king first passes before

> a very high mountain, which is called *caput Turkiae*, because those that come from Apulia and, navigating in that sea, draw close to Turkey, see this mountain first. It marks the frontier between lands of the emperor of Constantinople and those of the sultan of Iconium; from this point begins Romania, which is called Greece.

At the other end of the Greek world, the surroundings of the island of Corfu are described in detail:

> At the entry to the island of Corfu, there is a dangerous sand bank which extends from the middle of the island to the coast of Romania; and the sea at that place is not deeper than four and a half ells ... and in certain places the sea is so narrow between Corfu and Romania that people can hear one another on either shore ... And at the end of the island, in Romania, there is a deserted castle called Butrinto ... Then, when one has nearly arrived at the outlet of the canal, there is a deserted city called Cassiopia ... And almost facing, there is in Romania a deserted city called Santa Quaranta, where there is a good port, wide and deep. When leaving this port, there is a rock similar to a half-collapsed tower, which extends across the middle of the port, hidden under the water. For that reason, one should pass near the island of Corfu.[29]

This long citation brings together all the characteristics of the borrowings made by Roger of Howden from the pilot books: important landmarks that are visible from aboard ship (notably ruins), possible dangers, and distances. There is also a small catalogue of the principal islands *in mari Graeco*, of which certain ones are inhabited by pirates, while many are deserted, says the author, because of the fear they inspire.

---

[29] W. Stubbs, ed., *Chronica magistri Rogeri de Houedene*, III (London, 1870) Rerum Britannicarum Medii Aevi scriptores, 51, 165-166; W. Stubbs, ed., *Gesta regis Henrici secundi Benedicti abbatis*, I (London, 1867) Rerum Britannicarum Medii Aevi scriptores, 49.2: *Gesta Ricardi*: 72-252; here 194-197 for the journey of Richard.

Thanks to the uninterrupted exchanges and pilgrimages that developed after the First Crusade, those who were not sailors often had occasion to consult pilot books. It is thus understandable that the contents of these books were used in the writing of different types of texts. Thus, in the closing years of the thirteenth century, an anonymous Italian, preoccupied with the contradictions between traditional geographical representations and contemporary realities, especially from the point of view of the political affiliation of certain regions, composed a description of the world entitled *De divisione orbis terrarum*. He tried to take into account 'modern' sources (his adjective) and, in particular, portulans. For the Greek world, his notes touch on the large islands (Crete, Rhodes, Cyprus), commercial centres (Laiazzo), and a few cities on the Black Sea not mentioned in ancient sources, such as Trebizond, Sinope and Sebastopol.[30] The effect of this modest utilisation of a portulan, which he calls *compassus*, or *compassus orbis*, is to underscore the deficiencies of traditional descriptions, rather than to construct a more precise and complete image of the world. A few years later, the Venetian Marino Sanudo who spent a large part of his life drawing up and perfecting a crusade project entitled *Liber secretorum fidelium crucis*, used the information provided by portulans with a strategic or even logistic objective in mind, in order to characterise the places useful to a fleet of crusaders. Without saying so explicitly, he copied whole passages from the *Conpasso da navegare* concerning the coast of Syria, then Asia Minor from Caramela to the gulf of Makri (today Fetiye). By comparison to the *Conpasso*, the version of Sanudo adds considerations on the quality of the ports and on the availability of water, as for example: 'From Finigha (*Finike*) to Saint Nicolas of Stamiris (*Myra*), 15 miles: good port, safe on the sea side, but on the land side, beware; this port has a narrow entry and an outlet of fresh water in that entry'.[31] Marino Sanudo complements his text with an atlas of charts, among which there is a world map. Around the world map is a text devoted to the *insulae minores* that could not be represented because of the scale. These are the islands of the southern Adriatic, then the '*Agyos pelagos*, which we call the holy sea'; these

---

[30] 'Nam ultra Constantinopolim nunc a modernis quedam nominantur ciuitates, de quibus nulle istorie faciunt mentionem, sicut est Trapizonda ciuitas, ad quam Latini aplicant, et specialiter Ianuenses, qui habent dominium quem uocant Comino, quod sonat in lingnua nostra marchio, item Senopi ...'; 'Sciendum tamen hic quod duplex est Sebastia ... alia ad quam per mare Ponticum quod nos Constantinopolitanum appellamus, traffretant mercatores Latini.' The work is in the process of being edited by the author.

[31] J. Bongars, *Gesta Dei per Francos*, II (Hanover, 1611), 90.

islands can mark the stages and furnish fresh supplies for the fleet of crusaders. The *Conpasso* probably provided the ideas for that exposé.

In the fourteenth and fifteenth centuries pilgrims took, for the most part, regularly scheduled ships from Venice. The account of pilgrimages to the Holy Land become more numerous, and a recurrent number of notations concerning the navigation between Corfu and Cyprus come from portulans that must have been on board ship. Above all, these notations give the distances between the longer stages in the journey, perhaps because one then changed pilot. This concrete knowledge of the lengths of the journey of the pilgrims is so widespread that in western manuscripts we often find cursory information on the journey to the Holy Land, accompanied by numerical indications given in round numbers.[32] Furthermore, we find identical descriptive details in the works of many authors writing at widely different dates. The Augustinian monk Jacobus of Verona, in 1335, like the notary Nicolaus of Martoni, in 1294, note that near the island of Cerigo, there are three dangerous islands, which bear colourful names used by sailors: for Jacobus they are 'Ova, As, Porrum';[33] for Nicolaus they are, 'Ovi, Assu et Patassu'.[34] The same Nicolaus and, in 1483, the German pilgrim Paul Walther, both note the church on top of the mountain of Cape Malea, a landmark visible between the Peloponnese and Crete.[35] It is tempting to think that these notations are too numerous and too systematic to be the fruit of the travellers' direct experience, or of discussions with sailors. Moreover, certain travellers have left us explicit references to portulans. A Norwegian pilgrim, who accompanied Saint Louis's crusade as far as Cagliari (1270), wrote that the Mediterranean is entirely 'divided into miles (*per miliaria distinctum*)', a statement that can be made only with reference to a book where all the distances have been gathered together.[36] Another pilgrim, an Irishman who in 1323-24 described the coasts and ports and noted the distances, cited with regard to the perimeter of Crete the 'sailors who describe the

---

[32] For example: 'A Venetiis ad Parentium sunt 100 m. Italica; a Parentio ad Corphouam 100 [sic]; a Corphoua ad Modonam 300; a Modona ad Cretam 300; a Creta ad Rhodum 300 ...': London, British Library, Sloane MS 683, f. 42r.

[33] U. Monneret de Villard, *Liber peregrinationis di Jacopo da Verona* (Rome, 1950), 15.

[34] L. Le Grand, 'Relation du pélerinage à Jérusalem de Nicolas de Martoni, notaire italien (1394-1395)', *Revue de l'Orient latin* 3 (1895), 580.

[35] '... qui mons est in terra firma et est capud Romanie. Et est in dicto monte quadam ecclesia cum uno remita': Nicolas de Martoni, ed. Le Grand (as in n. 34), 580; M. Sollweck, *Fratris Pauli Waltheri Guglingensis itinerarium in Terra Sancta et ad Sanctam Catharinam*, Bibl. des literarischen Vereins 192 (Stuttgart, 1892), 83.

[36] G. Storm, *Monumenta historica Norwegiae. Latinske Kildeskriften til Norge Histories i Middelalderen* (Christiania, 1880), 166.

islands of the sea' (*marinarios insulas maris describentes*).[37] One extreme case is that of the account of Nompar de Caumont in 1418. This noble Gascon reproduces the structure of a portulan exactly, from place to place, but without reproducing the orientations according to the winds. I will cite only what he wrote of the islands to the south of Kythera already mentioned:

> *Item*, before this foresaid Setvill, there is a little deserted reef in the sea, whose name is Lou ... and close to the foresaid reef, there are three other reefs whose names are Three, Two and Ace, and in this place is the beginning of the Archipelago, a part of the sea which is full of islands, inhabited as well as deserted.[38]

Conclusion

The Mediterranean portulans knew a greater success than the small number of surviving manuscripts may have led us to think. These technical aids quickly spread to milieux well beyond those interested in their daily navigational use and they became tools for the preparation of the voyage and companion volumes for travellers with different interests: royal officers preparing crusading expeditions, merchants, pilgrims. They also served to elaborate geographical descriptions. With regard to the Greco-Byzantine world, they furnished a relatively more precise knowledge of the islands. Their cultural, as well as their practical, role should not be underestimated.

---

[37] M. Esposito, ed., *Itinerarium Symonis Semeonis ab Hybernia ad Terram Sanctam*, Scriptores Latini Hiberniae 4 (Dublin, 1960), 44.

[38] Marquis de la Grange, ed., *Seigneur de Caumont, Voyaige d'oultremer en Jherusalem* (Paris, 1858; repr. Geneva, 1975), 40-41: 'Item; davant seluy dit Setvill, a ung petit roc en la mer désert, qui a nom Lou ... et près de cest dit roc, a trois autres rocs désert à qui disent: tria, deux et as; et en celluy lieu comence l'on entrer en l'Arcepellée, lequel est une partie de mer moult copieuse de ylles poblées et désertes'.

4. Roads and travel in Macedonia and Thrace in the middle and late Byzantine period[*]

K. Belke

Thrace, and partly Macedonia as well, were the 'bottle-neck' through which all overland traffic from Constantinople to the west and north (Greece, Italy, Danube basin and central Europe) and vice versa had to pass. The available documentation for roads and traffic in these regions is therefore much richer than for other areas of the Byzantine empire.[1] The aim of the first part of this paper is to analyse some reports on the use of roads, especially those which allow a glimpse of the actual condition of roads and travel in this area in different periods. These reports pertain above all to the two most important long distance roads, the *Via Egnatia* from Constantinople to Dyrrachion and Apollonia (later Aulona),[2] and the so-called *Military Road* from

---

[*] I would like to thank P. Soustal and M. Popović, Vienna, for help and advice.

[1] From the sources relating to roads in Macedonia and Thrace, a selection had to be made for the purposes of this contribution; I restricted myself to some passages from Byzantine chroniclers and historians, as well as hagiographic texts, reports on diplomatic exchanges with the west, historians of the crusades and, for the late Byzantine period, letters. For the final part of this paper, use has been made of documents, above all those of Mount Athos.

[2] The *Via Egnatia* — the origin of the name is still disputed — is called so only by Strabo VII 7.4 after Polybios XXXIV 12 (whose original text is lost for this passage); cf. also Strabo VII 7.8 and fragments 10, 13, 21, where, strictly speaking, the name is applied to the western part up to Thessalonike (or Kypsela and the Hebros) only. The designation has been extended by modern scholars to the whole length of the road to Constantinople and to all periods, its modern successors included. Still important for the history of the *Via Egnatia* are Th. L. F. Tafel, *De via militari Romanorum Egnatia, qua Illyricum, Macedonia et Thracia iungebantur, dissertatio geographica* (Tübingen, 1842; repr. London, 1972); E. Oberhummer, 'Egnatia via', *RE* 5/2 (1905), 1988-93; see, further, N. G. L. Hammond, 'The western part of the Via Egnatia', *JRSt* 64 (1974), 185-194; N. G. L. Hammond and M. B. Hatzopoulos, 'The Via Egnatia in western Macedonia, I: the routes through Lyncus and Eordaea in western Macedonia', *American Journal of Ancient History* 7 (1982), 128-149 and II:

From *Travel in the Byzantine World*, ed. Ruth Macrides. Copyright © 2002 by the Society for the Promotion of Byzantine Studies. Published by Ashgate Publishing Ltd, Gower House, Croft Road, Aldershot, Hampshire, GU11 3HR, Great Britain.

Constantinople across the Balkan peninsula via Adrianople and Serdica (Sofia) to Belgrade.[3] In the second part, on the basis of documents from Mount Athos some observations are made concerning the different categories of roads and their history, especially in the late Byzantine period. Archaeological remains and questions relating to the exact course of roads are not to be discussed here.

As with many roads of the Roman empire, the main roads on the Balkan peninsula also were constructed first as military roads. Cicero characterises the *Via Egnatia* — without calling it by its name — expressly as a 'military road'[4] and most reports we have on the use of the trans-Balkan roads concern marches of armies along it. Second comes administration, and only in the third place did these roads serve the needs of merchants and private travellers.

The safety, which in times of peace prevailed on the trans-Balkan roads during the Roman and early Byzantine periods, came to a definite end with the invasions of Slavs, Avars and Bulgars, and the breakdown of Byzantine rule over most of the Balkan peninsula at the beginning of the seventh century at the latest. All roads, except for the immediate hinterland of Constantinople and possibly the road to Thessalonike,

---

'The Via Egnatia from Mutatio Ad Duodecimum to Civitas Edessa', *American Journal of Ancient History* 8 (1983), 48-53; P. Collard, 'Les milliaires de la Via Egnatia', *BCH* 100 (1976) I (Études), 177-200; F. Papazoglou, *Les villes de Macédoine à l'époque romaine* (Athens, 1988), passim; P. Soustal, *Thrakien (Thrake, Rodope und Haimimontos)*, TIB 6 (Vienna, 1991), 136-138 (hereafter Soustal, *Thrakien*).

[3] The *Military Road* owes its conventional name to the author of the 'classical' monograph on this road, C. Jireček, *Die Heerstrasse von Belgrad nach Constantinopel und die Balkanpässe* (Prague, 1877; repr. Amsterdam, 1967), 5, 7, who seems to have been confirmed in his naming of it by a Latin inscription (*CIL* III 6123) which indicates that *via militaris* was its Roman designation; the inscription mentions, however, *vias militares* of Thrace in general (cf., on this point, M. Popović, *Die Reiseliteratur des 14. bis 16. Jahrhunderts als Quelle zur Via Traiana und zu den an ihr lebenden Völkern*. Unpublished MA Thesis. Vienna, 2000, 9f.). On the road itself see Soustal, *Thrakien* (as in n. 2), 132, 134; for an overview of other important roads of the eastern Balkan peninsula cf. V. Beševliev, 'Bemerkungen über die antiken Heeresstraßen im Ostteil der Balkanhalbinsel', *Klio* 51 (1969), 483-495 (repr. in V. Beševliev, *Bulgarisch-Byzantinische Aufsaetze* [London 1978], no. XXVI); Beševliev, *Die protobulgarische Periode der bulgarischen Geschichte* (Amsterdam, 1980), 22-29 (hereafter Beševliev, *Protobulgarische Periode*); P. Schreiner, 'Städte und Wegenetz in Moesien, Dakien und Thrakien nach dem Zeugnis des Theophylaktos Simokattes', in R. Pillinger, ed., *Spätantike und frühbyzantinische Kultur Bulgariens zwischen Orient und Okzident. Referate gehalten im Rahmen eines gemeinsam mit dem Bulgarischen Forschungsinstitut in Österreich organisierten Arbeitsgespräches vom 8. bis 10. November 1983* (Vienna, 1986), 25-35.

[4] Cicero, *De provinciis consularibus* 2 (4); cf. Oberhummer, 'Egnatia via' (as in n. 2), 1989; Jireček, *Heerstrasse* (as in n. 3), 5 and n. 8; T. Pekáry, *Untersuchungen zu den römischen Reichsstraßen* (Bonn, 1968), 10-13.

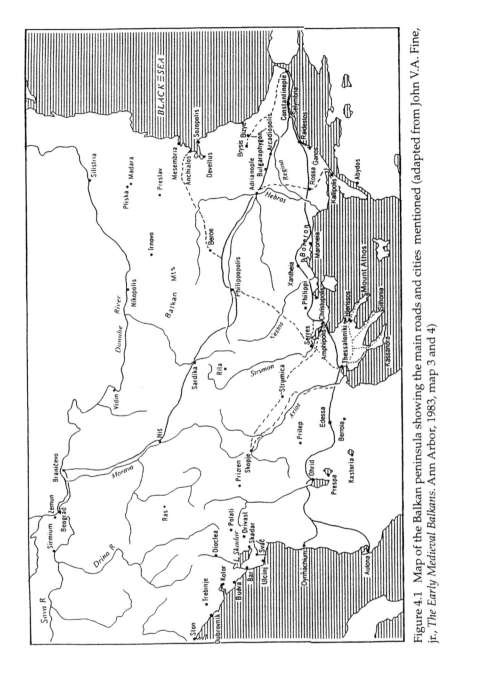

Figure 4.1 Map of the Balkan peninsula showing the main roads and cities mentioned (adapted from John V.A. Fine, jr, *The Early Medieval Balkans*. Ann Arbor, 1983, map 3 and 4)

were practically cut off for more than a century.[5] Traffic from Constantinople to Macedonia, Epiros, Italy and central Europe and vice versa, which usually had gone along the *Via Egnatia*,[6] was now replaced by sea traffic. Byzantine delegations to the Frankish kings were obliged (or preferred) to travel by sea (although there were exceptions, see below), usually via Rome and/or Venice in the eighth, ninth and tenth centuries.[7]

The first indication of a recovery was the famous expedition of the emperor Justinian II to Thessalonike in 688. By means of a victory over the Bulgarians, the emperor was able to fight his way free to Thessalonike. But on the way back his army was attacked by Bulgarians in a *kleisoura* and suffered severe losses.[8] It is still open to debate which group of Bulgarians they were and where the ambush was laid; in other words, which way the Byzantine army marched to and from Thessalonike, along the *Via Egnatia*,[9] or on roads further to the north.[10] The sources hardly enable us to answer these questions,[11]

---

[5] See the general picture drawn by D. Obolensky, 'The Balkans in the ninth century: barrier or bridge?' BF 13 (1988), 47-66, esp. 48-50 (hereafter Obolensky, 'Balkans'); I. Ch. Dimitroukas, *Reisen und Verkehr im Byzantinischen Reich vom Anfang des 6. Jhr. bis zur Mitte des 11. Jhr.* (Athens, 1997), 346f. (hereafter Dimitroukas, *Reisen und Verkehr*).

[6] Cf., as an example, the reports of the papal legates to Justin I after the death of Anastasius; s. L. Duchesne, *Le Liber Pontificalis* I (Paris, 1886, 2nd edn. 1955; repr. 1981), 270; A. Thiel, *Epistolae Romanorum pontificum genuinae et quae ad eos scriptae sunt, a S. Hilaro usque ad Pelagium II*, I (Braunsberg, 1867), 849-852 (letters 59, 60); Dimitroukas, *Reisen und Verkehr*, 343f.

[7] Cf. Dimitroukas, *Reisen und Verkehr*, 252-256, 346f.

[8] Theoph. 364 (A.M. 6180); Nikephoros Patriarch of Constantinople, *Short History*, ed. and trans. C. Mango, CFHB 13 (Washington, D.C., 1990), 92 (chap. 38); H. Ditten, *Ethnische Verschiebungen zwischen der Balkanhalbinsel und Kleinasien vom Ende des 6. bis zur zweiten Hälfte des 9. Jahrhunderts* (Berlin, 1993), 220f.

[9] So Beševliev, *Protobulgarische Periode*, 169f., and other Bulgarian researchers; Soustal, *Thrakien* 77f. The Bulgarians in this case would be those of Kuber, who tried to establish a Bulgaro-Slavic principality around Thessalonike; for them see Lemerle, *Saint Démétrius* II (as in n. 11), 143-162.

[10] The latter interpretation of sources is the one adopted, amongst others, by Martha Gregoriou-Ioannidou,'Ἡ ἐκστρατεία τοῦ 'Ιουστινιανοῦ Β' κατὰ τῶν Βουλγάρων καὶ Σλάβων (688)', *Byzantiaka* 2 (1982), 111-124, and I. Karagiannopulos, Ἡ Επικοινωνία Θεσσαλονίκης-Κωνσταντινουπόλεως κατὰ τους 7.-9. αι.', *Επιστημονική Επετηρίς της Φιλοσοφικής Σχολής Θεσσαλονίκης* 22 (1984), 211-229, esp. 214f.; the military expedition in this case would have been directed primarily against the Bulgarians of Asparuch, whose centre was at the lower Danube.

[11] See the synopsis by Ditten, *Verschiebungen* (as in n. 8), 219f. The argument that the Bulgarians of Asparuch are meant and, as a consequence, that Justinian II probably marched along more northern routes, may be seen in the fact that Theoph., 364 (A.M. 6179) and Nikephoros Patr., *Short History* 92 (chap. 38) expressly state that the emperor broke the treaty his father had concluded with the Bulgarians; it is much more probable

but one can certainly not conclude, as has been done from this military expedition and from the foundation of the *kleisoura* (later the theme) of Strymon by the same emperor at an unknown date,[12] that the land routes between Thessalonike and Constantinople were not disrupted until the end of the seventh century.[13] Justinian's expedition was, however, an important step in improving the political and military situation and thus, but probably only later, in reopening overland routes in the Balkans.[14]

The eighth century was a period of constant warfare in the Balkans, but during the second half, Byzantium was able to build a number of fortifications in Thrace and to start a programme of repopulation of the devastated countryside.[15] The extent of the secured area can be estimated from the increase of the number of bishops present at the council of Nicaea in 787, compared with the councils of 680/81 and 690,[16] and from the itinerary of a journey of the empress Eirene in Thrace in 784. She went out in complete safety with a large force and much pomp and visited (and contributed to rebuilding and/or fortification of) towns such as Beroe (Stara Zagora), Philippopolis (Plovdiv) and Anchialos (Pomorie). The journey also shows that the roads between these cities must have been repaired by that time.[17] Some other observations also point to this. When the Bulgarian khan Krum devastated and plundered the suburbs of Constantinople in 813 after the treacherous attempt on his life, he had an enormous amount of booty carried away on carts (ἅμαξαι),[18] and so did another army sent by Krum to plunder

---

that they are referring to the treaty of 681 with Asparuch they had mentioned themselves (Theoph., 359 [A.M. 6171]; Nikephoros, *Short History* 91 [chap. 36]; cf. F. Dölger, *Regesten der Kaiserurkunden des oströmischen Reiches* I [Munich-Berlin, 1924], 243) and not to the agreement between Constantine IV and Kuber, which is known only from the *Miracula S. Demetrii*: P. Lemerle, *Les plus anciens recueils des miracles de Saint Démétrius et la pénétration des Slaves dans les Balkans* I (Paris, 1979), 229 [§ 289] and II (Paris, 1981), 148f.). Gregoriou-Ioannidou, 'Ἐκστρατεία' (as in n. 10), 114-116, only considers the first possibility (see esp. p. 124).

[12] Constantine Porphyrogennetos, *De thematibus*, ed. A. Pertusi, StT 160 (Vatican City, 1952), 88-89, 166-168; See P. Lemerle, *Philippes et la Macédoine orientale à l'époque chrétienne et byzantine* I, texte (Paris, 1945), 124-128.

[13] Karagiannopulos, 'Ἐπικοινωνία', (as in n. 10), 216; Dimitroukas, *Reisen und Verkehr*, 350f.

[14] See Obolensky, 'Balkans' (as in n. 5), 50.

[15] Beševliev, *Protobulgarische Periode* 206f.; Soustal, *Thrakien* 79f.

[16] Cf. R.-J. Lilie, '"Thrakien" und "Thrakesion". Zur byzantinischen Provinzorganisation am Ende des 7. Jahrhunderts', JÖB 26 (1977), 7-47, esp. 40-45; Soustal, *Thrakien*, 81.

[17] Theoph. 457 (A.M. 6276); Lilie, 'Thrakien' 41; Beševliev, *Protobulgarische Periode*, 229.

[18] Theoph. 503; cf. Beševliev, *Protobulgarische Periode*, 256f.

Thrace at the end of 813. This group of Bulgarians went as far as Arkadioupolis (Lüleburgaz); however, to cross the Regina (Ergene) river, they first had to build a wooden bridge.[19] For the transport of siege machinery of all kinds on his intended expedition against Constantinople in spring 814, Krum prepared 5,000 iron-clad carts but he died before the expedition began.[20]

Corresponding to the increased safety in these regions, we find the first concrete reports on civilian travel along trans-Balkan roads in the ninth century.[21] A famous example is the adventurous and still dangerous journey of St. Gregory of Dekapolis who, on his way to Rome probably in the early 830s, went overland from Christoupolis (Kavala) to Thessalonike. At the crossing of a river, the Strymon, he fell into the hands of Slavic robbers (Σκλαβηνοὶ λῃσταί) who, surprisingly, let him go and even carried him over in a boat, from where he continued his journey unhindered.[22] The same *Life* shows us the imperial administration at work along the *Via Egnatia* between Thessalonike and Constantinople some years later: George, a *protokankellarios* and deputy *strategos* of Thessalonike was to travel from Thessalonike to Constantinople by land through 'difficult and horrible places'. He was in fact arrested twice by the emperor's subordinates, in Christoupolis (Kavala) and in the region of Bouleron, and escaped prison or even death only by intervention of a monk Anastasios who accompanied him; at Maroneia, however, the two travellers chose to continue their journey by sea, in spite of the danger from Arab or other pirates. After some time, George, now *kandidatos*, returned to Thessalonike the way they had come.[23]

Other journeys show a more official character, such as the delegation of Louis II to the Byzantine emperor Basil I, led by Anastasius Bibliothecarius in 869/70, and the legates of Pope Hadrian II to the council of Constantinople in the same years. The papal legates were welcomed by an imperial *spatharocandidatus* in Thessalonike, who conducted them as far as Selymbria, where they were received

---

[19] *Scriptor incertus, De Leone Bardae Armenii filio* (in Leo gramm., *Chronographia*, ed. I. Bekker [Bonn 1842]), 347; cf. Beševliev, *Protobulgarische Periode*, 260.

[20] *Scriptor incertus*, 347f.; cf. Beševliev, *Protobulgarische Periode*, 260f.

[21] Dimitroukas, *Reisen und Verkehr*, 347.

[22] *Ignatios Diakonos und die Vita des hl. Gregorios Dekapolites*, ed. G. Makris (Stuttgart, 1997), 86; for the date see C. Mango, 'On the re-reading of the Life of St. Gregory the Decapolite', in Δώρημα στὸν ’Ιωάννη Καραγιαννόπουλο = *Byzantina* 13/1 (1985), 633-646, esp. 637; see Obolensky, 'Balkans', 55f.; Dimitroukas, *Reisen und Verkehr*, 350f.

[23] Ed. Makris, *Gregorios Dekapolites* (as in n. 22), 112-116; Dimitroukas, *Reisen und Verkehr*, 351f.

even more honorifically and escorted to the capital.[24] Both parties left Constantinople together in March 870. Again they travelled along the *Via Egnatia* to Dyrrachion under the guidance of a *spatharios* Theodosios.[25]

These examples may suffice to illustrate that in the ninth century the *Via Egnatia* had revived as a main artery for diplomatic exchange with the west, at least until the outbreak of the wars between tsar Symeon (893-927) and the Byzantines and the revolt of the Kometopouloi in Bulgaria in the second half of the tenth century.[26] To sum up, it may be said that the *Via Egnatia* as a main land route between Constantinople and the coast of the Adriatic sea was open to traffic during much of the ninth century in times of peace, but was still very vulnerable in periods of war.

The other great trans-Balkan road of antiquity, the so-called *Military Road* (the 'Heerstrasse' of Constantine Jireček) led over Bulgarian territory; it was therefore reopened as a whole much later than the *Via Egnatia*, that is to say, only after the conquest of the Bulgarian empire in 1018.[27] But it was with the conversion of the Hungarians and the hospitality that King Stephan and his successors displayed to pilgrims from the countries of central and western Europe that the *Military Road* gained importance as a short and direct 'Pilgrim's Road' to Constantinople (and the Holy Land). These pilgrims were the immediate predecessors of the crusaders.[28]

Like the pilgrims, the crusaders too had a choice between two main roads to get to Constantinople: crusader armies from northern France and Germany usually moved through Austria and Hungary to Belgrade and along the *Military Road* (via Niš, Sofia, Philippopolis, Adrianople), while those from southern France and Italy would march to Brindisi, Bari or Otranto, from where they embarked for Dyrrachion or Aulona, and continued along the *Via Egnatia*.

Some crusader armies which marched through Hungary had carts with them for their equipment, baggage and food supplies, and perhaps also for their women and children. Peter the Hermit crossed the

---

[24] L. Duchesne, *Le Liber Pontificalis*, II (Paris, 1892), 180.
[25] *Liber Pontificalis*, II, 184; Anastasius Bibliothecarius, *PL* 129.39B.
[26] See 'Symeon', *ODB* 3.1984, and 'Kometopouloi', *ODB* 2.1140-1141, respectively.
[27] Jireček, *Heerstrasse*, 81f.
[28] Dimitroukas, *Reisen und Verkehr*, 356, 360f. For pilgrimages to Palestine through the Byzantine empire, before the crusades in general, see S. Runciman, 'The pilgrimages to Palestine before 1095', in K. Setton, ed., *A History of the Crusades*, I (Madison, London, 1969), 68-78, esp. 75-78. Pilgrims from Italy and France preferred the way via Apulia and Dyrrachion (Runciman, 'The pilgrimages', 75).

Balkan peninsula with his army in 1096, a short time before one of the main armies of the First Crusade under Geoffrey of Bouillon. After the difficult passage over the Sava river and after burning down Belgrade, Peter and his followers 'entered the enormous and spacious woods of the Bulgarians, with the carts for foodstuffs and with all equipment and the booty from Belgrade' (*ingentia et spaciosissima Bulgarorum nemora ingreditur, cum vehiculis cibariorum et omni apparatu, et spoliis Bellegravae*). They reached Niš, at that time capital of the Byzantine theme of Bulgaria, in eight days, and crossed some river (probably the Nišava) on a stone bridge. When fighting arose after a quarrel, the pursuing Byzantines under their *doux* Niketas captured the crusaders' carts and waggons (*currus et plaustra*), led away the women and children, as well as all their things, weapons and especially all their food and, a little later, the cart with Peter's treasury as well. The surviving crusaders now began to suffer from hunger, 'because they had lost their waggons and carts, more than two thousand, on which they carried the grain, barley and meat for eating' (*quia plaustra et currus, frumentum, ordeum carnesque ferentes ad edendum, supra duo milia amiserant*).[29]

The armies of the unfortunate Second Crusade under the German king Conrad III and the French king Louis VII marched separately through Hungary and along the *Military Road* across the Balkans, each with their baggage carts.[30] Odo of Deuil comments on the considerable number of *bigae et quadrigae* (two- and four-horse carts) in the army of Louis VII:

> ... the carts afforded more hope than usefulness. We say all these things to caution subsequent pilgrims; for, since there was a great number of four-horse carts, if one was damaged, all were delayed to the same extent; but, if they found many roads, all thronged them at the same time, and the packhorses, in avoiding the obstruction they presented, very frequently ran into more serious hindrances. For this reason the death of horses was a common occurrence, and so were the complaints about the short distance travelled each day.[31]

---

[29] Albertus Aquensis, *Historia Hierosolymitana*, in Recueil des Historiens des Croisades, Historiens occidentaux, IV (Paris, 1879), 278-281; S. Runciman, *A History of the Crusades*, I (Cambridge, 1951), 125-127.

[30] For carts in the German army, see Otto of Freising and Rahewin, *Gesta Frederici seu rectius Cronica*, chap. 48, F.-J. Schmale, ed., A. Schmidt, trans. (Darmstadt, 1965; repr. 1974), 222.

[31] Odo of Deuil, *De profectione Ludovici VII in orientem*, ed. and trans. V. G. Berry (New York, 1948), 24-25.

The baggage and food of the Third Crusade, led by the German emperor Frederick Barbarossa, were carried on a considerable number of carts again along the *Military Road* on to Adrianople.[32] The *Historia de expeditione Friderici* states that this road was called a 'frequently trodden route or public road' (*trita semita seu strata publica*), which probably corresponds to Greek *leophoros* and surely to *demosia hodos* ('public road', a term inherited from the Romans and used into the post-Byzantine period). At some places in the so-called *silva Bulgariae* (north of Niš) the crusaders' army was diverted from this road to another (parallel) one, which was 'rocky and not public' (*saxosa et non publica*) and allegedly obstructed by order of the Byzantine emperor.[33] Perhaps this diversion was in reality due not to the bad will of the Greek guides, but to necessity, because the main road was in bad condition. In 1172, Henry the Lion's carts could pass over this same stretch of the road only with extreme difficulty because of the swampy ground, and they suffered from so many breakdowns that he decided to leave the carts behind and to load supplies onto pack animals.[34] Considerable difficulties of passage along the *Military Road* in general are mentioned north of Niš, in the passes between Niš and Straliz (Sofia) and again in the *clausurae, clusae* behind Sofia.[35]

When the crusaders of Frederick Barbarossa passed the winter of 1189-90 at Philippopolis (Plovdiv) and Adrianople (Edirne), they lived off the country and plundered the villages and towns of Thrace. In some cases we learn that the immense booty was carried away on horses and carts, from Beroe (Stara Zagora, 80 km north-east of Plovdiv),[36] and generally 'a great number of carts that went out for booty and depopulated the whole country returned laden with loot and food' (*iam numerositas curruum in predam egregiens totam terram depopulando spoliis et victualibus honusta redibat*).[37] It becomes clear that where the terrain was flat or rolling as in the Maritsa plain in western Thrace, carts could circulate on roads practically all over the countryside.

But conditions could also change suddenly. The crusader army left

---

[32] For the march of Barbarossa from Belgrade along the *Military Road* to Adrianople and on secondary roads to the shore of the Dardanelles see E. Eickhoff, *Friedrich Barbarossa im Orient* (Tübingen, 1977), 58-80.

[33] A. Chroust, *Quellen zur Geschichte des Kreuzzuges Kaiser Friedrichs I, MGH*, Scriptores rerum Germanicarum, n.s. 5 (Berlin 1928), 27, 35 (hereafter Chroust, *Quellen*).

[34] Arnold of Lübeck, *Chronica Slavorum*, ed. J. M. Lappenberg, MGH (Hanover, 1868; repr. 1995), 15.

[35] Chroust, *Quellen*, 27f., 35, 37, 132, 135, 137-140.

[36] Chroust, *Quellen*, 141f.

[37] Chroust, *Quellen*, 142.

Adrianople in March 1190 in order to reach Kallipolis (Gelibolu) to cross the Dardanelles, i. e. they left the main road to Constantinople and moved on secondary roads. Unusually heavy and incessant rainfall hindered the progress of the army and especially the carts, and near Rossa (Rusköy, Keşan) a great number of the knights began *ob difficultatem viarum* to leave the carts and waggons behind and to load the pack horses.[38] Some carts and men were submerged by the swollen flood of a river when they tried to cross it.[39] The last carts were left behind at Kallipolis; for the march through Asia Minor, the crusaders relied exclusively on pack animals.[40]

I have dwelt on the use of carts by the crusader armies in some detail, because the fact that vehicles were used allows us a glimpse of the actual condition of roads at that time. It was still possible to cross the Balkan peninsula with carts, but even the main roads were very narrow, in mountain crossings rocky, sometimes swampy, and they could soon become overcrowded with carts. It is easy to understand why no carts at all are mentioned for those groups of crusaders who came to Constantinople along the *Via Egnatia* after having crossed the Adriatic sea. An oversea ship passage with a great number of carts would have been too expensive or even impossible.

The conquest of Constantinople by the armies of the Fourth Crusade changed the conditions of the Byzantine roads in the Balkans completely. There was no longer a centralised state to watch over the long distance roads on the Balkan peninsula, and even after the reconquest of Constantinople by Michael VIII, neither the *Via Egnatia* nor the *Via Militaris* ever returned entirely to Byzantine control. In the empire's shrinking territory the late Byzantine Balkan roads soon again all ended in Thrace and Macedonia somewhere in the hinterland of Adrianople and Thessalonike and, even in those parts that remained Byzantine, Serb, Bulgarian, Catalan, Mongol and Turk invasions and/or bands of robbers (including Greeks) made travel a dangerous adventure.

Apart from some information we find in Byzantine historians,[41] there are a handful of sources, travel letters, which describe at least

---

[38] Chroust, *Quellen*, 70.
[39] Chroust, *Quellen*, 152.
[40] Chroust, *Quellen*, 72, 152.
[41] E.g. a report on the fruitless delegation of 1269 to settle the marriage of Anna, daughter of Michael VIII, with the Serbian prince Milutin; they went along the *Via Egnatia* via Berroia to Ochrid and then turned to the north, before they fell into ambushes of Serbian robbers and returned (George Pachymeres, ed. A. Failler, *Georges Pachymérès, Relations historiques*, II, CFHB 24/2 (Paris, 1984), 452-456; for the historical situation, see the commentary by A. Failler.

some aspects of the roads and travel in the late Byzantine empire.[42] The well-known *Presbeutikos* of Theodore Metochites is a report on the delegation he led to King Uroš II Milutin at Skopje in 1299, in which the final stipulations for the marriage of the Serbian king with Simonis, the five-year-old daughter of Andronikos II, were fixed. The route was along the *Via Egnatia* to Thessalonike and from there through the valley of the Axios (Vardar) river to the Serbian capital Skopje. The group — Metochites and a Serbian ambassador on his way home to Skopje, with their respective servants — left Constantinople in winter. Travelling was therefore very hard, and they all suffered severely from icy north winds, rain and much snow. They often had to dismount the horses and walk. The horses slid and fell down, as did the carts which often broke down. The report of Metochites is interesting also with regard to administration. The *Via Egnatia* (of course not named as such) is expressly called *hodos basileos*, which naturally corresponds to the more common *basilike hodos*. For official delegations the emperor himself had to provide the necessary food supplies (probably, therefore, also the carts). The peasant population which lived in the villages along the road was responsible only for night quartering and was given, in compensation, exemption from all additional taxes and other compulsory services.[43]

If the *Presbeutikos* was more an official report than a letter, the account of Nikephoros Gregoras on a delegation to the Serbian court in 1326 for the safe return of Eirene, daughter of Theodore Metochites and widow of John Palaiologos who had died at Skopje, was originally a letter to a friend[44] which was eventually incorporated in Gregoras' *Roman History*.[45] Concerning the Thracian part of the journey we learn

---

[42] See A. Karpozelos, 'Ταξιδιωτικές περιγραφές και εντυπώσεις σε επιστολογραφικά κείμενα', in N. G. Moschonas, ed., *Η επικοινωνία στο Βυζάντιο. Πρακτικά του Β' Διεθνούς συμποσίου, 4-6 Οκτωβρίου 1990* (Athens, 1993), 511-541 (hereafter, Karpozelos, 'Perigraphes').

[43] Theodore Metochites, *Presbeutikos*, ed. L. Mavromatis, *La fondation de l'empire serbe. Le kralj Milutin* (Thessalonike, 1978), 89-119, esp. 90-94; cf. E. Malamut, 'Sur la route de Théodore Métochite en Serbie en 1299', in *Voyages et voyageurs au moyen âge, XXVIe Congrès de la Société des Historiens médiévistes de l'Enseignement Supérieur Public, Limoges-Aubazine, mai 1995* (Paris, 1996), 165-175.

[44] Letter to Andronikos Zaridas, whom Gregoras had met on his way to Skopje, but whom he could not meet again on his way back, contrary to his intention, because he was led along another road: ed. P. A. M. Leone, *Nicephori Gregorae epistolae*, II (Bari, 1982), 115-124. Gregoras sent this same letter, with a different introduction and ending, to a certain Athanasios as well (ed. Leone 103-115); see J.-L. van Dieten, *Entstehung und Überlieferung der Historia Rhomaike des Nikephoros Gregoras, insbesondere des ersten Teiles: Buch I-XI*, Thesis (Cologne, 1975), 153-159; Karpozelos, 'Perigraphes', 523f.

[45] Nicephori Gregorae *Byzantina historia*, ed. L. Schopen, I (Bonn 1829), 374-383; see

only that there were rumours of an imminent invasion of Skyths (Mongols); the rural population therefore fled from the villages to fortresses, and the houses where the members of the embassy were to find night quarters were often empty. Crossing the Strymon near Amphipolis at its mouth was an adventure; the whole party of 140 men and pack animals had to cross the river singly or in groups of two or three in only one small ship, which took nearly a day. They then left the *Via Egnatia* and marched, in darkness, through dense woods of bushes along a completely unmaintained road on the right bank of the Strymon river; shoes and clothes were torn to pieces by branches of the trees and thorns. Luckily they met some Slavic-speaking watchmen who were equipped with light arms in order to keep thieves off the estates; they led them to the next village. Allegedly, the next day they reached Stroumitsa (which is virtually impossible considering the distance), where they celebrated Easter, and from there they travelled to Skopje in three days. As for the way back, we are told only that Gregoras separated from Eirene and her entourage after one day. The latter followed the direct way to Thessalonike, while Gregoras himself returned to Constantinople as quickly as possible; he was guided by a Serb on a different, even more uncomfortable road.[46]

Matthew, metropolitan bishop of Ephesos, describes in a letter his journey to the metropolitan see of Brysis (Pınarhisar, c. 80 km east of Adrianople) in Thrace, which he was given in 1332 as an *epidosis*.[47] He is the only traveller who, following the (probably bad) advice of his guides, did not keep to the *Via Egnatia*, but took a more direct inland

---

the German translation by J. L. van Dieten, *Nikephoros Gregoras, Rhomäische Geschichte (Historia Rhomaïke)*, Bibliothek der griechischen Literatur 2/1 (Stuttgart, 1979), 73-78; commentary, 180-185, where the history of the text is discussed and its different introductions and its variations from the text of the *History* are translated into German; Karpozelos, 'Perigraphes', 529-531.

[46] Although geographical details are lacking, some speculation on Gregoras' route back to Constantinople is allowed. Zaridas lived a comfortable three days' march east of Amphipolis, near the mouth of the Strymon river (Leone, *Nicephori Gregorae epistolae*, II, 116). A march of about 30 km a day was a good average, about 20 km (or a little more) could be regarded as comfortable. Zaridas' home may therefore have stood at or near Christoupolis (today Kavala), which was, along the course of the *Via Egnatia*, about 65 km distant from Amphipolis. On the return journey, Gregoras' guide must have led him along a route further to the north and east in order to avoid Christoupolis, probably on a mountain road to the valley of the (upper) Nestos, through which a Byzantine road led to Xantheia (Xanthi), where the *Via Egnatia* was reached again (Soustal, *Thrakien*, map).

[47] D. Reinsch, *Die Briefe des Matthaios von Ephesos im Codex Vindobonensis Theol. Gr. 174* (Berlin, 1974), letter 64, pp. 192-201 (text); 369-383 (German translation); see Karpozelos, 'Perigraphes' 534-536.

road.[48] After the first night at an unknown place, *Prota*, adventures began, because the guides had left Matthew during the night and taken a short cut. The main road could hardly be seen, so that Matthew, his son, and the servants soon lost the way and only by chance found a man who could show it to them. On the second night one of the party encountered native robbers and murderers at the innkeeper's (*kapelos*), where he went to buy wine. The whole remote and lonely region was notorious for its robbers. On the next day, they saw little hills of earth with crosses which they took for graves of slain and robbed travellers. After a difficult river crossing they reached Brysis via Bizye (Vize).

Finally, there is the letter of a George Oinaiotes which describes the adventures and impressions of a four-day private journey on horseback which Oinaiotes made probably in the later 1320s with some companions from Constantinople to Ganos, some 20 km south-west of Rhaidestos (Tekirdağ). Such a journey would involve going to Rhaidestos along the *Via Egnatia* and then on a difficult secondary road through the mountains. Although the whole region, at least to the west of Selymbria (Silivri), had been repeatedly sacked and pillaged by Catalans and Turks over the last 20 years and had, in addition, suffered from the civil war between Andronikos II and his grandson Andronikos III, our travellers could spend the nights at rest-houses (the first near modern Küçük Çekmece, the second at or near Selymbria, the third at Rhaidestos where, however, they were invited by the patriarchal exarch), and there were also some inns along the road, where they could buy lunch.[49] These rest-houses were entirely private establishments; the quality of the houses and the character of the innkeepers and hostesses could vary considerably.

In conclusion, from travel letters it can be said that the only overland road that was kept in at least an acceptable condition was the *Via Egnatia*, for which facilities for travellers and some sort of imperial administration are attested as late as the end of the thirteenth century. Along this road there was also some sort of infrastructure for private travellers, such as inns and hostels. All other roads (except, perhaps, for the road to Adrianople, the beginning of the

---

[48] Reinsch, *Briefe* 192: '... καὶ τὴν 'επ' ἀριστερὰ καταλιπόντες πρὸς ἠιόνα τὴν ἐπὶ δεξιὰ βαδίζομεν' ('ließen wir den Weg zur Linken liegen, der zur Küste führt, und schlugen den Weg zu unserer Rechten ein'). Reinsch in his translation (p. 369) connects πρὸς ἠιόνα with τὴν ἐπὶ δεξιά, which for geographical reasons seems less probable.

[49] H. Ahrweiler, 'Le récit du voyage d'Oinaiôtès de Constantinople à Ganos', in W. Seibt, ed., *Geschichte und Kultur der Palaiologenzeit. Referate des Internationalen Symposions zu Ehren von Herbert Hunger (Wien, 30. November bis 3. Dezember 1994)* (Vienna, 1996), 9-27 (with Greek text by G. Fatouros); see Karpozelos, 'Perigraphes', 531-534.

old *Military Road*, for which, however, there is no information) were extremely neglected, so that anyone not from the area could hardly follow them without guides.

Finally, I turn to quite a different kind of source which sheds light mainly on local roads, but allows some glimpses of road administration as well: the documents of monasteries, for our purposes those of Mount Athos, which exist from the middle Byzantine into the Ottoman period. Usually, only the existence of roads, not their destinations, are mentioned in the descriptions and delimitations of estates and other property of the monasteries. Geographically, mainly the Holy Mountain itself, the Chalkidike peninsula, Thessalonike and its hinterland, and the lower Strymon region are described. The overwhelming majority of the roads mentioned here are local ones (between villages, or leading to fields or forests); long-distance roads are only mentioned where estates border on them.

Without going into detail, a general picture emerges from the documents. They show us an astonishingly dense network of local roads, some of which were obviously paved.[50] J. Lefort has recorded and, as far as possible, localised and mapped all the roads that are mentioned in the western part of the Chalkidike,[51] but the overall picture seems to be quite similar in all areas. Furthermore, the roads have differentiated designations according to their importance, function or appearance. These categories of course overlap.

With respect to function, we find *agelodromi(o)n* (a road or track for herds),[52] a term that could also become a proper name of a road,[53] *hamaxegos, hamaxege* or *hamaxike* (*dromos* or *hodos* understood), or the like, a local carriageable road for the farmers' oxen carts, never for wheeled long distance traffic which in Byzantium virtually did not exist,[54] and *xylophorikon, ton xylophoron hodos* (a road or track the

---

[50] Apart from those roads, which are styled *plakotoi* in the sources (see *infra*, p.87), remains have been found at various places in the countryside; see J. Lefort, 'De Bolbos à la Plaine du Diable', *TM* 7 (1979), 465-489, esp. 465.

[51] J. Lefort, *Villages de Macédoine, 1. La Chalcidique occidentale* (Paris, 1982).

[52] P. Lemerle, A. Guillou, N. Svoronos, D. Papachryssanthou, *Actes de Lavra* II (Paris, 1977), 90, l. 278 (1300), 108, l. 413 (1321); M. Živojinović, V. Kravari, Chr. Giros, *Actes de Chilandar* I (Paris, 1998), 40, ll. 38, 40f. (1318).

[53] D. Papachryssanthou, *Actes de Xénophon* (Paris, 1986), 3, l. 57 (1300), 12, l. 92 (1318), 13, ll. 68f. (1320), 25, l. 35 (1338), App. II, l. 35 (before 1338).

[54] E.g., J. Lefort, N. Oikonomidès, D. Papachryssanthou, V. Kravari, H. Métrévéli, *Actes d'Iviron* I (Paris, 1985), 29, ll. 44, 51f. (1047); II (Paris, 1990), 50, ll. 11, 15f., 51 (1101), 52, ll. 494f., 497 (1104); III (Paris, 1994), 56, l. 160 (1152), 70, ll. 262, 340, 347, 369f., 417, 438f. (1301); IV (Paris, 1995), 86, ll. 217, 354, 384f., 442 (1341).

purpose of which is especially to transport wood from the forests).[55] *Palaiostraton*[56] or *palaios dromos (palaia hodos, strata)*[57] obviously means a more or less unfunctioning road.

With respect to appearance, there is *monopation* (a narrow path for pedestrians or pack animals),[58] at the low end of scale, and *plakotos (plakote)*, a paved road, at the upper end.[59] *Plakotos*, too, occasionally became a proper name for a stretch of road.[60]

As regards importance, there are — above all — the higher ranking roads such as *demosia* (or *demosiake) hodos, basilike hodos*, and the rather unspecific terms such as *katholike hodos*,[61] or *megale hodos* in later sources.[62] Other terms, such as *leophoros*, do not occur in the documents.

The *basilike hodos* from the early Byzantine period certainly denotes a road for which emperors have some sort of responsibility for organisation and maintenance (directly, through governors of provinces or the *logothetes tou dromou* and his staff). The name occurs in crusader sources (*via regia*, in Asia Minor)[63] and in the *Presbeutikos* of Theodore Metochites of 1299 (*hodos basileos*). It has been stated that in the late Byzantine period the term could mean any road of some importance.[64] Can we corroborate this from the documents of the Athos monasteries? *Basilikai hodoi* are specified by name from 1017 to at least 1496, and it turns out that many of them are part of old long-distance roads. In 1062

---

[55] *Actes de Lavra* II, 98, ll. 43f. (1304); *Actes d'Iviron* III, 70, ll. 400f. (1301), 75, l. 534 (1318); IV, 86, l. 410 (1341).

[56] *Actes de Chilandar* I, 21, l. 6 (ca. 1300); *Actes de Lavra* II, 90, ll. 75, 82, 107, 353 (1300), 108, ll. 15, 17f., 27 (1321).

[57] *Actes d'Iviron* II, 50, l. 65 (1101), 52, l. 486 (1104); *Actes de Chilandar* I, 9, l. 86 (1274), 12, l. 10 (1293), 40, l. 24 (1318); *Actes de Lavra* II, 108, l. 19 (1321); P. Lemerle, G. Dagron, S. Ćirković, *Actes de Saint-Pantéléèmôn* (Paris, 1982), 13, text B, l. 15 (1363), Appendix II l. 17 (1312); N. Oikonomidès, *Actes de Dionysiou* (Paris, 1968), 20, ll. 26f. *(pepalaiomene hodos)*.

[58] Frequently mentioned, e. g. *Actes d'Iviron* I, 22, ll. 18f. (1016 or 17).

[59] *Actes d'Iviron* I, 10, l. 56 (996), 19, l. 2 (1013), 29, l. 55 (1047); *Actes de Saint-Pantéléèmôn*, 3, l. 23 (1044?); the *plakotos* near the village of Radolibos most probably denotes the Via Egnatia; see J. Lefort, 'Radolibos: population et paysage', *TM* 9 (1985), 195-234, esp. 207: *Actes d'Iviron* II, 48, ll. 6, 8f. (between 1098 and 1103), 51, ll. 114, 116-118 (1103), 53, l. 142 (beginning of 12th cent.); III, 55a, text at l.15 (1142).

[60] *Actes de Lavra* II 108, ll. 492, 921f. (1321).

[61] E.g. V. Kravari, 'Nouveaux documents du monastère de Philothéou', *TM* 10 (1987), 261-356, esp. 313 (commentary), 314, no. 5, l. 25 (1355); P. Lemerle, *Actes de Kutlumus* (Paris, 1988), 51, l. 32 (1518).

[62] N. Oikonomidès, *Actes de Kastamonitou* (Paris, 1978), App. I, γ, l. 26 (p. 91) (forgery of the 16th cent.); *Actes de Kutlumus* 61, l. 23 (1613), 62, l. 12 (1613), 64, l. 8 (1619), 76, l. 38 (1800).

[63] *Epistola de morte Friderici imperatoris*, in Chroust, *Quellen*, 174 (as in n. 33); see Dimitroukas, *Reisen und Verkehr*, 324.

[64] P. Lemerle, *Actes de Kutlumus*, 43.

and in 1152 two stretches of a *basilike hodos* along the right bank of the Strymon river via Stroumitsa to Skopje are mentioned, the road over which Nikephoros Gregoras found it so difficult to travel in 1326.[65] The *basilike hodos* east of the Strymon river near its mouth, referred to in a comparatively late document (1394), must be the *Via Egnatia*. For this road two *poroi* (fords) across the river are mentioned;[66] an alternative crossing was, as we know from other sources, by boat.[67] According to the itinerary in a late Byzantine letter of Constantine Akropolites, it was possible to get from Christoupolis to Thessalonike also via Serres[68] (instead of following the *Via Egnatia*), and indeed the road to Serres and in the town itself was called a *basilike hodos* in several documents.[69] These are stretches of the old, Constantinople-centred long-distance — in other words — real 'imperial' roads.

The other *basilikai hodoi* which are attested in the documents of the Athos monasteries are all on the Chalkidike peninsula. Each of its three fingers (Kassandra, Sithonia and the Holy Mountain) had at least *one* imperial road, which went longitudinally through these sub-peninsulas.[70] The situation on Mount Athos itself is more difficult to assess because five stretches of a *basilike hodos* or *basilikai hodoi* are attested, some of which cannot be located exactly. It is therefore not quite clear whether there was one imperial road through the Holy Mountain — this seems to me to be more probable — or several.[71]

---

[65] *Actes d'Iviron* II (Paris, 1990), 35, l. 36 (1062); *Actes d'Iviron* III (Paris, 1979), 56, ll. 158, 223 (1152); see above, p. 84.

[66] V. Kravari, *Actes du Pantocrator* (Paris 1991), 16, ll. 13f.; 17, ll. 31, 35 (both 1394).

[67] See above, p. 78, p. 84.

[68] R. Romano, *Costantino Acropolita, Epistole* (Naples, 1991), letter 98, 193.

[69] *Actes de Kutlumus* 4, l. 5 (1287); J. Lefort, *Actes d'Esphigménou* (Paris, 1973), 9, l.-10 (1301); Kravari, 'Nouveaux documents du monastère de Philothéou' (as in n. 61), 314 (no. 5, l. 19 [1355]); A. Guillou, *Les Archives de Saint-Jean-Prodrome sur le mont Ménécée* (Paris, 1955), 26. The *basilike hodos* or a branch of it may also have led up the Strymon valley.

[70] Kassandra: *Actes de Xénophon*, 22, ll. 23, 25 (1333), mentioned in delimitation of a winter pasture in the north-west of the peninsula; Sithonia (Longos): a *basilike hodos* is mentioned twice, but I doubt that it is really the same road; it is perhaps two branches. Both start from Longos (= Sykia) in the southern part of the peninsula; the first one (*Actes de Lavra* II, 108, l. 744 [1321]) goes inland to the north, the other one (N. Oikonomidès, *Actes de Docheiariou* [Paris, 1984], 20, l. 25 [1341]; *Actes de Lavra* II, 97, l. 800 [1304]: road Longos-Sarti) equally goes north, but to Sarti at the eastern coast.

[71] P. Lemerle, A. Guillou, N. Svoronos, D. Papachryssanthou, *Actes de Lavra* I (Paris 1970), 61, ll. 22f. (1141): an inland road in the central part of Mount Athos; *Actes de Chilandar* I, 14, l. 45 (1294): at or near the western coast, but not to be located exactly; *Actes de Kastamonitou* 2, ll. 23-25 (1310), cf. p. 32, from Kastamonitou to Karyes; *Actes de Saint-Pantéléèmôn*, App. II, 12f., l. 24 (1312): probably an inland road north of Karyes; *Actes de Dionysiou* 39, 16 (1496), cf. p. 184f.: probably from Karyes to H. Paulos, if so, perhaps at least in part along the coast.

It would be logical to assume that the *basilikai hodoi* from the three fingers of the Chalkidike peninsula should have continuations to its natural administrative centre, Thessalonike, and perhaps to the Strymon valley as well. It is, therefore, astonishing to see that although there are numerous documents for many parts of the Chalkidike which mention hundreds of roads, only a small stretch of a *basilike hodos* is attested between Hierissos and Gomatou (6 km to the west).[72] Instead, we find *demosiai (demosiakai) hodoi* (public roads), which are attested much more frequently than the *basilikai hodoi* .

Although, according to the character of our documentary material, only those stretches of road are mentioned that are important for delimitations and related purposes, there are some exceptional instances where Thessalonike is spoken of as the destination of *demosiai hodoi*. Two are attested as leading to Thessalonike from western Chalkidike; they run parallel, and rather close, to each other.[73] The final destinations of *demosiai hodoi* further away from Thessalonike are not given in the documents, but at least some of these roads led to Thessalonike as well, such as the *demosia hodos* from H. Mamas to Katakale, attested only in 1503-04.[74] Its continuation to Thessalonike may be assumed, either along the coast via Bryai, or through the interior via Karbaioi or via Bromosyrta.[75]

In some later documents, a confusion between the terms *basilike hodos* and *demosia hodos* occurs. The clearest example is in the Kassandra peninsula. The *basilike hodos* in a document of the Xenophontos monastery of 1333 becomes a *demosia hodos* five years later.[76] In other instances, the identification of a *basilike hodos* with a *demosia hodos* in different documents can only be assumed, not proved. The stretch of a *demosia hodos* south of Lake Achinos (right bank of the Strymon river), attested in 1318,[77] probably corresponds to the two stretches of the *basilike hodos* in the same area mentioned above (and to the road of the delegation of Nikephoros Gregoras in 1326).

Both terms survive the period of Byzantine domination; there was a *basilike hodos* on Mount Athos in 1496 (to H. Paulou),[78] and a

---

[72] *Actes de Lavra* II, 90, ll. 304-307 (1300) and 108, ll. 609f. (1321): Hierissos-Gomatou; *Actes de Chilandar* I, 9, ll. 80f. (1274), cf. p. 61: obviously the same road east of Gomatou; *Actes de Lavra* I, 22, l. 14 (1017): continuation to the west, but still near Gomatou.
[73] *Actes de Lavra* II, 90, l. 83 (1300); 108, ll. 28f., 195 (1321).
[74] *Actes de Dionysiou* 43, ll. 12f., cf. p. 195f. (1503/04).
[75] Cf. Lefort, *Villages*, map 13.
[76] *Actes de Xénophon* 22, ll. 23, 25 (1333); 25, l. 54 (1338).
[77] *Actes de Chilandar* 40, l. 87 (1318), cf. map, p. 6.
[78] *Actes de Dionysiou* 39, l. 16 (1496); cf. p. 184f.

demosiake hodos is mentioned, e.g. in 1639.[79] In this post-Byzantine period, the terms must have lost their juridical and administrative significance, but this process certainly began much earlier. On the other hand, it is apparent that the majority of the *basilikai hodoi* are real, old long-distance roads. Generally, it does not seem to me that the term was extended indiscriminately to 'any important road'. The same may be true for *demosiai hodoi*, but for these no clear development can be discerned.

In this contribution, only the bare skeleton could be revealed of some long distance roads, of road conditions, of travel and travel facilities in Macedonia and Thrace, using a selection of narrative sources and letters. Only the most important of these roads, the *Military Road* and, at least in part, the *Via Egnatia*, were kept in a condition that made it possible for carts to traverse them, albeit with great difficulty, until the end of the middle and even into the late Byzantine period. Documents, more than narrative sources, allow us a glimpse of road administration. Terms such as *basilike hodos* and *demosia hodos* prove that road administration remained centralised, at least in principle, until the end of the empire. But documents also show that beside these 'highways' there was an astonishingly dense network of 'secondary roads' with different designations and functions. These were the roads that chiefly met the needs of the local administration and, above all, the local population in everyday life.

---

[79] *Actes de Kutlumus* 69, 1. 9; ἡ δεμουσιά is still occasionally used in modern Greek: see P. Koukoules, Βυζαντινῶν βίος καὶ πολιτισμός, IV (Athens, 1951), 319, n. 6.

5. Horses and horse-doctors on the road

A. McCabe

τοῦτο γάρ, οἶμαι, κάλλιστον καὶ πανταχῇ περισπούδαστον ζῷον ἀνθρώποις ἵππος ἂν εἰκότως εἶναι νομίζοιτο. ὁδοιπορούντι μὲν ἐπελαφρύνων τῷ δεσπότῃ τοὺς πόνους, πομπεύοντι δὲ σεμνοτέραν ἀποφαίνων καὶ περιβλεπτοτέραν τὴν πομπήν, ἔν γε μὴν τοῖς κατὰ πόλεμον ἀγῶσιν συγκινδυνεύων ....[1]

The horse truly ought, I think, to be considered the finest animal and in every way the most desirable to mankind. For [the horse] lightens the labours of his master while on the road, on parade he makes the procession more solemn and more splendid, and in contests of war he shares in the danger ....

In the early Byzantine period horses were used not only for private travel, but also on a large scale by two great institutions of the Roman state, the army and the public post.[2] To ensure that mounts and pack-animals stayed in good condition, horse-doctors (ἱππιατροί) travelled with the army[3] and were stationed at the *mansiones* or σταθμοί that punctuated the network of roads across the empire.[4] The experiences of

---

[1] From an encomium of the horse in the treatise of Hierokles: E. Oder and C. Hoppe, eds., *Corpus Hippiatricorum Graecorum*, I (Leipzig, 1924), 249.2-7.

[2] The hippodrome, for which horses were required in large numbers, and for which they were often transported over long distances, is too vast a subject to be broached in this note.

[3] O. Nanetti, 'ΙΠΠΙΑΤΡΟΙ', *Aegyptus* 22 (1942), 49-54; R. W. Davies, 'The supply of animals to the Roman army and the remount system', *Latomus* 28 (1969), 429-59; R. E. Walker, 'Some notes on cavalry-horses in the Roman army', Appendix in J. M. C. Toynbee, *Animals in Roman Life and Art* (London, 1973), 335-343.

[4] The Theodosian Code VIII.5.31 stipulates that these *mulomedici* were to be fed and clothed by the state: ed. T. Mommsen and P. M. Meyer (Berlin, 1905). Cf. E. J. Holmberg, *Zur Geschichte des Cursus Publicus* (Uppsala, 1933). A grave stone found at Karakilise, the probable site of the Byzantine port of Pylai on the gulf of Nikomedeia, an important stopping-place for people and livestock on the way to the capital, commemorates the wife

From *Travel in the Byzantine World*, ed. Ruth Macrides. Copyright © 2002 by the Society for the Promotion of Byzantine Studies. Published by Ashgate Publishing Ltd, Gower House, Croft Road, Aldershot, Hampshire, GU11 3HR, Great Britain.

some of these men, and the sufferings of their patients, are recorded in the encyclopaedia of horse-medicine known as the *Hippiatrika*.[5]

Related in form to the better-known late antique compendia of human medicine, poetry, and the law,[6] the *Hippiatrika* is a composite text, assembled by an unknown editor in late Antiquity out of excerpts from a number of veterinary handbooks of the third and fourth centuries A.D. These excerpts are collated subject-by-subject into chapters on fever, lameness, colic, etc., so that under the heading of each disease, texts of various authorities are assembled for the purpose of reference or comparison.[7]

In the *Hippiatrika* are to be found many descriptions of ailments said to result from travel, ἐξ ὁδοιπορίας: from conditions of exhaustion (Fig. 5.1) and extreme hunger to accidents like spraining a shoulder, being bitten by a snake or falling into a ditch.[8] The *Hippiatrika* also contains remedies simplified or adapted for use on the road, when ingredients may be hard to find.[9]

Two of the authors represented in the *Hippiatrika* refer specifically to their experience of travelling with the army. The first, Apsyrtos, belongs to the late third or early fourth century; the second, Theomnestos, evidently composed his treatise somewhat later, for he

---

of a horse-doctor. See S. Şahin, *Bithynische Studien* [= *Inschriften Griechischer Städte aus Kleinasien* 7] (Bonn, 1978), II. 20, 47-48 and 117; pl. X. On Pylae, see C. Mango, 'The empress Helena, Helenopolis, Pylae', *TM* 12 (1994), 143ff.

[5] The text exists in five recensions, in some twenty manuscripts which range in date from the tenth century to the sixteenth: A.-M. Doyen-Higuet, 'The *Hippiatrica* and Byzantine veterinary medicine', *DOP* 38 (1984), 111-120; also K.-D. Fischer, 'Ancient veterinary medicine: a survey of Greek and Latin sources and some recent scholarship', *Medizinhistorisches Journal* (1988), 191-209. The modern edition of the text is that of Oder and Hoppe, *Corpus Hippiatricorum Graecorum*, I and II (Leipzig, 1924 and 1927), hereafter CHG.

[6] Such as the *Synagogai iatrikai* of Oribasios, the *Cycle* of Agathias, and Justinian's *Digest*. On the process of excerpting and compilation, see T. Honoré, *Tribonian* (London, 1978), 139ff. Paul of Aegina, in the prooimion to his medical encyclopaedia, explains that compilations are particularly useful for doctors, who are often compelled to practice their art far from their libraries, in deserted places, or even at sea: *Epitomae medicae libri septem*, ed. J. L. Heiberg (Leipzig, 1921), 3.

[7] In the manner of composite scholia or catenae, on which see N. G. Wilson, 'A chapter in the history of scholia', *Classical Quarterly*, n.s. 17 (1967), 244-256; and R. Devreesse, 'Chaînes exégétiques grecques', *Dictionnaire de la Bible, Supplément* I (Paris, 1928), cols. 1084-1233.

[8] CHG I, 252-253; 262f; 125ff; 308ff; 280f.

[9] *Euporista*, commonly available or easily formulated medicines, form a genre of medical literature in their own right; Dioscorides compiled a treatise on the subject, and Oribasius simplified and condensed his seventy-book *Synagogai* for use while travelling, *en apodemiais*: cf. *Synopsis ad Eustathium*, ed. J. Raeder (Leipzig, 1926), 1.1.

αὐ σῶμα ἕλκος ᾖ· ἐξ ὁλύμοῦ ἰῶ καὶ ἡ λατρεία· λαμωμ οιδία
βιερῶ· λε͂ ͂τοῦ κος χίνω κόπος καὶ οἶσας· διά πασαι πο σω
μα αὐτου διώσας ἕξω τοῦ λοί πτά͂ι· ὕδωρ ἥμισει ὄιον· ὥστε τὴν
αὐτὴν ἱκαμὼς ἡμεσθαι· εἶτα λύσας ἐχϊνου δυα λωι τὴν τλᾶ
ασαμψῶν τοῦ σώματος· ἐκπλύνον οἴνωι ἀκράτωι· ἐὰν δὲ
τοῦτο μὴ ἔχῃς· ἐλέας φύλα βιερά μαστίξον· καὶ εἰ
σου κοσκίμωι τοὶ κμὸ ἔμπασε· αὖ σοδιώσας πρὸ πομ τὴν
γ λῶ ασαμ βιοτ ἥμισει ὠρίου· εἶτα ἐκπολῶν μηδὲν πϊ· μέχρι
αὐ ὑ παμμ :~ ♦♦♦♦♦♦♦♦♦ κόπος ἐξ ὁδοι πορία :~ ♦♦♦

τοῦ σῶ βιμ κόπου σμ̈ φλεμο τομείοσθω παραυτίκας· εἶ ταρ
εὐμη λωδοκεῖν φλεμο πομεία· ἀλλὰ τύρω σαι πο σω δοκιμάσ
πορρω ἀλειφέοσθαι δὲ ἑλαίωι καὶ οἴνωι· ποιῶ ὅμοια καὶ τὰ σκε
λη· καὶ ταῖς χερσίν ἀνασαλῶ σαί πο τρίψεσθαι· μὴ ἔστω
δια τὸ πάνυ σκληρω· ἀλλὰ μ̈ κο πατρίσιν· ἥ πίσειν ὑπὸ ωλω

Figure 5.1 A horse suffering from exhaustion, *Parisinus graecus* 2244, f. 3v

refers to Apsyrtos's work.[10] Apsyrtos's treatise is in the form of a collection of letters purporting to respond to questions posed by cavalry soldiers and horse-doctors from all over the empire. This far-flung correspondence may simply be a stylistic device,[11] but Apsyrtos's statement, in his preface, that he campaigned with the τάγματα (the Roman legions) along the Danube, is borne out by the many allusions in his text to army life, travel, and contact with foreign peoples.[12]

Apsyrtos praises Spanish horses as being hardy travellers (ἰσχυροὶ ἐν ταῖς ὁδοιπορίαις).[13] He suggests that a horse exhausted from travelling be given little cakes made of barley and sweet wine, and cautions that phlebotomy not be performed upon a horse that is tired (ὑπόκοπος) in this way.[14] He warns that laminitis (κριθίασις), inflammation of tissues of the hoof, will often afflict a horse who has consumed a large quantity of grain while fresh from travelling (ἐξ ὁδοιπορίας ὤν).[15] For horses with ravenous hunger (βουλιμία), Apsyrtos offers an alternative treatment to be used on the road (ἐπὶ τῆς ὁδοῦ), which calls for simpler ingredients — bread and wine — than the fine flour and pine-nuts prescribed for use at home (ἐν οἴκῳ).[16] Apsyrtos warns that if, while on the road, a horse does not urinate all day (ὅταν ὁδοιπορῶν ἢ τροχάζων δι' ὅλης ἡμέρας μὴ οὐρήσῃ διὰ τῆς ὁδοῦ), dysury (δυσουρία) may result; the remedy that he prescribes is one, he tells us, that he learned from Sarmatians.[17] Apsyrtos devotes a good deal of attention to lameness — as the saying goes 'no foot, no horse' —

---

[10] For a discussion of the chronology of the two authors, see G. Björck, 'Apsyrtus, Julius Africanus et l'hippiatrique grecque', *Uppsala Universitets Årsskrift* 4 (1944), 7-12.

[11] On this device see J. Sykutris, art. 'Epistolographie', *RE* Supp. V (Stuttgart, 1931), col. 205; and A. M. Ieraci Bio, 'L'ἐρωταπόκρισις nella letteratura medica,' in C. Moreschini, ed., *Esegesi, parafrasi, e compilazione in età tardoantica*, Atti del 3º Convegno dell'Associazione di studi tardoantichi, Pisa 1993 (Naples, 1995), 187ff. Apsyrtos evidently had a considerable influence on veterinary writing: in the other texts gathered in the *Hippiatrika*, there are not only many references to his treatise, but instances of wholesale appropriation of its content and imitation of its literary form. The veterinary manual of Hierokles consists of a metaphrasis of Apsyrtos's work into a more elegant literary style; while that of Pelagonius is also in the form of a letter-collection. On Pelagonius see J. N. Adams, *Pelagonius and Latin Veterinary Terminology in the Roman Empire* (Leiden, 1995).

[12] *CHG* I, 1. He was evidently not a native of that region: the notice in the *Souda* under his name states that Apsyrtos was from Prousa or Nikomedeia, though evidence in the *Hippiatrika* suggests that he may in fact have been from Clazomenai (see *CHG* II, VI), corroborated by a mention of the river Meles, *CHG* II, 45. On the Meles see W. M. Ramsay, *The Historical Geography of Asia Minor* (London, 1890), 115.

[13] *CHG* I, 373.
[14] *CHG* I, 57-58, 252.
[15] *CHG* I, 49.
[16] *CHG* I, 262.
[17] *CHG* I, 166ff.

and weakness of the feet must have been of particular concern at a time when horses were on the whole not shod.[18] Apsyrtos gives instructions for the preparation of a hoof-dressing for horses with soft feet (μαλακόποδες) that are worn away by road travel (ἐν τῇ ὁδοιπορίᾳ).[19] He recommends cautery for swelling of knees and fetlocks as a result of travelling or heavy loads (ἐκ τῶν ὁδοιποριῶν καὶ φορτίων);[20] and notes that mules, used as pack-animals, are predisposed to certain conditions, such as sores on the feet (μάρμαρον) from travelling over rough terrain (ἐξ ὁδοιπορίας καὶ τραχείας ὁδοῦ).[21]

Our second author, Theomnestos, also travelled on the Danube frontier. While discussing a condition known as τέτανος (which in this case seems to be the result not of infection, but simply of extreme cold), Theomnestos digresses to sketch the grim details of his experience crossing the Alps with the emperor and his horse-guard in winter. The emperor has been identified as Licinius, who travelled from Carnuntum to Milan in 312 for his marriage to Constantine's half-sister Constantia.[22]

> Tetanos occurs in horses and other beasts of burden from no other cause than cold, when the body suffers and the nerves are affected as well. It is called tetanos because the whole body is tensed (τετάσθαι ὅλον τὸ σῶμα), especially the head and ears and neck. The horse can live as long as its heart does not freeze, but when the heart does freeze, the horse dies.
>
> I learned this once when I happened to be at Carnuntum in Pannonia, accompanying the emperor, spending time with him as a friend. All of a sudden he had to make haste because of his marriage, so at the beginning of the month of February, from Carnuntum he travelled to Italy at full speed, making two or three segments of the journey at one stretch.
>
> When we had traversed all of Noricum and had begun the ascent into the so-called Julian Alps,[23] there was a sudden and heavy

---

[18] *CHG* I, 362-363. Diocletian's price-edict of 301: *Diokletians Preisedikt*, ed. S. Lauffer (Berlin, 1971), 7.20 (p.119), sets the fees to be paid to a horse-doctor for trimming hooves. On shoes and shoeing, see A. Hyland, *Equus: The Horse in the Roman World* (London, 1990), 122ff.
[19] *CHG* I, 362-363.
[20] *CHG* I, 327. Cf. *Cod. Theod.* VIII.5.8 and 47 for regulation of the amount of weight to be carried by animals of the post.
[21] *CHG* I, 238.
[22] By M. Haupt, 'Varia, LIV', *Hermes* 5 (1871), 23-25. Cf. T. D. Barnes, *The New Empire of Diocletian and Constantine* (Cambridge, Mass., 1992), 81.
[23] On the route through the Julian Alps, see R. Chevallier, *Les voies romaines* (Paris, 1997), 192-195.

snowstorm around the first hour of the day. The mounted soldiers were freezing to death; they remained stiffened in place upon their horses. The sign that the men were dead was that their lips were drawn back and their teeth were showing. And when the horse happened still to be alive, it would just follow along, bearing the soldier's corpse, the corpse still clutching its weapon and the reins, remaining rigid and still somehow united to the horse, so that it was quite a task for the living to take the corpse down. If the horse died too, it would freeze stiff and remain standing. And this befell many men and horses and mules. Only those couriers (ἡμεροδρόμοι) who were sent ahead to the cities before the emperor did not die, nor did their horses. The reason for this is clear: their constant motion warmed the coldness, keeping them alive.

Then a horse of my own, one of the best, who was being ridden by a young servant, was seized by tetanos. And this grieved me very much, for nothing is better than a fine swift horse (σφόδρα με τὸ πρᾶγμα ἐλύπει· οὐδὲν γὰρ ἵππου καλοῦ καὶ γοργοῦ προκριτέον). This horse was Gaulish, eight years old, and unstoppable in galloping after stags. I really wanted to save that horse (σφόδρα οὖν ἐμέλησέ μοι σῶσαι τὸν ἵππον).[24]

So when we descended the mountains and arrived at the first city, I obtained a plenty of wood — my host (ξένος) was most excellent and provided me with smokeless wood[25] — and I put the horse in a small stable alone and burned the smokeless wood in a circle around him — he was very nearly dead. But around the time of the cock-crow, he began to stir. I had in my flask the dregs of some spiced wine (κονδῖτον): because the horse could not eat or even move his jaws, I dipped clean bread into it, and force-fed it to him three times as he lay there. And I had with me also a restorative (ἄκοπον) that I had prepared for those winters from simples (ἁπλὰ φάρμακα); I diluted it in henna-oil and anointed the horse with it. And immediately he began to perspire and to move and to eat.

I will set forth the properties and proportions of this remedy, for with it you may treat any tetanos in a horse or other beast of burden, and chase away any chill, and heal the ones that are frozen — even if they are half-dead you may restore them to their normal state. No medicine more warming than this one has ever been written down by a doctor or a horse-doctor, nor will one ever be written. Here it is:

---

[24] On affection for horses expressed in the letters of Roman soldiers in Egypt, see L. Robert, *Hellenica*, X (Paris, 1955), 32-33.

[25] See J. Haldon, 'The organisation and support of an expeditionary force: manpower and logistics in the middle-Byzantine period', in *Byzantium at War*, National Hellenic Research Foundation, Institute for Byzantine Research, International Symposium 4 (Athens, 1997), 111-151, which gives references to late antique sources.

Spurge, 2 oz; castor, 4 oz; marsh-salt, 6 oz; bdellion 3 oz; pepper, 1 lb; fox fat, 2 oz; opopanax, 4 oz; asafoetida, 3 oz; ammoniac incense, 6 oz; old pork fat, 1 lb; pigeon dung, 6 oz; all-heal juice, 2 oz; nitron, 5 oz; fine nitron, 3 oz; gum ladanum, 1 lb; pellitory, 1 oz; laurel berries, 3 oz; cardamom, 8 oz; rue seed, 6 oz; chaste-tree seed, 4 oz; parsley, 2 oz; dried iris, 5 oz; hyssop, 3 oz; balsam fruit, 3 oz; balsam juice, 1 lb; iris oil, 1 xestes; nard oil, 2 xe; laurel oil, 1 xe; henna oil, 3 xe; very old oil, 4 xe; lamp-black, 1 xe; turpentine resin, 1 lb.

Dissolve the soluble ingredients separately, then add them uncooked to the rest and heat them moderately; then strain the mixture into a vessel. Use the medicine with wine ... the older it is, the more effective it is. If in time it becomes hard, dilute it with henna oil to the consistency of gum, and use it ...[26]

In this vivid passage, felicitously preserved by the excerpter and by the medieval editors of the *Hippiatrika*,[27] Theomnestos shows us the darker side of an imperial adventus, and provides a chilling reminder of the danger and discomfort that faced horses and horsemen on the road.

---

[26] *CHG* I, 183-185 (text from cod. Berolinensis gr. 134, with additions from Parisinus gr. 2322). A German translation of the text was published by E. Oder, 'Winterlicher Alpenübergang eines römischen Heeres nach der Schilderung eines griechischen Veterinärs', *Veterinärhistorisches Jahrbuch* 1 (1925), 48-50.

[27] And even by a medieval translator into Arabic: I am grateful to Dr R. Hoyland for his help with the Arabic text in Parisinus ar. 2810 and Köprülü 959.

6. Travelling with the plague[*]

D. Ch. Stathakopoulos

Diseases, like ideas, travel along with people, their dissemination over a wide geographical frame being a true reflection of the nature and capacities of the actual state of communications of a given society in a specific period. The Justinianic plague is no exception to this pattern. The study of its dissemination will enable us to look at the internal connections of the Byzantine world at the moment of its greatest territorial expansion.

More specifically, we shall follow the first outbreak of the Justinianic plague as closely as our source material allows us, in an effort to make visible the contemporary communication networks both by sea and by land. Furthermore we will look into the possibility of using additional, alternative sources to historiography and chronography for establishing the route of the infection.

Procopius records that the plague broke out in Pelusium, at the extreme eastern branch of the Nile's mouth, a year before it reached Constantinople.[1] This occurred in mid-spring 542, as the internal chronology of the *Persian Wars* makes clear; therefore the plague visited Pelusium in 541.[2] It need not concern us from where the epidemic came to this city. It suffices to say that it probably had a central/east

---

[*] For more information, see now my monograph *Loimos kai limos. A Systematic Survey and Typology of Epidemics and Famines in the Late Roman and Early Byzantine World (284-750)*, Doctoral Thesis submitted at the University of Vienna in 2000, to be published in 2002 in the series BBOM. I would like to thank Professor Ewald Kislinger for his valuable suggestions.

[1] *BP* II. 22.6-9, ed. C. de Boor and P. Wirth, I (Leipzig, 1962), 250-251.

[2] For a minute investigation of Procopius' chronology, see E. Kislinger and D. Stathakopoulos, 'Pest und Perserkriege bei Prokop. Chronologische Überlegungen zum Geschehen 540-545', *Byz* 69 (1999), 76-98, esp. 85-86 (hereafter Kislinger-Stathakopoulos, 'Pest').

From *Travel in the Byzantine World*, ed. Ruth Macrides. Copyright © 2002 by the Society for the Promotion of Byzantine Studies. Published by Ashgate Publishing Ltd, Gower House, Croft Road, Aldershot, Hampshire, GU11 3HR, Great Britain.

African origin.[3] We will escort the plague on its journey from Egypt to various places in the Mediterranean basin. This journey is not altogether hypothetical. One man had the 'luck' of travelling along, but fortunately, not *with* the plague: the Monophysite bishop John of Ephesos. In the second part of his *Church History* which has survived only in a fragmentary manner, he devotes more than twenty pages to what he experienced during this journey and gives us one of the most remarkable descriptions of the devastation brought about by the pandemic. We know from his own account that he was in Palestine towards the end of 541[4] and that he left the region, heading for Constantinople via Syria and Asia Minor during the height of the plague. John first records the outbreak in Alexandria, then relates how the plague reached Palestine: bronze boats manned by black, headless figures travelling mostly at night were seen proceeding to Gaza, Askalon, and Palestine in general. Simultaneously with their appearance the epidemic visited these sites.[5] This seems an easily dismissible piece of pious fiction, but this is not quite the case, as epigraphical evidence, the funerary inscriptions of this realm, shows.

There are four funerary inscriptions found in Nessana, one of the largest cities of the Negev region, dated between 27 October and 4 November 541.[6] In less than ten days six people were buried (one tombstone, no. 112, was laid for three siblings), with an age range between six and twenty-eight. They did not suffer a violent death — or they would all share a common date of death — and they had survived the difficult years of early infancy.[7] Everything speaks in favour of an epidemic as cause of death. Naturally this is not recorded on their epitaphs, according to common Byzantine practice. One cannot be certain that the epidemic that claimed these victims in Nessana was indeed the plague, but let us at least take this into consideration as we travel around the region looking for more evidence.[8] Our next stop is at

---

[3] A detailed analysis in favour of this theory can be found in: D. Keys, *Catastrophe: an investigation into the origins of the modern world* (London, 1999), 15-23.

[4] For the date see Kislinger-Stathakopoulos, 'Pest', 86-87, n. 69.

[5] Ed. J. P. N. Land, in *Anecdota Syriaca*, II (Louvain, 1868). The second part of the *Church History* of John of Ephesos survives only in the *Chronicle* of Pseudo-Dionysios, an eighth-century author. As this text is Syriac, I have based my work on the English translation: Pseudo-Dionysius of Tel-Mahre, *Chronicle*, Part III, trans. W. Witakowski, Translated Texts for Historians 22 (Liverpool, 1996), 77.

[6] G. E. Kirk and C. B. Welles, 'The Inscriptions', in H. D. Colt, ed., *Excavations at Nessana*, I (London, 1962), 168 (no. 80), 179-181 (nos. 112-114).

[7] C. Dauphin, *La Palestine byzantine. Peuplement et populations*, BAR International Series 726, II (Oxford, 1998), 398-402.

[8] The first scholars to draw attention to epigraphic material as a source for the route

the nearby town of Rehovot, north-east of Nessana, probably to be identified with the Byzantine location Betomolachon; another tombstone with the date 3 November 541 was discovered here, along with an additional one bearing only the same year.[9] Finally, one funerary inscription in Eboda, a Negev town situated a short distance to the south between Nessana and Rehovot, bears the date 12 December 541;[10] this may be taken as mere coincidence.

Following the narrative of John, it seemed promising to try and locate more epigraphical evidence in order to trace the plague's diffusion further and, at the same time, to strengthen this line of argumentation. This material had to be sought in those Palestinian coastal cities John mentions as the ones infected after Egypt: Askalon and Gaza. The scarce epigraphical data of Askalon does not include any material in that direction, but Gaza's inscriptions provided what seems to be the necessary link. Three epitaphs, dated 14 and 17 August and 1 September 541, can be regarded in the context of the plague's outbreak.[11] Therefore, the route of the plague leads from Gaza, where it seemed to have been present in the second half of August 541, to Nessana approximately two months later, at the end of October and the beginning of November, passing through Rehovot at around the same time, and finally arriving about a month later, in mid-December, at Eboda. This construction is based on the acceptance of a number of hypotheses. They are all plausible; none, however, can be proved. Certainly the density and chronological proximity of these funerary inscriptions is unparalleled in their respective collections. The plague's movement from the coast inland was a fact noticed already by contemporary authors.[12] The period in question is the same one mentioned by Procopius and the route of the infection is compatible to the one recorded by John. Furthermore there is evidence that these

---

of the plague were J. Durliat, 'La peste du VIe siècle', in *Hommes et richesses dans l'empire byzantin*, I (Paris, 1989), 108, and L. I. Conrad, 'Die Pest und ihr soziales Umfeld im Nahen Osten des frühen Mittelalters', *Der Islam* 73 (1996), 95.

[9] Y. Tsafrir, 'The Greek inscriptions', in *Excavations at Rehovot in the Negev*, I Qedem 25 (Jerusalem, 1988), 161 (nos. 11 and 10a).

[10] A. Negev, *The Greek Inscriptions from the Negev*, Studium Biblicum Franciscanum, Collectio Minor 25 (Jerusalem, 1981), 30-31 (no. 17).

[11] C. Glucker, *The City of Gaza in the Roman and Byzantine Periods*, BAR International Series 325 (Oxford, 1987), 124-127 (nos. 9-11). After the publication of the joint article on the plague with E. Kislinger in 1999 (see above, n. 2) I discovered that Dauphin, *La Palestine byzantine* (as in n. 7), 512-513, had independently arrived at the same conclusion.

[12] BP II. 22.9, p. 250; John of Ephesos, *History of the Church*, part II, 77 (as in n. 5).

cities traded with one another and there are roads or paths that testify to this connection.[13]

The intervals between the outbreaks in the various places, especially between Gaza and Nessana, seem quite long — around two months for a distance of about fifty miles — but there are possible explanations for this. First of all we cannot be certain that the epigraphical evidence at our disposal covers the entire period of the plague's visitation to the cities in question. On the contrary, the epitaphs are part of a random sample which can merely indicate a trend, possibly the epidemic's peak in the cities. Modern epidemiology, moreover, has developed models that shed light on the mechanism of the plague's dissemination. The plague is a zoonose of rodents — especially rats — originally infected by rat fleas that spread the disease from wild rodents to those living among human populations. It is dependent on the passive transportation of infected rat fleas. The disease has to run its full course among the rats, a process which must be repeated in each area it touches. Furthermore, the infected rat population has to have been decimated prior to the epidemic's spread to human hosts, as rat fleas attack humans — as a rule — only after they can find no murine hosts.[14]

The next certain date of the plague's presence in another region concerns Constantinople, in mid-spring 542.[15] According to the contemporary writer John of Lyda, spring begins on 7 February and lasts until 8 May;[16] this would set mid-spring around 23 March. The emperor Justinian's edict 7, issued on 1 March 542, mentions that 'mortality has traversed all places'. Thus, in a manner which is quite distanced — even for a legal text — the edict implies that the plague had not yet reached the city itself when the text was being promulgated in late February 542.[17] The plague in all probability did not reach Constantinople aboard the grain shipments coming from Alexandria in

---

[13] J. Shereshevski, *Byzantine Urban Settlements in the Negev Desert*, Beer-Sheva 5 (Beersheva, 1991), 4; K. C. Gutwein, *Third Palestine. A Regional Study in Byzantine Urbanization* (Washington, D.C., 1981), 347-350; T. Canaan, 'Byzantine caravan routes in the Negeb', *Journal of the Palestine Oriental Society* 2 (1922), 139-144.

[14] O. Benedictow, *Plague in the Late Medieval Nordic Countries* (Oslo, 1992), 75-80; Kislinger-Stathakopoulos, 'Pest' 90-91.

[15] See n. 1.

[16] *De Ostentis LX*, ed. C. Wasmuth (Leipzig, 1887), 122.14-15; See M. McCormick, 'Bateaux de vie, bateaux de mort. Maladie, commerce, transports annonaires et le passage économique du Bas-Empire au Moyen Âge', in *Morfologie sociali e culturali in Europa fra tarda antichita e alto Medioevo*, Settimane di studio del Centro italiano di studi sull'alto Medioevo 45 (Spoleto, 1998), 53.

[17] Ed. R. Scholl and G. Kroll, *Corpus Iuris Civilis*, III (Berlin, 1895), 763-767.

mid-autumn 541.[18] The third annual shipment of the grain fleet sailed from Alexandria in the second half of August.[19] If our calculations based on the funerary inscriptions are correct, then the epidemic that infected Gaza in the second half of August 541 must have broken out in Pelusium about a month before and cannot therefore have reached Alexandria before September 541 — provided that we trust Procopius' account, according to which the epidemic reached Alexandria from and after Pelusium. This is a matter of routes. Usually the distance between Pelusium and Gaza, some 130 miles, was covered by water, while the route from Pelusium to Alexandria, at 200 miles, was covered by land — all according to the evidence of the *Itinerarium Antonini*.[20] An example of the slowness of dissemination by land is provided by a contemporary papyrus document from Antaiopolis, some 560 km south of Pelusium, dated to December 541; it makes no mention of the plague whatsoever — since, in all probability, the pandemic had not reached that region yet.[21] Indeed, the fact that the plague is recorded in the capital in late March/early April 542 corroborates the hypothesis that it did not reach the city with the grain shipments from Alexandria as early as September 541; otherwise the outbreak would have occurred much earlier.

In the six-month period between the outbreaks in Gaza and Constantinople, a number of other cities and regions were infected. The most direct testimony is given by John of Ephesos:

> At the same time that in the region of the capital these things were as yet known (only) by rumour, since they were still remote, and also before the plague (reached) Palestine, we were there. (Then) when it was at its peak we went from Palestine to Mesopotamia and then came back again when the chastisement reached there also, as well as (going) to other regions — Cilicia, Mysia, Syria, Iconium, Bithynia, Asia, Galatia and Cappadocia, through which we travelled in terror (on our way) from Syria to the capital (during) the height of the plague.[22]

---

[18] Kislinger-Stathakopoulos, 'Pest', 90.

[19] Edict 13.6 of Justinian (dated to 538/539); see Kislinger-Stathakopoulos, 'Pest', 92; J. Durliat, *De la ville antique à la ville byzantine. Le problème des subsistances*, Collection de l'École française de Rome 136 (Rome, 1990), 239-244.

[20] Ed. O. Kuntz, 151.2-154.5 (Leipzig, 1929), 21. The *Itinerarium Antonini* is a handbook of routes in the Roman empire that has come down to us in a form dated to the reign of Diocletian (284-305); see J. Fugmann, *RAC* 19, 10-11.

[21] P. Cair. Masp. III 67320 = *Papyrus grecs d'époque byzantine*, ed. J. Maspero, Catalogue général des antiquités égyptiennes du Musée du Caire 73, III (Cairo, 1916), 111-113.

[22] *History of the Church*, part II, 80 (as in n. 5).

It does seem strange that someone travelling during the ravaging of such a pandemic would not choose a more swift way to reach Constantinople from Palestine — for example, by embarking on a ship. However, we have to take into consideration that John was on a mission to convert pagan populations in Asia Minor, a task entrusted to him by Justinian around 542 which he pursued with great zeal.[23] In another text of his, the *Life* of John of Hephaistopolis, he mentions that he met the holy man in Rhodes and accompanied him to Tralles and then to Ephesos.[24] We should look, therefore, at any information we have concerning the outbreak in Palestinian, Syrian and Asia Minor sites in the early spring and summer of 542. Again, we face the problem of vaguely dated narrative which we are asked to put into the general context. An outbreak in the hinterland of Jerusalem recorded in the *Life* of Cyriacus by Cyril of Scythopolis can be dated to 542; it probably occurred after the Negev cases, and was possibly even transported from this region, in the early months of the year.[25] A donor inscription from the city of Zora, in the Hawrān, commemorating the death of Bishop Varos, 'on whom God brought on the evil death of the groin and the armpit', dated vaguely to 542-543, is probably to be set in the spring of 542; as the site is far from the coast, the epidemic must have reached it by land and therefore required a longer period.[26] In the early summer of 542 the plague reached Antioch and the neighbouring cities of Epiphaneia and Apameia. According to the testimony of Evagrius, who was infected with the plague as a schoolboy in one of the latter cities, the pandemic arrived at Antioch two years after the city's capture by the Persians,[27] in June 540.[28] Therefore the outbreak can be dated to early summer 542. The next stop of the plague was presumably Myra, on the Lycian coast. The outbreak is mentioned, but not dated, in the *Life* of St. Nicholas, abbot of the monastery of Sion.[29] Since Myra and its port Andriake were often used as intermediate landing points in the

---

[23] *History of the Church*, part II, 72 (as in n. 5); F. R. Trombley, 'Paganism in the Greek world at the end of antiquity: the case of rural Anatolia and Greece', *Harvard Theological Review* 78 (1985), 329-336.

[24] *Lives of the Eastern Saints*, ed. and trans. E. W. Brooks, *PO* 18, 526-540.

[25] Ed. E. Schwartz (Leipzig, 1939), X, 229.

[26] J. Koder, 'Ein inschriftlicher Beleg zur justinianischen Pest in Zora (Azra'a)', *BSl* 56 (1995), 13-18.

[27] Ed. J. Bidez and L. Parmentier (London, 1898), IV, 29, 177-179.

[28] Date: June of the third indiction (= 540) provided by Malalas, ed. I. Thurn, *Ioannis Malalae Chronographia*, CFHB 35 (Berlin, New York, 2000), 405.65-66.

[29] *The Life of Saint Nicholas of Sion*, ed. and trans. I. Ševčenko and N. P. Ševčenko (Brookline, Mass., 1984), 52, pp. 82-83.

maritime route from Alexandria to Constantinople,[30] we can assume that the plague was spread to the city by water, setting the outbreak around the same time as the Syrian cities. These options, however, must remain open. The same can be said of the outbreak in Sykeon in Galatia which is recorded in the *Life* of Theodore of Sykeon, again undated.[31] We can assume that the pandemic reached this city after and from Constantinople, or equally that the plague had reached Galatia by land coming from the Syrian mainland before Constantinople.

At the same time the plague worked its way into the western Mediterranean. The pandemic continued to ravage the African coast in radial expansion starting from Alexandria. Unfortunately, the restricted archaeological evidence for the coastal cities of North Africa does not allow us to monitor the visitation and its course. Our only information derives again from epigraphical material. The evidence consists of four epitaphs of siblings from the city of Sufetula (today Sbeitla in Algeria, by the Tunisian border) who died one closely after the other from 24 January to 8 February 543.[32] Again we can rule out violent death, and we propose to identify the disease that killed these children with the plague.

Ultimately the disease must have reached the other great contemporary capital, Rome. According to Marcellinus Comes the plague struck Italy in the year 543-544.[33] Surveying the epigraphic material from the ten volumes of the *Inscriptiones Christianae Urbis Romae*, one comes across a large number of epitaphs dating from the last months of 543 and early 544. There are eleven epitaphs from the period in question, nine of which cover a period of four months, while six of these carry an absolutely secure date; the rest bear dates with more than one possible reading. The securely dated epitaphs start at 8, 10 and 28 November 543 and end with 11, 13 and 28 February 544.[34] In order to obtain a figure of comparison for this data I surveyed the above-

---

[30] M. Zimmermann, 'Die lykischen Häfen und die Handelswege im östlichen Mittelmeer', *ZPE* 92 (1992), 201-217.

[31] *Vie de Théodore de Sykeon*, ed. A. J. Festugière, 2 vols. (Brussels, 1970), I, 8, pp. 7-8.

[32] N. Duval, 'Nouvelles recherches d'archéologie et d'épigraphie chrétienne à Sufetula (Byzacène)', *Mélanges d'archéologie de l'école française de Rome* 68 (1956), 247-298.

[33] Ed. T. Mommsen, MGH AA 9, 2, = Chronica Minora saec. IV-VII/2, (Berlin, 1894), 37-108; Mommsen's text with trans. and commentary by B. Croke, *The Chronicle of Marcellinus*, Byzantina Australiensia 7 (Sydney, 1995), 50, 135-136.

[34] *Inscriptiones Christianae Urbis Romae*, eds. I. B. de Rossi, A. Silvagni, A. Ferrua, *et al.*, 10 vols. (Rome, 1922-1991). The number of the ICUR NS volume and the inscription number are in parentheses: 8 November (I 1452); 543, 10 November (II 4287); 543, 28 November (VII 17624); 544, 11 February (II 5087); 544, 13 February (II 5087); 544, 28 February (II 5087).

mentioned ten volumes and collated the dated epitaphs of the sixth century. No similar frequency could be found; the highest occurrence of closely dated epitaphs is four (for the years 522 and 530). One has to admit that the information provided by this material is quite limited and at the same time open to various interpretations. However, since we can assume that the sample of funerary inscriptions that has come down to us is a random one, the possibility that this series reflected an increased mortality in the city during this period is at least plausible. If we connect this outbreak with the one recorded in Sufetula, we can suppose that given Rome's dependency on north African grain and the commercial connection that enabled this, the plague reached Rome from a north African port.

We have reached the end of our journey through the Mediterranean. Even if our hypothetical construction is based on sometimes insecure foundations, one result from it is absolutely clear: the communication between coastal areas and their hinterland, between central cities of a region and smaller ones, between the capitals of the late Roman empire and the cities that provisioned them, worked quite well in the mid-sixth century — with fatal results for the contemporary populations.

Section II
Getting around — the purposes of travel

7. Maritime trade and the food supply for Constantinople in the middle ages[*]

J. Koder

The purpose of this paper is thematically limited. I would like to offer an approach to some aspects of the transportation of goods, combined with a discussion of the problems of providing sufficient quantity and variety of food for Constantinople.[1] I shall restrict my paper chronologically to the period between the late sixth and the twelfth century. Therefore, I am mainly concerned with the period *after* the major demographic changes of the great Justinianic pestilence, *after* the territorial and political losses in the Balkans, and *after* the Muslim expansion in the former dioceses of Oriens and Aegyptus. But it is also in these centuries mainly *before* the crusades that Byzantium still had at least a partial control over the merchant shipping in the Black Sea, the straits, the Aegean and main coasts of the eastern Mediterranean, and that Byzantine merchants could still rely on Byzantine fleets or ships.[2] I cannot offer definitive conclusions but only general approaches

---

[*] I am greatly indebted to David Jacoby (Jerusalem) and to Ewald Kislinger (Vienna) who read drafts of this paper and made valuable remarks and additions. In this chapter the following abbreviations will be used:

rt	registered tonnage	mill	million	dm	decimetre
t	tonne(s)	hl	hectolitre	m³	cubic metre
l	litre	cm³	cubic centimetre	ha	hectare
qx	metric hundredweight (100kg)				

[1] With respect to the methodological approach, there will be some similarities with the paper given by H. Galsterer, 'Plebiculam pascere — Die Versorgung Roms in der Kaiserzeit', *Critica Storica* 27 (1990), 21-40.

[2] As G. Prinzing, 'Zur Intensität der byzantinischen Fern-Handelsschiffahrt des 12. Jahrhunderts im Mittelmeer', in E. Chrysos, D. Letsios, et al., *Griechenland und das Meer. Beiträge eines Symposions in Frankfurt im Dezember 1996* (Mannheim, 1999), 141-150, demonstrated, after 1133 there is no certain documentation for *Byzantine* long-distance merchant shipping.

From *Travel in the Byzantine World*, ed. Ruth Macrides. Copyright © 2002 by the Society for the Promotion of Byzantine Studies. Published by Ashgate Publishing Ltd, Gower House, Croft Road, Aldershot, Hampshire, GU11 3HR, Great Britain.

which could turn out to be useful for similar reflections on other medieval Byzantine urban settlements also.

The food supply of Constantinople: general remarks

What kind of food was needed in the course of a year and for how many inhabitants of Constantinople? The population figures of Constantinople after the sixth century are even more uncertain than for the early period.[3] I am very reluctant to accept the large number of 400,000 inhabitants for the years 1203-04, given by Geoffrey de Villehardouin.[4] Perhaps the figure of some 160,000 inhabitants, proposed by Ewald Kislinger some years ago,[5] is nearer to the truth. But any realistic number, even a number as low as 50,000 inhabitants, would signal that — under medieval conditions — we are concerned with a megalopolis, a type of settlement which was not able to survive from its hinterland alone; it could not survive without a supply system.

I have no intention of continuing here the discussion concerning the population figure of Constantinople. I propose — as I did some years ago when discussing the supply of Constantinople with fresh vegetables and grain[6] — a medium, hypothetical, but not impossible figure of 100,000 people.[7]

What did the average *homo constantinopolitanus* normally eat? Gathering the information from a variety of sources, such as monastic typika,[8] the Ptochoprodromos poems,[9] the Geoponika, the Farmer's

---

[3] Especially for the early period, cf. D. Jacoby, 'La population de Constantinople à l'époque byzantine: un problème de démographie urbaine', *Byz* 31 (1961), 81-109.

[4] Geoffrey de Villehardouin, *La conquête de Constantinople*, ed. E. Faral (Paris, 1973), II, 251.

[5] He relies on the possible capacity of the bakeries: 21 pistrinae according to the *Notitia urbis Cpl.* 243: E. Kislinger, 'Pane e demografia: L'approvvigionamento di Costantinopoli', in *Nel nome del pane = Homo edens* 4 (Trento, 1995), 279-293, esp. 289f.

[6] J. Koder, *Gemüse in Byzanz. Die Frischgemüseversorgung Konstantinopels im Licht der Geoponika* (Vienna, 1993), 99ff.

[7] As the following calculations have in any case a rather provisional character I will not take into consideration that different quantities of provisions need to be provided for different ages.

[8] E.g., P. Gautier, 'Le Typikon du Christ Sauveur Pantocrator', *REB* 32 (1974), 1-145, here l. 424ff; P. Gautier, 'Le Typikon du sebaste Grégoire Pakourianos', *REB* 42 (1984), 5-145, here l. 742ff.

[9] *Ptochoprodromos*, ed. H. Eideneier (Cologne, 1991); for the documentation of a broad variety of different levels of nutrition cf. esp. poem II, 24ff., 73-76, 100-112, and many passages of poem IV.

Law,[10] the Book of the Eparch, military treatises,[11] a dietary calendar,[12] and a significant group of letters,[13] we find at first glance a large variety of goods: living animals for slaughter, meat, lard and fat, fresh and salted fish, oil, eggs, milk, butter, cheese, honey, wine, vinegar, fresh and dried fruits, onions, legumes, and other fresh and pickled vegetables, salt, rice, bread and other cereal products, and all these of different qualities.[14] With regard to quality, we should certainly mention the four 'niveaux de préparation' which Evelyne Patlagean proposed some time ago[15] in order to define social categories of nutrition. I think, however, that only the third and fourth levels ('préparés sans/avec cuisson') are relevant for us.

Concerning the annual demand, we have to make a general distinction between normal food and Lenten fare. Lenten fare was in effect every Wednesday and Friday (except for the fifty days after Easter) and in three more Lenten days of the weeks preceding Christmas, Easter, the feast of Peter and Paul and of the Dormition of the Virgin. So, at least for the faithful, Lenten fare (in its different stages of *apokreas, tyrine* and *xerophagia*) lasted nearly half of the year,[16] and during these periods, as confirmed by canons and monastic typika, meat was always excluded from meals, and often also fish, eggs

---

[10] The *Nomos Georgikos* reflects the conditions in a countryside *without olives* in the period of the *Ecloga* or some decades earlier. Cf. Sp. Troianos, Οἱ πηγές τοῦ βυζαντινοῦ δικαίου (Athens, Komotini, 1999), 119-120. The most recent edition of the *Nomos Georgikos* (*Vizantiiskij zemledelcheskij Zakon*, ed. I. P. Medvedev, E. K. Piotrovskaja and E. E. Lipsic (Leningrad, 1984) gives information (directly or indirectly) about sheep, pig and cattle breeding, and about the following products: cereals (passim), legumes (§60), grapes (§61) and wine (passim), ewe's milk (to be sold, §34), figs (§61), orchard products in general (§§31-33) and firewood (§§39-40).

[11] J. F. Haldon, *Constantine Porphyrogenitus, Three Treatises on Imperial Military Expeditions*, CFHB 28 (Vienna, 1990), 102-105 (hereafter Haldon, *Three Treatises*).

[12] Cf. e.g. R. Romano, ed., 'Il calendario dietetico di Ierofilo', *Atti della R. Accademia Pontaniana*, n.s. 47 (1998), 197-222.

[13] A. Karpozelos, 'Realia in Byzantine Epistolography X-XII c.', *BZ* 77 (1984), 20-37; see also A. Markopoulos, ed., *Anonymi professoris epistulae* (Berlin, 2000), letter 24.

[14] Cf. e.g. E. Kislinger, 'Cristiani d'Oriente: regole e realtà alimentari nel mondo bizantino', in J.-L. Flandrin, ed., *Storia dell'alimentazione* (Rome, Bari, 1997), 250-265.

[15] E. Patlagean, *Pauvreté économique et pauvreté sociale à Byzance, 4e-7e siècles*, Civilisations et Sociétés 48 (Paris, The Hague, 1977), 38: Ramassés — Cultivés — Préparés sans cuisson — Préparés avec cuisson.

[16] 14 September, the six weeks before Christmas, 5 January, the seven weeks before Easter, at least two weeks before the feast day of saints Peter and Paul, two weeks before the Dormition, 29 August, and every Wednesday and Friday of the non-Lenten weeks of the year except Easter time (until Pentecost): in total at least 144 days.

and cheese, less often, oil and wine.[17] Otherwise, meat, most types of fish and cheese, as well as many kinds of imported wine were too expensive for the greater part of the population. Especially informative is poem II of Ptochoprodromos, in which the anonymous poet provides us with a catalogue of the basic equipment of every household, namely grain, various vegetables and spices, olive oil, linseed oil, kitchen utensils, firewood and charcoal, torches and candles, soap, shoes and various pieces of clothing. He ends with the statement: 'All this they need every year at home, rich and poor, servants and masters, monks and laymen, young and old ....'[18] From this we can observe that bread, gruel or pap dishes (such as *trachanas*)[19] and soups (*chylos*),[20] olives, legumes, onions and fresh or preserved vegetables (boiled or prepared in *halmaia* /pickle, or as salad, *lachana oma*), nuts and fruits (also dried fruits, such as figs) were staple food all the year round. Local wine (*oinos enchorios*),[21] often of inferior quality, or vinegar, mixed with water, was the normal drink.[22]

Not all of these products had to be brought from far away. For perishable goods, many fruits and vegetables, there must have existed a short distance supply, not only by land from Thrace,[23] but also by boat from the Asiatic coasts of the Bosphoros and the Marmara Sea.[24] The Book of the Eparch and other sources[25] confirm this additionally for meat, namely living animals for slaughter (cattle, sheep, goats, pigs), and I suppose that animal products, such as cheese, butter and (salted)

---

[17] Cf. J. Herbut, 'De ieiunio et abstinentia in ecclesia byzantina', *Apollinaris* 39 (1966), 158-200, 303-332, 382-432.

[18] Ed. Eideneier, Poem II, 24ff., esp. 73-75:
Ταῦτα δὲ πάντα χρῄζουσι κατ' ἔτος εἰς τὸ ὁσπίτιν
καὶ πλούσιοι καὶ πένητες, καὶ δοῦλοι καὶ δεσπόται,
καὶ μοναχοὶ καὶ κοσμικοί, καὶ γέροντες καὶ νέοι ...

[19] S. Hill and A. Bryer, 'Byzantine porridge: tracta, trachanas and tarhana. Food in antiquity', in J. Wilkins, *et al.*, *Food in Antiquity* (Exeter, 1995), 44-54.

[20] P. Lemerle, *Les plus anciens recueils des miracles de Saint Démétrius et la pénétration des Slaves dans les Balkans*, I (Paris, 1979), 245, p. 212.

[21] J. Haldon, *Three Treatises* (as in n. 11), 103, l. 147.

[22] Cf. E. Kislinger, 'Φοῦσκα und γλήχων', *JÖB* 34 (1984), 49-53. Water supply was a problem for Constantinople: see C. Mango, 'The water supply of Constantinople', in C. Mango and G. Dagron, eds., *Constantinople and its Hinterland* (Aldershot, 1995), 9-18.

[23] For transports from the hinterland of Constantinople, see E. Papagianne, 'Μοναχοί καὶ μαύρη αγορά στο 12° αιώνα. Παρατηρήσεις σε προβλήματα του επαρχικού βιβλίου, *Byzantiaka* 8 (1988), 61-76.

[24] Cf. Koder, *Gemüse* (as in n. 6), 69ff. and Koder, 'Fresh vegetables for the capital', in Mango and Dagron, eds., *Constantinople and its Hinterland*, 49-56.

[25] E.g. Leo of Synada: M. P. Vinson, *The Correspondence of Leo, Metropolitan of Synada and Syncellus*, CFHB 23 (Washington, D.C., 1985), no. 54, pp. 86-91.

fat, to some extent, also came from the Asian hinterlands of Constantinople. The Book of the Eparch likewise informs us that fresh fish from the Marmara Sea and the straits was sold every morning in the fish market.[26] Other goods, such as rice, sugar and various spices, are luxury products and were not transported in significant quantities.

Supply cargo for Constantinople over medium and long distance

We should, therefore, exclude the above-mentioned types of basic foodstuffs from the catalogue of significant cargo for medium and long distance transportation with vessels. The remaining goods are grain, oil and olives, wine, legumes, dried fruits, and generally not easily perishable victuals (as, for example, dried fish and the vital salted fish), which were not (or not in sufficient quantities) produced in the hinterland of Constantinople.

Additionally, we should mention at least two goods which are absolutely necessary for everyday life, namely salt and firewood. Strangely, I could not find relevant information about the supply of these two goods in medieval Constantinople. Thanks to the Athonite documents we dispose of information about the production and distribution of salt in the Chalkidike area and in Thessalonike in the late medieval period, but we can only guess that Constantinople was supplied from salt pans in the Black Sea and the Marmara Sea.[27] Likewise I could not find information about the usual form and packing of salt for trade and transport.[28] As for firewood and charcoal, I would assume that the reserves in the European hinterland of Constantinople were not sufficient, because even in the late centuries, when the number of inhabitants was rather low, the inhabitants could run short of firewood, for example during the blockade by Michael VIII Palaiologos at the end of 1260.[29] Therefore, fuel was probably brought from the

---

[26] Cf. G. Dagron, 'Poissons, pêcheurs et poissoniers de Constantinople', in Mango and Dagron, eds., *Constantinople and its Hinterland*, 57-73.

[27] Kl.-P. Matschke, Leipzig, kindly informed me about the state of research. On salt in general see *ODB* 3, 1832-1833; for Rome cf. P. Herz, *Studien zur römischen Wirtschaftsgesetzgebung, Die Lebensmittelversorgung*, Historia Einzelschriften 55 (Stuttgart, 1988), 195f.; on the production in the Genoese salt-pits in the Black Sea see M. Balard, *La Romanie Génoise (XIIe—début du XVe siècle)* Bibliothèque des Écoles françaises d'Athènes et Rome 235 (Rome, 1978), 708-711.

[28] Euphrosyne Rizopoulou-Egoumenidou, University of Cyprus, Nicosia, kindly informed me that sacks made of the fibre of palm trees were the traditional means of packing salt in Cyprus.

[29] Nikephoros Gregoras, ed. L. Schopen (Bonn, 1829), I, 81.5-11. Cf. also a letter of the patriarch Athanasios in which he refers to the same problem, when he mentions boiling

coast of Asia Minor, as happened also in Ottoman times, in the sixteenth century, when the town of Casilik in the Izmit gulf was a staple harbour for firewood.[30]

Within the above-mentioned group of food supplies we should concentrate our attention on grain, wine, legumes, oil and olives,[31] because only in these goods are the following four factors combined: absolute necessity for the subsistence of all social strata of the population, non-availability in sufficient quantities near Constantinople, important quantity, bulkiness of cargo. This is confirmed by other written sources which are helpful because they mention the ship-cargo only incidentally; for example, the Miracles of St. Demetrios mention wine, oil and legumes as well as — of course — grain (οἶνος, ἔλαιον, ὄσπριον, σῖτος as cargo for Constantinople. In one special case (miracle 8 of the first collection),[32] Demetrios stops a grain transport heading for Constantinople, which had reached Chios from the east, and he diverts the grain to Thessalonike.[33] A second example, the famous inscription of Abydos, does not belong chronologically to our period, because it dates to c. 492, but it is of an official nature. This inscription mentions the tariffs to be paid by the transporters of wine, oil, legumes, lard and grain (*oinegoi ... elegoi kai osprigoi kai lardegoi ... sitegoi*).[34] A third important example which is also of an official

---

gruel for the poor: *The Correspondence of Athanasius I Patriarch of Constantinople*, ed. A.-M. Maffry Talbot, CFHB 7 (Washington, D.C., 1975), no. 78, pp. 194-197, here 196.39-42.

[30] W. Sahm, ed., *Die Tagebücher des Reinhold Lubenau*, II (Koenigsberg in Preussen, 1930), 111f.; cf. J. Koder, *Der Lebensraum der Byzantiner. Historisch-geographischer Abriß ihres mittelalterlichen Staates im östlichen Mittelmeerraum* (Graz, Vienna, Cologne, 1984), 53f. Casilik is the modern Kazıklıköy.

[31] Similarly, H. Magoulias, 'The Lives of the saints as sources of data for the history of commerce in the Byzantine empire in the VIth and VIIth century', *Kleronomia* 4 (1971), 311. R. Frankel, *Wine and Oil Production in Antiquity in Israel and Other Mediterranean Countries* (Sheffield, 1999), 38f., also states that 'the fruit of the vine and the olive, together with wheat, are the three traditional staple products of Mediterranean dry farming'.

[32] Ed. Lemerle (as in n. 20), I, 70-72, pp. 102-103 ; cf. Ph. Malingoudis, 'Die Hungersnot in Thessalonike (ca. 676-678)', *JÖB* 40 (1990), 145-154. See also P. Speck, 'De miraculis Sancti Demetrii', *Varia* 4, ΠΟΙΚΙΛΑ ΒΥΖΑΝΤΙΝΑ 12 (1993), 255ff., esp. 402ff., and Speck, 'Nochmals zu den Miracula Sancti Demetrii', *Varia* 5, ΠΟΙΚΙΛΑ ΒΥΖΑΝΤΙΝΑ 13 (1994), 317ff., esp. 361ff. and 369, with comments of Speck in n. 109, which I do not understand: What is a 'vorgeschobener Aufkaufposten'? What are the advantages in case of famine in Constantinople, if the cargo has to be reloaded one more time (in the harbour of Chios) from one ship to another? Are bigger or smaller ships quicker, and why?

[33] Similar demands for grain and other victuals are mentioned in the second collection of the Miracles of St. Demetrios: ed. Lemerle, I, 209, p. 188: ... σιτοφόρους ὁλκάδας μετὰ καὶ ἑτέρων διαφόρων εἰδῶν πλείστας; 245, 212, 268, 218, 280, 220-21, 281, 221: σιτοφόρα σκάφη.

[34] J. Durliat and A. Guillou, 'Le tarif d'Abydos', *BCH* 108 (1984), 581-598; cf. D.C. Gofas,

nature is the *Nomos Rhodion Nautikos*.[35] It survived thanks to the initiators of the Macedonian legislation. Its main part (III) was introduced into the collection later known as the *Basilika* by order of the patriarch Photios, while the shorter second part was written by the emperor Leo the Wise.[36] I believe the patriarch and the emperor are responsible only for the final text of the *Nomos Rhodion Nautikos*, as it has come down to us, and that the main stages of the formation of the *Nomos* have to be dated much earlier indeed.[37]

The *Nomos Rhodion Nautikos* is not mainly concerned with goods being transported, and therefore it refers to cargo only by the way. The law mentions[38] precious items, such as gold, silver, pearls and silk, textiles of minor value, especially raw linen and linen clothing, slaves, and finally grain, wine and oil.[39] The victuals in the cargo mentioned in the *Nomos Rhodion Nautikos* are of some importance for us, if we keep in mind the time and manner of introduction of the Rhodian Law into Macedonian legislation; it confirms that grain, wine and oil were important transportation goods to be imported by ship to Constantinople not only in late antiquity, but also in the middle ages.

'Λόγω πρόβας σίτου. A contribution to the interpretation of an early Byzantine fiscal inscription', *Revue Internationale des droits de l'antiquité* 3/22 (1975), 233-242.

[35] Cf. Troianos, *Πηγές* (as in n.10), 123-124; most recent edition: *Basilicorum libri LX*, eds. H. J. Scheltema and N. van der Wal, series A, VII, Libri LIII Appendix Restituta (Groningen, 1974), 2464-2479. For practical reasons the text of the *Nomos Rhodion Nautikos* will be quoted as in the edition of W. Ashburner, *Nomos Rhodion Nautikos, The Rhodian Sea-Law* (Oxford, 1909, repr. Aalen, 1976), his parts II and III corresponding to parts I and II in the Basilika edition.

[36] Cf. A. Schminck, 'Probleme des sog. "Νόμος 'Ροδίων ναυτικός"', in E. Chrysos and D. Letsios, *et al.*, *Griechenland und das Meer* (as in n. 2), 171-178.

[37] This is confirmed, for example, by the use of the word *chrysinos*, which is the only concrete reference to a coin in the *Nomos Rhodion Nautikos* (2.16, 3.7). Terminologically, the *chrysinos* corresponds to the Latin *aureus* (cf. Codex Iustinianus, *Corpus Iuris Civilis* II, ed. P. Krueger [Berlin, 1915], 6.4.4.10; G. W. H. Lampe, *A Patristic Greek Lexicon* [Oxford, 1961], 1535, and *Thesaurus Linguae Graecae*, CD-Rom, version E [University of California, 2000] of 5.46 g which had been obsolete since the fourth century. It was substituted with the solidus by Constantine (307 or 324 respectively). Until the reign of Justinian the *chrysinos* was 'nur mehr gelegentlich als Festmünze ausgeprägt': W. Hahn, *Moneta Imperii Byzantini*, I (Vienna, 1973), 21. Of course the Byzantine reader of the *Nomos Rhodion Nautikos* in the ninth century understood *chrysinos* simply as the gold coin, the solidus, but the terminology belongs to the early period or even to the roots of the Rhodian Sea Law. Thus, the textual history of the *Nomos Rhodion Nautikos* may, in some respect, be comparable to that of the Book of the Eparch.

[38] For the transportation of goods cf. D. G. Letsios, *Νόμος 'Ροδίων Ναυτικός. Das Seegesetz der Rhodier. Untersuchungen zu Seerecht und Handelsschiffahrt in Byzanz* (Rhodes, 1996), 134-143.

[39] *Nomos Rhodion Nautikos* 3.38f.

Quantities and containers of transported food

The next step is an attempt to quantify: the quantities consumed depend, among other conditions, on human weight and the level of physical stress. Following basically Foxhall-Forbes and the WHO report from 1973, I would like to propose for *homo constantinopolitanus* a standard weight between 55 and 65 kg (for ages 15-40) and a demand of 3,800 calories.[40] How much grain, wine, legumes, oil and olives had to be brought to Constantinople every year and what proportion was brought by ship?

For grain I proposed some time ago[41] an annual demand of 200-300 kg per person per year. But as Andreas Müller[42] demonstrated, the higher figure would mean that victuals containing starch, namely bread (and grain dishes) might have supplied nearly 90% of the total requirements; and since the results of Jean Durliat also are convincing,[43] I would now plead for the lower value. Therefore, the annual demand of grain for 100,000 inhabitants should be 20,000 t or a little more. However, we should keep in mind that grain was also brought by carts from the European hinterland to the granaries of Constantinople,[44] although we are not informed about the quantities (which were in any case important enough to be mentioned in connection with the famine in the years after 1071). This quantity of grain, 20,000 t or a little more, corresponds to a volume of up to 26,000 m^3 (or 9,200 rt).[45] In antiquity,

---

[40] 62 kg: L. Foxhall and H. A. Forbes, 'Sitometreia. The role of grain as a staple food in late antiquity', *Chiron* 12 (1982), 47f.; 2852-3822 calories: WHO, Energy and Protein Requirements, in *WHO Technical Report* Series 522/FAO Nutrition Meetings Report Series 52 (Geneva, 1973), 79-84, quoted from A. E. Müller, 'Getreide für Konstantinopel. Überlegungen zu Justinians Edikt XIII als Grundlage für Aussagen zur Einwohnerzahl Konstantinopels im 6. Jahrhundert', *JÖB* 43 (1993), 13; cf. also Kislinger, 'Pane' (as in n. 5), 286.

[41] Koder, *Gemüse*, 101.

[42] Müller, 'Getreide' (as in n. 40), 13-15.

[43] J. Durliat, *De la ville antique à la ville byzantine. Le problème des subsistences*, École française de Rome 136 (Rome, 1990), 253ff. and 569: productivity of 10 qx/ha wheat for 5 persons, and esp. Durliat, 'L'approvisionment de Constantinople', in Mango and Dagron, *Constantinople and its Hinterland*, 22, n. 12: 2 qx grain for 1 person annually. Cf. Foxhall and Forbes, 'Sitometreia' (as in n. 40), Herz, *Studien* (as in n. 27), and Kislinger, 'Pane' (as in n. 5), with more bibliography; K. Karaple, 'Τὸ σιτάρι, τὸ ψωμί καὶ ὁ βυζαντινὸς στρατός', in 'Ο ἄρτος ἡμῶν, Ἑλληνικὴ Τράπεζα Βιομηχανικῆς Ἀνάπτυξης (Athens, 1994), 100-111, discusses the provisions for the army, without significant new results.

[44] From Rhaidestos: Michael Attaleiates, *Historia*, ed. I. Bekker (Bonn, 1853), 201-204; cf. P. Magdalino, 'The grain supply of Constantinople, ninth-twelfth centuries', in Mango and Dagron, *Constantinople and its Hinterland*, 39ff.

[45] 1 kg = 1.2-1.3 l: cf. Müller, 'Getreide' (as in n. 40), 2f.

corn was, to some extent, kept in amphoras, but in Roman and Byzantine times the handling of grain to and from granaries, as for example in Tenedos,[46] and also in the Rhodian Sea Law,[47] suggests that normally it was transported in sacks (made of sack-cloth) or — cheaper but less efficient in handling — loose (as bulk cargo).[48]

I have not been able to find information in the sources until now with regard to the quantity of legumes in demand.[49] But legumes were a basic element of normal and of Lenten food, as important providers of vegetable protein. I therefore assume that at least once every week they were on the menu of the average family. Relying on some 20 modern Greek Lenten recipes,[50] I propose a minimum consumption of c. 100 g per person per week (for 1 meal) of peas, chick peas, lentils, broad beans or beans of other varieties. In other words, the annual need per person was at least 5 kg (therefore, at least 5,000 t for 100,000 inhabitants). These 5,000 t correspond to a volume of 4,300-6,000 m^3 (or 1,500-2,100 rt).[51] Until now I have not found any hints in the sources about the packing material of legumes, but I think that the logical way of packing for transportation would be in sacks (for shipping) or in bags (for pack-animals).

The consumption of wine, often mixed with (warm) water,[52] was common to all social levels of Byzantium, although the quality of this drink was often poor and the distinction between wine and vinegar was not so clear, as we can infer from the remarks of Ptochoprodromos (especially poem IV). Monastic typika of the eleventh and twelfth centuries mention donations of 16 (*thalassia*) *metra* (for hospital orderlies), 18 (for priest and inhabitants of the *nosokomeion*), 24 (for

---

[46] Procop., Aed. 5.1.7-16; cf. J. Koder, TIB 10: *Aigaion Pelagos* (*Die nördliche Ägäis*) (Vienna, 1998), 287-291.

[47] *Nomos Rhodion Nautikos* 3.38 (eds. Scheltema and van der Wal, p. 2477) discusses the possibility that grain might be soaked by bilge water: λη΄.' Ἐὰν πλοῖον μεστὸν σίτου ἐν ζάλῃ καταληφθῇ, ὁ ναύκληρος διφθέρας παρεχέτω καὶ οἱ ναῦται ἀντλείτωσαν. εἰ δὲ ἀμελήσωσι καὶ βραχῇ ὁ φόρτος ἐξ ἀντλίας, οἱ ναῦται ζημιούσθωσαν: 'If a ship loaded with grain is caught in a gale, let the captain provide skins and the sailors work the pumps. If they are negligent and the cargo is soaked by bilge water, let the sailors pay the penalty' (trans. by W. Ashburner, *The Rhodian Sea-Law* [as in n. 35]).

[48] Cf. A. J. Parker, 'Cargos, containers and storage: the ancient Mediterranean', *International Journal of Nautical Archaeology* 21 (1992), 93-95.

[49] According to the Book of the Eparch (13.1), *osprion pan eidos* was sold by the *saldamarios*.

[50] M. D. Kokkinou and G. S. Kophina, Σαρακοστιανά. Συνταγές για νηστίσιμα φαγητά καί γλυκά, 2nd edn. (Athens, 1990), esp. 161-173.

[51] Peas: 860 cm^3/kg; big beans: 1,200 cm^3/kg.

[52] Cf. E. Kislinger, 'Thermodotes — ein Beruf?', *Klio* 68 (1986), 123-127.

monks) and 36 *metra* (for the abbot) for one year.[53] From the context we can assume that the amount of 16-24 *metra* corresponds to the annual consumption of one person (I take the 36 *metra* for the abbot to be exceptional). This means from 1/2 l to 1 bottle a day (or 180-250 l/year). The quantities estimated by Durliat and Galsterer lie between these two values, namely 2 hl and 1.5-1.8 hl respectively per person per year.[54] If we take the lower quantity as a mean value for the Constantinopolitan drinker and suppose (according to Galsterer) that only every second person belonged to this group, the annual demand for wine in Constantinople was at least 900,000 *thalassia metra* (more than 9,000,000 l) for 100,000 inhabitants.

Wine was brought both by sea, from medium and long distances,[55] as well as from the hinterland of Constantinople, but we are not informed about the quantities. However, it was not distance alone that was related to price or quality, because Ptochoprodromos[56] mentions good wine from Chios, Samos,[57] Crete and bad wine from Varna (which evidently also had to be brought by ship), and he praises the excellent wine from nearby, namely from Thrace. Transportation was in amphoras. The Farmers Law mentions *pithoi* (jugs) and *bouttia*, but these 'barrels' seem to be a late medieval addition to the text, according to its most recent editor.[58] In the context of military expeditions, paired flasks (*zygophlaskia*) and wine skins (*askia*) are also mentioned, but this only for minor quantities and in the case of transport by land.[59] Therefore, the normal container was the amphora.

---

[53] The Pantokrator Typikon (as in n. 8), ll. 1227, 1357, 1369, 1387: 16 *metra* = 164 l; 18 *metra* = 184.5 l; P. Gautier, 'La Diataxis de Michel Attaliate', REB 39 (1981), 5-143, here l. 869-870, 891,1026: 24 *metra* = 246 l; 36 *metra* = 369 l; cf. E. Kislinger, 'Zum Weinhandel in frühbyzantinischer Zeit', Tyche 14 (1999), 141-156, esp. 153f.

[54] Durliat, *De la ville*, 569 (0.5 ha, 10hl, 5 persons/year); Galsterer, 'Plebiculam' (as in n.1), 34f.

[55] Until the early seventh century wine from all over the Mediterranean reached Constantinople: cf., e.g., Durliat, 'L'approvisionment' (as in n. 43), 27-28 and n. 45, and Frankel, *Wine* (as in n. 31); for the fifth-seventh century, see also J. Schaefer, 'Amphorae as material indices of trade and specialization', AJA 84 (1980), 230-231 (summary of paper).

[56] Ed. Eideneier, poem IV, 181, 298, 332, 395f.

[57] A similar mention can be found in a letter of Theodoros Laskaris to George Akropolites: ... τὸν Σάμιον οἶνον, τὸν λεπτότατόν τε καὶ διειδέστατον: *Theodori Ducae Lascaris epistulae*, ed. N. Festa (Florence, 1898), letter 54, 81. 81-82.

[58] *Nomos Georgikos*, ed. I. P. Medvedev, et al. (as in n. 10), 69: Ὁ ἐν νυκτὶ κλέπτων οἶνον ἐκ πίθου ἢ ἐκ ληνοῦ [ἢ ἀπὸ βουττίου] ... ; cf. *Lexikon der byzantinischen Gräzität*, ed. E. Trapp, W. Hörandner, et al., I (Vienna, 2001), 293a. However, according to the Book of the Eparch, 13.1., the *saldamarios* also was licensed to sell *bouttia*, but we do not know what they were for.

[59] Haldon, *Three Treatises*, 102f.

Among the amphoras found in the context of shipwrecks, those which certainly were used for wine have, in a significantly high number, a capacity of 36 l or a little more (e.g. the type Saraçhane CA2a). This type of wine amphora seems to have been common in the middle ages, as the findings near ancient Ganos confirm which date from the tenth/eleventh century.[60] The quantity of 9,000,000 l therefore would correspond to c. 250,000 amphoras.[61]

Olives and olive oil were more important than they are today as a major component of the diet, compared with other edible fat[62] as, for example, linseed-oil. Again relying on modern Greek, Turkish and Levantine recipes, a minimum mean daily consumption of up to 50 cm^3 per day per person or 15-18 l/year is likely.[63] Consequently 100,000 inhabitants would need 1.5-2 mill. l of oil/year. In the early Byzantine centuries, probably until the early seventh century, oil was imported in part from Syria and Palestine,[64] but also later on most of the oil must have been brought by ship. The reason is that, despite the olive's ability to expand cultivation onto poor, thin soils, the climate of Constantinople and Thrace is not favourable for olive growing.

Oil was transported in amphoras. Again, for military purposes leather flasks (*skortzidia*) are mentioned for imperial oil.[65] But the normal container, it seems, was the amphora of which there were special types for oil.[66] Until now, between the fifth and the tenth centuries three sizes with a capacity of 20, 30 and nearly 40 l[67] have

---

[60] Cf. N. Günsenin, 'Le vin de Ganos: les amphores et la mer', in M. Balard, *et al.*, *ΕΥΨΥΧΙΑ. Mélanges offerts à Hélène Ahrweiler*, I (Paris, 1998), 281-287.

[61] In her paper on 'The Medieval Trade in the Sea of Marmara from the Evidence of Shipwrecks' (2 April 2000), however, Nergis Günsenin, Istanbul University, gave information about a smaller, eleventh-century type of amphora for wine, with a height of c. 40 cm and a capacity of c. 10 l, found in great numbers near Marmara adası. See Günsenin's chapter in this volume.

[62] In general, cf. H. Forbes, 'Ethnoarchaeology and the place of the olive tree in the economy of the southern Argolid, Greece', in M.-Cl. Amouretti and J.-P. Brun, eds., *La production du vin et d'huile en Méditerranée* (Athens and Paris, 1993), 213-226, with bibliography.

[63] Kokkinou and Kophina, Σαρακοστιανά (as in n. 50), 109-137.

[64] Cf. Durliat, 'L'approvisionment' (as in n. 43), 27f., n. 45 (Sarachane amphoras), and Frankel, *Wine* (as in n. 31).

[65] Haldon, *Three Treatises*, 102f.

[66] W. Hautumm, *Studien zu Amphoren der spätrömischen und frühbyzantinischen Zeit* (Fulda, 1981), 21ff. and 175: in the 'Eupalinos tunnel', Samos.

[67] 1:1.5:2: The equivalents of 19.88/29.82/39.76 l correspond to 70/105/140 *sualiai litrai* (1 *sualia litra* for oil = 0.284 l: cf. E. Schilbach, *Byzantinische Metrologie*, Handbuch der Altertumswissenschaft 12.4 (Munich, 1970), 115f.

been observed. A volume of 2 mill. l of oil therefore corresponds to 50,000-100,000 amphoras.

To recapitulate: the possible minimum quantities of absolutely necessary provisions to be transported by ship per person for one year might have been approximately 200 kg of grain, 5 kg of legumes, 90 l of wine and 18 l of oil. Perhaps this is what Anastasius II (713-715) had in mind when, in expectation of the Arab siege of Constantinople, he ordered that every inhabitant should provide food supplies for up to three years.[68]

The ships

How many ships were necessary for the supply of Constantinople? This depends on the mean size and capacity of cargo vessels during the Byzantine period, the mean transportation distance and time, and the number of passages during the season, as the sea was basically open *ex kalendis Aprilibus in diem kalendarum Octobrium*.[69] I do not believe that this Roman legal regulation was strictly observed during the middle ages (and certainly not in the Palaiologan period),[70] but during the winter period the traffic was in any case reduced for practical reasons to the necessary minimum.

Evidence for the capacity of the vessels comes from the archaeological documentation of shipwrecks. Out of the 1,259 ships registered in A. J. Parker's catalogue of ancient shipwrecks, one finds 19 examples (see Appendix 1) between the fifth and the twelfth century which provide sufficiently exact information about the size of ships. Their length varies between 6 and 35 m and the beam between 3 and 12 m.[71] Among these ships a group of nine is to be found with a

---

[68] Theoph., A.M. 6206 (p. 384); Anastasius Bibliothecarius, *Chronographia Tripertita*, in Theoph., II, 246.

[69] *mare clausum* in winter, between October and March: cf. Codex Justinianus, *Corpus Iuris Civilis*, II, ed. Krueger, 11.6 3.3 (De naufragiis); see also D. Claude, *Der Handel im westlichen Mittelmeer während des Frühmittelalters*, Untersuchungen zu Handel und Verkehr der vor- und frühgeschichtlichen Zeit in Mittel- und Nordeuropa, II, Abh. Ak. Göttingen, phil.-hist. Klasse 3.144 (Göttingen, 1985), 31-35, and L. Casson, *Ships and Seamanship in the Ancient World* (Baltimore and London, 1995), 270-272.

[70] Cf. J. Koder, 'Νησιωτικὴ ἐπικοινωνία στὸ Αἰγαῖο κατὰ τὸν ὄψιμο μεσαίωνα', in N. G. Moschonas, ed., *Η Επικοινωνία στο Βυζάντιο* (Athens, 1993), 445-455.

[71] Cf. the list in Appendix 1, based on A. J. Parker, *Ancient Shipwrecks of the Mediterranean and the Roman Provinces*, BAR International Series 580 (Oxford, 1992) (hereafter Parker, *Ancient Shipwrecks*), who is more complete than Casson, *Ships* (as in n. 69), 456ff. On the types of vessels, cf. Casson, *Ships*, 169ff., and Letsios, Νόμος ʹΡοδίων Ναυτικός (as in n. 38), 81-83 (with bibliography). J. H. Pryor, *Geography, technology and war. Studies in the maritime history of the Mediterranean, 649-1571* (Cambridge, 1992), 27, speaking about Yassı

significant similarity or approximation in size;[72] these ships have an average length of 20-25 m (43-53 *pechys*) and a beam of 5-8 m (11-17 *pechys*).[73] If we assume a depth of 2-3 m (4-7 *pechys*), the capacity of these vessels must have been roughly between 2,000 and 6,300 cubic *pechys* (or 70-230 rt).[74]

More information on this group is given for two vessels which had a capacity of 'over 1,100 amphoras' each (Parker No. 1240 and 71), one more ship (Parker No. 1239) with a cargo of some 900 amphoras (and a possible maximum of 1,200) and an 'estimated capacity c. 37 t, maximum 50-60 t',[75] and one (Parker No. 796) with 'at least 100 t'[76] capacity. This size can obviously be identified with the 'smallest, with under 75 tons of cargo, or 1500 amphoras — the commonest kind, found in all periods' in the definition of Parker.[77] It is corroborated, for example, by new findings in the harbour of Ganos, where in 1993 and 1994 seven wrecks with a cargo of wine amphoras were discovered; one of these held some 1,000 amphoras.[78] To sum up, it seems likely that the common middle

---

Ada A, remarks in connection with the capacity of ships, that 'Ordinary merchantmen of the Byzantine empire from the 7th to the 11th centuries were small, less than 250 tons deadweight tonnage ...'. Chr. H. Ericsson, *Navis Oneraria. The Cargo Carrier of late Antiquity, Studies in Ancient Ship Carpentry*, Acta Acad. Aboensis, Ser. A, Humaniora, 63/3, 9-108 (Abo, 1984), 72, talking about 'hull-weight and the corresponding need for power', is more cautious and states that 'a hull of 150-200 metric tons cannot be warped, hauled or towed by muscle power except in a complete calm and within a sheltered basin', whilst 'three or four men may in favourable conditions handle a coaster of 50-80 tons [deadweight] not using winches'. See also M. Goudas, ' Ἡ καταμέτρησις τῶν ἐμπορικῶν πλοίων καὶ ἡ νεολόγησις καὶ φορολογία αὐτῶν κατὰ τοὺς βυζαντινοὺς χρόνους', *Byzantis* 1 (1909), 35-47.

[72] Our examples: A. J. Parker, *Ancient Shipwrecks*, nos. 518, 1110, 1111 (20 x 5 m); 97 (20 x 6 m); 1240, 1239 (20 x 6.5-8 m); 8 (20-25 x 7 m), 335 (21 x 7-8.5 m), 71 (24 x 12 m), 796 (25 x 8 m).

[73] Casson, *Ships*, 173: 19-33 m long, 25-33 m broad; cf. ibidem 183f.

[74] 1 *pechys* = 4.68 dm, 1 cubic *pechys* = 102.50323 l or dm³ (= 6 *thalassioi modioi*, each with a capacity of 17.084 l or dm³). — 1 rt = 2.831 m³.

[75] 37/60 t possibly correspond to 900/1,200 amphoras (on the base: 20-25 amphoras/rt). — Possible calculation: 20 x 6.5 m, 43 x 14 x 4? pechys = 2408 cubic pechys = 87 rt.

[76] Parker, *Ancient Shipwrecks*, no. 796: 'at least 25 x 8 m'. Possible calculation: 53.5 x 17 x 4? *pechys* = at least 3,638 cubic *pechys* = 132 rt.

[77] Parker, *Ancient Shipwrecks*, 26f. Let me just mention one problem with Parker's remarks on the ships' sizes, namely that he equates in the first case 75 tons with 1,500 amphoras, in the second 75-200 tons with 2,000-3,000 amphoras and in the third case 'over 250 tons' with 'more than 6000 amphoras', which means that 1 amphora would have a weight of 50 kg *or* between 37.5 and 66.6 kg *or* 41.6 kg.

[78] Cf. the information from Günsenin, 'Le vin de Ganos' (as in n. 60), 283f.

Byzantine type of cargo-boat for medium and long distance had a capacity of between 70 and, at the most, 230 rt which — based on the findings — corresponded to a maximum number of 1,200 amphoras.[79]

Number of ships or freight units

How many ships brought their freight to the 'wooden jetties' (*proteichismata*, also *skalai*) around the 'Queen of Cities', as Michael Attaleiates calls it?[80] According to the above discussed quantities of medium and long distance supply, we can sum up what the annual minima would have been (see Appendix 2): c. 9,200 rt grain in sacks or loose, c. 1,500-2,100 rt legumes in sacks, c. 9 mill. l wine in amphoras (perhaps 250,000 amphoras with a capacity of 36 l), and c. 2 mill. l olive oil in amphoras (50,000-100,000 amphoras with a capacity of 20-40 l). The number of necessary ships or better, cargo units, at the end of Appendix 2 (40-130, 10-30, 200-400 and 80-160) is, as its great variability already shows, far from certain. Consequently, the total figure of between 330 and 720 units also can only be understood as a possibility, an approximation. Furthermore, within the period of *mare apertum* every merchantman could normally make more than one return journey between Constantinople and any destination in the eastern Mediterranean.[81] Thus, the number of necessary ships in this case might have been one half of this total, or less.

---

[79] In her paper (see above, n. 61), however, Nergis Günsenin mentioned two shipwrecks near Marmara adası, one with c. 21,600 amphoras and the other with c. 3,000 amphoras of the above-mentioned minor type, which, when filled, would have a weight of c. 12 kg. So the weight of the cargo would be at least 259 t and 36 t respectively.

[80] Attaleiates, *Historia*, 277-278. I shall not discuss the archaeological evidence concerning the location and number of the harbours of Constantinople, because I could only repeat or sum up what has been published recently by W. Müller-Wiener, *Die Häfen von Byzantion Konstantinupolis Istanbul* (Tübingen,1994) and A. Berger, 'Die Häfen von Byzanz und Konstantinopel', in Chrysos and Letsios, *et al.*, *Griechenland und das Meer*, 111-118.

[81] For the times given for sea travel, cf. Koder, 'Νησιωτικὴ ἐπικοινωνία' (as in n. 70), and Koder, TIB 10, 101-105; for the ancient period see Casson, *Ships*, 281-296. In an earlier draft of this paper I proposed that it might be possible to make the journey up to three times during the season. On this Professor Jacoby rightly commented in a letter — referring to J. H. Pryor, *Commerce, Shipping and Naval Warfare in the Medieval Mediterranean* (London, 1987) — that this was normally not possible for distances south of Anatolia, taking into consideration the wind patterns.

Appendix 1: Useful examples of shipwrecks in chronological order

The following list is based on Parker, *Ancient Shipwrecks*.[82] If Parker mentions only length *or* beam of a ship, the other figure is added approximately in [ ] on the base of a beam/length ratio of 1 : 2.5-3.0.[83]

(Parker No. 1240) late 4th/early 5th c. (Yassı Ada B, near Bodrum, TR): length 20 m [beam 6.5-8 m], cargo: over 1,100 amphoras
(Parker No. 375) 420-425 (Dramont E, France): 15-18 x 5-6 m, cargo: amphoras of Tunisian origin, several contained olive pits
(Parker No. 292) 5th-6th c. (Cefalo I): timber preserved over an area 35 x 6 m, cargo: amphoras, pottery
(Parker No. 518) 6th c. (Iskandil Burnu, near Rhodos, TR): c. 20 x 5 m, cargo: wine amphoras, jugs from Palestine
(Parker No. 71) 6th-7th c. (H. Stephanos, Chios, GR): c. 24 x 12 m, cargo: over 1,000 amphoras
(Parker No. 660) 500-650 (Marsa Lucch, Libya): at least 6 x 2 m, cargo: amphoras
(Parker No. 1001) 600-625 (Saint Gervais B, France): beam 6 m [length 15-18 m] and depth 2 m, estimated capacity 41-49 t [recte: 54[84]] (metric tons), 6,000-8,000 modioi; cargo: corn, esp. Triticum turgidum (Rivet wheat), re-used amphoras filled with pitch (retsini)
(Parker No. 787) 600-650 (Pantano Longarini, I): length 30 m [beam 10-12m], cargo: over 300 t[85]
(Parker No. 1239) 626 or little later (Yassı Ada A, near Bodrum, TR): length c. 20 m [beam c. 6.5-8 m], estimated capacity c. 37 t, maximum 50-60 t, cargo: c. 900 amphoras, all reused (possible maximum 1,200)[86]
(Parker No. 8) mid 10th c. (Agay, France): length 20-25 m, beam at least 7, cargo: amphoras and other
(Parker No. 97) mid 10th c. (Bataiguier, France): over 20 x over 6 m preserved hull, cargo: amphoras, pottery, lamps and other
(Parker No. 1110) 11th/12th c. (Northern Sporades B, GR): some 20 x 5

---

[82] Parker, *Ancient Shipwrecks* (as in n. 72), nos. 8, 71, 97, 165, 292, 335, 375, 518, 660, 663, 744, 787, 796, 1001, 1070, 1110, 1111, 1239, 1240.

[83] For this ratio cf. e.g. Parker, *Ancient Shipwrecks*, 373.

[84] 6,000 *modioi* correspond to 40.8 t on the ratio of 1 *modios* wheat = 8.6185 l or 6.8 kg, but 8,000 *modioi* are 54.4 t.

[85] Gross tonnage 400-500, cf. P. and J. Thockmorton, 'The Roman wreck at Pantano Longarin', *The International Journal of Nautical Archaeology and Underwater Exploration* 2.2 (1973), 243-266, esp. 260.

[86] 20 x 6.5-8 m = 43 x 14-17 x 4? *pechys* = 2,408-2,924 cubic *pechys* = 14,448-17,544 *thalassioi modioi* = 87-106 rt.

m, cargo: byz. amphoras
(Parker No. 1111) 11th/12th c. (Northern Sporades C): some 20 x 5 m, cargo: byz. amphoras
(Parker No. 1070) 1025 (Serçe Limanı A, near Marmaris, TR): waterline length about 14 m, very rounded, with flat bottom, length/beam ratio just over 3:1 [beam c. 4.5 m], maximum 37 t (but a better rating would be about 27 tons)[87], cargo: some 3 tons of broken glass vessels and glass cullet, amphoras with wine, raisins, sumac for tannery
(Parker No. 744) 1050-1100 (Nin A, Croatia): length 9 m [beam 3-3.5m], no cargo (was sunk to block the approach to Nin)
(Parker No. 165) 12th c. (Camarina C, I): length 25-30 m, but only 4 m wide (therefore a galley, whether transporting food or horses)
(Parker No. 796) mid 12th c. (Pelagos, Northern Sporades, GR): at least 25 x 8 m, at least 100 t[88], cargo: mill-stones, pottery, glazed sgraffito ware
(Parker No. 663) 1150-1200 (Marsala A, I): 15 x 3 m, cargo: Some 80 small amphoras, with stoppers of cork, have been raised
(Parker No. 335) c. 1200 (early 13th c.?) (Contarina, I): length 21 m [beam 7-8.5m], no cargo

Appendix 2: Approximate numbers of transportation vessels

Goods	Quantity	Transp. Form	No. of Ships
Corn	9,200 rt	sacks or bulk cargo	40-130
Legumes	1,500-2,100 rt	sacks	10-30
Wine	9 mill l	250,000 amph.(36l)	200-400
Olive oil	2 mill l	100,000 amph.(20l)	80-160
Total			330-720

---

[87] 14 x 4.5 m = 30 x 9.5 x 4? *pechys* = 1,140 cubic *pechys* = 6,840 *thalassioi modioi* = 41 rt.
[88] 'At least 25 x 8 m', 53.5 x 17 x 4? *pechys* = 3,638 cubic *pechys* = 21,828 *thalassioi modioi* = 132 rt (100 rt = 16,571 *thalassioi modioi*).

8. Medieval trade in the Sea of Marmara: the evidence of shipwrecks

N. Günsenin

We can learn much about the Byzantine world from the surviving writings of contemporary travellers, scholars, merchants, pilgrims, and conquerors while our own travels can be an important source of information as well. I began my own research journey in 1984, visiting Turkish museums along the northern, western and southern coasts of Anatolia from Trabzon to Antakya in search of examples of four major types of Byzantine amphoras dating from the tenth to the thirteenth centuries, the subject of my doctoral dissertation at the Sorbonne in Paris which was completed in 1990.[1]

Near the end of these efforts, in the summer of 1989, I discovered a major amphora production centre during a brief visit to a little coastal village, Gaziköy, located on the north-west shore of the Sea of Marmara, within the modern administrative district of Tekirdağ (Fig. 8.1). The amphoras produced there fit into the amphora typology I had developed in my dissertation. They were piriform amphoras belonging to my Type I. The discovery of this production centre during the final stages of the preparation of my dissertation served as a point of departure of several projects that I continue to work on with a number of colleagues from different disciplines. After that brief visit to Gaziköy, which stood at the end of a journey of thousands of kilometres, I went to Paris to research into any known documentation that might be relevant to the history of the region. However, written sources convey little about Gaziköy,

---

[1] See N. Günsenin, 'Recherches sur les amphores byzantines dans les musées Turcs', in V. Déroche and J.-M. Spieser, eds. *Recherches sur la Céramiques Byzantine*, Suppl. BCH XVIII (1989), 267-276; N. Günsenin, *Les amphores byzantines (Xe-XIIIe siècles): typologie, production, circulation d'après les collections turques*, Université Paris I (Panthéon-Sorbonne), Paris (1990), Atelier national de reproduction des thèses de Lille III.

From *Travel in the Byzantine World*, ed. Ruth Macrides. Copyright © 2002 by the Society for the Promotion of Byzantine Studies. Published by Ashgate Publishing Ltd, Gower House, Croft Road, Aldershot, Hampshire, GU11 3HR, Great Britain.

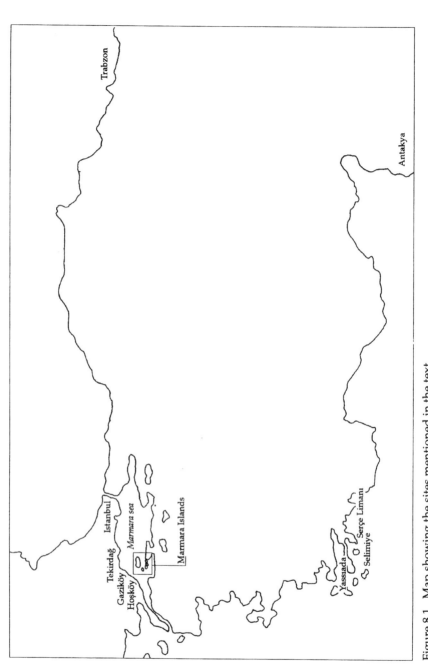

Figure 8.1 Map showing the sites mentioned in the text

known in ancient and medieval times as Ganos.[2] It is first referred to by Strabo, who says it was a Greek colony established during the first century B.C. Later, in the Byzantine period, from the tenth century onward, it appears in the written sources as a thriving monastic centre. Sailors passing through the straits made pilgrimages to the mountain of Ganos, which gave its name to the settlement. Consequently Ganos became known as a 'sacred mountain', comparable with the Bithynian Olympos and Athos. I realised then that I was not simply dealing with a straightforward amphora factory, but with an important medieval monastic settlement to which the factory was connected. However, none of the historical sources that I had found up to that point could enlighten me as to the possible contents for which these amphoras had been made. Until, that is, I came upon important Ottoman sources that made clear that the Ganos region had a reputation for wine production.

I had discovered, during the course of a number of archaeological surveys, the existence of even more amphora kilns, stretching for several kilometres along the littoral in the region of Ganos. The abundance of high quality clay deposits nearby conveniently provides the raw materials necessary for amphora, or any other ceramic, production on such scale. This is a particularly satisfying elucidation of the monastery as an economic unit producing a commodity in bulk for which they were also able to provide the necessary containers for long distance transport at a minimum cost. It can reasonably be surmised that the commodity in question was wine. Ottoman sources refer to the Greek population of the area being engaged in wine production; the 'young wine' was accepted as a tax payment in kind.[3] The sources even indicate that amphora production went on well into the Ottoman period, when wooden barrels had become the normal wine transport container in the Mediterranean.

---

[2] On Ganos see N. Günsenin, 'Ganos: centre de production d'amphores à l'époque byzantine', *Anatolia Antiqua* 2 (1993), 193-201; Günsenin, 'Ganos: résultats des campagnes de 1992 et 1993', *Anatolia Antiqua* 3 (1995), 165-178; P. Armstrong and N. Günsenin, 'Glazed pottery production at Ganos', *Anatolia Antiqua* 3 (1995), 179-201; N. Günsenin and H. Hatcher, 'Analyses chimiques comparatives des amphores de Ganos, de l'île de Marmara et de l'épave de Serçe Limanı (Glass Wreck)', *Anatolia Antiqua* 5 (1997), 249-260; N. Günsenin, 'Le vin de *Ganos*: les amphores et la mer', in M. Balard *et al.*, ΕΥΨΥΧΙΑ. *Mélanges offerts à Hélène Ahrweiler* I (Paris, 1998), 281-287; Günsenin,'Les ateliers amphoriques de Ganos à l'époque byzantine', *Production et commerce des amphores anciennes en Mer Noire*, l'Université de Provence, (1999) 125-128; H. Ahrweiler, 'Le récit du voyage d'Oinaiôtes de Constantinople à Ganos', in W. Seibt, ed., *Geschichte und Kultur der Palaiologenzeit* (Vienna, 1996), 18-21.

[3] Ö. L. Barkan, *XV ve XVI. Asırlarda Osmanlı İmparatorluğunda ziraî ekonominin hukukî ve malî esaslar*, I, *Kanunlar*, Istanbul (1943), LXV Kanun-i Reayây-i Livâ-i Gelibolu, 235-236 (translated by M.-M. Lefebvre, 'Actes ottomans concernant Gallipoli, la mer Egée et la Grèce au XVIe siècle', *Südost-Forschungen* 42 (1983), 128.

Today there are many active vineyards in the region which produce respected and sought-after wines. Even ceramic production continues, albeit on a much smaller scale than the days when the estates of Ganos flourished. The last surviving potter using traditional methods of production lives in the village of Hoşköy, the neighbouring village to Gaziköy and formerly known as Chora. Although the written evidence relates to the early Ottoman period, it must reflect a longer tradition, stretching back at least into the early middle Byzantine period.

One might expect, given the proximity of Ganos to the huge and demanding market of Constantinople, that the entire production simply went there, but the presence of Type I amphoras in all parts of the empire suggests the pattern of distribution was more complicated. Was the wine sold at Ganos to middlemen, who then sold it either in Constantinople or elsewhere? Or did the monastery transport most of its wine surplus to Constantinople to be sold for hard currency, while a certain amount was exchanged for commodities which the monastery did not produce? Evidence of this kind of barter exists in connection with the Athos monasteries. In either case, Constantinople was certainly an entrepôt through which goods were transported to other parts of the empire.

During our field seasons of 1991-92 and 1993, we tried to survey all the villages in the vicinity of Ganos and place them in a historical context. At the same time, together with colleagues from Tekirdağ museum, we carried out a rescue excavation of a kiln at Ganos that had recently been damaged by road construction.[4] Magnetic prospection by Albert Hesse and his assistant Florence Tixier pinpointed further kilns, indicating just how extensive amphora production along the Ganos-Chora shoreline had been.[5] With the help of Pamela Armstrong, we also investigated glazed pottery production of the region.[6]

I know well that an archaeological site is potentially a boundless repository of information, but my enthusiasm for underwater excavations, inspired by meeting George Bass and the Institute of Nautical Archaeology (INA) during the summer of 1979, led me to search for the ships that had set sail from Ganos laden with amphoras full of wine. With a knowledge of the currents and prevailing winds in the Sea of Marmara, I charted the route that ships departing from Ganos would have followed when sailing to Constantinople. Careful investigation of this route revealed that at certain junctures around the Marmara islands, there are clusters of shipwrecks. These wrecks highlight locations with

---

[4] See Günsenin, 'Ganos: résultats des campagnes de 1992 et 1993' (as in n. 2), 165-178.
[5] Günsenin, 'Ganos: résultats de campagnes de 1992 et 1993 ', 165-178.
[6] See Armstrong and Günsenin, 'Glazed pottery production at Ganos' (as in n. 2), 179-201. I thank Ms. Armstrong for revising and contributing to the present article.

especially difficult conditions for navigation, where a higher than average number of vessels would come to grief and founder.

The young team of underwater divers selected and trained for our project had already surveyed the ancient harbour of Ganos. In the summer of 1993, we departed temporarily from Ganos, and sailed to the island of Marmara (ancient Prokonnesos). A combination of investigations, both underwater and on land, on and around the Marmara islands followed, forming the second phase of the overall project. Fresh finds linked to historical information furthered our interests in the monastic network of Ganos-Prokonnesos-Constantinople, and convinced us of its importance.

INA had surveyed the waters around the Marmara islands in 1984, but our investigations were just one more logical step in our own overall research. Several underwater survey seasons have brought to light thirteen Byzantine shipwrecks and a sunken mound (höyük) dating from about 3200 B.C., (Kumtepe Ib) to about 1100 B.C. (Troy VIIb 2) off Türkeli (Avşa) island, while on the island of Marmara two amphora production sites were found.[7] Eight of the shipwrecks carried Ganos-type amphoras; another, a cargo of roof tiles; and another, a cargo of water pipes. The tile wreck is dated by its anchors, and the water pipe wreck by an associated amphora, to the seventh century.[8] Another seventh-century wreck was filled with amphoras like the globular ones found on the seventh-century Byzantine shipwreck at Yassı Ada. A thirteenth-century wreck carried amphoras belonging to the last major type of Byzantine amphora used in maritime commerce, the Type IV amphoras of my dissertation typology. Finally, a wreck of possibly the sixth century, off the north coast of Ekinlik island, contains architectural marbles (Fig. 8.2).

I would now like to concentrate on two of these shipwrecks which seem to me to be of particular importance to the medieval history of the sea of Marmara. One of them, *Tekmezar I*, was probably one of the biggest vessels of the Byzantine period, a *myriophoros* ('10,000-carrier') that could carry a considerable cargo, as I shall demonstrate. The amphoras carried by Tekmezar I are distributed over an area that measures 40 m by 20 m, that is a surface area of 800 square metres. The amphoras themselves are 40 cm high, with a maximum body

---

[7] On Marmara Sea underwater research, see N. Günsenin, 'Récentes découvertes sur l'île de Marmara (Proconnèse) à l'époque byzantine: épaves et lieux de chargement', *Archaeonautica* 14/1998 (1999), 309-316; Günsenin, 'From Ganos to Serçe Limanı: social and economic activities in the Propontis during medieval times, illuminated by recent archaeological and historical discoveries', *INA Quarterly* 26.3 (1999), 18-23.

[8] After examining the anchor drawings done in situ F. H. Van Doorninck thinks that the tile wreck should be dated to the Roman period.

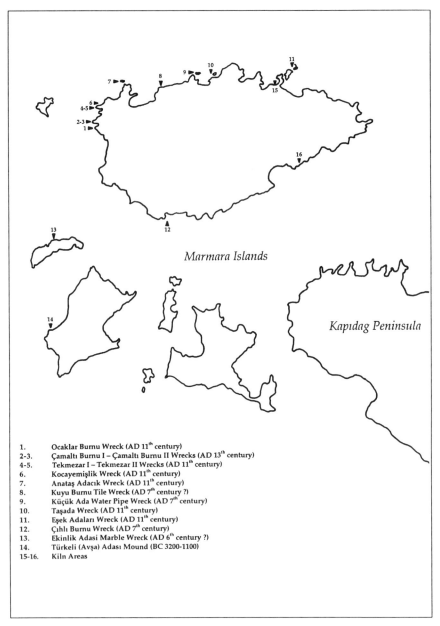

Figure 8.2 Discoveries to date around the Marmara Islands

circumference of about 90 cm. Thus nine amphoras would fill one square metre. Since three layers of amphoras are presently visible, just the visible cargo can be estimated at approximately 21,600 amphoras. There are certainly more amphoras buried out of sight, but even if not taking them into account we arrive at a cargo size of about 20,000 amphoras, at the absolute minimum. Since a full amphora weighed about 12 kg, the estimated weight of the cargo of Tekmezar I is about 200 tonnes. This size of cargo and consequent size of ship give a new perpective to the study of commercial shipping in the Byzantine period. The depth at which the wreck is lying, 35-45 m, and, even more so, the huge numbers of amphoras would make excavation difficult. It would, however, be worth making one sondage into Tekmezar I, to search for the hull and also to gather further statistics that would permit making a more accurate estimate of the ship's size and capacity.

The *Çamaltı Burnu I* Wreck, the shipwreck dating to the thirteenth century, has been chosen to be excavated for both archaeological and historical reasons. Relatively little is known of the ship-building technology of this period, and most of what is known derives from written texts rather than archaeological remains, while the type of amphoras on the wreck (Günsenin type IV) has not yet been studied in any detail. Moreover, the only archaeological material related to Byzantine maritime activities excavated and studied to date consists of three wrecks excavated by INA along the Anatolian coasts, namely, the *Yassıada I* (7th century), *Selimiye* (9th century) and *Serçe Limanı* (11th century) wrecks.[9] Thus the excavation of Çamaltı Burnu I Wreck would doubtless contribute a good deal of new information concerning Byzantine maritime activities, particularly in the sea of Marmara region during the thirteenth century, but of a general nature as well.

A brief summary of what we have learned during our first three field seasons will suffice here.[10] Type IV cargo amphoras on the wreck show a wide range of sizes (47 to 80 cm high) and capacities (17 to 115 litres,

---

[9] For the latest interpretation of the 7th-century Yassıada ship and bibliography, see F.H. van Doorninck, Jr., 'Yassıada Wrecks', in J. P. Delgado, ed., *Encyclopedia of Underwater and Maritime Archaeology* (London, 1997), 469-471. For the Selimiye (Bozburun) Wreck, see *INA Quarterly* 22.1 (1996), 12-14; *INA Quarterly* 22.3 (1996), 16-20; *INA Quarterly* 22.1 (1996), 3-8; *INA Quarterly* 25.2 (1998), 12-17; and *INA Quarterly* 25.4 (1998), 3-13. For most recent information and bibliography on the Serçe Limanı Wreck, see F. H. van Doorninck, Jr., 'The 11th-century Byzantine ship at Serçe Limanı: an interim overview', in C. G. Makrypoulias, ed., *Sailing Ships of the Mediterranean Sea and the Arabian Gulf*, I (Athens, 1998), 67-77; see also the chapter by van Doorninck in this volume.

[10] N. Günsenin, 'L'épave de Çamaltı Burnu I (l'île de Marmara, Proconnèse): résultats des campagnes 1998-2000', *Anatolia Antiqua* 9 (2001), 117-133. For the latest information on the continuing excavation see, www.nautarch.org.

measured to the base of the neck). The different capacities may be multiples of some standard unit of capacity, as are the capacities of the Byzantine amphoras from the Serçe Limanı shipwreck, but more accurate capacity measurements must first be made before any reliable conclusions about this are possible. Greek monogram stamps occur on the handles of the amphoras where they meet the shoulders. These monograms should indicate the names of the potters or the owners of the workshops that produced the amphoras and will undoubtedly raise some questions about the economic life of the empire. In addition to the cargo amphoras, there are several different types of storage jars similar in style that also appear to have been cargo but possibly carried some other commodity or commodities. Various ceramic wares not belonging to the ship's cargo and including one-handled jars, cooking pots, glazed plates, a sgraffito plate and a cup will undoubtedly make an important contribution to the Byzantine ceramic typologies of the period. The ship was also carrying as part of its cargo two or three dozen broken anchors destined to be repaired or used as scrap iron.

On Marmara island, we identified two kiln areas: one on the north coast, at Saraylar, the other on the southeast coast, at Topağaç. Both kiln areas seem to have produced Type I amphoras like those produced at Ganos. From our initial investigations undertaken with Pamela Armstrong, we realised that the beach location of both kiln areas was significant. At Saraylar, two kiln zones, one producing amphoras, the other roof-tiles, are curiously impermanent and in an exposed position in the sand on the beach. At one end of the beach are remnants of domestic occupation: walls can be seen along the shore, and glazed ceramics (Byzantine and Ottoman) can be found at the same location. Tile kilns may have been associated with these buildings. At Topağaç the destroyed kiln can be seen in section on the beach. Many amphora sherds and wasters can be seen in the section and on the sand below. Nearby is a small monastery, with more amphora sherds and wasters in its vicinity.[11]

Ganos Type I amphoras had a greater volume and scope of circulation than any other Byzantine amphora type during the period in which they were produced. The scale of production of these amphoras at Ganos and Marmara island begins to explain how this could be so. When I started my investigations at Ganos, I claimed that almost every amphora discovered along the Mediterranean and Black Sea coasts should be attributed to this production. My hypothesis was that ships could have

---

[11] See Günsenin and Hatcher, 'Analyses chimiques comparatives des amphores de Ganos, de l'île de Marmara et de l'épave de Serçe Limanı' (as in n. 2), 249-260.

loaded their cargoes of amphoras containing wine directly at Ganos or at some entrepôt, such as Constantinople. But this theory needed to be modified with the discovery of two small Ganos-type amphora production areas on the nearby Marmara island. A further complicating factor is the lack of an identified clay source on the island. Keeping the historical evidence in mind, we looked afresh at the Ganos-Prokonnesos link, both as part of the same geological system, and also as a mutual monastic system.

The next step was clearly a programme of scientific analysis of the products of the Ganos and Prokonnessos kilns, and in particular, comparison of their mineralogical contents. In Pamela Armstrong's words, 'Scientific analysis of the amphoras produced at Ganos can contribute to the wider problem of understanding how far these amphoras travelled, and trying to establish their network, which means the trade network of the monastery itself.' We collected samples from Ganos, Saraylar and Topagaç. These sherds formed one part of my programme of analysis. As Pamela Armstrong explained,

> Samples of amphoras produced at Ganos have just recently been subjected to a sequence of chemical analysis in order to work out the chemical profile of Ganos products. At a later date it is hoped to test other amphoras against this. For instance, there are no obvious sources of clay on the island of Marmara, yet a number of amphora kilns have been located there. All the island's kilns are on the shoreline. I intend to have the products from these kilns analysed to test the theory that the clay used was carried to the island from the Ganos area, where there was no shortage of clay, and that the amphoras were made on site, right where they were needed. This would be significantly easier than transporting empty amphoras. But it also implies much more about the Ganos estates, and whether the monastery had properties on island in the Sea of Marmara. At least one of the island kilns is located close to a monastery: was this an otherwise undocumented *metochion* of Ganos? It may never be possible to prove this fully, but undertaking a structured programme of scientific analysis of the ceramics will be the first step in showing, if it is true, that there were these otherwise undetectable links between wine-producing estates.[12]

The other part of the analysis concerned the amphoras found on the Serçe Limanı Glass Wreck. Through my work at Ganos, I had realised that amphoras in the Glass Wreck cargo must have been produced there.

---

[12] By personal communication.

I discussed this idea on a number of occasions with van Doorninck to whom I owe much of my understanding of nautical archaeology. His trust in my observations was evidenced by his permitting me to sample a number of amphoras from the Glass Wreck, for which I am most grateful.[13] We then had all the samples we needed to provide information comparing a 'production place' with 'other production places in the vicinity' and the 'only excavated archaeological evidence of this production'. The programme of analysis was accomplished with the help of Pamela Armstrong, as part of the Oxford Byzantine Ceramics Project, and carried out by Helen Hatcher, an analytical chemist at the Research Laboratory for Archaeology and the History of Art in Oxford.[14] We can now say with some confidence that all the piriform amphoras on the Glass Wreck ship had been made somewhere in the region around Ganos.

There is still the question of the source of the clay used in producing the amphoras at the kilns of Saraylar and Topağaç on Marmara island. If local clays were used at these sites, as was the case at Ganos, it would be quite difficult to differentiate between the clays, since they would all belong to the same greater geological formation. It does not appear that there would have been sufficient quantities of suitable clay available on the island, except possibly to a limited degree in the Topağaç area. The seaside locations of the Saraylar and Topağaç kilns may have in part been due to a need to transport from Ganos much, if not all, the clay they used. The relative dates of all the kilns we have found on Marmara island and in the Ganos region might make a useful contribution toward solving this problem, but suffcient data is not as yet available.

In any case, Marmara was certainly a wine- and amphora-producing island and possessed a significant number of monasteries. Another ongoing project we are working on with Pamela Armstrong concerns the economic activities of these monasteries and in particular whether they operated independently or were subordinate to Ganos. Their history is under investigation and we hope to find enough information for a future article.

The journey I have been taking with a number of valued colleagues from different disciplines is not yet over, but it is my hope that the road already travelled will awaken in others a new interest in the role of the Sea of Marmara region in the economic life of the empire and bring into

---

[13] I also thank him for revising and contributing to the present article.
[14] See Günsenin and Hatcher, 'Analyses chimiques comparatives des amphores de Ganos, de l'île de Marmara et de l'épave de Serçe Limanı', 249-260.

sharper focus the present poor state of our knowledge concerning the purposes and places of manufacture of the various types of Byzantine amphoras.

9. The Byzantine ship at Serçe Limanı: an example of small-scale maritime commerce with Fatimid Syria in the early eleventh century

F. van Doorninck, jr

In the third decade of the eleventh century, a Byzantine merchant ship, while on a return voyage from the Fatimid Syrian coast to the environs of Constantinople, sought anchorage, perhaps in bad weather, at Serçe Limanı, a natural harbour on the southern Anatolian coast directly north of the island and city of Rhodes. Only one anchor had been cast when the ship was driven shoreward, apparently by a strong gust of wind. The anchor cable held, but the anchor's iron shank broke. The ship ran against the rocks of shoreline cliffs and sank to a sandy seabed at the base of the cliffs, thirty-three metres beneath the surface.[1] The shipwreck, popularly known as the Glass Wreck, was excavated between 1977 and 1979 by the Institute of Nautical Archaeology and Texas A&M University, with the assistance of the Bodrum Museum of Underwater Archaeology.[2]

---

[1] The bottom part of the anchor was recovered a short distance away from the wreck site and was virtually identical in design, fabrication and size to two anchors still on the ship. Examination of the break revealed that it had occurred before there had been any significant oxidation of the anchor, that is, while the anchor was still in use.

[2] Early general reports on the excavated shipwreck include G. F. Bass, 'Glass treasure from the Aegean', *National Geographic* 153 (June 1978), 768-793 and Bass, 'The shipwreck at Serçe Liman, Turkey', *Archaeology* 32 (1979), 36-43; G. F. Bass and F. H. van Doorninck, Jr., 'An 11th-century shipwreck at Serçe Liman, Turkey', *International Journal of Nautical Archaeology* 7 (1978), 119-132. We initially believed the ship to be Islamic: G. F.Bass, 'A medieval Islamic merchant venture', *Archaeological News* 8.2/3 (1979), 84-94. For later overviews of the ship and its contents, see G. F. Bass, K. Cassavoy, C. Runnels, J. K. Schwarzer, II, J. R. Steffy and F. H. van Doorninck, 'The Glass Wreck: an 11th-century merchantman', *INA Newsletter* 15.3 (1988), 1-31; and F.H. van Doorninck, 'The medieval shipwreck at Serçe Limanı: an early 11th-century Fatimid-Byzantine commercial voyage',

From *Travel in the Byzantine World*, ed. Ruth Macrides. Copyright © 2002 by the Society for the Promotion of Byzantine Studies. Published by Ashgate Publishing Ltd, Gower House, Croft Road, Aldershot, Hampshire, GU11 3HR, Great Britain.

The ship's captain was apparently well acquainted with the coastline in the vicinity of Serçe Limanı, for the mouth of the harbour is almost impossible to detect from the sea, and the captain had attempted to anchor at what has always been the harbour's primary anchorage. Despite the danger from frequent strong, gusty winds along this coastline, a captain who knew the region well would have opted for the protection from hostile ships afforded by the intercoastal waterway passing between the mainland and the islands of Rhodes, Symi and Kos through the western part of the then well-populated and prosperous maritime theme of the Kibyrrhaiots.[3] Moreover, the ship had a very flat bottom with an only slightly projecting keel and was thus well suited for shallow-water coastal navigation.

The ship was a two-masted lateener with an overall length of only 15.6 m (50 Byzantine feet), a breadth one-third the length, and a box-like hold having a capacity of some 30 metric tons, or somewhere roughly around 3,000 *modioi*, depending on the cargo carried. Thus she was a modest-sized vessel, but at the same time relatively large when compared to those that we know were commonly used by Byzantine monasteries for the transport of produce during those times.[4]

The hull provides us with one of the earliest extant examples of Mediterranean frame-first construction, in which overall hull shape is determined primarily by frames (ribs) erected before planking, rather than by tenoned-together planking erected before frames, the method followed in the ancient Mediterranean world.[5] Immediately after the keel, stem and sternpost had been assembled, two complete and eight partial frames were erected amidships, and an unusually strong, complete frame near either end of the keel; the latter two frames would later support bulkheads partitioning off bow and stern compartments from the hold. The overall span of the frames was decreased towards either end of the hull, and the lateral rise of their bottom part increased, by successively greater multiples of the Byzantine finger (16

Graeco-Arabica 4 (1991), 45-52 and van Doorninck, 'Glasvraget–et byzantinsk skib fra 1000-tallet', in B. P. Hallager, ed., *Hvad Middelhavet gemmer* (Århus, 1997), 121-136.

[3] Two particularly useful sources on the Byzantine archaeological remains within this area are: C. Foss, 'The coasts of Caria and Lycia in the middle ages: a preliminary report', in *Fondation européene de la science, Rapports des missions effectuées en 1983* (Paris, 1987), 213-255 and V. Ruggieri, 'Rilievi di architettura bizantina nel golfo di Simi', *OCP* 55.1-2 (1989), 75-100 and 345-373.

[4] With the exception of one vessel of 6,000 *modioi*, all such boats cited by A. Harvey range in capacity from several hundred to 2,000 *modioi*: *Economic Expansion in the Byzantine Empire 900-1200* (Cambridge, 1989), 238-241.

[5] For a detailed description of the hull and its construction, see J. R. Steffy, *Wooden Ship Building and the Interpretation of Shipwrecks* (College Station, Texas, 1994), 85-91.

fingers = 1 foot). The bottom planking and some lower side planking were then fastened to the already erected framing, this being all the planking required to give the hull its overall shape. The builders were now able to shape and install the remaining framing, without great difficulty, and then finish the planking. Quite similar, but more developed, methods, employed first by Mediterranean and then by other European shipwrights in subsequent centuries, produced ships with hulls adequate for transoceanic exploration and colonisation. The recently recovered hull remains of an early tenth-century Byzantine ship appear to provide us with a yet earlier stage in the development of these methods.[6]

The home port of the ship and its crew was probably located somewhere along the northern shore of the Sea of Marmara in the general area of Rhaidestos, then an important supplier of grain, wine and oil to Constantinople. Analysis of the lead from some of the personal possessions and objects belonging to the ship shows that it had come from nearby lead mines in the eastern Rhodope mountains of south-eastern Bulgaria. Chemical analysis of the fabric of the cooking ware and food storage jars belonging to the ship[7] and of most types of Byzantine amphoras on board indicates that in quite possibly all cases their clay was from the Sea of Marmara north shore geological area.[8]

There was a strong Bulgarian ethnic presence on the ship. Many of the best parallels for shipboard tools and weapons are from Bulgaria, while many of the Byzantine amphoras have marks of potters and owners that together as a group occur only in medieval Bulgaria.[9] Many of the owners had Greek names, such as Leon,[10] NI(kolaos),[11]

---

[6] A brief, general description of the hull remains appears in F. M. Hocker, 'Bozburun Byzantine shipwreck excavation: the final campaign 1998', *INA Quarterly* 25.4 (1998), 3-13.

[7] Parallels for the ship's pottery have not yet been found, undoubtedly due in part to the fact that these vessels had been made by local potters who used relatively primitive, slow wheels.

[8] N. Günsenin and H. Hatcher, 'Analyses chimiques comparatives des amphores de Ganos, de l'île de Marmara et de l'épave de Serçe Limanı (Glass-Wreck)', *Anatolia Antiqua* 5 (1997), 249-260. It should be noted that Amphora 3 in Table 1 of the Günsenin-Hatcher article and the ship's cooking ware and storage jars have the same fabric.

[9] Some of these marks are illustrated by fig. 3, nos. 1-8, 16 and 23 in F. H. van Doorninck, 'The cargo amphoras on the 7th century Yassı Ada and 11th century Serçe Limanı shipwrecks: two examples of a reuse of Byzantine amphoras as transport jars', in V. Déroche and J.-M. Spieser, eds., *Recherches sur la céramique byzantine*, BCH Supplément 18 (Paris, 1989), 247-257.

[10] van Doorninck, 'The cargo amphoras' (as in n. 9), fig. 3, no. 14.

[11] van Doorninck, 'The cargo amphoras', fig. 3, no. 12, left.

M(ichael),[12] IŌ(annis), but there was also a MIR,[13] possibly standing for a misspelled Myron, but more likely a Slavic name, such as, for example, Miroslav. The amphoras appear to have had around a dozen different owners in all. The presence of 11 sets of weapons on the ship raises the possibility that most, if not all, of the owners were on the ship.

Those on board the ship were engaged in what appears to have been a rather marginal level of maritime commerce involving a few cargoes of fairly substantial size and quite a number of much smaller, seemingly personal cargoes.

One of the more substantial loads was 3 metric tons of glass cullet that was to be remelted and made into new glassware. Two tons were raw glass that had been broken up into small chunks to facilitate its transport. Two-thirds of the other ton consisted of glassware that had become misshapen and discarded during manufacture, again broken into small pieces for transport. The remaining cullet consisted of waste glass produced during every stage in the manufacture of glassware.[14]

Made at some glass factory on the Fatimid Syrian coast, then an important glass-making centre that produced glass famous for its unusually fine quality,[15] the cullet was most probably being transported to Constantinople, the most important glass-making centre in the Byzantine world. The cullet was almost certainly placed in wickerwork baskets and was being carried in place of stone ballast in the after quarter of the hold. Shipping glass cullet cheaply as ballast often made economic and/or technical good sense, since melting glass requires a much lower temperature (2000° F.) than making glass does (2600° F.) and a desired kind of glass cannot always be made from locally available raw materials. The famous glass-makers of Venice found it advantageous to import glass cullet from Syria during late medieval times,[16] and it would appear to have been a common practice

---

[12] van Doorninck, 'The cargo amphoras', fig. 3, no. 9.

[13] van Doorninck, 'The cargo amphoras', fig. 3, no. 18.

[14] Preliminary articles on the glassware cullet, as well as intact glassware, include G. F. Bass, 'The nature of the Serçe Limanı glass', *Journal of Glass Studies* 26 (1984), 64-69; F. H. van Doorninck, 'The Serçe Limanı shipwreck: an 11th century cargo of Fatimid glassware cullet for Byzantine glassmakers', in *1st International Anatolian Glass Symposium, April 26th-27th, 1988* (Istanbul,1990), 58-63; I. L. Barnes, R. H. Brill, E. C. Deal and G. V. Piercy, 'Lead isotope studies of some of the finds from the Serçe Liman shipwreck', in J. S. Olin and M. J. Blackman, eds., *Proceedings of the 24th International Archaeometry Symposium* (Washington, D.C., 1986), 1-12; and B. Lledó, 'Mold siblings in the 11th-century cullet from Serçe Limanı', *Journal of Glass Studies* 39 (1997), 43-55.

[15] W. Heyd, *Histoire du commerce du Levant au moyen-âge*, I (Leipzig, 1885), 179-180.

[16] D. Jacoby, 'Raw materials for the glass industries of Venice and the Terraferma,

at least as early as Fatimid times within the Byzantine world. Although glass from Corinth once thought to be Fatimid is of later Italian origin,[17] Fatimid glassware cullet from Syria was used in a glass factory at the Bulgarian capital of Preslav[18] and has been found on another Byzantine shipwreck 30 km to the east of Serçe Limanı.[19]

Dozens of sumac and grape seeds found in the glass cullet indicate that there may have been substantial amounts of sumac and raisins overlying the cullet. Both were important Syrian exports.[20]

No recognisable traces of any cargo and almost no stone ballast was found within the forward one-third of the hold. We think that some 3 tons of a cargo of relatively high density that disappeared without a trace must have been carried here. One possibility is plant ash, which was shipped as ballast from Syria to glassmakers in the western Mediterranean in later centuries.[21]

There had been at least 103 Byzantine amphoras on the ship.[22] Some eighty of them were also being shipped as ballast and probably contained wine, another important Syrian export.[23]

We were at first puzzled that the amphoras were Byzantine, but then it emerged that they had already been used many times over. This was evident from the reoccurring damage to the amphora mouths sustained when stoppers had been pried out on a number of different occasions. Every time some part of the mouth was pry damaged, the damaged area was carved down and rounded off to minimise the chance

---

about 1370-about 1460', *Journal of Glass Studies* 35 (1993), 65-90; L. Zecchin, 'Materie prime e mezzi d'opera dei vetrai nei documenti veneziani dal 1233 al 1347', *Rivista della Stazione Sperimentale del Vetro* no. 4 (July-August 1980), 171-176.

[17] D. Whitehouse, 'Glassmaking at Corinth: a reassessment', in D. Foy and G Sennequier, eds., *Ateliers de verriers: de l'antiquité à la période pré-industrielle* (Rouen, 1991), 73-82; for earlier views, see van Doorninck, The Serçe Limanı shipwreck' (as in n. 14), 62 and n. 19.

[18] G. Džinkov, 'Atelier médiéval de verrerie de Patleina', *Arheologija* 3.3 (1961), 30-36 (in Bulgarian with French summary).

[19] C. Pulak, 'Turkish coastal survey yields wrecksite inventory', *INA Newsletter* 12.2 (1985), 2.

[20] S. D. Goitein, *A Mediterranean Society*. I: *Economic Foundations* (Berkeley and Los Angeles, 1967), 154 and 213; Heyd, *Histoire du commerce* (as in n. 15), 177-178.

[21] Jacoby, 'Raw materials' and Zecchin, 'Materie prime' (as in n. 16).

[22] A study of the dimensions and capacities of the amphoras, which were made at many different workshops, has revealed a high level of dimensional standardisation and a well-developed liquid capacity system that together imply a considerable degree of central imperial control: F. H. van Doorninck, 'The piriform amphoras from the 11th-century shipwreck at Serçe Limanı: sophisticated containers for Byzantine commerce in wine', *Graeco-Arabica* 6 (1995), 181-189.

[23] Heyd, *Histoire du commerce*, 177.

of more damage. The stubs of broken handles were also rounded off. At the same time, marks of ownership had only rarely been changed on any of these amphoras, and all amphoras carrying the same mark of ownership had been stowed together in the same place on the ship, a further indication that amphora ownership had not changed. We have concluded that the owners had repeatedly used these jars to transport wine cargoes but had sold only the wine, keeping the amphoras for future transport of wine. A widespread occurrence of Byzantine piriform amphoras with carved-down areas of damage suggests that the reuse of amphoras in this way was not uncommon at that time.[24]

About fifty of the wine amphoras were stowed as ballast at the very bottom of a compartment at the stern in which the ship's stores, tools, commercial equipment, valuables and the like were kept. Some thirty of these amphoras – the lion's share – belonged to Michael who, we think, was probably the ship's captain. Three other individuals owned perhaps no more than three or four amphoras each. Just forward of midships, some thirty wine amphoras were stowed as ballast. Leon owned five of them, and someone with the monogram Rho-Ēta-Chi[25] owned three. Several other individuals each owned perhaps only one or two of the amphoras.

There were a number of other small, probably personal, packages that could have been packed together in a single, manageable basket or bale. One such package had been kept by someone who had occupied the small compartment located in the bow. It contained several Islamic glazed bowls[26] and eight pieces of Syrian glassware.[27] The midships

---

[24] Photographs of amphoras in which carved-down damage is visible appear in M. I. Artamonov, 'Belaja Veža', *Sovetskaja Arkheologija* 16 (1952), 68, fig. 19; I. Barnea, 'La céramique byzantine de Dobroudja, Xe-XIIe siècles', in V. Déroche and J.-M. Spieser, eds., *Recherches sur la céramique byzantine*, BCH Supplément 18 (Paris, 1989), 132, fig. 2; K. M. Gupalo and P. P. Toločko, 'The old Kievan lowland in the light of new archaeological investigations' (in Ukrainian), in P. P. Toločko, ed., *Starodavnij Kiev* (Kiev, 1975), 73, fig. 94; A. Milčev, 'Matériaux découverts dans les locaux artisanaux et de commerce au nord de la porte méridionale de la ville intérieure de Pliska' (in Bulgarian with French résumé), in J. Văzărova, ed., *Pliska-Preslav*, vol. 1 (Sofia, 1979), 168, fig. 94; and D. L. Talis, 'A medieval stamped amphora handle from the excavations of Balinsk town' (in Russian), *Arkheologičeskij sbornik* (= *Trudy Gosudarstvennogo Istoričeskogo Muzeja* 40) (1966), 97, fig. 1. I have personally seen Byzantine piriform amphoras with carved-down mouths at the archaeological museums of Constanţa, in Romania; Varna and Sozopol, in Bulgaria; and Çanakkale, Istanbul (Naval Museum), Izmir and Bodrum, in Turkey.

[25] van Doorninck, 'The cargo amphoras' (as in n. 9), fig. 3, no. 13.

[26] The Islamic glazed bowls on the ship, almost four dozen in all, find their closest parallels at Caesarea on the northern coast of Israel. Most of the bowls are examples of either splash ware, so called because various colours of glaze were poured or splashed on the bowl's interior to form a decorative pattern, or *champlevé* ware, a style of sgraffito ware

area of the hold held a number of packages containing Islamic pottery that included some two dozen glazed bowls, a half-dozen two-handled redware jugs, a half-dozen redware gargoulettes, and almost two dozen redware cooking pots with lead-glazed interiors, of a type the crusaders were later to take back to western Europe in great numbers. Small packages stowed in the stern compartment included another dozen Islamic glazed bowls, three- to four-dozen glass bottles, and a half-dozen whiteware gargoulettes.[28]

Captain Michael appears to have been not only the principal merchant on the ship, but also the ship's carpenter. Weighing equipment, money and other valuables, tools and materials for shipboard repairs, and locks were all kept closely together in the stern compartment. Indeed, most of the tools, some of the weighing equipment, and at least some of the locks had been kept together in a single large wicker basket.

The weighing equipment, well suited for a Byzantine-Fatimid trading venture, consisted of a Byzantine steelyard, three balances, two large sets of balance-pan weights, and sixteen glass weights for weighing Fatimid coins. The balance-pan weights in one set were disc-shaped and based on a Byzantine pound of about 319 g. Those in the other set were barrel shaped and based (for the most part) on a commodity dirham of 3.125 g. The glass weights include 1/8, 1/4, 1/2, 1, and 2 silver dirham and 1 gold dinar weights. Some bear legible dates, the latest being either 1024/25 or possibly 1021/22. The ship must have sunk not long after.

In keeping with a then normal practice, little coinage appears to have been on the ship.[29] Only three Fatimid gold coins, fifteen clippings from other Fatimid gold coins, and some forty Byzantine copper coins were recovered. The gold coins are quarter-dinars issued during the reign of al-Ḥākim (996-1020); one has a legible date of 1008/9, while a second was probably issued in 1007/8. The clippings

---

in which designs are rather deeply and broadly carved into the clay, or both styles appear together on the same bowl. Since the two styles had previously not been thought to be contemporaneous, the Serçe Limanı bowls have led to a reassessment of the chronology of Islamic glazed wares: M. Jenkins, 'Early medieval Islamic pottery: the eleventh century reconsidered', *Muqarnas* 9 (1992), 56-66.

[27] In all, there were at least eighty pieces of intact glassware on the ship.

[28] For illustrations of one of the gargoulettes (one-handled jugs with filters at the base of the neck) and its ornately decorated filter, see G. F. Bass and F. H. van Doorninck, 'An 11th-century shipwreck at Serçe Liman, Turkey' (as in n. 2), 127, fig. 10.

[29] According to Goitein, even important Jewish merchants of the Cairo Geniza did not carry much cash on their journeys: *Letters of Medieval Jewish Traders* (Princeton, 1973), 47, n. 12.

were used in place of silver coins, then in short supply and therefore reserved for local commerce.[30] The Byzantine copper coins, useful for the return voyage, are anonymous issues with Christ holding the Gospels on the obverse and the inscription: Jesus Christ King of Kings: on the reverse; unfortunately, they cannot give us a precise dating for the wreck. A small amount of jewellery, mostly found in close association with coins and including a gold earring made in Fatimid Syria and a half-dozen silver rings, probably served as bullion, which merchants generally preferred to carry in the form of jewellery. The paucity of coins and bullion coupled with the presence of three Byzantine lead document seals (and one blank) suggests that letters of credit may have been used to minimise potential losses at sea. One of the seals depicts the Ecstatic Meeting of saints Peter and Paul on the obverse, while a metrical inscription on the reverse reads: 'Guardian of the writing I have been placed, bond of Peter'.[31]

There is evidence of a high level of seamanship in the operation of the ship. The ballasting for the return voyage had been done with great skill and care. Stone boulders, cobbles and pebbles, and high-density items of cargo were used as ballast. As already noted, wine amphoras were stowed as ballast in the stern compartment and in the hold just forward of midships, while the aftermost quarter of the hold was ballasted with the glass cullet. The hold between the glass cullet and the amphoras was ballasted with stone boulders which chemical analysis shows were obtained somewhere along the Syro-Lebanese coast. These were laid out in a single layer so that they fit closely together to form a stable dry-masonry floor. Calculations based on the weights and distributions of both the stone and cargo ballast reveal that it had a more or less uniform density throughout the after part of the hull.

Ship's stores included a very complete set of carpentry tools, spare nails and tacks, spare pulley sheaves and axles, pitch for caulking seams — everything needed to make any kind of repair to the ship and its rigging. Judging from the location of a set of caulking irons on the ship, it would appear that some recaulking of the deck had been in progress when the ship sank.

Four anchors had been kept on the bulwarks in the bow, two on either side, ready for use; it had been the after anchor on the starboard side that broke at the Serçe Limanı anchorage. Five spare anchors had been

---

[30] Goitein, *Economic Foundations* (as in n. 20), 233.
[31] [+]ΦΡΟΥ[Ρ(ΟΝ) | ΤΗ]C ΓΡΑΦ(ΗC) | [ΤΕ]ΘΕΙΚΑ | [ΔΕ]CΜΟC | ΠΕΤΡΩ: My thanks to John Nesbitt for deciphering the inscription.

very carefully stacked on the deck nearby. Wooden chocks separated the anchors from each other and from the deck, and the entire pile was wrapped in two thicknesses of woven grass mats to protect both the anchors and crew. The arms of the anchors ended in chisel-like teeth designed to dig into the seabed. These were often broken during an anchor's use. Jagged edges were carefully filed down and rounded off, the tooth reshaped to minimise further damage and to keep the anchor as functional as possible.

It might be noted here that although the ship's nine anchors had originally been made in probably as many as five different workshops, their dimensions were highly standardised. Most, if not all, of the shanks had, or had had, a length of 6 imperial spans, or 1.4 metres, and six, or perhaps seven, of the anchors had arms exactly 2 Byzantine feet, or 0.625 metres, long. Seven of the anchor rings that were restorable all had the same diameter and cross-sectional dimensions, and all of the anchors used a wooden stock with a maximum cross-sectional diameter of 3 Byzantine fingers. The anchors were of three different weights: 150, 175 and 200 Byzantine pounds, or 48, 56 and 64 kg. The fact that these weights are multiples of one-quarter a Byzantine hundredweight is of interest in that anchor weights at thirteenth-century Genoa were multiples of one-quarter a Genoese hundredweight. The great degree of standardisation present in the dimensions and weight of our anchors suggests that by the eleventh century, Byzantine maritime law exercised, in the interest of safety, a high level of control over the number and weight of anchors carried by a ship of any particular size, as we know maritime law did in the western Mediterranean a couple of centuries later. The standardisation of dimensions made it easier for an official to determine whether or not a ship was carrying anchors of an adequate weight.

The crew had faced real dangers from both men and the elements during their voyage. Piracy was widespread in the Mediterranean at that time, and we hear of pirate attacks occurring along the south coast of Anatolia in around 1028.[32] Each of the eleven sets of weapons on the ship consisted of a thrusting spear and four or five javelins. The remains of perhaps three swords were also recovered. One of the swords had a bronze hilt decorated on either side by an elaborately-feathered bird, the *hamsa*, a motif of Indian origin then popular in the Black Sea region.[33] The preponderance of javelins suggests that the primary

---

[32] Goitein, *Economic Foundations*, 214 and 327-332.
[33] G. F. Bass and F. H. van Doorninck, 'An 11th-century shipwreck at Serçe Limanı, Turkey' (as in n. 2), 125, fig. 8.

defensive strategy was to engage attackers at a distance in the hope of preventing them from boarding. The spears would also have been effective anti-boarding weapons, particularly the three which had side lugs designed to limit the spearhead's penetration into an enemy's body.[34] The bronze sword hilt had a ring for a lanyard that could be tied to the wrist, a feature normally found on swords of mounted troops, but in this case an insurance against losing the sword overboard.[35]

The breaking of an anchor shank had brought the voyage to a sudden end, but this was not the first time during the voyage that an anchor shank had broken. The shanks of three other anchors had already broken earlier on. Since a buoy rope was usually attached to the lower end of the shank of an anchor when in use to mark its location, and an anchor cable was attached to the anchor ring at the shank's upper end, it was often possible to retrieve both parts of an anchor whose shank had broken and to repair it by forging the two broken ends back together. In the case of our three anchors, the job had been done very quickly, with the result that we can easily see where the repair was made.

Turning to shipboard life, we find evidence for three living areas on the ship: the stern compartment, the smaller bow compartment, and, for those of lower status, the midships deck area.

Cooking was done with charcoal, probably in a sandbox or the like, since no physical remains of a permanent cooking facility were detected. The fact that charcoal was found only just forward of the stern compartment suggests that most, if not all, cooking was done there. Somewhere between half a dozen and a dozen cooking pots, mostly Byzantine, were in use on the ship, and three or four copper cauldrons on board may also have been used.

Of the nine various-sized storage jars, located in the stern and midships living areas, most presumably carried food and water. The shipboard diet included meat (pig, goat, and possibly sheep), fish (tunny, tub gurnard, sea bass and drum), almonds, assorted fruits and olives. There is some reason to believe that there was one or more live goats on board, but this is not certain. Pork consumption was restricted to those living in the stern, and possibly the bow, compartment; this may have been true of fruit as well.

To catch fish there were 3 large nets with floats, a casting net, and a thirteen-tined spear. Many of the lead weights for the large nets are

---

[34] G. F. Bass *et al.*, 'The Glass Wreck: an 11th-century merchantman' (as in n. 2), 27.

[35] D. Alexander, '*Dhū'l-faqār* and the legacy of the Prophet, *mīrāth rasūl Allāh*', *Gladius* 19 (1999), 158.

decorated with geometric patterns in relief, often including rosettes, and several of the weights bear a cross or the name of Jesus in abbreviated form. Copper netting needles were employed to repair the nets, and some bone spindle whirls on board were probably being used to make line for net repairs. The multi-tined spear is of a type also represented by a seven-tined example found on a Venetian wreck of the second half of the sixteenth century.[36] Spears of this type could be disassembled by removing a key, so that the number of tines could be reduced or a broken tine could be repaired while the spear continued to be used.

Vermin has been a source of acute discomfort and disease on ships throughout the ages. Thus the cleaning, trimming and even total removal of hair was a very important aspect of shipboard life. This was certainly true on our ship, from which the remains of three different grooming kits were recovered: one from the bow compartment and two from the midships living area. The most complete of these, from the bow compartment, was kept in a woven vegetable-fibre container and included a wooden delousing comb, a pair of iron scissors, an iron razor, and perhaps also an iron knife and iron mirror. The container also held four Byzantine coins, a very interesting detail to those of us who keep our spare change in our toilet kits when travelling. Small amounts of orpiment (trisulfide of arsenic) found both in the bow compartment and in the midships living area may have been used together with quicklime and water as a depilatory.

Particularly in the case of a small coastal merchant ship, the crew occasionally would have camped on land while obtaining fresh water, wood, or diet supplements. To this end, there were two axes, a billhook, a mattock and a pick. Perhaps the ship also had a shovel with a wooden, iron-sheathed blade that did not survive.

Board games appear to have been a popular form of recreation on the ship, as has generally been the case on ships of more recent times, and, along with diet, reflect some degree of social stratification. A wooden chess set, of which a king, queen, bishop, two rooks and three pawns survive, had been kept in the stern compartment, while a backgammon piece and two small pieces of pottery cut into triangles of a similar size that were quite possibly gaming pieces were found in the midships living area.

We have learned, and continue to learn, a great deal that is new about maritime trade and travel in the Byzantine world of the early

---

[36] M. D'Agostino, 'Il Relitto del Vetro', *Bulletino di Archeologia Subacquea* 2-3.1-2 (1995-1996), 44-45.

eleventh century from our study of the Glass Wreck. The final excavation report will be published in three volumes. The first volume, devoted to the harbour's history, the ship itself, personal objects, tools, weapons, fishing equipment, metal vessels, locks, and plant and animal remains, is scheduled for publication by Texas A&M University Press in 2003.[37] The second volume, now nearing completion, will be devoted to all of the glass. The last volume will include all other cargo, coins, weighing and other commercial equipment, and conclusions.

---

[37] G. F. Bass, S. Matthews, J. R. Steffy, and F. H. van Doorninck, Jr., eds., *Serçe Limanı: An Eleventh-Century Shipwreck. I: The Ship and Its Anchorage, Crew and Passengers* (College Station, forthcoming, 2003).

10. Byzantine and early post-Byzantine pilgrimage to the Holy Land and to Mount Sinai

A. Kuelzer

Medieval pilgrimage to the 'Holy Land', to the countryside of Syria, Palestine and Egypt, is a well-known subject today; numerous academic studies have been made, numerous books have been written about the history of religion and migration, social history and 'daily life'.[1] Most of the sights and places, the churches and shrines of the important cities like Jerusalem or Bethlehem, the area along the banks of the River Jordan or the region around Mount Sinai, are well-known and have been dealt with repeatedly in archaeological and art historical studies.[2] Surprisingly, however, these studies take as their sources

---

[1] E.g., B. Kötting, *Peregrinatio religiosa* (Münster, Regensburg, 1950); J. Wilkinson, *Jerusalem Pilgrimage before the Crusades* (Warminster, 1977); J. Richard, *Les récits de voyages et de pèlerinages* (Turnhout, 1981); Cl. Zrenner, *Die Berichte der europäischen Jerusalempilger* (Frankfurt am Main, 1981); Fr. Hassauer, *Volkssprachliche Reiseliteratur. Faszination des Reisens und räumlicher ordo*, in *La littérature historiographique des origines à 1500*, I (Heidelberg, 1986), 259-283; G. Jaritz and A. Müller, eds., *Migration in der Feudalgesellschaft* (Frankfurt am Main, New York, 1988); B. Kötting, *Ecclesia peregrinans. Das Gottesvolk unterwegs. Gesammelte Aufsätze*, I-II (Münster, 1988); X. von Ertzdorff, D. Neukirch, R. Schulz, eds., *Reisen und Reiseliteratur im Mittelalter und in der Frühen Neuzeit. Vorträge eines interdisziplinären Symposiums vom 3.-8. Juni 1991 an der Justus-Liebig-Universität Gießen* (Amsterdam, Atlanta, 1992); X. von Ertzdorff, ed., *Beschreibung der Welt. Zur Poetik der Reise- und Länderberichte. Vorträge eines interdisziplinären Symposiums vom 8.-13. Juni 1998 an der Justus-Liebig-Universität Gießen* (Amsterdam, Atlanta, 2000). See, further, the important books by T. Tobler, *Bibliographia Geographica Palaestinae. Kritische Übersicht gedruckter und ungedruckter Beschreibungen der Reisen ins Heilige Land* (Leipzig, 1867) and by R. Röhricht, *Bibliotheca Geographica Palaestinae. Chronologisches Verzeichnis der auf die Geographie des Heiligen Landes bezüglichen Literatur von 333 bis 1878 und Versuch einer Kartographie* (Berlin, 1890; new ed. London, 1963). St. Yerasimos, *Les voyageurs dans l' empire ottoman (XIVe-XVIe siècles). Bibliographie, itinéraires et inventaire des lieux habités* (Ankara, 1991).

[2] Here too the scholarly literature is immense: J. D. Purvis, *Jerusalem, the Holy City. A Bibliography* (London, 1988) lists, on approximately 500 pages, articles and books which

From *Travel in the Byzantine World*, ed. Ruth Macrides. Copyright © 2002 by the Society for the Promotion of Byzantine Studies. Published by Ashgate Publishing Ltd, Gower House, Croft Road, Aldershot, Hampshire, GU11 3HR, Great Britain.

texts written in Latin, Slavonic or in western vernacular languages, while the Greek literature of the middle ages, the 'Byzantine point of view' is hardly taken into account.[3] Even Byzantine scholars are mostly interested in political events such as the Arab conquest or the history of the crusader states when dealing with *terra sancta*; others concentrate on the life and writings of some church fathers like Origen or Cyril of Scythopolis.

But what about the phenomenon of a Byzantine, a Greek orthodox pilgrimage? The religious significance of the area of Palestine, Egypt, and Syria, especially in middle and late Byzantine times, is usually neglected. At most, scholars refer to Constantinople, the New Jerusalem, which with its many relics and its ecclesiastical prominence had taken the place of the old Jerusalem in Palestine. Nevertheless, some relatively unknown sources tell us that there was Byzantine pilgrimage, even after the Arab conquest in the seventh century A.D., at a time when the east Roman empire no longer ruled the region. Although they have been disregarded by many modern scholars, there were numerous travellers with a religious motivation who wanted to see with their own eyes the places of the Old and the New Testament, who had the intention to pray and to pay their devotions there. The aim of this paper is to look at these pilgrims and to present the significance of the Holy Land for the Byzantines, as it emerges from the Greek sources. I shall begin with some remarks on the phenomenon of the holy place in general and the growing significance of pilgrimage in Christianity. After a short reference to the sources of early Byzantine times I shall give attention to those important writings which were composed in later times: on the one hand, the *proskynetaria*, guidebooks without any personal elements and, on the other, the travellers' accounts, written by pilgrims, ambassadors and others, sometimes full of personal observations. The text tradition of the *proskynetaria* starts in the thirteenth century and goes up to the eighteenth century, while the first traveller's account known to us was written by Epiphanios Hagiopolites after the year 638; the genre comes to an end with the works of Paisios Hagiapostolites and Jakobos

---

mention 'Jerusalem' or a synonym of the city in their title. Very important are F. M. Abel, *Géographie de la Palestine*, I-II (Paris, 1938), A. Ovadiah, *Corpus of the Byzantine Churches in the Holy Land* (Bonn, 1970) and the excellent new book by C. Dauphin, *La Palestine byzantine*. BAR International Series 726, I-III (Oxford, 1998). Concerning cartography see R. Cleave, *The Holy Land. A unique perspective* (Oxford, 1993).

[3] See A. Kuelzer, *Peregrinatio graeca in Terram Sanctam. Studien zu Pilgerführern und Reisebeschreibungen über Syrien, Palästina und den Sinai aus byzantinischer und metabyzantinischer Zeit* (Frankfurt a. M., 1994), esp. 2-5 (hereafter Kuelzer, *Peregrinatio graeca*).

Meloites in the second half of the sixteenth century.[4] Finally, I shall discuss 'daily life' in *terra sancta*, based on the Greek sources.

To begin with, some remarks about the terms 'holy' and 'holy places' are necessary in order to understand the phenomenon of pilgrimage in its deepest sense, to emphasise why *terra sancta* was still important for the Byzantines even when the significance of Constantinople had grown, as well as to demonstrate why the capital of the Byzantine empire was unable in the end to replace Jerusalem. In the field of the philosophy of religion there are difficulties in explaining the term 'holy' because one cannot simply express it in categories of rationality. It is filled with strong emotions and therefore essentially defined by reactions of emotion in individual subjects.[5] The 'holy' is part of the transcendental; it describes a characteristic feature of divinity. Objects, persons, or places are also able to have a share in the holiness; the divinity itself has chosen them or approved them for its cult. In religious studies the definition is more descriptive; here the 'holy' is 'everything, wherein a human being meets the divinity, which is part of one's religious awe, reference and worship'.[6] An object in which the 'holy' reveals itself changes its character but at the same time does not give up being itself, because it continues to be a part of its surroundings.[7] But now it is in contrast to the secular, to the *amorphe* or the disordered. The confessors of all higher developed religions agree with the idea that God or, more generally, the divinity, communicates to His or its chosen ones in an act of free grace, and, it is important, too, that the latter are able to understand these kinds of messages. A revelation, a theophany, a visualisation of the divinity, disturbs the former homogeneity of the space. The location is ennobled by the touch of godship and has a higher quality than its disordered surroundings. In a word, it has changed its character to a 'holy place'. Through the theophany, there is now a centre in the former unified and boundless space, a 'stairway to the cosmos', a bridge from one cosmic region to another. One has to stress that human beings are able only to recognise such places, not to establish them.[8] Mircea Eliade described a religious

---

[4] See Kuelzer, *Peregrinatio graeca*, 13-62, and below, nn. 20, 27 and 29.
[5] A. Lang, 'Heilig. Das Heilige: II. Religionsphilosophisch', *LThK* 5 (1960), 86-89, 86.
[6] B. Thum, 'Heilig. Das Heilige: I. Religionswissenschaftlich', *LThK* 5 (1960), 84-86, 84.
[7] M. Eliade, *Das Heilige und das Profane. Vom Wesen des Religiösen* (Frankfurt a. M., 1990), 15.
[8] This is very important in the case of Constantinople: the city itself was not touched by the 'holy'; here there is no 'holy place' in the original meaning of the word. The attempt to enhance its status by the many translations of relics from the time of Constantius II (337-361) onwards and by the creation of the legend of the apostle Andrew in a later period was remarkable but, in the end, without success. We have no evidence for a real *pilgrimage* to

person's striving for the 'holy' as 'the desire to live in objective reality and not to remain imprisoned in the endless relativity of one's own experiences'.[9] The final result of this kind of desire is a journey to the 'holy place', a journey to reality, to stay in this special and excellent atmosphere for some time at least. This is the decisive motive for all kinds of pilgrimage, much more important than other reasons for religious travelling: supplication, purification, benediction, aid in decision-making and others. Of course there are also secular motives for travelling, but in such cases, if there is no religious connection, one cannot use the term 'pilgrimage.'[10]

The belief that Jesus of Nazareth is ὁ ἅγιος τοῦ θεοῦ (Mark 1. 24; Luke 4. 34) forms the fundamental basis for Christian thinking about pilgrimage. He was the personal revelation of God, he lived in a fixed time at a place, exactly determinable, and ennobled this place in comparison with all the other places by His Holiness. In the middle of the second century, at the moment when the *parousia* was no longer expected to occur soon, when more and more people became interested in the historical person of Jesus of Nazareth, one is able to find the first traces of Christian pilgrims. At first, mostly clergymen like Melito of Sardes (second century) or Alexander of Cappadocia (third century) undertook a pilgrimage in order to verify the tradition but at the beginning of the fourth century many more people were involved in pilgrimage because of the spread of Christianity, the ending of persecution, and the greater security. The building work sponsored by the Empress Helena in Palestine from 326 was of great significance; the crowd of believers grew so quickly there that some church fathers, like Gregory of Nyssa (335-394) or John Chrysostom (344/54-407), tried to lead and control the phenomenon through their letters and homilies.[11] The number of 'holy places' grew constantly. Along with places which are directly connected with Jesus of Nazareth, now also many places well-known from the Old Testament were included in the visiting

---

Constantinople by Byzantines from Attica or Thessaly, from Crete, Asia Minor or elsewhere outside the capital; there is no *proskynetarion* comparable to those for the Holy Land. The churches and the shrines of the city were visited for purposes of devotion and veneration, but the actual place itself, Constantinople, was not regarded as 'holy'.

[9] Eliade, *Das Heilige und das Profane* (as in n. 7), 28-29.

[10] See L. Schmugge, 'Kollektive und individuelle Motivstrukturen im mittelalterlichen Pilgerwesen', in G. Jaritz and A. Müller, eds., *Migration in der Feudalgesellschaft* (Frankfurt am Main, New York, 1988), 263-289, 277-280; Kuelzer, *Peregrinatio graeca*, esp. 67-69.

[11] See Kötting, *Peregrinatio religiosa* (Münster, Regensburg, 1950), 421-426; Kötting, 'Gregor von Nyssas Wallfahrtskritik', *Studia Patristica* 5 (1962), 360-367. Sources: Gregory of Nyssa, epistula II: *PG* 46.1009-1016; John Chrysostom, homilia III: *PG* 49, 47-60.

programme. In addition, some pagan sites were associated with traditions of the Bible; for example, the pyramids of Gizeh, buildings regarded as Joseph's grain silos.[12] The cult of saints and relics which had emerged in the third century supported the formation of many new centres of pilgrimage.[13] The Arab conquest of Syria, Palestine, and Egypt in the seventh century was definitely not the end for Byzantine pilgrimage, as our sources state. However, two reservations must be expressed: firstly, in future, imperial figures like Helena, the mother of Constantine the Great, or Eudokia-Athenais, the wife of the Emperor Theodosius II, would not be among the travellers; secondly, the permanent settlement of pilgrims in *terra sancta*, not unusual even in the sixth century in the time of Cyril of Scythopolis,[14] became exceptional.

I have presented the above considerations in great detail in order to reveal the continuing importance of Byzantine pilgrimage to the Holy Land even in times when Constantinople, the centre of the east Roman empire, was growing and flourishing. They help us to clarify that the New Jerusalem, in spite of its steadily increasing treasure of relics and its ever-growing ecclesiastical power, was unable to take the place of Palestine completely. Two points especially show clearly that this is not simply an academic perception but a reflection of the thinking of the Byzantines. In the first place, one ought to remember that Constantinople in the high and later middle ages did not exclusively occupy the excellent position in the Greek conception of the world which many scholars want to concede to the city after having read the *Laudes Constantinopolitanae*. Quite the reverse, the whole genre of apocalyptic literature saw the New Jerusalem in a critical, often even in a negative manner, and always in sharp contrast to *terra sancta*.[15]

---

[12] See J. Wilkinson, 'Jewish Holy Places and the Origins of Christian Pilgrimage', in R. Ousterhout, ed., *The Blessings of Pilgrimage* (Urbana, Chicago, 1990), 41-53; H. S. Sivan, 'Pilgrimage, monasticism, and the emergence of Christian Palestine in the 4th century', in Ousterhout, ed., *The Blessings of Pilgrimage*, 54-65.

[13] See B. Kötting, 'Entwicklung der Heiligenverehrung und Geschichte der Heiligsprechung', in P. Manns, ed., *Die Heiligen in ihrer Zeit*, 2nd edn. (Mainz, 1966), 27-39; A. Kuelzer, 'Pilger. Byzanz', *LexMA* 6 (1993), 2151-2152; also, R. A. Markus, 'How on earth could places become holy? Origins of the Christian idea of holy places', *Journal of early Christian studies* 2 (1994), 257-271.

[14] The seven monks mentioned by the church father in his 'Lives of the monks of Palestine' were all former pilgrims. For the history of monasticism in Palestine, see D. Chitty, *The Desert a City* (Oxford, 1966) and J. Binns, *Ascetics and Ambassadors of Christ: the Monasteries of Palestine, 314-631* (Oxford, New York, 1994).

[15] See W. Brandes, 'Das "Meer" als Motiv in der byzantinischen apokalyptischen Literatur', in E. Chrysos, D. Letsios, *et al.*, *Griechenland und das Meer. Beiträge eines Symposions in Frankfurt im Dezember 1996* (Mannheim, 1999), 119-131; A. Kuelzer, 'Konstantinopel in der apokalyptischen Literatur der Byzantiner', *JÖB* 50 (2000), 51-76.

Secondly, the appreciation of Palestine as *terra sancta*, as we have mentioned before, is documented in the introductory sentences of many Greek *proskynetaria*: 'Listen, all you devout Christians, men and women, children, adults and all you orthodox Christians to this story telling of the holy places and announcing where our Lord Jesus Christ, the God of everyone, walked together with His pure mother, the most holy Theotokos, and all the apostles and the prophets. The root and the head of this holy and praiseworthy region is the holy and praiseworthy city of Jerusalem ... Not only the city itself is holy and is called holy, but all its surroundings and the whole region is holy. In the Old Testament this region is called the Promised Land.'[16]

From the fourth century until post-Byzantine times Greek pilgrims are to be found uninterruptedly documented in *terra sancta*. One encounters them in archaeological remains like the excavated inns and guesthouses in Bethlehem and Qalat Seman, or in churches and monasteries, some of which are in use today, in Jerusalem, along the banks of the River Jordan and on Mount Sinai, but also in small objects like *eulogia*, medallions and reliquaries from the 'holy city' or from Abu Mina.[17] More vivid is our picture of the pilgrims in literary sources: one can find them in epistolography, in the homilies, commentaries and other writings of the church fathers. Also the genre of hagiography gives examples of numerous saints who travelled in *terra sancta*: for example, Chariton in the fourth, Gerasimos and Nicholas of Sion in the fifth, Abraamios of Emesa, called 'the Syrian' in the sixth, and Theodore of Sykeon in the seventh century, to mention only the most famous. From later times there are Elias of Enna or Hilarion the Georgian in the ninth century, Lazaros Galesiotes around 1000, Christodoulos of Patmos in the eleventh century and many

---

[16] The quotation is by Anon. Monac. gr. 346 a. 1608/34: A. Papadopoulos-Kerameus, Προσκυνητάριον σὺν Θεῷ ἁγίῳ τῆς Ἁγίας Πόλεως Ἰερουσαλὴμ καὶ τῶν λοιπῶν Ἁγίων Τόπων, PPS 53 (St. Petersburg, 1900), 1: 'Ἀκούσατε πάντες οἱ εὐσεβεῖς χριστιανοί, ἄνδρες τε καὶ γυναῖκες, μικροί τε καὶ μεγάλοι καὶ ἅπαντες οἱ ὀρθόδοξοι χριστιανοί, ταύτην τὴν διήγησιν, ἡ ὁποία διηγᾶται καὶ λέγει διὰ τοὺς ἁγίους τόπους, ὁποῦ ἐκπεριπάτησεν ὁ κύριος ἡμῶν Ἰησοῦς Χριστὸς καὶ Θεὸς τῶν ἁπάντων καὶ ἡ πανάχραντος αὐτοῦ μήτηρ, ἡ ὑπεραγία Θεοτόκος, καὶ πάντες οἱ ἅγιοι ἀπόστολοι καὶ οἱ προφῆται. καὶ εἰς τοῦτον τὸν ἅγιον καὶ σεβάσμιον τόπον ἡ ῥίζα καὶ τὸ κεφάλαιον εἶναι ἡ ἁγία καὶ σεβασμία πόλις Ἰερουσαλήμ ... καὶ ὄχι μόνον ἡ πόλις εἶναι καὶ λέγεται ἁγία, ἀλλὰ καὶ τὰ περίχωρα καὶ ὁ τόπος ὅλος τριγύρου ἅγιος εἶναι. ὁ ὁποῖος τόπος ὀνομάζεται εἰς τὴν παλαιὰν Διαθήκην Γῆ τῆς Ἐπαγγελίας.

[17] See Wilkinson, *Jerusalem Pilgrims before the Crusades* (as in n. 1), 148-178; G. Vikan, *Byzantine Pilgrimage Art* (Washington, D.C., 1982); C. Hahn, 'Loca Sancta souvenirs: sealing the pilgrim's experience', in R. Ousterhout, ed., *The Blessings of Pilgrimage* (as in n. 12), 85-96. See also n. 2 above.

others.[18] These *Lives* are evidence for the existence of Byzantine pilgrimage to the Holy Land. However, further information about the details and practicalities of travel, about roads and guesthouses, distances and the duration of journeys can only be noted with some reservation. The intention of the genre lies in the emphasis on the marvellous, the virtue of a saint, the actions of God in history and so on, but definitely not in meticulous descriptions of historical or social facts of life. Therefore, hagiography is not the best form of literature to learn about the experience of the travellers. The concrete circumstances of the journeys, the roads and sights, the legends and traditions connected with particular buildings and places are best reflected in the Greek travellers' accounts as well as in the *proskynetaria*, guidebooks, composed mainly in the famous monastery of St. Sabbas near Jerusalem.[19]

The tradition of these Greek sources starts considerably later. In early Byzantine times all important writings which come down to us were composed in Latin, for example the *Itinerarium Burdigalense*, written in the year 333, the *Peregrinatio ad loca sancta*, written by the Spanish nun Egeria in c. 380, the *Proskynetarion de situ terrae sanctae*, composed by Theodosios the archdeacon in c. 520, or the *Itinerarium Antonii Placentini*, written in the year 570.[20] In contrast, the first account of a Greek pilgrim which is known today, the first redaction of *Ad modum descriptionis situs orbis enarratio Syriae, Urbis Sanctae, et Sacrorum ibi Locorum* by the monk Epiphanios Hagiopolites, dates from after 638.[21] This literary genre is characterised by a strong personal element. However, on the whole, there are not so many texts. This is perhaps a result of the deeply respected ideal of rhetoric in Byzantium which may have deterred many travellers from writing down their

---

[18] Chariton: see G. Garitte, 'La vie prémétaphrastique de s. Chariton', *Bulletin de l'Institut Belge de Rome* 21 (1941), 5-50; Chariton and Gerasimos: see H.-G. Beck, *Kirche und theologische Literatur im Byzantinischen Reich* (Munich, 1959), 203; for other saints mentioned: see E. Malamut, *Sur la route des saints byzantins* (Paris, 1993), passim.

[19] See A. Kuelzer, 'Wallfahrtsliteratur', *LexMA* 8 (1997), 1983f. For a different point of view on the value of hagiography for details of travel, cf. the chapters by McCormick and Pryor in this volume.

[20] The following are in *Itineraria et alia Geographica*, CCSL 175 (Turnhout, 1965): Itinerarium Burdigalense: P. Geyer and O. Cuntz, eds., 1-26; Itinerarium Egeriae: Aet. Franceschini and R. Weber, eds., 27-103; Theodosii de situ terrae sanctae: P. Geyer, ed., 113-125; Itinerarium Antonii Placentini: P. Geyer, ed., 127-174.

[21] There are two more redactions, the latest one from about 900; the first redaction from after 638 mentions only Jerusalem and some 'holy places' along the banks of the River Jordan; the later redaction of the treatise includes Egypt, Galilee and Mount Sinai. See H. Donner, 'Die Palästinabeschreibung des Epiphanios Hagiopolites', *ZDPV* 87 (1971), 42-91; Kuelzer, *Peregrinatio graeca*, 14-17.

experiences. It could be a real effort for simple pilgrims to become authors and men of letters. For obvious reasons most of the travellers' accounts are written by religious authors, often even clergymen, such as John Phokas in the twelfth century, Perdikas of Ephesos in the fourteenth century, Daniel of Ephesos in the fifteenth century or Paisios Hagiapostolites in the late sixteenth century. Others were written by ambassadors such as Constantine Manasses in the twelfth, Andrew Libadenos in the fourteenth or Theodosios Zygomalas in the sixteenth century. Jakobos Meloites who wrote his *Hodoiporikon* in 1588 was a merchant.[22]

In contrast to the few Greek travellers' tales there are many guidebooks or *proskynetaria* preserved. These are geographical commentaries on the Old and the New Testament, a kind of *gebrauchsliteratur*, written to guide the pilgrims through *terra sancta*. The first *proskynetarion* which has survived was composed in the middle of the thirteenth century; it is therefore about 900 years later than the *Itinerarium Burdigalense*, the description of the famous Bordeaux pilgrim.[23] Scholars cannot easily explain this late beginning, but one should remember the arbitrariness of the text tradition. Up to the fourteenth century the composition of the *proskynetaria* was very individual and without any specific form, but thereafter three traditions developed, one of them in political verse.[24]

But what do the sources say about 'daily life'? Which aspects of Byzantine pilgrimage to the Holy Land do we really know about? From the time of the crusades, pilgrims normally reached *terra sancta* by ship. Travel by land along the endless dusty roads of Asia Minor, a route which Theodore of Sykeon for example had used three times in the seventh century, was regarded as too dangerous. The pilgrim ships usually were provided by Venice, sometimes also by Genoa. Only exceptionally did the Byzantines have ships of their own. Starting in Constantinople, the journey was made through the Propontis and the

---

[22] Kuelzer, *Peregrinatio graeca*, 13-35. Sources: K. Horna, 'Das Hodoiporikon des Konstantin Manasses', *BZ* 13 (1904), 313-55. Th. Baseu-Barabas, 'Perdikas von Ephesos und seine Beschreibung Jerusalems: die Heiligen Stätten gesehen von einem Byzantiner des 14. Jahrhunderts', *Symmeikta* 11 (1997), 151-88. See below, nn. 29, 30, 32, 33. The account of Theodosios Zygomalas can be found in A. Papadopoulos-Kerameus, *PPS* 56 (St. Petersburg, 1903), 41-54.

[23] A. Papadopoulos-Kerameus, Μερικὴ Διήγησις ἐκ τῶν ἁγίων τόπων τῆς Ἱερουσαλὴμ διὰ τὰ πάθη τοῦ κυρίου ἡμῶν Ἰησοῦ Χριστοῦ καὶ ἄλλων τινῶν. Πονημάτιον Ἀνωνύμου γραφὲν μεταξὺ 1253 καὶ 1254, *PPS* 40 (St. Petersburg, 1895). See Kuelzer, *Peregrinatio graeca*, 41f.

[24] Kuelzer, *Peregrinatio graeca*, 35-62. See S. N. Kadas, Προσκυνητάρια τῶν ἁγίων τόπων (Thessalonike, 1986), 52-57.

Aegean to the islands of the Cyclades or the Dodecanese. Then some pilgrims went to Egypt; sometimes they visited Crete from where, as we know, connections existed to Alexandria and to Damietta at the Nile delta.[25] But most pilgrims sailed directly from the Aegean to Palestine, either along the coasts of Lycia, Pamphylia and Syria or directly across the Mediterranean. If they did the latter, they would stop at Cyprus: Epiphanios Hagiopolites, for instance, mentions a connection from the island to the town of Tyre.[26] The most important harbour for the pilgrims in late and early post-Byzantine times was Jaffa, because of its short distance to Jerusalem. The harbours of St. Symeon near Antioch and of Akkon or Ptolemais, which were often used even in the times of the crusaders, had later largely lost their significance.

In Palestine travellers used a road system which partly dated from pre-Roman times, had received its main extension in the days of the emperor Hadrian (117-38), and was only in some cases maintained and improved in later centuries.[27] At least in the middle ages the main connections were in good condition, as was, for example, the road from Jaffa to Jerusalem.[28] In the twelfth century John Phokas describes the paved road from Samareia to Jerusalem but the same author characterises the well-known street from the 'holy city' to Jericho as 'rough, narrow, and without any pavement'.[29] Little is known about the roads in Syria and Egypt; perhaps their condition was not especially good. However, Paisios Hagiapostolites, later metropolitan bishop of Rhodes, describes the road from Mount Sinai to the small town of

---

[25] Anon. Cod. Pauli Lambri saec. XV: A. Papadopoulos-Kerameus, ed.,'Ὀκτὼ ἑλληνικαὶ περιγραφαὶ τῶν ἁγίων τόπων ἐκ τοῦ ιδ', ιε' καὶ ις' αἰῶνος, PPS 56 (St. Petersburg, 1903), chap. 1.

[26] H. Donner, 'Die Palästinabeschreibung des Epiphanios Hagiopolites', ZDPV 87 (1971), 66.

[27] D. A. Dorsey, *The roads and highways of Ancient Israel* (Baltimore, London, 1991) (pre-Roman times); M. Avi-Yonah, 'Palaestina', RE Suppl. 13 (1973), 321-454, esp. 436-443: 'Das Straßennetz'. See, further, W. Heinz, *Straßen und Brücken im Römischen Reich* (Jona, Feldmeilen, 1988) and R. Chevallier, *Les voies romaines* (Paris, 1997).

[28] M. L. Fischer, B. Isaac, I. Roll, *Roman roads in Judäa: The Jaffa-Jerusalem roads*. BAR International series 628 (Oxford, 1996).

[29] J. Troickij,'Ἰωάννου τοῦ Φοκᾶ ἔκφρασις ἐν συνόψει τῶν ἀπ' Ἀντιοχείας μέχρις Ἱεροσολύμων κάστρων καὶ χωρῶν Συρίας, Φοινίκης καὶ τῶν κατὰ Παλαιστίνην ἁγίων τόπων', PPS 23 (St. Petersburg, 1889), chap. 14, for the first road, chap. 20, for the second road. See A. Kuelzer, 'Konstantinos Manasses und Johannes Phokas — zwei byzantinische Orientreisende des 12. Jahrhunderts', in X. von Ertzdorff and G. Giesemann, eds., *Erkundung und Beschreibung der Welt. Zur Poetik der Reise- und Länderberichte. Vorträge eines interdisziplinären Symposiums vom 19.-24. Juni 2000 an der Justus-Liebig-Universität Gießen* (Amsterdam, Atlanta), in press.

Rhaitou at the shore of the Red Sea in the second part of the sixteenth century; he calls it 'long but not unpleasant'.[30]

Most of the pilgrims probably travelled on foot. It seems that the use of donkeys, although legitimised by the events of Palm Sunday,[31] was a privilege of the members of the higher classes. Horses are not mentioned; these animals belonged more to soldiers or to secular travellers than to pilgrims on their way to the 'holy places'. Longer distances, especially straight through the deserts, were covered by using camels. There is some evidence concerning travel on camels in journeys from Jerusalem or from Cairo to the monastery of St. Catherine on Mount Sinai. In Rhaitou people were able to rent camels to cover the way from the Red Sea to Cairo. However, as Paisios Hagiapostolites complains, camels were very expensive to rent.[32] Coaches and carts, very usual in central European countries, were only rarely documented in *terra sancta*: with the exception of the well-known statement by the Latin pilgrim Arculf in the late sixth century we know only one further reference, a passing remark transmitted in the *Periegesis*, a traveller's account written by the Byzantine ambassador Andrew Libadenos in the fourteenth century.[33]

The sequence of visits to the 'holy places' normally started in Palestine and went through the Sinai peninsula westwards to Egypt. However, we know about some travellers like Daniel of Ephesos who started their pilgrimage in Egypt even in the late fifteenth century and

---

[30] A. Papadopoulos-Kerameus, 'Παισίου 'Αγιαποστολίτου Μητροπολίτου 'Ρόδου ιστορία τοῦ ἁγίου ὄρους Σινᾶ καὶ τῶν περιχωρῶν αὐτοῦ', PPS 35 (St. Petersburg, 1891), l. 1798. See A. Kuelzer, 'Die Sinaibeschreibung des Paisios Hagiapostolites, Metropolit von Rhodos (1577/92)', in X. von Ertzdorff and R. Schulz, eds., *Beschreibung der Welt. Zur Poetik der Reise- und Länderberichte* (Amsterdam, Atlanta, 2000), 205-218. For the roads cf. E. Honigmann, 'Syria', RE II 8 (1932), 1549-1727, esp. 1645-1650; St. E. Sidebotham, 'Römische Straßen in der Ägyptischen Wüste', Antike Welt 22 (1991), 177-189.

[31] Cf. N. Ohler, *Reisen im Mittelalter*, 2nd edn. (Munich, Zürich, 1988), 35-44.

[32] Kuelzer, *Peregrinatio graeca*, 98-100. The camels are mentioned in the treatises written by Daniel of Ephesos, Paisios Hagiapostolites and Jacobos Meloites: G. Destounis, 'Διήγησις Δανιὴλ μητροπολίτου 'Εφέσου καὶ περίοδος τῶν τόπων', PPS 8 (St. Petersburg, 1884), chap. 4; A. Papadopoulos-Kerameus,'Παισίου 'Αγιαποστολίτου', PPS 35 (St.Petersburg, 1891), ll. 1945-1960, 1965; Sp. K. Papageorgiou, "Οδοιπορικὸν 'Ιακώβου Μηλοίτου', Parnassos 6 (1882), 632-642, 635f. See also, in general, R. J. Forbes, 'The coming of the camel', in Ch. Singer, et al., *Studies in Ancient Technology*, II (Leiden, 1965), 193-209, and R. W. Bulliet, *The Camel and the Wheel* (New York, 1990).

[33] O. Lampsides,'Ανδρέου Λιβαδηνοῦ βίος καὶ ἔργα (Athens, 1975), 47, 16-18. For Arculf see J. Wilkinson, *Jerusalem Pilgrims* (as in n. 17), 16. Shipping routes are unimportant in this context, with the exception of the River Nile: Andrew Libadenos, Daniel of Ephesos and Jacobos Meloites are known to have gone from Alexandria to Cairo by ship: Kuelzer, *Peregrinatio graeca*, 100.

travelled — sometimes after a short stay at Mount Sinai — across the old Roman road along the Mediterranean which western sources often mention, via Gaza eastwards to the 'holy city' of Jerusalem.

But let us discuss the sightseeing programme the Greek pilgrims completed, going from the north, from Syria, to the south, to Egypt. In Syria they visited only a few places;[34] John Phokas, for example, stayed for some time in Antioch and its suburbs, then travelled southwards via Laodiceia, Gabala and Tripolis on the same coastal road the Bordeaux pilgrim had used some eight hundred years before. Sites not on the coast of the Mediterranean but in the interior of the country, like Damascus, were hardly ever visited by Greek pilgrims. The importance of the whole region with its few 'holy places', distant from each other, diminished substantially when pilgrims normally did not travel by land any longer but used ships to go directly to the harbour of Jaffa. Palestine, *terra sancta* in the narrow sense, was obviously the most important aim for all Christian pilgrims.[35] The long and extended sightseeing that pious believers had undertaken in the area from Galilee in the north to the southern shore of the Dead Sea in the first centuries A.D. was reduced in late and early post-Byzantine times to some selected landscapes. The lake of Galilee and the lake of Hula, now drained, the towns of Capernaum and Tiberias, Caesarea Philippi, Nazareth and Cana, also Mount Carmel and Mount Tabor were probably not visited by Greek pilgrims. The *proskynetaria* normally simply mention these place-names but without any detailed description, only 'to complete the picture'.

The most important destination for any Christian pilgrimage is the 'holy city' of Jerusalem,[36] which in the middle ages could be reached from Jaffa through Lydda-Diospolis, the place where St. George was made a martyr, and Nikopolis, one of the three villages connected with the biblical Emmaus. In Jerusalem itself the church of the Holy Sepulchre, built in 326 A.D., is a special place of prayer and devotion. After 1149, after several rebuildings and renovations, it included various renowned New Testament places, above all Mount Golgotha and

---

[34] In general, R. Dussand, *Topographie historique de la Syrie antique et médiévale* (Paris, 1927); I. Peña, *Lieux de pèlerinage en Syrie* (Milan, 2000).

[35] For their aims, see Y. Tsafrir, *Ancient churches revealed* (Jerusalem, 1993); G. S. P. Freeman-Grenville, *The Holy Land: a pilgrim's guide to Israel, Jordan and the Sinai* (New York, 1996); J. Murphy-O'Connor, *The Holy Land: an Oxford archaeological guide: from earliest times to 1700* (Oxford, New York, 1998). Cf. also n. 2.

[36] As a *pars pro toto* see F. E. Peters, *Jerusalem. The Holy City in the eyes of chroniclers, visitors, pilgrims, and prophets from the days of Abraham to the beginnings of modern times* (Princeton, 1985).

the Tomb of Jesus of Nazareth.[37] Although the Greek pilgrim writings describe numerous sights there they never fail to mention the miracle of the 'holy light' in the evening of the Anastasis which emphasises the sacred character of the place. The Greek pilgrims visited Mount Sion, the Mount of Olives and Gethsemane east of Kidron valley, the church of St. Anna, regarded as the House of the Theotokos and her parents, the site of Bethany two miles from the 'holy city' and some other sites. After this they went to Bethlehem or down to old Jericho and the River Jordan.[38] In the lower reaches of the river north of the Dead Sea there are some orthodox monasteries like St. John the Forerunner, St. Theodosios Koinobiarches, and the Laura of St. Sabbas, important places, visited by the pilgrims up to post-Byzantine times.

Many Greek pilgrims were not afraid of the hardships of the long journey down to the Sinai peninsula to visit Mount Sinai or Horeb, the 'holy place' where God was said to have revealed Himself to Moses, and to Mount Katrina and the monastery of St. Catherine, founded by Justinian I (527-65), where the believers could pay devotion to the Holy Bush, to some miraculous icons and, from the fourteenth century on, to the relics of St. Catherine of Alexandria.[39] From the second century A.D. and later, the whole area was inhabited by Christian ascetics who had the desire to stay in its special atmosphere, to live near this well-known 'stairway to the cosmos'. Especially from the sixth century, a great number of chapels, shrines and places of worship appeared which would be destinations of Christian pilgrims. A *proskynetarion* composed in the last days of the Byzantine empire, the so-called *Anonymus Allatii*, mentions 60 sacred places on Mount Sinai.[40]

Along an often mentioned road, people travelled northwards via the oasis of Pharan and Rhaitou at the shore of the Red Sea to Egypt.[41] Here the Greek pilgrims, like all the other travellers, visited Suez and the town of Aigyptos, the modern Cairo. They remembered the events

---

[37] Cf. Ch. Coüasnon, *The Church of the Holy Sepulchre in Jerusalem* (London, 1974).

[38] N. Glueck, *The River Jordan. Being an illustrated account of earth's most storied river* (Philadelphia, 1946).

[39] Cf. Kuelzer, *Peregrinatio graeca*, 260-266; also cf. J. J. Hobbs, *Mount Sinai* (Austin, 1995); M. Saad el Din, *Sinai: The site and the history: essays* (New York, 1998); D. Valbelle and Ch. Bonnet, eds., *Le Sinai durant l' Antiquité et le Moyen Age: 4000 ans d' histoire pour un désert* (Paris, 1998).

[40] Chap. 9 in L. Allatius, Ἀπόδειξις περὶ τῶν Ἱεροσολύμων, PG 133.973-999, here 984.

[41] S. Clarke, *Christian antiquities in the Nile valley: a contribution towards the study of the ancient churches* (Oxford, 1912); D. Frankfurter, ed., *Pilgrimage and holy space in late antique Egypt* (Leiden, Boston, 1998); J. E. Goehring, *Ascetics, society, and the desert: studies in Egyptian monasticism* (Harrisburg, Penn., 1999).

at the River Nile, so well known from the Old Testament, and kept on travelling to the pyramids of Gizeh. On the basis of Genesis 41. 46-49, Stephen of Byzantium considered these buildings in the sixth century A.D. to be Joseph's grain silos;[42] this tradition was readily reported in the middle ages, although in post-Byzantine times some travellers like Daniel of Ephesos in 1480-81 or Paisios Hagiapostolites at the end of the sixteenth century knew about their real function as sepulchres of Egyptian pharaohs.[43] The last-named traveller described his visit to one of the four pyramids of Gizeh in such a detailed manner that we are able to identify this building with the pyramid of Pharaoh Chefren.[44]

The Byzantine and early post-Byzantine travellers' accounts and *proskynetaria* give insight into aspects of daily life: for example, the condition of the roads, the number and character of buildings at a particular 'holy place', their state of preservation and the tales and legends connected with them, the distribution of property which the various Christian confessions had on specific sites and, last but not least, the relationship between orthodox pilgrims and members of different religious communities. Through these accounts the reader of today is able to understand many aspects of Byzantine pilgrimage to the Holy Land. Other aspects which are not connected with the 'holy' but with the 'disordered', with the secular world — the manifold problems of supply or accommodation[45] — are more hinted at than reported, while observations concerning social and cultural history, like the Arabs' way of arming, dressing or eating, are not mentioned at all. This disregard for the secular justifies the long theoretical reflections at the beginning, and was this chapter's most central concern. The special character of pilgrimage literature in Greek shows very clearly that the Holy Land was still of high importance in the world of Byzantine thought; continual *peregrinatio graeca in terram sanctam* allows us to see the often emphasised significance of Constantinople in a more relative way. This conclusion enables us to come closer to the reality of the much discussed *homo byzantinus*.[46]

---

[42] A. Meinecke, ed., *Stephani Byzantii Ethnicorum quae supersunt* (Berlin, 1849; repr. Graz, 1958), 540.

[43] Kuelzer, *Peregrinatio graeca*, 159f.

[44] A. Papadopoulos-Kerameus, 'Παισίου 'Αγιαποστολίτου', *PPS* 35 (St. Petersburg, 1891), ll. 2233-2239.

[45] Cf. C. Galatariotou, 'Travel and perception in Byzantium', *DOP* 47 (1993), 221-241.

[46] On *homo byzantinus* see A. Kazhdan, G. Constable, *People and Power in Byzantium. An Introduction to Modern Byzantine Studies* (Washington, D.C., 1982).

Section III
Being there

11. Bilingual word lists and phrase lists: for teaching or for travelling?

K. Ciggaar

'Quid boni dat [imperator]? Satis nummos et arma.'[1]

'What bounty does [the emperor] give? Sufficient money and arms.'

Learning languages has always been useful for travelling abroad or for meeting foreigners in one's own country. People living in the middle ages realised this. The thousands and thousands of travellers to the east, pilgrims, crusaders, adventurers and many others, could see that the building of the tower of Babel had had its effects on the eastern world as well.

Travelling to and in the Byzantine world made clear that Greek was not the only spoken language in the east. There were also Armenian, Syriac, Hebrew, Arabic, and the languages of other minorities in the Byzantine empire and of the numerous visitors from neighbouring areas. In spite of the great diversity of languages and the many people who travelled from one place to another, the study of languages for practical purposes hardly existed.[2]

Here I shall pay attention only to the linguistic problems of western travellers during the tenth, eleventh and twelfth centuries, largely the crusading period. For western Europe I shall mainly deal with the use of Latin.[3]

---

[1] W. J. Aerts, 'Froumund's Greek: an analysis of fol. 12v of the Codex Vindobonensis graecus 114, followed by a comparison with a Latin-Greek wordlist in MS Auxerre fol. 137ff.', in A. Davids, ed., *The Empress Theophano. Byzantium and the West at the turn of the first millennium* (Cambridge, 1995), 194-210, here 204.

[2] B. Bischoff, 'The study of foreign languages in the middle ages', *Speculum* 36 (1961), 209-224.

[3] Interesting phrase lists were compiled in the thirteenth century, e.g. G. Ineichen, 'Il

Learning Greek or the other languages spoken in the Byzantine empire was not really necessary for all those westerners who went eastward. There was plenty of opportunity to find interpreters if necessary. Depending on the social status of a visitor to Constantinople there was a wide choice, sometimes an obligation to use special interpreters. Ambassadors were given interpreters by the imperial court from the corps of professional interpreters. They were active during official, unofficial, and private conversations. Larger groups of pilgrims and crusaders were given guides upon entering Byzantine territory. They were able to speak a western language or had people in their services who could do so. Merchants could be served by compatriots living in one of the foreign colonies in Constantinople and elsewhere. Individual visitors, mostly pilgrims, who were given permission to visit Constantinople as tourists, could find local guides who had a few rudiments of a foreign language, enough to take them around the tourist highlights, or they could appeal to compatriots living in Constantinople where so many nationalities lived and worked together. There were also the children of mixed marriages who could handle more than one language.[4] Numerous references to interpreters can be found in historical and literary texts.[5]

An assessment of the level of knowledge of Greek among western Europeans is almost impossible. In consequence it will be difficult to write a survey of the knowledge of Greek in western Europe. References are not always very clear; the level of knowledge of the Greek language is hardly ever described.[6] The same goes for the knowledge of Latin by

---

glossario arabo-francese di messer Guglielmo e maestro Giacomo', *Atti dell'Istituto Veneto di scienze, lettere ed arti: Classe di scienze morali, lettere ed arti* 130 (1971-1972), 353-407; G. Maspero, 'Le vocabulaire français d'un Copte du XIIIe siècle', *Romania* 17 (1888), 481-512.

[4] For the Great Interpreter, a title signalled for the first time in the twelfth century, see D. A. Miller, 'The Logothete of the Drome in the middle Byzantine period', *Byz* 36 (1966), 438-70, esp. 452, and below note 5; a number of interpreters are known by their seals; see also *ODB*, s.v. Interpreters.

[5] In Latin texts *interpres*, e.g. Guillaume de Jumièges, *Gesta Normannorum ducum*, ed. J. Marx (Rouen and Paris, 1914), 112, in the new edn. with English translation by E. M. C. van Houts (Oxford, 1995), II, 82, where Robert of Normandy visits Constantinople; William of Tyre, *Chronicon*, ed. R. B. C. Huygens (Turnhout, 1986), 855 (in 1160-1161 a Greek mission came to the crusader states); in Old French *druguemant*, e.g. Chrétien de Troyes, Cligés, ed. A. Micha (Paris, 1957, 2nd edn. 1970), 119, ll. 3913-3914 (*Et fet par un suen druguemant,/qui greu savoit et alemant*); La chanson de Gérart de Roussillon, ed. and trans. M. de Combarieu du Grès and G. Gouiran (Paris, 1993), Lettres Gothiques, 48-49, IX (6): *L'empereur m'a fait accompagner par des interprètes et je me suis rendu au saint sépulcre*.

[6] W. Berschin, *Griechisch-Lateinisches Mittelalter* (Berne and Munich, 1980); English trans. J. J. Frakes, *Greek letters and the Latin Middle Ages*, rev. edn. (Washington, D.C., 1988), passim.

the Greeks. If we consider the Byzantine view of other people, i.e. a great contempt for everybody not Byzantine, we can safely assume that this knowledge was rather limited, not to say defective.

From the Byzantine side we have a short phrase list written in the twelfth century by John Tzetzes in the epilogue to his *Theogony*. The author pretends that he was able to greet people from various nations. That he was boasting becomes clear from the rather unpleasant way he salutes some people. He was either completely ignorant of the meaning of the words or he was a very unpleasant and rude person, or he thought he was being funny. His approach to the Latins, a term which designates a great variety of westerners, is neutral:

> To a Latin I speak in the Latin language:
> Welcome, my lord, welcome, my brother:
> *Bene venesti, domine, bene venesti, frater.*
> Wherefrom are you, from which theme do you come?
> *Unde es et de quale provincia venesti?*
> How have you come, brother, to this city?
> *Q[u]omodo, frater, venesti in istam civitatem?*
> On foot, on horse, by sea? Do you wish to stay?
> *Pezos, caballarius, per mare? Vis morare?*[7]

One wonders which people spoke Latin when they visited the Byzantine empire. The vernacular languages must have been in use by all those who did not belong to the Church. The fact that John Tzetzes wrote 'his languages' in Greek characters seems an indication that his linguistics were phonetic rather than grammatical. In other words, he wrote down what he had heard. If so, he listened rather carefully if we compare his results with western examples of similar exercises.

In times of peace it was all right to have a very limited knowledge of a language, partly based on phrase lists. Times of crisis, however, require a more sophisticated linguistic approach. Medieval travellers themselves were aware of this, as Odo of Deuil's report of the Second Crusade shows. When the many crusaders were before Constantinople, quarrels occurred. Odo of Deuil oberved that 'when one person accuses another in a very loud voice without understanding him, there is a brawl'.[8]

---

[7] H. Hunger, 'Zum Epilog der Theogonie des Johannes Tzetzes', *BZ* 46 (1953), 304-305, and *Byzanz, eine Gesellschaft mit zwei Gesichtern* (Copenhagen, 1984), 12-13; see N. G. Wilson, *Scholars of Byzantium* (London, 1983), 192; A. Kazhdan and A. Wharton Epstein, *Change in Byzantine culture in the eleventh and twelfth centuries* (Berkeley, 1985), 259, for the English translation from which I quote here.

[8] Odo of Deuil, *De profectione Ludowici VII. in Orientem*, ed. and trans. V. G. Berry (New

Such a crisis situation is also described by Niketas Choniates when the Greeks fled the capital after the Latin conquest of 1204. When a young girl was abducted by a Latin soldier, Niketas could free her only by asking help from Latin soldiers who had some knowledge of Greek.[9] In that same year an old Greek priest who knew the *romana lingua* imperfectly, was able to calm down a rude Latin abbot, Martin of Pairis, who had entered his church to get hold of relics. Gunther of Pairis describes the incident in his *Hystoria Constantinopolitana*, apparently not ashamed of the despicable behaviour of his abbot:

> The old man was truly terrified by the shouting rather than by the words, inasmuch as he heard the former but could not understand the latter. Knowing that Martin could not communicate in the Greek tongue, the old man began to speak the Roman language, which he had learned to an extent, in order to appease the man with flattery and mollify his anger (which really did not exist). In reply, the abbot was barely able to force out a few words of the same language, in order to communicate to the old man what he demanded of him.[10]

One wonders if the Greek priest used a few stereotyped phrases of the kind listed above. Whatever his knowledge of the language was, he succeeded in communicating with the intruder. I have related the episode in full to show what kinds of situations could occur and how difficult it could be if one was not able to communicate in another language.

The mixed population of Constantinople enabled Greeks and Latins alike to learn the colloquial language of the other group, phrases of everyday life, as appear in John Tzetzes's work. Some westerners seem to have learnt Greek in a more systematic way, in the *scola Greca* which was possibly an annexe to the 'Patriarchal School' of

---

York, 1948), 44-45: *Ubi enim alter alterum non intelligens cum clamosa voce impetit, garritus est.*

[9] *Nicetae Choniatae Historia*, ed. J.-L. van Dieten (Berlin, New York, 1975), 590; H. J. Magoulias, *O City of Byzantium, Annals of Niketas Choniates* (Detroit, 1984), 324-325.

[10] It has been suggested that the *romana lingua* which the old man 'had learned to an extent' (*quam ex parte noverat*) was Latin or a north Italian patois used for commercial purposes: *Gunther von Pairis, Hystoria Constantinopolitana*, ed. P. Orth (Hildesheim, 1994), 159, 201, index, suggests that it was Latin; *The Capture of Constantinople. The "Hystoria Constantinopolitana" of Gunther of Pairis*, English trans. A. J. Andrea (Philadelphia, 1997), 109-111, 172-173, n. 240, thinks that it was Italian. [Editor's note: since the abbot of Pairis was 'barely able to force out a few words of the same language', the 'romana lingua' cannot have been Latin. For a twelfth-century use of 'romana lingua' to mean French, see *Gesta Herwardi*, ed. T. D. Hardy and C. T. Martin, in Gaimar, *L'Estoire des Engles*, Rerum britannicarum medii aevi scriptores (1888-89), I, 385.]

Constantinople. A late eleventh-century western pilgrim studied Greek there. Another westerner was allowed to use the library of this institution.[11]

Diplomats in the west could learn the basics of Greek, including some polite phrases, from returning compatriots who had resided in the Greek capital or from Greek monks who occasionally travelled in western Europe. For official missions interpreters were needed. The Byzantine court disposed of a corps of such professionals.[12]

In the eleventh century bishop Benno II of Osnabrück promoted a school of languages where Greek and Latin were taught. The many embassies going from Germany to the Byzantine empire formed the justification for this initiative for practical training. By issuing a false diploma, the bishop pretended that the school had been founded by Charlemagne. It was an important initiative which he introduced as follows: 'And therefore we have affirmed this, because we have ordained that in this place there should be perpetually a Greek and a Latin school, so that there should never be a shortage of clerics able to speak the two languages.' It was an interesting start, the more so since both Latin and Greek were part of the curriculum.[13]

This brings us to the topic of this paper: the bilingual word lists, called glossaria or glossaries, which existed in various monastic libraries. As we have seen, the bishop of Osnabrück placed his language school under the aegis of Charlemagne. It was during Charlemagne's reign that the interest in Greek and the teaching of Greek increased. The contacts between the western empire and Byzantium were frequent. A number of matrimonial alliances was planned.[14] There were also contacts concerning theological questions like the adoration or veneration of images.

---

[11] *Le Guide du Pèlerin de Saint-Jacques de Compostelle*, ed. J. Vielliard (Paris, 1984), 65; K. N. Ciggaar, 'Une description de Constantinople dans le *Tarragonensis* 55', *REB* 53 (1995), 125, ll. 265-266.

[12] J. M. McNulty and B. Hamilton, 'Orientale lumen et magistra Latinitas: Greek influences on western monasticism (900-1100)', in *Le Millénaire du Mont Athos, 963-1963, Etudes et Mélanges,* I (Chevetogne, 1963), 181-216. For the interpreters at the Byzantine court see also Miller, 'The Logothete' (as in n. 4), passim.

[13] W. Ohnsorge, *Abendland und Byzanz* (Darmstadt, 1958; repr. 1979), 277, 538-539; Berschin, *Griechisch-Lateinisches Mittelalter* (as in n. 6), 9-10: *Et hoc ea de causa statuimus, quia in eodem loco Grecas et Latinas scolas in perpetuum manere ordinavimus et nunquam clericos utriusque linguare gnaros ibi deesse.*

[14] A. Davids, 'Marriage negotiations between Byzantium and the West and the name of Theophano in Byzantium (eighth to tenth centuries)', in *The Empress Theophano* (as in n. 1), 104.

The interest in the Greek language as such can be seen in the compilation of Latin-Greek word lists where sometimes Greek characters were used for Greek words. These word collections go back to earlier sources and offer sometimes strange etymologies. It is clear that they do not give contemporary spoken Greek. The length of these glossaries varies from a few words to several hundreds of words, like the Laon glossary (Municipal Library, 444) which almost constitutes a small dictionary. A number of glossaries from St. Gall and elsewhere mentions the names of Byzantine charitable institutions like xenodochium, nosochomium, etc., which at an early date had found their way into Latin and gradually lost their Greek connotation if we are to judge from the regular use of these terms to designate such institutions in the west. The reading of these glossaries is not a very exciting experience. This may be one of the reasons why reference is not often made to them. A great number of them has been published by J. Goetz.[15]

These glossaries were compiled out of scholarly interest. They were consulted for synonyms and were used for teaching in the monastic schools. Since most of these glossaries are only word lists, and since the vocabulary was a sort of classical Greek rather than the spoken language, they were probably not used for travelling purposes. This goes also for the few phrase lists, some of which have been published by Goetz.[16] It is interesting to note that Otto III, half-Greek from his mother Theophano, had in his library two glossaries.[17] Otto had Greek teachers, like John Philagathos and Gregory of Burtscheid, who probably taught him Greek. We can only guess what his glossaries were like. Otto's library eventually came to Bamberg, residence of Henry II. When Wolfger of Prüfening, educated at the monastery of Saint Michael in Bamberg, made his compilation of glossaries, he most certainly had access to the library of the Bamberg monastery. The manuscript *Monacensis* Clm. 13002, written in 1158, which contains his compilation, offers phrase lists going back to earlier sources, and which may have been used by Otto III. Some of the phrases remind one of grammar school exercises. One of these, the so-called *colloquia Monacensia*, is explicitly meant for children (*parvulis pueris incipientibus*) which suggests that they were used for school teaching,

---

[15] G. Goetz, *Corpus Glossariorum Latinorum*, I-VII (Leipzig, 1888-1901; repr. 1923); *Lexikon des Mittelalters*, s.v. Glossen, Glossare; *ODB*, s.v. Glossaries, bilingual.

[16] Goetz, *Corpus Glossariorum*, III, e.g. 210-220, 285f., 635-659.

[17] F. Mütherich, 'The Library of Otto III', in P. Ganz, ed., *The Role of the Book in medieval culture* (Turnhout, 1986), 16; for the Ottonians, J. Shepard, 'Byzantium and the West', *New Cambridge Medieval History*, III (Cambridge 1999), 605-623.

rather than for travelling purposes.[18] Otto had to learn Greek for his political education; he dreamt of a *Renovatio imperii*, and a good insight into the Greek world was necessary. Were it not for his untimely death, he would have married a Greek princess and may have planned to travel to the east one day himself. For colloquial Greek, however, he would have been prepared by a native speaker and not by learning the phrase lists in question.

One of the phrase lists of the *Monacensis* Clm. 13002 has been published as a conversation between a crusader and his Byzantine friends.[19] I think we should reconsider this attribution for several reasons. Firstly, the language used in the conversation does not betray any influence of the spoken language of the crusader period, the twelfth century for example. Secondly, Wolfger of Prüfening was probably not interested in modern texts, but was rather an antiquarian collector. Last, but not least, the proper names which figure in the text, Gaius and Lucius, were not very current in Byzantium.[20] One should be very careful in drawing conclusions from the fact that the Munich manuscript was written in the year 1158. Another phrase list in this manuscript introduces the text as follows: 'because I see many who want to discuss in Latin and in Greek, but in Greek it is not easy because of the many difficult words'.[21] One feels tempted to see evidence of a revival of interest in the Greek language in the twelfth century. However, the same wording can be found in a ninth century manuscript of Montpellier (Municipal Library, H 306), introducing another glossary; it was probably copied word for word by a later compiler.[22]

From the above it should be clear that these early bilingual word lists and phrase lists, including a few tenth century siblings, did not function as preparation for a journey eastward. A number of still unpublished glossaries from Ripoll (northern Spain) may reveal more

---

[18] Goetz, *Corpus Glossariorum*, III, 644f., esp. 645; for the manuscript see H.-G. Schmitz, *Kloster Prüfening im 12. Jh.* (Munich, 1975), 111-117, and for Wolfger, 234-238; Berschin, *Griechisch-Lateinisches Mittelalter*, 200, 210.

[19] Goetz, *Corpus Glossariorum*, III, 648-650; M. Triantaphyllides, *Neoellenike grammatike* (Athens, 1938), I, 195-196; G. Thomson, *The Greek Language* (Cambridge, 1960), 51, who dates the conversation to the eleventh century.

[20] Goetz, *Corpus Glossariorum*, 647, 648, 649, 651. The name Lucius occurs only twice in the *PLP*, fasc. 6 (1983), nos. 15149, 15150 (both in the fifteenth century); the name Gaius does not occur at all. Other internal evidence against contemporary Greek influence is the use of artos for bread (647), and oil from Spain (650, 653), which suggests a Spanish origin or connection for the text.

[21] Goetz, *Corpus Glossariorum*, III, 641.

[22] Goetz, *Corpus Glossariorum*, III, 654: *quoniam video multos cupientes Latine disputare et Graece neque facile posse propter difficultatem et multitudinem verborum.*

contemporary linguistic elements since commercial contacts between Catalonia and Byzantium did develop rather quickly from the tenth century onwards.[23]

Travellers who wanted to survive daily life in a foreign country or who wanted to be friendly or make a friendly impression, needed different linguistic help. If they could manage a few phrases to obtain food, drink and accommodation, they were all right, and they had to learn them by heart. If they were literate they need take only a very small piece of parchment for the journey. However, few such linguistic guides have survived. They were either left behind and passed on to others when the journey to Byzantine lands was completed, or lost or thrown away because of intensive use. Two lists have been discovered so far. Others may have survived unnoticed, noted down in an empty corner of a manuscript. A third list seems to have survived only indirectly through a French *roman courtois*.

Interesting is the very short list of phrases and words in a manuscript in the Municipal Library of Avranches, MS 236, fol. 97v, written in the eleventh century. The manuscript comes from Mont Saint-Michel. It is known that the monastery had contacts with the east, and that Greek priests came to Mont Saint-Michel. Norman nobles served in the Byzantine army in the eleventh century. A direct link with a specific person cannot be found. The list is very short, and gives the words and phrases of both languages in Latin characters. There are few errors in the transcription of the Greek language. One finds simple phrases such as: give me bread, give me fish, give me cheese, and meat and beans and apples. Give me a drink, wine, and water and milk. Good appetite, cheers, and a few other phrases and a few words for daily use, such as house, bed, horse, etc. At the end there is a hint of religion where *agnus Dei* (probably known from services in church) is rendered as AMNOS TUTHEU). This bears no relation to the rest of the manuscript.[24]

If one wanted more than simple survival in foreign lands another list could be used, like the one found in a manuscript in the Municipal

---

[23] N. D'Olwer, 'Les glossaires de Ripoll', *Bulletin Du Cange* (= *Archivum latinitatis medii aevi*) 1928, 137-143; L. Llauró, 'Los glosarios de Ripoll', *Analecta Sacra Tarraconensia* 4 (1928), 271-341.

[24] *Catalogue général des manuscrits des bibliothèques publiques de France*, X, Départements, Paris 1889, 115; W. J. Aerts, 'The Latin-Greek wordlist in MS 236 of the Municipal Library of Avranches, fol. 97v', *Anglo-Norman Studies* 9 (1987), 64-69; G. Nortier, 'Les Bibliothèques médiévales des abbayes bénédictines de Normandie', III. La Bibliothèque du Mont Saint-Michel', *Revue Mabillon* 47 (1957), 138; J. J. G. Alexander, *Norman Illumination at Mont St Michel, 966-1100* (Oxford, 1970), 13 (Anastasius, a Greek monk from Venice, visited the monastery).

Library in Auxerre, MS 212 (179), fol. 133v, which was copied in the twelfth century in the monastery of Saint-Pierre-le-Vif, in Sens. The manuscript contains an autograph of the chronicle of the monastery, but information about Byzantium or travellers to the east is scarce. Byzantine treasures are kept in the cathedral of Sens, betraying contacts with Byzantium. However, this is not exceptional since crusaders and pilgrims from all over western Europe and especially from France travelled all the way to Constantinople. For contemporary history in this chronicle there is only an allusion to the sending of the French princess Agnes to Constantinople as a fiancée for Alexios II Komnenos. The rest of the manuscript has no relation with Byzantium or the Greek world. It is not possible to give a proper dating for the list which is, like the list in Avranches, a combination of phrases and words. It is clear, however, that the text was copied more than once, rendering the sense of some Greek words, which were given in Latin characters, so obscure that the recent editor of the text was not able to reconstruct all the Greek. It may have been tradition to copy these specific phrase lists. Even in the Auxerre manuscript one finds the text in two copies with minor differences, as if they were to be cut up and distributed. It may be no coincidence that in this part of the manuscript a few pages are missing. This list is more elaborate than the list in the Avranches manuscript. Various scholars have referred to it as one used by crusaders.[25]

The two phrase lists have certain things in common, words of greeting, asking for bread, terms for clothing, etc. But the differences are remarkable. In the Auxerre list there are sentences asking how the Greek emperor is doing, and how he behaves with the Franks, a term designating all sorts of westerners (*Quid audisti de imperatore greco; ti aquis to apeto vasilio romeco? Quid facit imperator? ti pissem vasilios. [...] Francis calom*). More interesting is the question what the emperor gives and the answer that he gives much money and weapons (*Quid boni dat? Pola lacotina que armata*). Then the traveller asks how to get to

---

[25] L. Delisle, *Le Cabinet historique* 23 (1877), 10-15; Aerts, 'Froumund's Greek', 203-208. For the *strategos*, see H. Glykatzi-Ahrweiler, 'Recherches sur l'administration de l'empire byzantin aux IXe-Xe siècles', *BCH* 84 (1960), 36-52 (repr. in Ahrweiler, *Etudes sur les structures administratives et sociales de Byzance* (London, 1971), no. VIII; the term *strategetes* occasionally occurs: see R. Guilland, *Recherches sur les institutions byzantines* I (Berlin, Amsterdam, 1967), 395. *Chronique de Saint-Pierre-le-Vif de Sens, dite de Clarius*, ed. and trans. R.-H. Bautier (Paris, 1979), 210-211 (who gives the manuscript as no. 212, xiii-xvii); J. Ebersolt, *Orient et Occident. Recherches sur les influences byzantines en France avant et pendant les croisades* (Paris, 2nd edn., 1954), 40 n. 6, 47 and n. 2, 65, 79 119 and n. 9; J. Ebersolt, *Orient et Occident, Recherches sur les influences byzantines en France pendant les croisades* (Paris, 1929), 14, 84.

the castle or *kastron* (*Ubi est via ad castellum? po ne strata oto castro?*), and what the *strategetes* is like (*Qualis homo est prefectus? Pios atropos ene estraiget?*), if he is married and has children (*Habet conjugem et infantes? Equit innecam que pedia?*). The interlocutor hears that the *strategetes* will certainly be good to him (*faciet tibi bonum. pissem si calon*). Elsewhere in the list he asks for benedictions — from a *pater, despota, mater*, and a *roda* (derived from *prota*?) — which suggests that he went to monasteries and convents.[26] One finds the names of some weapons *macherium (cultellum), spatim (spatam), que condarium (et lanceam)* and a military outfit (*loricam*, without an equivalent in Greek, however). It is interesting to find in this text the term *olocotinon/olocotina (lacotina)*. In Greek this name for a *nomisma* does not occur very often.[27]

If I am not mistaken the vocabulary in the Auxerre manuscript, which was recently re-edited by W. J. Aerts, suggests that it was meant for future mercenaries who asked about the emperor, i.e. the political situation in Byzantium, a situation which could change very quickly. I do not think that it was meant for crusaders, as some scholars have assumed. The mercenary was paid in gold (*pola lacotina* = olokotina) and received arms. He had apparently to report to a military commander in a castle somewhere and had to find his way there. If this hypothesis is right the phrase list teaches us something about the Byzantine empire. So far we hardly know from western or Byzantine sources how mercenaries were paid, how they were armed or whether they carried their own arms, and how they got to their regiment or that they had to report to the (military) governor of the province. We know that some leaders of mercenaries, like Harald of Norway, were paid in gold, and that the rest of the mercenaries were happy with food, clothes and a few *nomismata*.[28] From the phrase list in Auxerre we may

---

[26] I thank Jan Olof Rosenqvist for corroborating the hypothesis *roda/prota* by referring me to the *Life* of St. Athanasia of Aegina. See L. Carras, 'The Life of St Athanasia of Aegina. A critical edition with introduction', in A. Moffatt, ed., *Maistor* (Canberra, 1984), 213-214 (English translation in A.-M. Talbot, ed., *Holy women of Byzantium. Ten saints' Lives in English translation* (Washington, D.C., 1996), 144-145.

[27] Aerts, 'Froumund's Greek', 203-208, with commentary; N. A. Bees, 'A propos de la monnaie ΟΛΟΚΟΤΙΝΟΝ', *Revue numismatique* 16 (1912), 84-90. I am grateful to the staff of the Rijksmuseum het Koninklijk Penningkabinet, Leiden, for helping me to find this reference.

[28] Bischoff, 'Study of foreign languages' (as in n. 2), 219; C. Morrisson, 'Le rôle des Varanges dans la transmission de la monnaie byzantine en Scandinavie', in R. Zeitler, ed., *Les Pays du Nord et Byzance* (Uppsala, 1981), 136; Kekaumenos, *Soveti i rasskazi Kekaumena*, ed. G. G. Litavrin (Moscow, 1972), 278, repeated three times. For a German translation of this text see H.-G. Beck, *Vademecum des byzantinischen Aristokraten* (Graz, Vienna, Cologne, 1964), 138.

conclude that not only the great leaders of foreign mercenaries were paid in gold, but those of lower rank as well. Furthermore, it seems that paying one's respects to the clergy of monasteries may have been part of the itinerary of mercenaries; some monasteries may have had the obligation to house the military or help them otherwise. We know that religious institutions could be exempted from accommodating the army, but this may not have applied to individual mercenaries or small groups who had to report to their bases.[29] The use of *vasilio romeco*, 'Roman emperor', suggests that the informant for the list was a Greek, possibly a member of a recruiting mission sent to the west, or someone returning to his homeland after a longer period of service in Byzantium and with a good knowledge of Greek traditions: he knew the real title of the Byzantine emperor. In the west we do not often hear of military leaders returning home after their journey to Byzantium. On an earlier occasion I suggested that the phrase list in Avranches (Normandy) might be related to the two sons of Stigand of Mézidon, Odo and Robert, who both served in Byzantium in the second half of the eleventh century and returned home with great wealth. One of them brought home gold, the other was reputed to handle the Greek language very well, and it may be possible to connect the phrase list in Auxerre, rather than the list in Avranches, with one of them.[30] One thing is clear from the quoted lines: the text has suffered from being copied a number of times, showing that there was a certain demand for such texts. One needs some imagination to find the clue to some Greek words rendered in Latin characters. I hope to have given more sense to the text by proposing a solution for two enigmatic terms, *roda* and *estraiget*.[31]

It is a pity that up to now only two bilingual word/phrase lists for practical use, i.e. for travelling, have survived from the eleventh and twelfth centuries. Apart from travel, the use of such lists must have been very limited. Another possible use may be that of Aimon de Varennes in his *Florimont* (1188). A. Hilka, the editor of the text, has

---

[29] For exemptions and exemption charters see P. Lemerle, *The agrarian history of Byzantium from the origins to the twelfth century* (Galway, 1979), 225-226, and J. Shepard, 'The English and Byzantium: a study of their role in the Byzantine army in the late eleventh century', *Traditio* 29 (1973), 60-63.

[30] K. Ciggaar, 'Byzantine marginalia to the Norman conquest', *Anglo-Norman Studies* 9 (1987), 48-55. Recently the suggestion has been made that Odo Stigand was a *tagmatophylax* (a title which only occurs on seals) rather than a *thalamepoulos*: see E. Amsellem, 'Les Stigand: des Normands à Constantinople', *REB* 57 (1999), 286; also, G. Zacos, *Byzantine Lead Seals*, II (Berne, 1984), nos. 596, 597, 1003.

[31] Maspero, 'Vocabulaire d'un Copte', 481-485, 512, had similar problems.

intepreted the source of the Greek in the romance as a Greek phrase list. *Florimont*, a *roman courtois* of 13,680 lines, is the story of Philip, ancestor of Alexander the Great, whose activities in the Balkans involved the founding of Philippopolis. The French writer says in his work that he found the story for his text in Philippopolis (l. 33: *A Felipople la trova*).[32] One should bear in mind that Philippopolis possessed a Latin monastery dedicated to Saint George outside the walls of the city. A library and a small scriptorium must have been part of it. The crusaders sometimes buried their dead in this church.[33] As for the Greek phrases in the text, Aimon de Varennes may indeed have had recourse to a phrase list such as the one in Auxerre. Overseas Latin monasteries may also have kept such lists. Several expressions and words occur in both lists. If Aimon used a list like the Avranches list, then he combined some of the words with fantasy. Here I shall give the examples:

> *offenda calo* (l. 693), Deus, boin signor (l. 695)
> *uto vassilleo* (l. 694), cest empereor (l. 696)
> *matoteo* (l. 713), Se m'aïst Deux (l. 716)
> *calimera, vasilio* (l. 1303), Que boen jor eüsse(nt) li rois (l. 1306)
> *Cast[r]o* (l. 6332) est: chastiaus en fransois

The expression *calimera, vasilio,* may not have occurred in any phrase list, since the average traveller was not received by the emperor. Even high-placed persons, like the Bulgarian king in *Florimont*, were not allowed to address the emperor in such a way. Since Aimon visited the area, as he explicitly states in his text (ll. 29-36, 167-176, 10213-10216), he may have remembered a few words from the language spoken around him during the journey. He wrote down his story in Châtillon, in the Lyonnais, where he may have had at his disposal such a list or he could have consulted it elsewhere in the region. It is thought that his family came from the area of Berzé. One should bear in mind that the seigneurs of Berzé had a tradition of going to the east. An interesting trace of Aimon's visit to Philippopolis can be seen in his rendering of the name of the nearby river, the Maritsa. He calls it the *Podomen* (l. 852), perhaps misled by the inhabitants who might have referred to the Maritsa as 'the river' (*potamos*), instead of calling it always by its

---

[32] *Aimon von Varennes: Florimont*, ed. A. Hilka (Göttingen, 1932), cii-cvi, esp. ciii, and l. 33.

[33] Odo of Deuil, *De profectione*, ed. and trans. Berry, 44-47.

proper name.[34] His use of 'besants' (ll. 11594, 12439) appears to confirm his familiarity with life in the east.

It has been suggested that Aimon did not know how to pronounce the Greek language and rendered it in a defective way, or that he wanted to enhance his story with some exotic phrases. It seems that he introduced phrases of everyday life, some *realia*, to make this ancient story more real. Constantinople was probably left out to avoid too much anachronism.[35]

In the context of travelling in the Byzantine world it may be useful to look at Aimon's geographical description of parts of the Byzantine empire, where consciously or unconsciously he refers to contemporary events. When he describes Gallipoli (Kallipolis) he tells us that there were three crossings a day in his time. This is a unique statement. We otherwise only occasionally hear of people who crossed the Hellespont from Gallipoli to the Asian side. Gallipoli was a naval base and as such had facilities for the officials who had to travel. Private people had possibly to rely on private enterprise.[36]

The conclusion from the above is simple. The various bilingual glossaries from Carolingian times were used for teaching in monastic schools, were consulted out of scholarly interest, and were used to explain 'difficult' words. They had nothing to do with travelling. The very few bilingual lists that have survived up to now from the crusader period could be very useful for travellers. They are short and their contents are practical. They may have been carried along and thrown away after frequent use. They may even have been used for literary purposes.

A good reading of these lists reveals a few details of the life of travellers, what they had to ask for and what they thought they

---

[34] There is no need to refer to an *Itinerarium* to explain Aimon's name for the Maritsa, as does Hilka, *Aimon von Varennes: Florimont*, c-ci (who cites the *Ravennatis anonymi cosmographia*, ed. M. Pinder and G. Parthey (Berlin, 1860), 185: 'Potamia'). Other travellers may also have been misled in the same way about a river's name. Likewise, the term *protosabato* (l.10826) need not be a mistake for *protostrategos*: Hilka, *Aimon von Varennes*, cv. Westerners may have been familiar with the title of *protosebastos* from members of the imperial family; A. Fourrier, *Le courant réaliste dans le roman courtois en France au Moyen Age. Les débuts (XIIe siècle)* (Paris, 1960), 487-492.

[35] E. Schulze-Busacker, 'French conceptions of foreigners and foreign languages in the twelfth and thirteenth centuries', *Romance Philology* 41 (1987), 39; Fourrier, *Le courant réaliste*, 447-485, esp. 482-485.

[36] Hilka, *Aimon von Varennes*, ll. 173-176: *A Galipol une citeit,/Ou Aymes ot jai maint jor esteit,/Illuec est li bras plus estrois,/Passeir le puet le jor .III. fois*. So far it has been assumed that the ferry crossing from Gallipoli 'became more common' from the thirteenth century: see *ODB*, s.v. Kallipolis, which needs to be corroborated by source references.

ought to know in the other language. As for the phrase/word list in Auxerre it is my guess that it was destined for commanders of a group of mercenaries who travelled in the Byzantine empire. Let us hope that more of these lists will turn up and give us a glimpse of the life of travellers in the Byzantine world.

12. Sightseeing in Constantinople: Arab travellers, c. 900-1300

A. Berger

The reports of Arab writers about the Byzantine empire and about Constantinople consist of two main groups. On the one hand, we have the primary texts, where travellers give an account of what they have seen and experienced themselves; on the other hand, we have short passages in chronicles or in geographical treatises which were compiled from older sources without personal knowledge. It is clear that these secondary texts are based on earlier travellers' accounts, and in some cases we can trace the information back to the original source. But these secondary texts were transmitted for a long time without any contact with reality, so that slowly a kind of standard description of Constantinople developed which contains legends and elements of fantasy.

I will start this paper by introducing to you this secondary description, and show how it was gradually expanded. Substantial parts of it appear already in the writings of Ibn Khurradadhbih in the ninth and of al-Mas'udi in the tenth century; other elements are added by al-Marwazi, al-Idrisi and al-Harawi in the twelfth century; and the final form is known from Yaqut and al-Qazwini in the thirteenth, Abu'l-Fida' and al-Firuzabadi in the fourteenth, and from al-Wardi in the fifteenth century.[1] The last form of this description, that of al-Wardi, was later translated several times into Turkish and therefore also formed the picture that educated Ottomans may have had about

---

[1] An incomplete bibliography is given by J. P. A. van der Vin, *Travellers to Greece and Constantinople. Ancient Monuments and Old Traditions in Medieval Travellers' Tales*, 2 vols., (Istanbul, 1980).

From *Travel in the Byzantine World*, ed. Ruth Macrides. Copyright © 2002 by the Society for the Promotion of Byzantine Studies. Published by Ashgate Publishing Ltd, Gower House, Croft Road, Aldershot, Hampshire, GU11 3HR, Great Britain.

the Christian past of their capital Istanbul.[2] The text of this second-hand description, which became the 'traditional description' by Ottoman times, begins as follows:

> Constantinople is one of the famous cities of the Romans. Its shape is that of a triangle, two sides of it lie to the sea, one to the solid land, where the Golden Gate is. The circuit of the city is nine miles. It has a solid wall of 21 ells height. Around it there is another wall which is called 'the smaller outer wall', of ten ells height. The wall has a hundred gates, of which the biggest is the Tightly Closed Door; it is covered with gold.

This first section, which contains some topographical and geographical information on Constantinople, was repeated with minor changes from the time of the geographical author Ibn Khurradadhbih (825–912).[3] All this is neither very wrong nor very original, and even the given ell measurements are quite correct.

> In the town there is the palace which belongs to the wonders of the world, because in it there is an *ibudhrun*, that means a vestibule of the palace. This is a lane where you pass between two rows of statues from bronze, of excellent work, in the shape of men, horses, elephants, ferocious animals and others. These statues are bigger than those copies that would correspond to their prototypes. In the palace and around it there are still many such wonders.

The second section appears first in the mid-twelfth century in the work of al-Idrisi.[4] It gives additional evidence that at least from the tenth century onwards only the southern part of the Great Palace was still inhabited; the famous Chalke gate at its northern end gradually went out of use, and the actual main entrance was through the hippodrome, through a gate leading directly from the hippodrome into the new

---

[2] F. Taeschner, 'Der Bericht des arabischen Geographen Ibn al-Wardi über Konstantinopel', in H. Mžik, ed., *Beiträge zur historischen Geographie, Kulturgeographie, Ethnographie und Kartographie vornehmlich des Orients* (Leipzig, 1929), 84-91.

[3] *Kitâb al-Masâlik wa'l-Mamâlik (liber viarum et regionum) auctore Ibn Khordâdbeh*, ed. M. J. de Goeje, *Bibliotheca geographorum arabicorum* 6 (Leiden, 1889), 104-105, 76 (translation). Also in al-Mas'udi (895–956): C. Barbier de Meynard and Pavet de Courteille, *Les prairies d' or*, 2 vols. (Paris, 1863).

[4] P.-A. Jaubert, *La Géographie d' Idrisi*, 2 vols. (Paris, 1837–41), 298-299. A text similar to this section is also found in al-Marwazi (died after 1120): V. Minorsky, 'Marvazi on the Byzantines', *Mélanges Henri Grégoire II*, Annuaire de l' Institut de philologie et d' histoire orientales et slaves 10 (1950), 461.

centre of the palace.⁵ However, since two rows of statues are mentioned in the *ibudhrun* which can hardly be identified with the single row on the spina of the great hippodrome, we must assume that the description speaks rather about the covered hippodrome which at this time had become the main vestibule of the palace or that it confused both structures.⁶

The remaining sections of this secondary description can be found for the first time in al-Harawi's handbook about the places of pilgrimage which was written in the late twelfth century. Although it is thought that al-Harawi travelled to Constantinople himself, it must be stated that his picture of the city is largely dominated by legends and travel guides' stories.⁷

> In the town there is a tower which is fastened with iron and lead. It stands on the *maydan*. Whenever wind arises, it inclines to the right and left, back and forward from the place where it stands. They put earthenware below it, and it gets crushed to powder. In the town there is also a tower from bronze, which is one piece and has no door.

These are the two obelisks of the hippodrome, the Egyptian one and the so-called obelisk of Constantine Porphyrogennetos.

> Also there is a tower in the town close to the house of the infirm, completely covered with yellow bronze resembling gold, in a good

---

⁵ This becomes clear, e.g., from the description of a procession in Constantine VII Porphyrogennetos, *De cerimoniis aulae Byzantinae*, ed. I. Reiske, I (Bonn, 1829), 507, 11–15; another procession through the hippodrome to Hagia Sophia was described by Harun b. Yahya around 900 (see below n. 15). The wall of Nikephorus II Phokas (963–969) included only the southern part of the palace area: see E. Mamboury and Th. Wiegand, *Kaiserpaläste von Konstantinopel* (Berlin, 1934), 18-19.

⁶ On the hippodrome in Arab descriptions of Constantinople, see now S. Métivier, 'Note sur l'hippodrome de Constantinople vu par les Arabes', *TM* 13 (2000), 175-180. On the covered hippodrome, see R. Janin, *Constantinople byzantine. Développement urbain et répertoire topographique*, 2nd edn. (Paris, 1964), 119-120; A. Berger, *Untersuchungen zu den Patria Konstantinupoleos* (Bonn, 1988), 263-265.

⁷ Ch. Schefer, 'Aboul Hassan Aly el Herewy, Indications sur les lieux de Pelèrinage', *Archives de l' Orient latin* 1 (1881), 587–609; A. A. Vasiliev, 'Quelques remarques sur les voyageurs du moyen-âge à Constantinople', *Mélanges Ch. Diehl* (Paris, 1930), 294–296. Also in Yaqut (1179–1229): *Jacut's Geographisches Wörterbuch*, ed. F. Wüstenfeld, IV (Leipzig, 1869), 95-96; in al-Qazwini (1203–83): *Zakarija Ben Muhammed Ben Mahmud el-Cazwinis Kosmographie*, ed. F. Wüstenfeld, II (Göttingen, 1848), 406ff.; in Abu'l-Fida' (1273–1331): *Géographie d'Aboulféda*, ed. M. Reinaud and Baron MacGuckin de Slane (Paris, 1840), 212-213; and in al-Firuzabadi (1329–1415): *Al-Qamus al-muhit*, 4 vols. (Cairo, 1289 = 1872/73), s.v. qst.

way and manner. On it there is the grave of Constantine, the founder of Constantinople. On his grave stands the brazen statue of a horse, and on the horse a figure which has the appearance of Constantine; he rides, and the feet of the horse are fixed firmly with lead, except the right front foot which is in the air. He has his right hand raised which points to the countries of the Muslims, and in his left hand is a sphere. This tower can be seen one day's journey from the sea and half a day's journey from the land. They say that in his hand there is a talisman that wards off the enemy, and that there is a Greek inscription on the sphere: 'I ruled the world, until it became in my hand like this sphere, and likewise I have left this world without owning anything from it.'

The object described here is, of course, the column of Justinian.[8] Although the church of Hagia Sophia would be the most natural point of reference to describe its position, instead the hospital of Sampson is mentioned which was actually invisible from the column, since it was situated behind the church.[9] It becomes most obvious here that in the traditional description churches and other Christian monuments are completely ignored. The reason for this was probably not only lack of interest from the side of the visitors, but also that it was not easy for Muslims to get permission to see a church from inside, as we shall presently see.

The description of the column is somewhat surprising, but I hope to demonstrate later how Justinian became Constantine in the imagination of the Arab writers, and how his grave was moved from the church of the Apostles far in the west of Constantinople to the top of the column.

Also there is a tower of white marble on the market *Istabrin*. It is decorated with figures from top to bottom, and its railing is of one piece of bronze. There is a talisman, and if somebody goes up it he sees the whole town. Also there is a bridge which belongs to the wonders of the world. Its length makes the reporter so unable to describe it that he is accused in the end of a lie. Finally there are so many pictures there that they cannot be described.

Only the last section of the account leads us away from the old centre around the Great Palace, the hippodrome and Hagia Sophia. The tower is probably the column of Theodosius in the forum usually called

---

[8] Janin, *Constantinople byzantine* (as in n. 6), 74–76; W. Müller-Wiener, *Bildlexikon zur Topographie Istanbuls* (Tübingen, 1977), 248-249; most recently, C. Mango, 'The columns of Justinian and his successors', *Studies on Constantinople* (Aldershot, 1993), no. X, 3–8.

[9] Janin, *Constantinople byzantine*, 561-562; Müller-Wiener, *Bildlexikon*, 113; Berger, *Untersuchungen* (as in n. 6), 399-400.

Tauros,[10] but the name *Istabrin* suggests rather that the source is speaking about a place name Staurion. Actually there was a place called Staurion half-way between the forum of Constantine and the Tauros which was named after a monumental cross on a column. Close to this column stood a monumental Tetrapylon, covered with brazen reliefs and crowned with a weather-vane on the top of its high pyramidal roof, from which it got the popular name Anemodoulion. The Anemodoulion is now lost, but the surviving descriptions suggest that it must have been nearly as impressive as the Tauros column[11]. I would therefore like to propose that this passage of the traditional description confused the monuments. The location is that of the Anemodoulion, the description that of the column except for the talisman, which may be identified with the weather-vane of the Anemodoulion. Finally, the long bridge in the city is, of course, the aqueduct of Valens.

This is the traditional Arab description of Constantinople, to which some authors add remarks on Greek philosophy or an account of the hippodrome games.

Let us now have a look at the writings of those authors who had actually been to Constantinople, namely Harun b. Yahya who visited the city before 912, and Ibn Battuta who was there in 1332.

Harun b. Yahya's report[12] has come down to us through the geographical work of the contemporary geographer Ibn Rusta. Harun b. Yahya was brought from Syria to Constantinople as a prisoner of war. Since he was the only Arab visitor who described Hagia Sophia and the Nea church in some detail, and since he made a journey to Rome after his release before returning home, it is probable that he was a Christian.[13] However, the audience to which he told his adventures was certainly one of Muslims, as special attention is paid to the conditions of life the Muslim prisoners enjoyed in Constantinople.[14]

---

[10] Janin, *Constantinople byzantine*, 64–68; Müller-Wiener, *Bildlexikon*, 258–265; Berger, *Untersuchungen*, 323–327.

[11] Janin, *Constantinople byzantine*, 100-101; A. Berger, 'Das Chalkun Tetrapylon und Parastaseis, Kapitel 57', *BZ* 90 (1997), 7–12.

[12] A. Vasiliev, 'Harun-ibn-Yahya and his description of Constantinople', *Seminarium Kondakovianum* 5 (1932), 149–163; G. Ostrogorsky, 'Zum Reisebericht des Harun-ibn-Jahja', *Seminarium Kondakovianum* 5 (1932), 251–257; H. Grégoire, 'Un captif arabe à la cour de l'empereur Alexandre', *Byz* 7 (1932), 666–673.

[13] Vasiliev, 'Harun-ibn-Yahya', 162.

[14] Vasiliev, 'Harun-ibn-Yahya', 157. On this, see L. Simeonova, 'In the depths of tenth-century Byzantine ceremonial: the treatment of Arab prisoners-of-war at imperial banquets', *BMGS* 22 (1998), 75-104.

Harun b. Yahya describes in great detail the centre of Constantinople around the hippodrome, and gives an account of a Christmas banquet which was held in the emperor's palace, and of a solemn imperial procession from the palace through the hippodrome to Hagia Sophia.[15] The description has elements of fantasy and legend. Above all, the numbers he gives are greatly exaggerated; for example, Harun tries to make us believe that the number of participants in the procession to Hagia Sophia was more than 50,000. It would take me too far away from my purpose here to analyse all this, so I will confine myself to one short passage which was excerpted by al-Harawi and thus became part of the Arab traditional description, namely that on the column of Justinian. Harun b. Yahya writes:

> Ten paces to the west of the church there is a column of a hundred ells height; it is built column on column and surrounded by chains of silver. On top of the column there is a square slab of marble of four ells square. On it there is a sockle of marble, on which Astilyanos lay, the builder of this church. On this sockle is a brazen horse, and on the horse the statue of Justinian.[16]

We know that Hagia Sophia was built in reality by Anthemios of Tralles and Isidoros of Miletos, and no one has been able to explain why in the legendary *Diegesis peri tes Hagias Sophias* there is only one architect, and why he is called Ignatios.[17] The *Diegesis* seems to go back to the seventh or eighth century, but in the late tenth century the following story was added at the end.[18] Ignatios becomes so famous by the work he has done, that Justinian fears he might be overthrown and Ignatios made emperor instead. Therefore, when the column in front of Hagia Sophia is built and Ignatios works on the top, Justinian lets the scaffolding be removed and expects Ignatios to die from hunger. But during the night Ignatios cuts his clothes into strips with a knife, binds them together and pulls a rope up which his wife has brought secretly; then he fixes the rope around the foot of the horse, slides down to the earth and escapes, and later is pardoned by the emperor.

---

[15] Vasiliev, 'Harun-ibn-Yahya', 158–159; see also A. Berger, 'Imperial and ecclesiastical processions in Constantinople', in N. Necipoğlu, ed., *Byzantine Constantinople: Monuments, Topography and Everyday Life* (Leiden, Boston, Cologne, 2001), 73-87.

[16] Vasiliev, 'Harun-ibn-Yahya', 160.

[17] *Diegesis*, in Th. Preger, ed., *Scriptores originum Constantinopolitanarum* I (Leipzig, 1901), 74–108; E. Vitti, ed., *Die Erzählung vom Bau der Hagia Sophia* (Amsterdam, 1986).

[18] *Diegesis*, in Preger, ed., *Scriptores originum Constantinopolitanarum* II (Leipzig, 1907), IV §31; Vitti, *Die Erzählung*, 488–490, 505–507; see also G. Dagron, *Constantinople imaginaire* (Paris, 1984), 261–263.

It is clearly this story Harun b. Yahya has in mind when speaking about the block of marble, on which the builder of the church lay. The name he bears, Astilyanos, is the Byzantine name Stylianos, and we can assume that it was a part of this story from the beginning, since this word, which actually means 'stylite', is obviously understood here as 'the man who built the *stylos*', that is, the column of Justinian.

We do not know from any Byzantine source about a tradition that makes a man called Stylianos the builder of Hagia Sophia and of the column of Justinian. But it is possible that such a tradition existed. In a thirteenth-century manuscript with Christian epigrams the famous inscription on the fountain of Hagia Sophia, Νίψον ἀνομήματα μὴ μόναν ὄψιν, is labelled τοῦ κυροῦ Στυλιανοῦ, which means 'by kyr Stylianos'.[19] We do not know the identity of this Stylianos and how old the attribution actually is. The name Stylianos does not appear in Byzantium before the ninth century, and the first historical person to bear it was Stylianos, surnamed Mappa, archbishop of Neocaesarea and adversary of Photios.[20] If he was indeed the author of the inscription, as has been assumed,[21] and if he is the historical prototype of the Astilyanos mentioned by Harun b. Yahya, the legend about the origin of the column must have originated within the one generation between his death and the visit of Harun b. Yahya, long before it appeared in the *Diegesis peri tes Hagias Sophias*, now with Ignatios as the hero.

Since the Stylianos story was unknown to modern scholars, the name Astilyanos in Harun b. Yahya's report was usually interpreted as Justinian,[22] although the emperor is mentioned immediately thereafter with his own name as the rider on the horse. And since the later Arab writers did not know the story either, the 'sockle of marble, on which Astilyanos lay, the builder of this church' became quite naturally the grave of the first builder of Hagia Sophia and that is, of course, Constantine the Great, the founder of the city.

Now I will turn to Ibn Battuta (1304–69), the most famous Arab traveller of the middle ages, who was also the last one known to have

---

[19] Appendix Planudea in a later addition to cod. Pal. 523: *Epigrammatum Anthologia Palatina*, ed. F. Dübner II (Paris, 1840), 608.
[20] On this person, see F. Dvornik, *The Photian Schism* (Cambridge, 1948) *passim*; also *Vita Euthymii*, ed. P. Karlin-Hayter (Brussels,1970), commentary 184-188.
[21] K. Preisendanz, *RE* 18/3 (1949), 133.
[22] Vasiliev, 'Harun-ibn-Yahya', 60; van der Vin, *Travellers* (as in n. 1), 492.

stayed in Constantinople personally.[23] Ibn Battuta has left us a long account of his various voyages which in the years between 1325 and 1354 led him to many countries, from India in the east to Morocco in the west. He did most of his travelling in the lands of the Muslims; Constantinople was the only major Christian city he saw. Ibn Battuta arrived there from the north through Bulgaria in the company of a Byzantine princess who had been given in marriage to a khan of the Mongols, and had obtained permission by her husband to visit her family.[24] From its chronological context in Ibn Battuta's work, the voyage must be dated to the year 1332 or 1334.[25] However, there are a number of prosopographical and chronological problems that can be explained only with difficulty. For instance, the princess in whose company Ibn Battuta travelled is only called the *khatun*, the 'lady'; she bears no name and is otherwise unknown. She was probably an illegitimate daughter of Andronikos III.[26]

Ibn Battuta's report about his stay in Constantinople begins with the arrival and entry there which are described with the following words:

> Our entry into Constantinople the Great was made about noon or a little later, and they rang their bells until the very skies shook with the mingling of their sounds. When we reached the first of the gates of the king's palace we found it guarded by about a hundred men, who had an officer of theirs with them on top of a platform, and I heard them saying *Sarakinu, Sarakinu*, which means 'Muslims'. They would not let us enter, and when the members of the khatun's party told them that we had come in her suite they answered 'They cannot enter except by permission', so we stayed by the gate. One of the khatun's party sent a messenger to tell her of this while she was still with her father. She told him about us, whereupon he gave orders to admit us and assigned us a house near the residence of the khatun.[27]

---

[23] H. A. R. Gibb, *The Travels of Ibn Battuta, A.D. 1325-1354*, 3 vols. (Cambridge, 1958-1971).

[24] Gibb, *The Travels of Ibn Battuta*, II (1962), 497-514.

[25] For the problems of the chronology mentioned below see I. Hrbek, 'The chronology of Ibn-Battuta's travels', *Archiv Orientální* 30 (1962), 473-483.

[26] Gibb, *The Travels of Ibn Battuta*, II, 505; *PLP*, fasc. 9 (1989), no. 21158.

[27] Gibb, *The Travels of Ibn Battuta*, II, 504. I have retained the translation 'they rang their bells' from the first edition (1929), instead of 'they beat their church-gongs', as a more accurate reflection of Palaiologan Constantinople. See H. Hellensleben, 'Byzantinische Kirchtürme', *Kunstchronik* 19 (1966), 309-311.

Some days later, Ibn Battuta was received by the emperor, who asked him about Jerusalem and the Holy Land. At the end of the audience he gave him a guard for his ride through Constantinople:

> He was pleased with my replies and said to his sons, 'Honour this man and ensure his safety.' He then bestowed upon me a robe of honour and ordered for me a horse with saddle and bridle, and a parasol of the kind that the king has carried above his head, that being a sign of protection. I asked him to designate someone to ride about the city with me every day, that I might see its wonders and curious sights and tell of them in my own country, and he designated such a guide for me. It is one of the customs among them that anyone who wears the king's robe of honour and rides on his horse is paraded through the city bazaars with trumpets, fifes and drums, so that the people may see him. This is most frequently done with the Turks who come from the territories of the sultan Uzbak, so that they may not be molested; so they paraded me through the bazaars.[28]

On the following days Ibn Battuta went around in Constantinople. What he tells us about the physical appearance of the city is evidently based on his own experience. He does not mention a single monument known from the Arab traditional description about which I have spoken; furthermore, he describes some new developments of his time, for example the Italian colony of Galata.[29] However, as we can assume from the passage just quoted, there was always a guide with him who gave him explanations which he can have understood only by the help of an interpreter.[30] And sometimes it is difficult to understand which of the inexplicable things Ibn Battuta claims to have seen in Constantinople were invented by his guide and which by himself. Even so, occasionally we learn things that may be historical and are unknown from elsewhere. His description of Hagia Sophia is particularly interesting: 'I can describe only its exterior; as for its interior I did not see it. It is called by them *Aya Sufiya*, and the story goes that it was built by Asaf, the son of Barakhya, who was the son of the maternal aunt of Solomon.'[31] The name Aya Sufiya is explained here as Asafiya and thus connected to Asaf, the loyal vizier of Solomon in Islamic tradition. Ibn Battuta is our first source for a story that has later

---

[28] Gibb, *The Travels of Ibn Battuta*, II, 506.
[29] Gibb, *The Travels of Ibn Battuta*, II, 508-509.
[30] Gibb, *The Travels of Ibn Battuta*, II, 505, 506.
[31] Gibb, *The Travels of Ibn Battuta*, II, 509.

become part of the Ottoman legend of Hagia Sophia.[32] After a short description of the exterior Ibn Battuta proceeds:

> At the door of the church there are porticoes where the attendants sit who sweep its paths, light its lamps and close its doors. They allow no person to enter it until he prostrates himself to the huge cross at their place, which they claim to be a relic of the wood on which the double of Jesus (on whom be peace) was crucified.[33]

If such a custom existed already some centuries before, this may explain why no Arab visitor except Harun b. Yahya described this central monument of Constantinople. However, later during his stay Ibn Battuta visited some monasteries and their churches, so apparently there was no general rule by which visits to churches were prohibited to Muslims. Another story connected to Hagia Sophia certainly does not come from Islamic tradition, but it is also hard to believe that a Greek guide told it to Ibn Battuta:

> ... the pope comes to it once in the year. When he is at a distance of four nights' journey from the town the king goes out to meet him and dismounts before him; when he enters the city, the king walks on foot in front of him, and the king comes to salute him every morning and evening during the whole period of his stay in Constantinople until he departs.[34]

Was this story the product of Ibn Battuta's limited knowledge of Christianity and of the differences of opinion which existed between Byzantium and the west? We will probably never know.

One day Ibn Battuta went out to visit the former Emperor George in a monastery and had the opportunity to talk with him. This presents us with a major chronological problem, for Andronikos II had died in February 1332 and his name as a monk was Antonios, whereas Ibn Battuta arrived in Constantinople only in mid-September of the same year, if not two years later. Ibn Battuta writes:

> Inside each of these monasteries is a little building designed for the ascetic retreat of the king who built it, for most of these kings on reaching the age of sixty or seventy build a monastery and put on

---

[32] S. Yerasimos, *Légendes d'empire. La fondation de Constantinople et de Sainte Sophie dans les traditions turques*, Bibliothèque de l'Institut français d'études anatoliennes 31 (Paris, 1990), 127.
[33] Gibb, *The Travels of Ibn Battuta*, II, 510.
[34] Gibb, *The Travels of Ibn Battuta*, II, 510.

cilices, which are garments of hair, invest their sons with the kingship and occupy themselves with devotions until their death.[35]

This is, of course, nonsense, since we know very well that Andronikos II gave up his throne only after a long civil war against his grandson Andronikos III, but it is easy to imagine why Ibn Battuta's guides told him such a story. However, it is still unclear why the guides identified an old monk as the father of the emperor.

Finally I would like to draw your attention to a third and perhaps not so well-known Arab traveller, namely the merchant Hajji 'Abd Allah who lived in Constantinople for twelve years in the early Palaiologan period. On his return to Damascus in 1293 he told his story to the chronicle writer al-Ghazari, also known as al-Dimashqi (1260–1338), where we read the following account:

> Constantinople is a great city that can be compared to Alexandria; it lies on the seashore, and if you want to cross it you have to walk from morning until mid-day. There is a place as big as two thirds of the city of Damascus, which is enclosed by a defence wall and has a gate that can be opened and closed. It is reserved especially for the Muslims so that they can live there. Likewise there is another place where the Jews live. Every evening both gates are closed at the same time with those of the city. There are a hundred thousand churches minus one, but the Great Church makes the number complete. When I asked them about this they told me that the emperor of Constantinople has a hundred thousand kings in his service minus one, of which everybody had his own church, and the emperor built the church which he called the Great. This church is one of the biggest and most admirable buildings that can be seen anywhere. The place where they stand during their prayers is completely surrounded with pierced lattices. The deacons put their censers below and go away, and the incense comes up from below their clothes.[36]

These details sound like second-hand knowledge, and we can assume that Hajji 'Abd Allah too was probably never permitted to go inside the Great Church. It is interesting, however, to see what he tells us about the exterior:

---

[35] Gibb, *The Travels of Ibn Battuta*, II, 511.
[36] M.-A. F. Mehren, ed., *Cosmographie de Chems-ed-din Abou Abdallah Mohammed ed-Dimichqui* (St. Petersburg, 1866; repr. Leipzig, 1927), 227.

> On the walls of this church all towns of the world and all professions are represented. If somebody wants to select a profession for his son, he takes him with him for three days, brings him to the church, shows him all professions and then decides for the profession he liked most. They have depicted there all professions and where the tools for these professions come from, but above all the others they have put a smith; he holds his member and urinates on the others. When I asked them they said that this was the case because the tools for all professions come from the smith.

Given that Hajji 'Abd Allah himself had spent twelve years in Constantinople, what he tells us here is surprising. If the urinating man ever existed, he was almost certainly not on the wall painting, but an otherwise unknown statue that stood in the hippodrome on a fountain of the spina as an early version of the famous *mannekenpis* in Brussels.[37] The wall paintings or reliefs must have shown a procession of guilds or simply an imperial triumph; in any case they were not on the walls of Hagia Sophia, but on a secular building nearby, possibly in the old palace or in the hippodrome. However, it is difficult to imagine a position on the walls of the spina which we would have to assume if water from the statue was really supposed to have touched them. Hajji 'Abd Allah goes on:

> At the door of the church I have seen two buildings similar to minarets whose construction resembles that of the lighthouse of Alexandria. On the top of one of them there is a brazen horse, but hollow; on its back sits a rider in the form of a man from hollow cast bronze. In one of his hands he holds a globe from bronze, the biggest in the world, which is also hollow, and raises his other hand. On the other minaret is the figure of a man, hollow and brazen; he kneels on both knees, has a globe in his hand and a flat headcovering on which there are pearls from glass, jewels and other things. I have asked the priest about the two minarets, and he told me that the rider had ruled the whole world, and that it was this that the globe meant.

The first minaret can easily be recognised as Justinian's column. As to the second minaret, there is only one monument of Constantinople that fits Hajji 'Abd Allah's description, namely the column of the Emperor

---

[37] The existence of fountains on the spina is well attested. The base of the Egyptian obelisk was used as one: see Müller-Wiener, *Bildlexikon* (as in n. 8), 65; a fountain with a female statue on the top is mentioned in the *Patria Konstantinoupoleos*, ed. Th. Preger, *Scriptores originum Constantinopolitanarum* II (Leipzig, 1907), III §202.

Michael Palaiologos which was erected to commemorate the return of Constantinople to Byzantine rule in 1261.[38] It was the last triumphal monument to be built in the city, and the mystery of the origin of the kneeling statue is yet unsolved. However, this column stood far away from Hagia Sophia at the church of the Apostles. It is possible that the different location was mentioned in Abd Allah's original report and disappeared only later in al-Ghazari's chronicle. The passage about Constantinople ends with the following words:

> Inside the church of Hagia Sophia there is a number of libraries in which you find all sciences; among them are also certain ones which are called the 'libraries of towns'. And in all of them the names of the towns are written in books, the rivers and sources which are there, where their wealth comes from, which disadvantages and advantages they have, and even which treasures and hidden riches are there, with the indication where they can be found. Actually they were not able to take away all the things they had when the Muslims came; so they buried them and made a note in these books which they keep in the library of the church of Constantinople for the future, because they believe that these pages will lead them back.

Here ends the tale of Hajji 'Abd Allah and also this paper. Again we have seen how close reality and fantasy can be in the accounts of the Arab travellers. It is a pity that the Byzantines were not able to recover their hidden treasures, nor the Ottomans, who must have found the 'library of towns' when they conquered Constantinople in 1453. So it must be left to our imagination which wondrous things might have been described there.

---

[38] On this see Th. Thomov, 'The last column in Constantinople', *BSl* 59 (1998), 80–92.

13. Constantinople: the crusaders' gaze

R. Macrides

If this chapter were simply about what the crusaders who passed through Constantinople in 1097, 1147 and 1203-04 said they saw in the capital of the Byzantine empire, it would be a very short one indeed. For of the thousands of crusaders who travelled through Byzantine territory, a small number only saw the city itself within the walls and, of these, only four have left a written account of their impressions: Fulcher of Chartres for the First Crusade, Odo of Deuil for the Second, and Geoffrey of Villehardouin and Robert of Clari for the Fourth. This meagre list can be augmented by two further accounts of 'crusaders', that of William, archbishop of Tyre, who came to Constantinople from the crusader states in the twelfth century, and Gunther of Pairis who wrote a second-hand report for abbot Martin of Pairis, a participant in the Fourth Crusade.

Accounts of Constantinople by crusaders are not only few in number. They are also almost useless in providing 'hard facts' about either the monuments of Constantinople or the topography of the city. Thus, those who study the city's architectural history and urban development find them a disappointing source of information.

However, the accounts by the crusaders together with the descriptions of other foreign travellers to Constantinople[1] are valuable

---

[1] Benjamin of Tudela, the Spanish Jew who travelled to the east in the 1160s: *The Itinerary of Benjamin of Tudela. Travels in the Middle Ages*, eds. M. A. Singer, M. N. Adler, A. Asher (Malibu, 1987), 69-73; a translation is also provided by Andrew Sharf, *Byzantine Jewry* (London, 1971), 134-136. For the Russian pilgrims who came to Constantinople, beginning in 1200 with Anthony of Novgorod, but mainly in the later fourteenth century: George P. Majeska, *Russian Travelers to Constantinople in the Fourteenth and Fifteenth Centuries* (Washington, D.C., 1984). For Anthony of Novgorod, until George Majeska's new edition and translation appears: B. de Khitrowo, *Itinéraires russes en Orient* (Geneva, 1889), 87-111. For Arab travellers, see M. Izeddin and P. Therriat, 'Un prisonnier arabe à Byzance au IXe siècle, Haroun-ibn-Yahya', *Revue des études islamiques* 15 (1941-47), 41-62; V. Minorsky, 'Marvazi on the Byzantines', *Mélanges Henri Grégoire* = *Annuaire de l'Institut de Philologie et*

From *Travel in the Byzantine World*, ed. Ruth Macrides. Copyright © 2002 by the Society for the Promotion of Byzantine Studies. Published by Ashgate Publishing Ltd, Gower House, Croft Road, Aldershot, Hampshire, GU11 3HR, Great Britain.

for the idea of the city which emerges, the impressions it made on them, their points of comparison, their choice of sights and monuments and their manner of description. Furthermore, the foreigners' descriptions are all the more important as a source since no inhabitant of Constantinople has left a description of the city he or she lived in and therefore took for granted.

The armed pilgrims whom we call crusaders did not, in general, have the opportunity to see Constantinople at their leisure. The treatment they received from Byzantine emperors reflects the apprehension felt towards the large, undisciplined armies encamped before the city walls. Fulcher of Chartres relates how the first crusading army pitched tent before Constantinople in 1097, resting there for fourteen days.

> We were not able to enter that city, since it was not pleasing to the emperor (for he feared that by chance we might plot some injury to him); it was necessary that we buy outside the walls our daily supplies, which the citizens brought to us by his order. Only five or six of us at the same time were permitted to go into the city each hour; thus some were coming out and others were going in to pray in the churches.[2]

Odo of Deuil, a clergyman in the entourage of the French king, Louis VII, on the Second Crusade, had less restricted access to the city, as the king's party were guests of the emperor Manuel and were accommodated in a palace in the north-west of the city. He remarks, 'those who had the opportunity entered these places, some to see the sights, others to worship faithfully. The king also visited the shrines, conducted by the emperor.'[3]

---

d'Histoire orientales et slaves 10 (1950, 455-69; Al-Harawi, Guide des Lieux de Pèlerinage, trans. J. Sourdel-Thomine (Damascus, 1957); The Travels of Ibn Battuta, trans. H. A. R. Gibb, II (Cambridge, 1962), 506-514; see also A. Berger, 'Sightseeing in Constantinople: Arab travellers, c. 900-1300', in this volume. Western travellers on diplomatic business or on return from pilgrimage to Jerusalem in the fifteenth century: Bertrandon de la Brocquière, 'The travels of Bertrandon de la Brocquière', Early Travels in Palestine, ed. T. Wright (London, 1928); Ruy Gonzalez de Clavijo, Embassy to Tamerlane, 1403-1406, trans. Guy le Strange (London, 1928); P. Tafur, Travels and Adventures, 1435-1439, trans. M. Letts (London, 1926); E. Legrand, Description des îles de l'archipel grec par Christophe Buondelmonti, Florentin du XVe siècle (Amsterdam, 1897, repr. 1974), 241-246; see also in this volume M. Angold,'The decline of Byzantium seen through the eyes of western travellers'.

[2] Fulcheri Carnotensis Historia Hierosolymitana (1095-1127), ed. H. Hagenmeyer (Heidelberg, 1913), 175-176; Fulcher of Chartres, A History of the Expedition to Jerusalem, 1095-1127, trans. F. R. Ryan (New York, 1973), 78.

[3] Odo of Deuil, De profectione Ludovici VII in orientem, ed. and trans. V. G. Berry (New York, 1948), 66, 67.

Villehardouin and Robert of Clari are the only two crusaders who had a great deal of time in Constantinople, months and perhaps years to get to know the city, as its conquerors in 1204. The detail and length of description of Constantinople in the crusading chronicles is not, however, related to the length of time their authors spent in the city, but rather to their interest and purpose in writing; Villehardouin says very little about the city in contrast to Robert. Yet, however much the crusaders may have differed in their presentation of the city, their expression of their initial impression is similar. It is one of amazement at its wealth and size which is summed up by the statements, 'For no man on earth ... could number them or recount them to you',[4] or 'its interior surpasses anything that I can say about it'[5] or, as Fulcher puts it, 'It is a great nuisance to recite what an opulence of all kinds of goods is found there ....'[6]

Constantinople was outside the experience of these men who had never travelled beyond the kingdom of France before they undertook their expeditions to the east. They had not seen Rome, the one city in Europe which was at all comparable — no longer in size or wealth but in its preservation of the remains of late antique monuments.[7] Each visitor to Constantinople compared the city with a part of the world which was familiar to him. Just as Benjamin of Tudela who travelled extensively in the east claimed that there was no city like Constantinople in all the world except for Baghdad,[8] and Stephen of Novgorod likened entering Constantinople to entering a great forest,[9] Villehardouin and Robert of Clari make comparisons with towns in France or Flanders. Commenting on the destruction caused by the third and last fire set by the crusaders to facilitate their final assault in 1204, Villehardouin says, 'more houses were burned than there are in the three largest cities of the kingdom of France'.[10] Robert, on the other hand, claimed that the first fire of 1203

---

[4] Robert of Clari, *La Conquête de Constantinople*, ed. P. Lauer (Paris, 1924), §92, 89-90; *The Conquest of Constantinople*, trans. E. H. McNeal (New York, 1936, repr. Toronto, 1996), 112.

[5] Odo of Deuil, ed. and trans. Berry, 64, 65.

[6] Ed. Hagenmeyer, 177; trans. Ryan, 79.

[7] For a twelfth-century description of Rome, see *Magister Gregorius, Narracio de Mirabilibus Urbis Romae*, ed. R. B. C. Huygens (Leiden, 1970); trans. J. Osborne, *Magister Gregorius, The Marvels of Rome* (Toronto, 1987). See also H. Bloch, 'The new fascination with ancient Rome', in R. L. Benson and G. Constable, eds., *Renaissance and Renewal in the Twelfth Century* (Oxford, 1982, repr. 1985), 615-636.

[8] *The Itinerary of Benjamin of Tudela* (as in n. 1), 70; Sharf, *Byzantine Jewry* (as in n. 1), 135.

[9] Majeska, *Russian Travelers* (as in n. 1), 44, 45.

[10] *La Conquête de Constantinople*, ed. E. Faral, II (Paris, 1973), §247, 48-51.

'burned an area of the city of Arras', a prosperous trading town of Flanders which he, as a knight from Picardy, could have known personally.[11]

The crusading authors express wonder at seeing this rich and mighty city — 'Oh, excellent and beautiful city', exclaimed Fulcher[12] — and admiration for the beauty, size and number of monuments contained in it. But wonder and awe for the unexpected give way to a feeling of exclusion and alienation and then to a desire to possess. We can see in Odo of Deuil's description of Constantinople during the Second Crusade the expression of alienation from the Greek inhabitants of the city which contributed to the call for its conquest by a French bishop.[13] In his account of the city Odo writes with admiration about the palaces, that of Constantine, the Great Palace, and the Blachernai, as well as the Philopation, to the north-west of the city. He describes the walls and towers, the churches and expecially the cathedral, Hagia Sophia.[14] His description is important not for anything specific he says about these monuments but for its manner of presentation. Both the city and its inhabitants are portrayed in terms of contrasts, in terms of the dichotomy between surface exterior and inner reality, deceptive appearances and true nature. For Odo, although the exterior view is delightful, and presents a peaceful and pleasing sight, the interior of the city is 'squalid and fetid and in many places harmed by permanent darkness, for the wealthy overshadow the streets with building and leave these dirty, dark places to the poor and travellers'.[15] The contrast between external appearance and internal reality is applied also to the people of the city who 'would not have exhibited such unremitting servitude to the French if they had had good intentions. They were concealing the wrongs which were to be avenged afterwards.'[16] The behaviour of the emperor is likewise suspect. The emperor's favours to the French are recalled by Odo 'so that there may be manifest the treachery of him who simulated the friendship which we are accustomed to show only to our most

---

[11] Ed. Lauer, §46, 47; trans. McNeal, 73. On Arras, see N. J. G. Pounds, *An Economic History of Medieval Europe* (London and New York, 1974), 238-241, 260; J. Lestocquoy, *Les villes de Flandre et d'Italie* (Paris, 1952), 10, 52-56. On the fires in Constantinople, T. F. Madden, 'The fires of the fourth crusade in Constantinople, 1203-1204: a damage assessment', *BZ* 84-85 (1991-92), 72-93.
[12] Ed. Hagenmeyer, 176; trans. Ryan, 79.
[13] Ed. and trans. Berry, 68-71.
[14] Ed. and trans. Berry, 48-49, 62-67.
[15] Ed. and trans. Berry, 64, 65.
[16] Ed. and trans. Berry, 66, 67.

intimate friends, while he harbored a feeling which we could not have appeased save by our very death'.[17]

The attitude toward Constantinople and its inhabitants expressed by Odo was accompanied by the conviction that the inhabitants of that city were not worthy of it. Villehardouin voiced the same sentiment in his remark, 'Judge for yourselves ... whether a people who could commit such great cruelties against each other deserve to hold the land or to lose it.'[18] For the western traveller to Constantinople, like the New World explorer, wonder was the prelude to, as well as the agent of, appropriation. The movement from dazed wonder, to estrangement, to destructive fever was expressed by one such explorer, Bernal Diaz, when he recounted his reaction to Mexico: 'I say again that I stood looking at it and thought that never in the world would there be discovered other lands such as these ... today all is overthrown and lost, nothing left standing.'[19] Something of this reaction can be found in Villehardouin's wonderment at Constantinople, even in its destruction: 'more houses were burned than there are in the three largest cities of the kingdom of France'.[20]

Robert of Clari's wonder before the city of Constantinople found expression in a more detailed account of the capital than that given by other crusading authors. While Fulcher, Odo, Villehardouin and Gunther write in general terms about the palaces, churches, monasteries and relics, Robert gives, in contrast, something like a guided tour.[21]

Robert of Clari has never been taken very seriously as a crusading chronicler and the same is true of his description of Constantinople: 'colourful but not trustworthy', 'naive, with a child-like spontaneity',[22] are judgments applied to his work as a whole. Villehardouin has traditionally been held to be *the* authority on the crusade. He took part in

---

[17] Ed. and trans. Berry, 68, 69.

[18] Ed. Faral, II §224, 22-25; §271, 78-81; §272, 80-81; trans. Shaw, 85, 99, 100.

[19] *The Conquest of New Spain*, cited in S. Greenblatt, *Marvelous possessions: the wonder of the New World* (Oxford, 1991), 130-139, here 133; O. Augustinos, *French Odysseys* (Baltimore and London, 1994), 53-54, note 14, points to the similarity in the feelings expressed by Diaz and the crusaders upon first seeing Constantinople.

[20] Ed. Faral, II §247, 48-51; trans. Shaw, 92.

[21] J. P. A. van der Vin, *Travellers to Greece and Constantinople. Ancient Monuments and Old Traditions in Medieval Travellers' Tales*, 2 vols. (Istanbul, 1980), I, 65-80 for crusading accounts in general; 74-80 for Robert of Clari.

[22] The most recent expression of this judgment is by D. E. Queller and T. F. Madden, *The Fourth Crusade: the conquest of Constantinople* (Philadelphia, 1997), 139-140; see also P. Noble, 'The importance of Old French chronicles as historical sources of the Fourth Crusade and the early Latin Empire of Constantinople', *Journal of Medieval History* 27/4 (2001), 399-416, here 410-413.

the main negotiations in the course of the crusade. Further, he is one of the 'high men' — in Robert's words — who was awarded a fief in the new Latin empire set up after 1204. But Villehardouin is also partly responsible for his good reputation through self-advertisement: he mentions himself no fewer than 48 times in his text. Besides, his work was first edited in the sixteenth century, almost 300 years before Robert's.[23] It therefore had a longer time to establish itself. Today it is Villehardouin who is a Penguin classic.[24]

Robert, on the other hand, was a poor knight from Picardy, with enough land — 6 hectares — to qualify as a knight, but not enough to feed himself.[25] Robert had no power or authority on the crusade. He has a small repetitive vocabulary. He makes mistakes in facts and figures and he is in an English translation which only recently came back into print.[26] This does not add up to an imposing picture. Yet it is Robert who has attempted to produce the more ambitious work which is revealed through a high degree of organisation and respect for literary conventions.[27] He provides a formal opening and conclusion to his work, maintains a strict chronological order, and justifies his flashbacks into past Byzantine history by connecting present behaviour with past events.[28] Thus he explains how the young Alexios came to ask for the crusaders' help by giving a history of dynastic succession from the reign of Manuel Komnenos.[29] To elucidate Boniface of Montferrat's interest in going to Constantinople with the crusading army he explains that his brother Conrad had been married to a Byzantine princess and had been treated badly at the Byzantine court.[30]

---

[23] For these arguments see P. M. Schon, *Studien zum Stil der frühen französischen Prosa* (Frankfurt a/M, 1960), esp. 72-102; J. Dufournet, *Les écrivains de la IVe croisade, Villehardouin et Clari*, 2 vols. (Paris, 1973); G. Jacquin, *Le style historique dans les récits français et latins de la quatrième croisade* (Paris, Geneva, 1986), 7-8, for comparisons of Villehardouin and Robert.

[24] The Shaw translation for Penguin was published in 1963 and has been reprinted several times.

[25] Dufournet, *Les écrivains*, II (as in n. 23), 341.

[26] The McNeal translation of 1936 in the Columbia University Press series was reprinted in 1996 by the University of Toronto Press in association with the Medieval Academy of America.

[27] P. F. Dembowski, *La Chronique de Robert de Clari: étude de la langue et du style* (Toronto, 1963), 120-122; Dufournet, *Les écrivains*, II, 356-359, 366.

[28] C. P. Bagley, 'Robert of Clari's *La Conquête de Constantinople*', *Medium Aevum* 40 (1971), 109-115; E. McNeal, 'The story of Isaac and Andronicus', *Speculum* 9 (1934), 324-329; Dembowski, *La Chronique* (as in n. 27), 120-122; Dufournet, *Les écrivains* (as in n. 23), II, 356-359.

[29] Ed. Lauer, §§18-28, 16-29; trans. McNeal, 46-57.

[30] Ed. Lauer, §§33-38, 32-39; trans. McNeal, 59-66.

Furthermore, we have Robert's interest in material culture to thank for information known from no other source: the value of a fief in the new Latin empire,[31] the coronation ceremony of the new Latin emperor,[32] representations of Isaac II on church façades,[33] and the bathing habits of the women of Constantinople.[34]

In keeping with this interest in material culture is Robert's detailed description of Constantinople, a guided tour which follows this order: the Boukoleon palace or Great Palace, the Blachernai palace, Hagia Sophia, the church of the Holy Apostles, the gate of the 'Golden Mantle',[35] the Golden Gate, the hippodrome, assorted statues and columns and relics. He introduces the description into his narrative after his account of the conquest of the city, 'when the city was captured and the pilgrims were quartered',[36] as if it were then that the crusaders saw the city for the first time. Yet we know from Villehardouin, Gunther and Robert himself that the crusaders had been allowed inside in 1203, when the young Alexios was put on the throne: 'And they went to the city whenever they wanted to, ...' [37] Furthermore, he makes hardly a reference to the changes the monuments and the life of the city underwent as a result of the conquest.[38] Thus, he succeeds in giving a

---

[31] Ed. Lauer, §107, 102-103; trans. McNeal, 123; P. Lock, *The Franks in the Aegean, 1204-1500* (London and New York, 1995), 48-49.

[32] Ed. Lauer, §§96-97, 93-95; trans. McNeal, 115-117; Lock, *The Franks*, 167-68.

[33] Ed. Lauer, §25, 28; trans. McNeal, 56. The passage is discussed by P. Magdalino and R. Nelson, 'The emperor in Byzantine art of the twelfth century', *BF* 8 (1982), 160-162, repr. in P. Magdalino, *Tradition and Transformation in Medieval Byzantium* (Aldershot, 1991), no. VI. The Continuator of William of Tyre provides independent confirmation that there were representations of Isaac, although the image is not described in detail: *La Continuation de Guillaume de Tyre (1184-1197)*, ed. M. R. Morgan (Paris, 1982), 15, 29; trans. P. W. Edbury, *The Conquest of Jerusalem and the Third Crusade* (Aldershot, 1996), 15, 22.

[34] Ed. Lauer, 81, 98, p. 80-81, 95-96; trans. McNeal, 102, 117; P. Magdalino, 'Church, bath and *diakonia* in medieval Constantinople', in *Church and People in Byzantium*, ed. R. Morris (Birmingham, 1990), 174.

[35] Identified by A. Berger, 'Das Chalkun Tetrapylon und Parastaseis, Kapitel 57', *BZ* 90 (1997), 7-12, here 9, as the Tetrapylon.

[36] Ed. Lauer, §82, 81-82; trans. McNeal, 102.

[37] Ed. Lauer,§§ 52, 55, 52, 55-56; trans. McNeal, 77, 80; ed. Faral, I §192, 194-195; trans. Shaw, 76; *Guntheri Pariensis Historia Constantinopolitana*, in P. Riant, ed., *Exuviae sacrae constantinopolitanae*, I (Geneva, 1877), 13; new edition by P. Orth, *Gunther von Pairis, Hystoria Constantinopolitana* (Hildesheim and Zurich, 1994), 166; trans. A. J. Andrea, *The Capture of Constantinople: The Hystoria Constantinopolitana of Gunther of Pairis* (Philadelphia, 1997), 94.

[38] Some of the columns and statues he describes are known to have been smashed or at least partially destroyed before the conquest itself: Gunther states of the column from which Mourtzouphlos was thrown, 'some people smashed these images with stones and iron hammers and largely deformed them, believing that in this way they could turn an unfavourable omen back on us' (ed. Riant, I, 21, 111-112; ed. Orth, 166; trans. Andrea, 117).

timeless quality to the crusaders' victory. It is for this reason that the description reads like a set piece.

Although Robert's attention to the city, its monuments and relics, is something which distinguishes his account from all other crusader accounts, little attention has been paid to it.[39] This is the case for several reasons. First, a glance at a map of the city shows that his 'tour' does not make topographical sense. It is an itinerary for an armchair traveller, not for a visitor on foot, for its organisation is thematic and not geographical: palaces, churches, gates, hippodrome, statues, columns. Nor does he tell us anything about the city that we did not know already. Moreover, he gets names and identifications wrong. For Robert the name Hagia Sophia means Holy Trinity,[40] not Holy Wisdom. He calls the church of the Holy Apostles, the Seven Apostles.[41] He identifies the equestrian figure of an emperor on a column in front of Hagia Sophia as the Emperor Heraclius, not as Justinian.[42] Finally, Robert's description of the city's monuments has been dismissed for failing to convey the intrinsic artistic merit of the antique statues and columns, for showing an interest in the 'fairy tale' element, instead of giving precise descriptions which would help us to reconstruct the appearance of the city.[43]

However, the picture is more complicated than this judgment would allow. If we look closely at Robert's descriptions, we often find a Greek source specified. The Greeks are named as sources for the identification of specific monuments and icons, for generalisations about the city, for beliefs in the protective powers of a monument:

> ... he took with him the icon, an image of Our Lady, which the Greeks call by this name.[44]

Gunther is referring to a time before April 1204: 'when they saw the ladders erected on our ships ....' Likewise, Choniates relates that in 1203, a mob smashed the statue of Athena in the forum of Constantine because it seemed to beckon the armies from the west: see below, p. 202-204 and n. 71.

[39] With the notable and recent exceptions of B. Bjørnholt, 'Perceptions of art: Niketas Choniates and Robert of Clari on the sack of Constantinople in 1204', abstract of a paper in the *Bulletin of British Byzantine Studies* 26 (2000), 78-79, and P. Schreiner, 'Robert de Clari und Konstantinopel', in C. Sode and S. Takács, eds., *Novum Millennium. Studies on Byzantine history and culture dedicated to Paul Speck* (Aldershot, 2001), 337-356.

[40] Ed. Lauer, §85, 84-85; trans. McNeal, 106.
[41] Ed. Lauer, §87, 86; trans. McNeal, 107-108.
[42] Ed. Lauer, §86, 86; trans. McNeal, 107.
[43] van der Vin, *Travellers* (as in n. 21), 74-78.
[44] Ed. Lauer, §66, 65; trans. McNeal, 89.

> For the Greeks attest that two parts of the wealth of this world is in Constantinople and the third is scattered throughout the world.[45]
>
> On this gate there was a golden globe which was made by such enchantment that the Greeks said as long as it was there no thunderbolt would fall in the city.[46]
>
> The Greeks said that this was Heraclius the emperor.[47]
>
> And the Greeks said that it was the first image of Our Lady ever made or painted.[48]

The specific identification of the source of the information is unique among crusader writers and other foreign visitors who write in more general terms, 'they say'.[49]

Furthermore, Robert's attentiveness to what the 'Greeks say' plays a significant part in what has up to now been labelled as his naïveté, unreliability, and fairy tale quality. It seems that his errors and naive pronouncements come from the Greeks, directly or indirectly. For example:

> In front of this church of Saint Sophia there was a great column .... On top of this column there lay a flat slab of stone .... On this stone there was an emperor made of copper on a great copper horse .... The Greeks said that this was Heraclius the emperor.

At least two other travellers to Constantinople misidentified the equestrian statue of Justinian, al-Harawi in the late twelfth century and Pero Tafur in the early fifteenth. It is likely that they gave mistaken information on the basis of what they had heard in the city. This can be inferred from Tafur's statement, 'This knight, they say, is Constantine'.[50]

Until now, the assumption has been that the Greeks told tales to gullible visitors, like Robert, who then transmitted erroneous information about Constantinople. I would suggest that the Constantinopolitans neither purposely misled foreigners, nor were themselves misinformed

---

[45] Ed. Lauer, §81, 80-81; trans. McNeal, 101.
[46] Ed. Lauer, §88, 86-87; trans. McNeal, 108. See also above, n. 35.
[47] Ed. Lauer, §86, 86; trans. McNeal, 107.
[48] Ed. Lauer, §114, 107; trans. McNeal, 126.
[49] See *infra*, p. 203 and n. 95.
[50] Pero Tafur, *Travels and Adventures*, ed. Letts (as in n. 1), 141. For al-Harawi, *Guide de Lieux de Pèlerinage*, trans. Sourdel-Thomine (as in n. 1), 114. On the equestrian statue of Justinian, see C. Mango, 'The columns of Justinian and his successors', in C. Mango, *Studies on Constantinople* (Aldershot, 1993), no. X, 1-20.

about their city. Constantinopolitan writers of the twelfth century show that statues in the capital were identified variously, at different times, and that their meaning could be reinterpreted, depending on circumstances. Neither the identification of a statue, nor its meaning was constant. The 'errors' of Robert and others reflect contemporary interpretations.[51]

In two other instances when Robert gives the wrong explanation for a Greek name, the errors show, I would argue, an attentiveness to Greek more than an ignorance of the language. For example, Robert calls the church of the Holy Apostles the 'Seven' Apostles, a mistake which could derive from a mishearing of the Greek adjective for 'all holy', *panseptoi*, which sounds like the French word for 'seven', sept.[52] Likewise, when Robert calls Hagia Sophia the Holy 'Trinity', he is not so much betraying his lack of knowledge of Greek as translating into understandable terms a concept foreign to the west: the dedication of a church to an abstract quality of one of the Trinity.[53]

If the Greeks and the Greek language are behind Robert's identifications and statements about monuments, so too are the beliefs he

---

[51] On the changing meanings or identifications of statues, see Niketas Choniates, ed. van Dieten, 643, 649; trans. Magoulias, 353, 358: 'Some claimed that the horse was Pegasos and its rider Bellerophontes; others contended that it was Joshua, the son of Nave'; likewise, a pair of female statues in the forum of Constantine is described as representing the 'Roman' woman and the 'Hungarian' woman at the time of the Emperor Manuel's Hungarian war (van Dieten, 151, trans. Magoulias, 86), but Arethas in the tenth century refers to one statue as 'earth' and another as 'the sea': see E. Mathiopulu-Tornaritu, 'Klassisches und Klassizistisches im Statuenfragment von Niketas Choniates', *BZ* 73 (1980), 25-40, here 32. See, also, the comments of J. Shepard, 'Cross-purposes: Alexius Comnenus and the first crusade', in J. Phillips, ed., *The First Crusade* (Manchester, 1997), 119; L. James, '"Pray not to fall into temptation and be on your guard": pagan statues in Christian Constantinople', *Gesta* 35/1 (1996), 12-20, here 13; H. Saradi-Mendelovici, 'Christian attitudes toward pagan monuments in late antiquity and their legacy in later Byzantine centuries', *DOP* 44 (1990), 47-61.

[52] Ed. Lauer, §87, 86; trans. McNeal, 108. Dembowski, *La Chronique*, 62, points out that Robert's 'hellenisms are approximate transcriptions of forms he heard but never read'. A similar mishearing could be at the origin of a false etymology given by Liudprand of Cremona in the tenth century for the Nea or New Church: *ecclesiam autem ipsam nean hoc est novam alii vocant, alii vero ennean, quod nostra lingua novennalem sonat, appellant, eo quod ibidem ecclesiasticarum horarum machina novem pulsata ictibus sonet*, in *Antapodosis*,§ 34, 90, ed. J. Becker, *Die Werke Liudprands von Cremona* (Hanover and Leipzig, 1915); trans. F. A. Wright, *Liudprand of Cremona, The Embassy to Constantinople and other Writings* (London, 1930, repr. 1993), 34, 84-85. On this etymology see J. Koder and Th. Weber, *Liudprand von Cremona in Konstantinopel* (Vienna, 1980), 31. Later western (Buondelmonti) and Russian travellers also refer to the church as the 'Enea' or 'Nine (Ranks of Angels)': see Majeska, *Russian Travelers*, 36-37, 96-97, 248 and n. 66.

[53] Ed. Lauer, §87, 86; trans. McNeal, 106.

transmits about these monuments. This is evident from his description of the two carved columns in Constantinople:

> There are two columns .... On the outside of these columns there were pictured and written by prophecy all the events and all the conquests which have happened in Constantinople or which were going to happen. But no one could understand the event until it had happened, and when it had happened the people would go there and ponder over it, and then for the first time they would see and understand the event. And even this conquest of the French was written and pictured there and the ships in which they made the assault when the city was taken, and the Greeks were not able to understand it before it had happened, but when it had happened they went to look at these columns and ponder over it, and they found that the letters which were written on the pictured ships said that a people, short haired and with iron swords, would come from the west to conquer Constantinople.[54]

Robert refers twice to these columns, in his description of the city's monuments and again, later, in his account of the manner in which Alexios Mourtzouphlos was put to death.[55] The latter is the context in which Villehardouin describes the column:

> On that column from which he fell were figures of various kinds, carved in the marble, and among them was one representing an emperor falling headlong. Now, a long time before, it had been prophesied that there would be an emperor in Constantinople who would be cast down from that column. In this way were this likeness and this prophecy shown to be true.[56]

This description is unusual for Villehardouin who otherwise gives no more than a general impression of the city. A third description of the column appears in Gunther of Pairis's second-hand report of the Fourth Crusade.

> Also, so they say, various representations of events since antiquity were sculpted on it, which are said to depict in sundry scenes the prophesies of a Sibyl, largely concerning their kingdom. Among these were scenes of ships, with ladders of a sort projecting from them, on which armed men were climbing. They seemed to be storming and capturing a city which was also sculpted there. Until

---

[54] Ed. Lauer, §92, 89-90; trans. McNeal, 110-111.
[55] Ed. Lauer, §109, 103-104; trans. McNeal, 124.
[56] Ed. Faral, II §§307-308, 114-117; trans. Shaw, 109.

that time the Greeks had disregarded the sculpture, thinking that nothing was less possible than that such a thing could ever befall a city such as their own. However, when they saw the ladders erected on our ships, they finally then pondered this sculpture and began to fear more seriously what they had held in contempt for so long.[57]

The column from which Mourtzouphlos was hurled and to which all three authors refer was one of two historiated columns; it stood in the forum Tauri,[58] while the other was in the forum of Arcadius or the Xerolophos. Although only fragments of these columns survive, their appearance is known from written sources and the drawings of later visitors to Constantinople. Depictions of the column erected by Arcadius in 402/3 to commemorate the defeat of Gainas show that the scenes carved on it in spiral bands portrayed a military campaign and victory.[59]

While Villehardouin describes a scene different from the one Robert and Gunther comment on, and Robert refers to an inscription, 'letters', as well as carving, all three authors relate a connection between prophecy and the carved scenes. The future was portrayed in the carved column and awaited decipherment by the people of Constantinople who were engaged in a 'permanent interrogation'[60] of the column; 'the people would go there and ponder over it' but nevertheless 'could not understand the event until it had happened'.[61]

The three authors' attribution of prophetic meaning to the carvings echoes the Greeks' explanation of this and other commemorative monuments in the city. Although the inhabitants of Constantinople left no descriptions of the city which give an overall impression of it, they recorded information about its history and its monuments in the so-called *Parastaseis Syntomai Chronikai* or 'Brief Historical Notes'.[62] This

---

[57] Ed. Riant, I, 21, 111-112; ed. Orth, 166; trans. Andrea, 116-117.

[58] Niketas Choniates, *Historia*, ed. van Dieten, 609; trans. Magoulias, 334.

[59] R. Janin, *Constantinople byzantine* (Paris, 1964), 81-84. For representations of the column of Arcadius see J. H. W. G. Liebeschuetz, *Barbarians and Bishops* (Oxford, 1990), Appendix II: the column of Arcadius, 273-278, and plates; see now too *Byzance retrouvée, érudits et voyageurs français (xvie-xviiie siècles)*, Byzantina Sorbonensia, catalogue of an exhibition held in the chapel of the Sorbonne, Paris 2001, no. 20, 55-56.

[60] The phrase is used by G. Dagron and J. Paramelle, 'Un texte patriographique: le 'récit merveilleux, très beau et profitable sur la colonne de Xèrolophos', *TM* 7 (1979), 497.

[61] Robert of Clari, ed. Lauer, §92, 89; trans. McNeal, 110-111; Gunther of Pairis, ed. Riant, 21, 112; ed. Orth, 166; trans. Andrea, 117: 'they finally then pondered this sculpture'.

[62] *Scriptores Originum Constantinopolitanarum*, ed. Th. Preger, I (Leipzig, 1901), 1-73. The text is reprinted, with translation and commentary, in A. Cameron and J. Herrin, eds., *Constantinople in the early eighth century: the Parastaseis Syntomai Chronikai* (Leiden, 1984).

work from the late eighth, early ninth century[63] consists of a series of entries or notes, in no particular order, on topics of Constantinopolitan topography and monuments, especially statues. It presents itself as the product of a group, the activity of inhabitants of the city who collected information on the monuments of the capital. Its sources are written and oral, that is, not only what 'people say' but also what was reported orally by those who read books or know how to decipher inscriptions.[64] Whether or not one believes that the *Parastaseis* is the product of group activity or of one author-editor, and whether or not a real or fictional friend requested the work,[65] the text does reveal a desire to explain and transmit knowledge about the monuments of the city. But the *Parastaseis* is less interested in describing the monuments than in recounting their past history and in revealing their present and future effects and powers.

The *Parastaseis* was incorporated into a late tenth-century compilation known as the *Patria* which is the main source of information about the history of Constantinople, its foundation and monuments, gathered from a variety of sources. Like the *Parastaseis*, it is literature about the city, written by inhabitants of the city for their own edification.[66] In both works of patriographical literature, late antique monuments like the two historiated columns are seen as prophetic monuments, announcing or even conditioning the future of the city. Of the two columns described by Robert, Villehardouin and Gunther, the *Patria* records that they had engraved on them 'the last events of the city and the conquests (it was to endure)'.[67] The accounts of Robert and Gunther show that centuries after the *Parastaseis*, the inhabitants of Constantinople were engaged in activities similar to those of their predecessors. They were searching for the deeper significance of the monuments of their environment.[68]

Although Robert is not the only crusade author who transmits the Constantinopolitans' beliefs in the prophetic powers contained in the column, his work contains more numerous reflections of the inhabitants'

---

[63] The early to mid-eighth century date assigned to the text by Cameron and Herrin, *Parastaseis*, 17-29, has recently been questioned. For the later dating see O. Kresten, 'Leon III. und die Landmauern von Konstantinopel', *Römische Historische Mitteilungen* 36 (1994), 21-52; also I. Ševčenko, 'The search for the past in Byzantium around the year 800', *DOP* 46 (1992) = *Homo Byzantinus, Papers in Honor of Alexander Kazhdan*, 279-293.

[64] Cameron and Herrin, *Parastaseis*, 12-14, 38-45; G. Dagron, *Constantinople imaginaire: études sur le recueil des "Patria"* (Paris, 1984), 38.

[65] For the former proposition in each case see Cameron and Herrin, *Parastaseis*, 9-29; for the latter, Dagron, *Constantinople imaginaire*, 29-48.

[66] Dagron, *Constantinople imaginaire*, 48-60.

[67] Ed. Preger, *Scriptores*, II, §47, 176-177.

[68] Dagron, *Constantinople imaginaire*, 149. For examples of such practices later than the *Parastaseis*, see Dagron and Paramelle, 'Un texte patriographique' (as in n. 60), 491-523.

attitudes towards the monuments of their city. Further evidence of the 'Greeks' perceptions comes from Robert's description of the statues in the hippodrome and elsewhere in the city. He singles out two made of copper in the form of women which 'stood in front of the Change':

> Neither of them was less than a good 20 feet in height. One of these held its hand out toward the west, and it had letters written on it which said, 'From the West will come those who will capture Constantinople'. The other figure held its hand out toward a vile place and said ... 'Here is where they will throw them'.[69]

The place Robert calls the 'Change' where the 'rich money changers' were, 'with great heaps of besants and of precious stones in front of them' can be identified with the forum of Constantine where silversmiths and bankers are known to have had their stalls.[70] Niketas Choniates relates that in the Forum of Constantine there was a statue of Athena, 30 feet high, with its right arm outstretched to the south but 'those who know nothing at all of the points of the compass contended that the statue was looking toward the west, as if beckoning with her hand the armies from the west'. In 1203 people smashed the statue, thinking to avert, in this way, the danger from the encamped crusading armies.[71] Even if this is not the statue described by Robert, Choniates, an inhabitant of Constantinople and eyewitness to the Fourth Crusade, gives evidence of the inhabitants' belief in the prophetic powers of a pointing female statue, at a time when the crusaders were encamped outside the city.

Robert mentions more statues in the hippodrome which likewise had powers. In the 'Games of the Emperor',

> there were figures of men and women, and of horses and oxen and camels and bears and lions and many other kinds of animals, all made of copper, and all so well made and formed so naturally that there is no master workman in heathendom or in Christendom so skillful as to be able to make figures as good as these. And formerly they used to play by enchantment, but they do not play

---

[69] Ed. Lauer, §91, 88-89; trans. McNeal, 110.

[70] M. F. Hendy, *Catalogue of the Byzantine Coins in the Dumbarton Oaks Collection: Alexius IV to Michael VIII, 1081-1261*, IV.1 (Washington, D.C., 1999), 109, 128-129.

[71] Ed. van Dieten, 558-59; trans. Magoulias, 305-306; on this statue, see R. J. H. Jenkins, 'The bronze Athena at Byzantium', *Journal of Hellenic Studies* 67 (1947), 31-33 and E. Mathiopulu-Tornaritu, 'Klassisches und Klassizistisches im Statuenfragment von Niketas Choniates' (as in n. 51), 25-40, esp. 32-36, who conjectures that this classical statue was holding a shield which was lost by the twelfth century; hence, the 'beckoning hand'.

any longer. And the French looked at the Games of the Emperor in wonder when they saw it.[72]

The description of the statues which stood on the spina, along the central divide of the race course, brings nothing new to our knowledge of the appearance of the hippodrome.[73] Yet, with the statement, 'And formerly they used to play by enchantment', Robert appears to imply that the statues were animated and took part in the 'Games'. No other source refers to automata in the hippodrome. It seems more likely that Robert is attributing powers to the statues, also assigned to them by Byzantine and other foreign authors. The word *'stoicheiosis'* or 'bewitchment' is used of the effect Apollonios of Tyre was reputed to have worked on these statues, according to the *Patria* and other sources which incorporate patriographic literature.[74] Niketas Choniates mentions Apollonios' services to the inhabitants of Byzantium, in his description of a bronze eagle with a snake in its claws which he set up in the hippodrome to 'bring them relief from the snake bites which plagued them'.[75] In 1403 Ruy Gonzales de Clavijo also commented on the talismanic role of another bronze sculpture in the hippodrome, the serpent column, saying that it served 'for an enchantment', protecting the people from a plague of serpents and other reptiles.[76] In the same way, Robert's use of the word 'enchantment' would seem to reflect the Constantinopolitans' belief in the 'bewitchment' of the statues.[77] For Robert, however, this 'enchantment' gave the statues the power to 'play' in the Games.

---

[72] Ed. Lauer, §90, 87-88; trans. McNeal, 109-110.

[73] See S. G. Bassett, 'The antiquities in the hippodrome of Constantinople', DOP 45 (1991), 87-96; Th. F. Madden, 'The serpent column of Delphi in Constantinople: placement, purposes and mutilations', BMGS 16 (1992), 111-145.

[74] *Patria*, ed. Preger, *Scriptores*, II, 79, 191; George Kedrenos, ed. I. Bekker, I (Bonn, 1838), 346-347. See, too, Cameron and Herrin, *Parastaseis*, 33-34, 193, 254. On *stoicheiosis* see C. Blum, 'The meaning of στοιχεῖον and its derivates in the Byzantine age', Eranos 44 (1946), 315-325.

[75] Ed. van Dieten, 651; trans. Magoulias, 359. Choniates refers to the 'enchanted' (*stoicheiode*) palladia of the city set up along the wall to ward off the enemy which the Latins destroyed after their conquest of the city, out of fear for their effects: ed. van Dieten, 643; trans. Magoulias, 353, who does not translate the word *stoicheiodē*.

[76] *Embajada a Tamorlán*, ed. F. Lopez Estrada (Madrid, 1943), 43.17-18: 'por un encantamiento que fuera fecho'; trans. Guy le Strange (as in n. 1), 71.

[77] That Robert is not referring to automata, or to the life-like nature of the statues (as does the author of the Norse sagas, describing the visit of king Sigurd in the reign of Alexios I: *Heimskringla. The Norse king Sagas by Snorre Sturlason* [London and Toronto, 1930], trans. S. Laing, 12, p. 286) but rather to their inherent powers is indicated by his use of the word 'enchantment' also in another passage, when he comments on the golden globe on a gate of the city 'which was made by such enchantment that the Greeks said as long as it was there no thunderbolt would fall in the city' (ed. Lauer, §88, 86-87; trans. McNeal, 108).

Robert does not merely, I would argue, parrot the Greeks' views of things. He has absorbed the lore about the city which both educated and non-educated inhabitants of Constantinople believed and handed down. The very fact that he spends so much space on sculpture and the meaning of the carvings shows this. It was these that the inhabitants of Constantinople found necessary to study and record, as the *Parastaseis* and other, later, patriographical literature show.[78]

These, also, were the monuments most prominent in the tours of the city arranged for visiting dignitaries, as two twelfth-century sources, one Greek, the other Latin, reveal. Anna Komnene describes the visit of the Turkish emir in the late eleventh century, at the beginning of her father's reign: 'The emperor did not cease from giving Abul Qasim money each day and inviting him to the baths, the horse races and hunting but also to view the columns erected on the avenues.'[79] Almost a century later, in the reign of Alexios' grandson Manuel I, King Amalric of Jerusalem visited Constantinople. William of Tyre who describes the visit in great detail, reports:

> The king was escorted throughout the whole city both within the walls and without. He visited the churches and monasteries of which there was an almost infinite number; he looked upon triumphal arches and columns adorned with trophies. Great nobles who knew the places well were his guides, and on his inquiring the nature and purpose of each object he was given full information by the oldest and best-informed men.[80]

From these accounts it can be seen that the Turkish emir and the king of Jerusalem were given slightly different tours; the Muslim would not have been interested in the churches and monasteries. But both were shown the monumental sculpture, the columns and arches on the main avenues.

Another emphasis in Robert's account is the attention he pays to icons.[81] Again this implies a reception of what is important to the

---

[78] For examples later than the *Parastaseis* see Dagron and Paramelle, 'Un texte patriographique' (as in n. 60), 491-523.

[79] *The Alexiad*, VI.x.10, ed. B. Leib (Paris, 1943), II, 71.18-22; *The Alexiad of Anna Comnena*, trans. E. R. A. Sewter (London, 1969), 204; J. Shepard, '"Father" or "scorpion"? Style and substance in Alexios's diplomacy', in M. Mullett and D. Smythe, eds., *Alexios I Komnenos*, I (Belfast, 1996), 68-132, here 78-79.

[80] William of Tyre, ed. R. B. C. Huygens, *Willelmi Tyrensis Archiepiscopi chronicon*, CCCont Med 63A (Turnhout, 1986), 24, 945.12-17; *A history of the deeds done beyond the sea*, trans. E. A. Babcock and A. C. Krey (New York, 1976), 382; P. Magdalino, *The empire of Manuel I Komnenos* (Cambridge, 1993), 242-243.

[81] Gunther of Pairis does not refer to icons and does not list any in his catalogue of relics (ed. Riant, 24-25, 121-125; ed. Orth, 175-180; trans. Andrea, 125-130). Villehardouin

Greeks, their interests, concerns, and point of view, for no other crusader account gives as much attention to icons. The French were not interested in them as devotional objects. They did not take them as 'holy loot', as the Louvre exhibition in 1992-93 which brought together Byzantine objects from French provincial collections amply illustrated.[82] It was the Venetians, rather, who took icons.[83] Yet Robert describes three images on panels, and their significance for the Greeks: 'the image of Our Lady ... which the emperors carry with them when they go to battle';[84] 'the first image of Our Lady that was ever made or painted';[85] and 'an image of St Demetrius ... that gave off so much oil that it could not be removed as fast as it flowed from the picture'.[86]

Robert presents the Greek view of things not only in his description of the city but also in his narration of events. In 1207 a siege of the city of Thessalonike, then under the control of the marquis Boniface of Montferrat, by the Vlach Johanitsa, was miraculously brought to an end by the death of the Vlach. Robert reports,

---

mentions only the icon lost by Mourtzouphlos (ed. Faral, II, 228; trans. Shaw, 86), as does the *Devastatio Constantinopolitana* (ed. Ch. Hopf, *Chroniques Greco-romanes inédites ou peu connues* (Berlin, 1873), 91; now in a new edition and trans. by A. J. Andrea, 'The *Devastatio Constantinopolitana*, a special perspective on the fourth crusade: an analysis, new edition and translation', *Historical Reflections/Réflexions historiques* 19 (1993), 107-149, here 136, 147). This icon was of great interest to the French because they regarded it as a trophy: 'They (the Greeks) fully believe that no one who carries it in battle can be defeated, and we believe that it is because Mourtzouphlos did not have the right to carry it that he was defeated' (ed. Lauer, 66; trans. McNeal, 89). Aubry of Three Fountains devotes a very large section of his account of the conquest of Constantinople to the way in which the icon was lost: *Albericus Trium Fontium, Chronica*, ed. G. H. Pertz, MGH Scriptores 23 (Hanover, 1874), 883.18-42.

[82] R. Cormack, 'The French construction of Byzantium: reflections on the Louvre exhibition of Byzantine art', *Dialogos: Hellenic Studies Review* 1 (1994), 28-41: 'But what the viewer of 1990 is now likely to remark is the virtual absence of icons from the French experience of Byzantine art.' For icons in the west, see K. Ciggaar, *Western Travellers to Constantinople: the West and Byzantium, 962-1204* (Leiden, New York, Cologne, 1996), 327.

[83] H. Belting, *Bild und sein Publikum im Mittelalter*, trans. M. Bartusis and R. Meyer, *The Image and its Public in the Middle Ages* (New Rochelle, c. 1990), Appendix C: Western Art after 1204: the importation of relics and icons, 203-221. The eleventh-century *Life* of Symeon the New Theologian relates the story of a Venetian who buys an icon in Constantinople: *Vie de Syméon le Nouveau Théologien*, ed. I. Hausherr, with P. Gabriel Horn (Rome, 1928), §152, 226-227. See also J.-C. Schmitt, 'L'occident, Nicée II et les images du VIIIe siècle', *Nicée II, 787-1987*, eds. F. Boespfulg and N. Lossky (Paris, 1987), 271-301, esp. 282-297.

[84] Ed. Lauer, §66, 65-68; trans. McNeal, 89.

[85] Ed. Lauer, §114, 107; trans. McNeal, 126.

[86] Ed. Lauer, §83, 83; trans. McNeal, 105. These images which Robert refers to as 'ansconne' or 'ymage ... painte en un tavle', are in addition to his descriptions of the Image of Edessa and Veronica's Cloth (ed. Lauer, §§83, 92, 82-84, 89-90; trans. McNeal, 104, 112).

Now there lay in this city the body of my lord St Demetrius, who would never suffer his city to be taken by force. And there flowed from this holy body such great quantitites of oil that it was a fair marvel. And it came to pass, as John the Vlach was lying one morning in his tent, that my lord St Demetrius came and struck him with a lance through the body and slew him.[87]

The story of St. Demetrios' killing of Johanitsa appears also in later thirteenth-century Greek sources, in encomia for the saint on his feast day. In those encomia, this, the latest miracle performed by Demetrios for his city, is added to all the other stories about the salvation of Thessalonike through its patron saint.[88] Yet the story was first recorded by Robert.[89]

Robert of Clari was not, it should be stressed, favourably disposed to the inhabitants of Constantinople or to the Greeks in general. If anything, he attacks them for their treachery even more virulently than does Villehardouin himself.[90] But his work shows that he absorbed 'Greek' attitudes and ideas, perhaps in spite of himself.

Indeed, Robert's account of Constantinople has more in common with those by the Russian pilgrims and the Arab travellers to Constantinople than it does with other crusading narratives. But the account which is closest to Robert's in content is the anonymous late eleventh-century description of Constantinople in the Cistercian monastery of Santes Creus, north of Tarragon, which is transmitted along with two collections of miracles of the Virgin.[91] The anonymous author, a layman from western Europe, leaves a record of the city whose emphases are like Robert's but whose account is without any hostility to the Greeks.[92] The

---

[87] Ed. Lauer, §116, 107-108; trans. McNeal, 127.

[88] John Stavrakios, 'Λόγος εἰς τὰ θαύματα τοῦ Ἁγίου Δημητρίου', ed. I. Iberites, Μακεδονικά 1 (1940), 369-372; Constantine Akropolites, 'Λόγος εἰς τὸν μεγαλομάρτυρα καὶ μυροβλύτην Δημήτριον', ed. A. Papadopoulos-Kerameus, 'Ἀνάλεκτα Ἱεροσολυμιτικῆς σταχυολογίας I (St. Petersburg, 1891; repr. Brussels, 1963), 211-213.

[89] Aubry of Three Fountains, MGH Scriptores 23, 886.28-29, writing after Robert of Clari, likewise reports that Johanitsa was killed by St. Demetrios: LexMA, s.v. Albericus v. Troifontaines.

[90] E.g. ed. Lauer, §55, 56; §60, 60; §61, 61; §62, 62; §70, 70; §78, 77; trans. McNeal, 80, 84, 85, 86, 93, 94, 98; Dufournet, Les écrivains, II, 381. See, too, Bagley, 'Robert of Clari's La Conquête de Constantinople', 111-112.

[91] K. N. Ciggaar, 'Une description de Constantinople dans le Tarragonensis 55', REB 53 (1995), 117-140 (text, 119-128).

[92] Ciggaar, 'Une description de Constantinople', 129-131, dates the text to a time not long before the First Crusade. See, too, now J. Shepard, 'Cross-purposes: Alexius Comnenus and the First Crusade', in J. Phillips, ed., The First Crusade (Manchester, 1997),

author had lived in Constantinople for some time where he had consulted books and studied Greek.[93] His description of the city, like Robert's, is not an organised tour or itinerary. He too shows an interest in icons and relics and the same churches, Hagia Sophia, the Holy Apostles, and the Blachernai.[94] He is the only other writer besides Robert to use the phrase 'the Greeks say' and he too repeats the claim that 'Two thirds of the world's wealth is in Constantinople, it is said and believed'.[95]

The anonymous late eleventh-century description shows how much of the lore about the city could have been transmitted to westerners by a westerner who had lived and studied in Constantinople and therefore had an insider's view. Robert's knowledge of the city could have derived from such a written source. Yet it is possible that some of his information was transmitted to him orally, by a long-term Latin inhabitant of the capital. A large number of these Latins, both men and women, joined the crusader camp in 1203 after a conflict with the Greeks which resulted in the first of the three fires of 1203-04. Villehardouin states that they were 15,000 in number. They aided the crusaders in their later assault, as Villehardouin and Gunther state.[96] They helped the crusaders in another way also. Gunther of Pairis specifies that those 'whom the Greeks had expelled' told the crusaders 'before the city was stormed' where they could find 'a large hoard of money' and 'precious relics' which the Greeks had brought from neighbouring churches and monasteries 'in the vain hope of security'.[97] These westerners who were Amalfitans and Pisans, according to Choniates, but also Franks, Venetians and Germans, according to Gunther,[98] had ample time then to pass on information about the city — its strategic secrets, the whereabouts of its treasures, and the stories about its monuments which we find recorded in Robert's description. They would be a source for what 'the Greeks say'.

---

119. However, Ciggaar's inference (133-134) that the author is from northern France or Flanders because of his admiration of marble and oil, rare in that part of the world, is not entirely convincing.

[93] Ciggaar, 'Une description', 125.265-266; 128.384.
[94] Ciggaar, 'Une description', 120-127.
[95] Ciggaar, 'Une description', 119.4-6, 17; 120.54; 121.76; 97; 122.137.
[96] Ed. Faral, I §§203-205; trans. Shaw, 79-80; trans. Andrea, 18, 107. The *Devastatio* relates, without giving figures, that none of the westerners who lived in the city remained there after the fire: ed. Hopf, 89-90; ed. and trans. Andrea, 'The *Devastatio Constantinopolitana* (as in n. 81), 134, 145.
[97] Ed. Riant, 19; ed. Orth, p. 156; trans. Andrea, 109.
[98] Ed. van Dieten, 552-553; trans. Magoulias, 302-303; ed. Riant, 18; ed. Orth, 156; trans. Andrea, 107.

To describe Robert of Clari's description of Constantinople as 'tall tales told by the Greeks of Constantinople to the simple-minded traveler from the West'[99] is to dismiss both Robert and the inhabitants of Constantinople and to misunderstand them. Rather, one of the conquerors of that city who was determined to record all he had seen and heard, gave further life to Constantinople as a Greek city long after it had ceased to be Greek, by preserving in his account of the Fourth Crusade what the Greeks said and thought about their city. Thus, paradoxically, in Robert of Clari's account we see Constantinople through the eyes of the Greeks.

---

[99] McNeal, *The Conquest of Constantinople*, introduction, 18.

14. The decline of Byzantium seen through the eyes of western travellers

M. Angold

Byzantium once again became a focus of western travel accounts towards the end of the middle ages, which was a great period of travel writing in the west. It was then that it began to take shape as a distinct branch of western literature. The first faltering and largely unsuccessful step was taken by Rustichello of Pisa, who sought to use romance as a narrative framework for Marco Polo's gazeteer of the east.[1] Far more successful were the *Travels* of Sir John Mandeville, which entirely transformed the pilgrim narrative by turning travel into exploration of God's creation rather than just the journey to the centre of the Christian world — Jerusalem.[2] The transformation was all the more successful because of the way a knight — an English knight — was chosen as the fictitious narrator. This meant, among many other things, that the knight's quest which had been at the centre of Romance could now in practice and on paper be assimilated to the pilgrim narrative. The author of Mandeville's *Travels* succeeded where Rustichello failed: in turning travel into romance.

This new genre of literature could take a variety of forms. It might

---

[1] J. Larner, *Marco Polo and the Discovery of the World* (New Haven and London, 1999), 46-67; J.-P. Rubiés, *Travel and Ethnology in the Renaissance. South India through European Eyes, 1250-1650* (Cambridge, 2000), 74-84.

[2] *Mandeville's Travels*, ed. M. Letts, Hakluyt Society, ser. ii, 101-102 (London, 1953).Vol. I contains the Middle English Egerton text; vol. II the Old French Paris text. See D. R. Howard, *Writers and Pilgrims. Medieval Pilgrimage Narratives and their Posterity* (Berkeley, 1980), 53-76; S. Greenblatt, *Marvellous Possessions* (Oxford, 1991), 26-51; C. K. Zacher, *Curiosity and Pilgrimage: the Literature of Discovery in fourteenth-century England* (Baltimore, 1976); J. R. S. Phillips, 'The quest for Sir John Mandeville', in M. A. Meyer, ed., *The Culture of Christendom. Essays in Medieval History in Commemoration of Denis L. T. Bethell* (London and Rio Grande, 1993), 243-257.

From *Travel in the Byzantine World*, ed. Ruth Macrides. Copyright © 2002 by the Society for the Promotion of Byzantine Studies. Published by Ashgate Publishing Ltd, Gower House, Croft Road, Aldershot, Hampshire, GU11 3HR, Great Britain.

be a straightforward and reasonably accurate account, held together by a narrator who often adopted the pose of the knight errant. It might be more or less fictitious in the manner of the *Travels of the Infante Pedro*, which purported to be the eastern travels of Henry the Navigator's elder brother.[3] As important was the way this new genre assimilated older forms of travel writing by opening up a more personal approach. This applies to diplomatic reports and even more to pilgrimage narratives which had become largely stereotyped and devoid of interest. These now took on new life in the later middle ages, as they came increasingly to be presented as a personal quest. Allegory too could be turned into a story of travel, as Philip de Mézières did in his *Songe du vieil pelerin*.[4] Travel also came to form an important element in chivalric biography, to judge from the amount of space devoted to it in the *Book of Deeds* of Marshal Boucicaut.[5] This is very largely a narrative of travel; travel provided one of the ways in which a knight could fulfil the chivalric ideal. One has only to think of the perfect gentle knight of Chaucer's *Canterbury Tales*, whose fictitious life of adventure on the frontiers of Christendom echoes episodes of Boucicaut's life. Chaucer has his knight fighting for a Turkish emir against other heathen Turks.[6] It was the same with Boucicaut. As a young man he had served the Ottoman emir Murad I for three months 'on the offchance that he might make war against any old Saracens'.[7]

The starting point for these developments is Sir John Mandeville's *Travels*, which appeared in the mid-fourteenth century.[8] One of the many surprises about this text is the importance it attached to Byzantium;[9] so much so that the author completely transforms his main source, the *Pilgrimage* of William of Boldensele, where only a few lines are devoted to the latter's stay at Constantinople in 1332.[10]

---

[3] F. M. Rogers, *The Travels of the Infante Dom Pedro of Portugal* (Cambridge, Mass., 1961).

[4] Philippe de Mézières, *Le Songe du vieil pelerin*, ed. G. W. Coopland (Cambridge, 1969), 2 vols.

[5] *Le Livre des fais du bon Messire Jehan le Maingre, dit Bouciquaut*, ed. D. Lalande (Geneva, 1985). See D. Lalande, *Jean II le Meingre, dit Boucicaut (1366-1421). Etude d'une biographie héroique* (Geneva, 1988).

[6] Geoffrey Chaucer, *The Canterbury Tales*, trans. N. Coghill, 1st edn. (Harmondsworth, 1951), Prologue, 20-21.

[7] *Livre des fais*, I, xvi: 61-62.13-25.

[8] Manuscripts give variously 1356, 1357, and 1366 as the date when the *Travels* were completed.

[9] See I. M. Higgins, *Writing East. The "Travels" of Sir John Mandeville* (Philadelphia, 1977), 64-77.

[10] C. L. Grotefend, *Die Edelherren von Boldensele oder Boldensen* (Hanover, 1855), 30-31.

'Mandeville' did this so that he could use his description of Constantinople as a way of announcing the themes of the book. Constantinople was the first staging post on the route to discovery leading ultimately to the confines of paradise. As such, it required a numinous quality, a quality which it had lost, in western eyes, with the sack of 1204, when its great collection of relics was scattered.

'Mandeville' restores Constantinople to its traditional position as a treasure house of relics. There is no doubt that by the middle of the fourteenth century the Byzantines had succeeded in replacing many famous relics lost in 1204 and its aftermath, including the relics of the Passion, now kept on a table in the north aisle of St. Sophia.[11] William of Boldensele itemised those that he saw: a large fragment of the True Cross, the seamless Tunic, the Sponge, the Reed, and a single Nail from the Cross.[12] To this list 'Mandeville' added both the Lancehead and the Crown of Thorns, but to give greater authenticity to his narrative he admitted that he had seen the portion of the Crown of Thorns kept in the Sainte-Chapelle. He even claimed to have one of the Thorns in his personal possession.[13] He echoes his source when he hails St. Sophia as 'the best kirk of the world and the fairest'.[14] He duly notes the equestrian statue of Justinian which stood beside it, but contradicts his source by insisting that it no longer holds the orb which was the symbol of universal lordship.[15] It was an economical way of suggesting that the Byzantine empire was now of little account politically. 'Mandeville' does not connect this with schism, as westerners usually did at the time.[16] Instead, he provides an accurate and very largely objective account of the religion of the Greeks; again there is nothing like it in his source or, for that matter, in any other travel account. There is a surprising lack of rancour. He has the Greeks refusing John

---

[11] G. P. Majeska, 'St. Sophia in the fourteenth and fifteenth centuries: the Russian travelers on the relics', *DOP* 27 (1973), 71-87. The Byzantine emperor John VI Kantakouzenos (1347-54) was in a position to sell off *pro necessitate* some of the relics housed in the imperial palace: G. Derenzini, 'Esame paleografico del codice X.IV.1 della Biblioteca Communale degli Intronati e contributo documentale alla storia del "Tesoro" dello Spedale di Santa Maria della Scala', *Annali della Facoltà di Lettere e Filosofia dell'Università di Siena* 8 (1987), 59-74.
[12] Grotefend, *Die Edelherren von Boldensele* (as in n. 10), 31.6-8.
[13] *Mandeville's Travels*, ed. Letts, I, 9; II, 235.
[14] Ed. Letts, I, 5; II, 232; cf. Grotefend, *Die Edelherren von Boldensele*, 30-31.
[15] *Mandeville's Travels*, ed. Letts, I, 5-6; II, 232-233. Cf. Grotefend, *Die Edelherren von Boldensele*, 31.1.
[16] E.g. Ludolph von Suchem, *Description of the Holy Land and the Way thither*, Palestine Pilgrims Text Society 27 (London, 1895), 7.

XXII's offer of reunion on the grounds of the Latins' pride and avarice.[17] This elicits no comment on the part of the author. Latin pride and avarice were certainly stumbling blocks as far as John Kantakouzenos was concerned during his negotiations over the Union of Churches in 1367.[18] 'Mandeville' does include details that underlined the hostility of the Greeks to the Latins; for instance, the often repeated complaint that they wash altars that have been used for Latin services. He admits that the Greek church is guilty of simony and fails to suppress usury. He quite correctly singles out Purgatory as an area where Greeks and Latins disagree. However, he — quite incorrectly — accuses the Byzantines of subscribing to 'aphthartodocetism'.[19] Surprisingly, he nowhere condemns the Greeks as schismatics.

'Mandeville' works into his description of Constantinople another detail that is entirely his own. He brings in Stagira as the birthplace of Aristotle and also the site of his tomb, on which there was an altar: 'And there make they a solemn feast ilk a year, as he were a saint. And upon his altar they hold their great counsel and assembly, and they trow that, through inspiration of God and him they will have the better counsel.'[20] I think that it is safe to say that this was sheer make-believe, but the author is picking up on the beginnings of an interest among westerners in classical lore. He also manages a fleeting reference to Mount Athos,[21] which again reflects a new western interest.

'Mandeville' is much less critical of Byzantium on religious grounds than might have been anticipated. He catches a moment when the question of the orient began to matter again after the disappointments produced by the failure of the second council of Lyons (1274). Vatican Register 62 is a monument to this renewed interest. In it a papal clerk has gathered together documents that plot the development of papal relations with oriental powers, including Byzantium. Like 'Mandeville's' *Travels*, Vatican Register 62 can be dated to the mid-fourteenth century. This is not to suggest that the clerk responsible for the Register was somehow influenced by Mandeville's *Travels*; only that 'Mandeville' had an exceptional ability to reflect the concerns of his own time.[22]

---

[17] *Mandeville's Travels*, ed. Letts, I, 13; II, 237-238.

[18] J. Meyendorff, 'Projets de concile oecuménique en 1367: un dialogue inédit entre Jean Cantacuzène et le légat Paul', *DOP* 14 (1960), 149-177, here 172.106-112.

[19] *Mandeville's Travels*, ed. Letts, I,13-14; II, 238-239

[20] Ed. Letts, I, 12; II, 236-237

[21] Ed. Letts, I, 12; II, 237

[22] J. Muldoon, 'The Avignon papacy and the frontiers of Christendom: the evidence of Vatican Register 62', *Archivum Historiae Pontificae* 17 (1979), 125-195, at 131, 159-160.

A generation later Philip de Mézières reviewed western Christendom's relations with the east, including Byzantium. Mézières used his fame as a crusade propagandist to set himself up as the conscience of the age. As a young man he had been close to both Peter Thomas, the papal legate, and Peter, king of Cyprus (1359-69), who had led the Alexandria crusade of 1365. He had also set up the crusading order of the Passion of Jesus Christ which attracted a surprising number of fashionable recruits, including Marshal Boucicaut.[23] In his allegory, *Le Songe du vieil Pelerin*, completed around 1390, Philip de Mézières used the journey of Queen Truth and her companions as a means of surveying the world. They made a special journey to Constantinople which allowed Mézières to consider the state of Byzantium.[24] He condemns the schism with Rome, but he has Queen Truth admitting that in its origins this was as much Rome's fault as it was Byzantium's. There had been a council, where the Greeks had found Roman pride and avarice insufferable. Here Philip de Mézières echoes Mandeville almost word for word.[25] Whatever past rights and wrongs, Constantinople was now in a state of abject decline. Queen Truth and her company entered the Great Church, but it had lost all the magnificence she remembered from earlier days. It was now dirty and rank, like some old tavern or dilapidated warehouse. The empire had been reduced to Constantinople, Philadelphia, and the city of Gallipoli, recently returned thanks to the count of Savoy.[26] Philip de Mézières puts the blame for this miserable state of affairs on the reigning Emperor John V Palaiologos (1341/54-91) — 'tel chief de scisme et de heresie'. Twice in the past twenty years he had publicly repudiated the schism, once before the papal legate Peter Thomas in 1357 and then again in the presence of Pope Urban V at Rome in 1369, but on each occasion he had failed to honour his pledge.[27] Philip de Mézières had a special interest in the reunion of churches, because Peter Thomas was his spiritual mentor. The failure of the Byzantine emperor to fulfil his undertaking over the reunion of churches was a betrayal of Peter Thomas's memory, of which Philip de Mézières was the self-appointed guardian.[28]

---

[23] N. Jorga, *Philippe de Mézières, 1327-1405, et la croisade au moyen age* (Paris, 1896), 63-76, 273-327.
[24] Mézières, *Songe* (as in n. 4), I, xv: I, 233-234.
[25] Mézières, *Songe*, I, lviii: I, 355-356.
[26] Mézières, *Songe*, I, xv: I, 234.
[27] Mézières, *Songe*, I, xxiii: I, 259.
[28] Philippe de Mézières, *The Life of Saint Peter Thomas*, ed. J. Smet, Textus et Studia Historica Carmelitana 2 (Rome, 1954), 75-80.

Needless to say, Constantinople was not at the centre of Philip de Mézières's allegory, nor was it the focus of his most savage criticism. This is reserved for the papacy which is blamed for the Great Schism — an infinitely more serious matter than the schism between Rome and Byzantium. *Le songe du vieil pelerin* was a call for the reform of Latin Christendom as a prelude to a new crusade. Philip de Mézières understood the crusade in a thoroughly old-fashioned way as an expedition to rescue the Holy Sepulchre. When a crusade materialised in 1396 — the so-called Nikopolis crusade — it did not meet with his approval, because it was directed not towards the Holy Land, but against the Ottoman Turks. Its defeat at the battle of Nikopolis called forth a bitter response from Philip de Mézières in his *Epistre lamentable et consolotaire*. It was among other things a call to the princes and chivalry of western Christendom to avenge the defeat. He blames the arrogance of the crusaders. He was certainly dismayed that the Hungarian contingent at Nikopolis had included Bosnians, Serbs, Vlachs, Albanians, and Bulgarians, who were schismatics in his eyes.[29] It was a question of one rotten apple spoiling the barrel,[30] but this was a remark made in passing. The weight of Mézières's criticism was not directed against the Orthodox. He has nothing to say about the Greeks, except to insist that chivalry should never be used against Christians, be they Catholic or schismatic. Instead, it had a duty to defend all Christians until the pride of the Ottoman ruler Bayezid had been brought low. It was a call that made the security of Constantinople in the face of Ottoman aggression a responsibility of the west.[31]

This is a theme that emerges from *The Book of Deeds* of Marshal Boucicaut, one of the participants in the disastrous crusade of Nikopolis. He had been captured and only escaped execution thanks to the last-minute intervention of John the Fearless, the future duke of Burgundy. He was then selected to negotiate with Bayezid over the payment of ransom. This eventually entailed his release so that he could raise the money from the Latin rulers of the Levant. His apparent success meant that he returned to France with his reputation enhanced.

---

[29] In *Oeuvres de Froissart*, ed. Kervyn de Lettenhove, XVI (Brussels, 1872), 453.

[30] K. Petkov, 'The rotten apple and the good apples: Orthodox, Catholics, and Turks in Philippe de Mézières' crusading propaganda', *Journal of Medieval History* 23 (1997), 255-270. This image, used by Philip de Mézières, gives Petkov his title, but otherwise the schismatics are scarcely mentioned in the *Epistre*. Petkov fails to use the passage in the *Songe*, where Mézières admits that papal pride and avarice must bear much of the blame for the schism. As a result, his assessment of Mézières's views on the Orthodox is not well balanced.

[31] *Oeuvres de Froissart*, ed. Kervyn de Lettenhove, XVI, 495.

He was the natural choice to command an expedition to bring aid to Constantinople, which set off in 1399.[32] He emerges from the pages of *The Book of Deeds* as an admirer of the Byzantine Emperor Manuel II Palaiologos (1391-1425). Boucicaut spent nearly a year at Constantinople. He shored up its defences and carried out a series of punitive raids against Turkish territories across the Bosphoros. The threat to Manuel II Palaiologos came not only from the Turks, but also from his nephew John VII Palaiologos who disputed his right to the throne of Constantinople. Boucicaut effected a reconciliation between uncle and nephew. Then, leaving behind a small French garrison, he escorted Manuel to the west to seek aid.[33]

One of the lessons of *The Book of Deeds* of Marshal Boucicaut is that Byzantium provided an arena where western knights could show off their prowess. But more than that, it tallied with Mézières's plea that western chivalry take Christians, even if they were schismatics, under their protection. It was the boast of the Marshal's biographer that 'the noble and ancient city of Constantinople' was only saved thanks to the French garrison that Boucicaut had left behind. He concluded: 'there can be no doubt that this was very pleasing to God and a great honour to the king of France and the French, who gave proof of their valour there, and a great blessing for Christianity.'[34]

Boucicaut's involvement with Manuel Palaiologos did not end there. The surprise defeat of the Ottomans in 1402 at Ankara by Tamburlane meant that Manuel Palaiologos was able to return from exile in the west to Constantinople. By that time, Boucicaut, in another turn of his extraordinary career, had become governor of Genoa. In 1403 he was in command of the Genoese fleet entrusted with the responsibility of safeguarding Genoa's interests in the Levant. As he rounded the Peloponnese on his way to Rhodes he received word that Manuel Palaiologos was at Mistra and wished to see him. He therefore put in near the modern Gytheion where the Byzantine emperor came to meet him. The latter was once again in need of the Marshal's assistance; this time to return to Constantinople. To this end Boucicaut put four galleys at the emperor's disposal.[35] Boucicaut saw the restoration of Manuel Palaiologos to Constantinople as part of God's plan. Tamburlane's great victory over the Ottomans was divinely inspired revenge not only for the defeat of the crusaders at Nikopolis, but also for the exile of the Byzantine emperor. The Marshal's biographer

---

[32] Lalande, *Boucicaut* (as in n. 5), 63-74.
[33] Lalande, *Boucicaut*, 82-93.
[34] *Livre des fais*, I. xxxv, ed. Lalande (as in n. 5), 153.46-49.
[35] Lalande, *Boucicaut*, 97-107.

concluded: 'God who knows how to remedy all situations, did not wish his Christian people to be subjugated by enemies of the true faith.'[36] In the circumstances this was a thought that applied more to Byzantium than it did to Latin Christendom. The assumption was that both were now united in the struggle against the Turks.

While in command of the Genoese squadron Boucicaut's path crossed that of another traveller who has left an account of his voyage: this was Ruy González de Clavijo, who was at the head of a Castilian embassy *en route* to the court of Tamburlane at Samarkand. He reached Rhodes in August 1403 only to discover that Boucicaut and the Genoese fleet had departed some six weeks previously.[37] Clavijo seems to have had a special interest in Boucicaut. It is conceivable that he had come across Boucicaut when in 1387 the latter visited the Castilian court in the company of the duke of Bourbon.[38] From Rhodes Clavijo made his way to Mitylene, where he was told about the settlement that Boucicaut brokered between Manuel Palaiologos and his nephew John VII Palaiologos.[39]

Clavijo received an enthusiastic reception at Constantinople. The Emperor Manuel Palaiologos provided a guard of honour to escort him to the Blachernai Palace, where the emperor received him in his private chamber. Manuel Palaiologos also did him the honour of sending his son-in-law and companion in exile, the Genoese Hilario Doria, to guide him around the sites of the city.[40] Clavijo provides descriptions of the churches and monasteries he saw during his tour: the Prodromos in Petra, the Peribleptos, St. John Stoudios, St. Sophia, St. George of the Mangana, the Blachernai. These are surprisingly detailed and rank among the most accurate and vivid descriptions of Byzantine monuments surviving from the middle ages. Clavijo's systematic presentation of Constantinople stands out from the somewhat inconsequential sketches of other travel narratives. He also refrains from passing judgment, content to exercise his considerable powers of description. He pays due regard to the wealth of the materials, decoration, and fittings that caught his eye. He informs his reader about mosaic technique: 'This mosaic work is made of very small stones, which are covered with fine gilt and blue, white, green, or red enamel, according to the colour which is required to depict the figures, so that this work is very marvellous to

---

[36] *Livre des fais*, I, xxxvii, ed. Lalande, 159.79-82.
[37] *Embajada a Tamorlan*, ed. F. López Estrada (Madrid, 1943), 19-20; trans. G. Le Strange (London, 1928), 42.
[38] Lalande, *Boucicaut*, 23-26.
[39] *Embajada a Tamorlan*, 27-28; trans. Le Strange, 51-53.
[40] *Embajada a Tamorlan*, 34-35; trans. Le Strange, 61-62.

behold.'[41] Clavijo noted that the large monasteries were set in 'gardens and water and vineyards' so that they were like large towns.[42] Throughout the city there were many fields and orchards; it was not densely populated and everywhere there were ruins. The aqueduct of Valens was used for irrigation.[43] This all contrasted with Pera across the Golden Horn, which in area was much smaller, but more densely populated with good and handsome houses.[44]

Clavijo has left a sober and accurate description of Constantinople as befitted an ambassador. It did enough to satisfy the curiosity of the Castilian court, but the purpose of his journey lay thousands of miles to the east, which may explain why he passes no judgment for good or for ill on the Greeks. Though he is too diplomatic to spell it out, his assessment of Byzantium is plain: its great days belonged to the past.[45]

Boucicaut's spiritual successor was the Burgundian Ghillebert de Lannoy.[46] He arrived at Constantinople in 1420 after a bewildering journey from Flanders via the Baltic and eastern Europe. On reaching his destination his first act was to present the Byzantine emperor with jewels he had been entrusted by the king of England and the letters of peace sent jointly by the kings of England and France. Lannoy was expected to advance the cause of the Union of Churches and spent several days with the emperor and the papal envoys discussing the matter but he says nothing about the outcome. Lannoy was touched by the way he was treated at Constantinople: the emperor himself had shown him the relics of the city and on his departure made him a special gift of relics, which he carefully itemised.[47]

If Lannoy has left no detailed description of the city, he did convey the meaning of his journey to Constantinople. He hoped that it would provide him with an opportunity to fight Saracens. When he heard that civil war had broken out among the Ottomans he hired a ship and put on armour hoping that there would be a battle. 'But', he goes on, 'the emperor of Constantinople impounded my ship and refused to let me go, fearing for my life, which caused me great dissatisfaction. I therefore decided to complete my journey to Jerusalem by sea.'[48] What

---

[41] *Embajada a Tamorlan*, 35; trans. Le Strange, 62.
[42] *Embajada a Tamorlan*, 40; trans. Le Strange, 68.
[43] *Embajada a Tamorlan*, 57; trans. Le Strange, 88.
[44] *Embajada a Tamorlan*, 58; trans. Le Strange, 89.
[45] *Embajada a Tamorlan*, 57; trans. Le Strange, 88.
[46] N. Housley, *The Later Crusades. From Lyons to Alcazar 1274-1580* (Oxford, 1992), 395.
[47] *Oeuvres de Ghillebert de Lannoy, voyageur, diplomate et moraliste*, ed Ch. Potvin (Louvain, 1878), 65-66.
[48] *Oeuvres de Ghillebert de Lannoy*, ed. Potvin, 67.3-6.

was the point of staying on in Constantinople, if you were forbidden to fight!

Lannoy is not critical of the Greeks but Bertrandon de la Broquière, another traveller with Burgundian connections, was most distrustful of them. He reached Constantinople late in 1432 after an overland journey from Syria with a Turkish caravan. He made his preference for the Turks all too clear: 'I found more friendship among the Turks and would sooner trust myself to them than to the Greeks.'[49] He also thought that the 'Greeks hate the Christians more than the Turks do'.[50] The local Greeks at first took Bertrandon for a Turk and treated him with deference, but as soon as they discovered that he was a Frank they set about cheating him: 'They would gladly have beaten me, for they hated the Christians very much at that time.'[51] He explained this in terms of their belief that the pope had held a general council in which they were condemned as schismatics. It is no surprise that Bertrandon gave it as his opinion that the Union of Churches negotiated since then at Florence was done 'more from poverty and hunger than from love for the Church of Rome'.[52]

This is a remark that indicates that Bertrandon had reflected on the Greek problem while he was writing up an account of his travels. He never spells out his line of thought, but it emerges from his account of his arrival at Belgrade at the end of his journey across the Balkans. Bertrandon was surprised to discover that this vital frontier fortress was not entrusted to local people, but was garrisoned by German mercenaries. He was told that in the face of a Turkish assault local forces would have been unreliable. This confirmed his worst fears that the Balkans along with Constantinople were all but lost to the Turks, because the local Christian population, be it Greek or Serb, no longer had the will to resist. 'This is a great pity for all of Christendom' which he understood in a good Latin fashion.[53] He appreciated Constantinople's strategic and commercial value to the west; the strength of its walls and its deep-water anchorage in the Golden Horn.[54] It was still full of Latin merchants. The Venetians were the most powerful and enjoyed independent status. The continued safety of

---

[49] *Le voyage d'Outremer de Bertrandon de la Broquière*, ed. C. H. A. Schefer (Paris, 1892), 149; trans. G. R. Kline (New York, 1988), 95.
[50] *Broquière*, ed. Schefer, 139; trans. Kline, 87.
[51] *Broquière*, ed. Schefer, 148-149; trans. Kline, 94.
[52] *Broquière*, ed. Schefer, 149; trans. Kline, 95.
[53] *Broquière*, ed. Schefer, 216; trans. Kline, 137-138.
[54] *Broquière*, ed. Schefer, 151, 153; trans. Kline, 97, 98-99.

the city depended very largely on them. Bertrandon noted that in the recent past it had been saved from the Turks only by the timely arrival of the Venetian fleet. His comment is interesting: 'I think God protected it for the holy relics that are there more than for anything else.'[55] The unwritten thought is that the Greeks did not deserve the relics housed in their city.

Because Bertrandon de la Broquière was travelling incognito and had no official status, he did not have access to the imperial court. He was accordingly less impressed by Byzantine majesty than other more favoured travellers. He regarded the Byzantine emperor not as a generous host, but as an uncertain quantity. He has a story of a Byzantine emperor who had backed down in the face of Turkish threats and had razed some of the city's defences, thus endangering its security.[56] This is a garbled version of John V Palaiologos's destruction, on Turkish orders, of the fortress that he constructed around the Golden Gate. The present emperor was in Bertrandon's estimate 'very much under the control of the Grand Turk'.[57] The Turks and Turkish ways were beginning to infiltrate Constantinople. The Turkish community was autonomous. A Christian slave escaping from a Turkish household would be sent back immediately.[58] Bertrandon noted that it was from the Turks that Byzantine aristocrats had learnt their equestrian tricks.[59]

Bertrandon de la Broquière was not oblivious to the glamour of Constantinople, represented by the beauty of the Byzantine empress.[60] He recognised its utility to 'Christendom' in the struggle with the Turks. Its relics alone meant it was worth fighting for, but the Greeks could not be trusted. Byzantium was a liability as far as Bertrandon was concerned. This represents a marked change of attitude compared with western travellers of a generation earlier. It can be explained in part by personal experience. Unlike Clavijo, Boucicaut, and Lannoy, Bertrandon was visiting Constantinople incognito and had no official status. He had no entry into the imperial court at Constantinople.

But it must have been more than this. His views agreed with those of the young Castilian Pero Tafur who followed Bertrandon to Constantinople six years later on the eve of the departure of the

---

[55] *Broquière*, ed. Schefer, 164; trans. Kline, 104.
[56] *Broquière*, ed. Schefer, 151-152; trans. Kline, 97.
[57] *Broquière*, ed. Schefer, 164-165; trans. Kline, 104.
[58] *Broquière*, ed. Schefer, 165; trans. Kline, 105.
[59] *Broquière*, ed. Schefer, 158; trans. Kline, 101.
[60] *Broquière*, ed. Schefer, 156; trans. Kline, 100.

Byzantine court to the council of Florence.[61] Unlike Bertrandon, Pero Tafur was able to gain access to the imperial court, claiming some spurious kinship with the imperial family.[62] John VIII Palaeologos apparently believed him, but he was happy at that moment to recruit likely looking young westerners into his entourage. Tafur was treated very generously by the Byzantine court: taken out on hunting expeditions and given guided tours of the churches and relics of the city. However, imperial favour did not fool the young Castilian. He saw as clearly as Bertrandon the weakness of the Byzantine imperial regime: 'The Emperor's state is splendid as ever, for nothing is omitted from the ancient ceremonies, but, properly regarded, he is like a bishop without a see.'[63] This was reflected in the imperial palace, which 'must have been very magnificent, but now it is in such a state that both it and the city show well the evils the people have suffered and still endure'.[64]

Tafur fails to explain what these evils were, but they are likely to have resulted from Turkish pressure. While he was there, he experienced a Turkish demonstration against the city. Much to his relief the Turks were bought off: he did not think that with so few men available Constantinople could have put up much of a defence.[65] In the same way as Bertrandon de la Broquière Pero Tafur was not particularly impressed by the Turks' battle array, but it was something of an irrelevance because 'there are here neither ships nor fortresses, nor is there any protection except by fighting', while western aid remained a remote possibility.[66] Looking back on his stay at Constantinople after the city had fallen, he noted that long before his arrival 'the Greeks were as subject then [to the Turks] as they now are'.[67] He blamed the fall of Constantinople partly on the west, but mostly on the Greeks themselves. He remembered them as 'sad and poor, showing the hardship of their lot which is, however, not so bad as they deserve, *for they are a vicious people steeped in sin*'.[68] These are harsh words. Whereas Bertrandon de la Broquière condemns the Greeks as

---

[61] See A. A. Vasiliev, 'Pero Tafur, a Spanish traveller of the fifteenth century and his visit to Constantinople, and Trebizond, and Italy', *Byz* 7 (1932), 75-122.

[62] *Andanças e viajes de un hidalgo español — Pero Tafur (1436-1439)*, ed. F. López Estrada (Barcelona, 1982), 139-149; trans. M. Letts, *Pero Tafur. Travels and Adventures 1435-1439* (London, 1926), 117-123.

[63] *Pero Tafur*, ed. López Estrada, 181; trans. Letts, 145.

[64] *Pero Tafur*, ed. López Estrada, 180; trans. Letts, 145.

[65] *Pero Tafur*, ed. López Estrada, 184-185; trans. Letts, 147-148.

[66] *Pero Tafur*, ed. López Estrada, 185; trans. Letts, 148.

[67] *Pero Tafur*, ed. López Estrada, 168; trans. Letts, 137.

[68] *Pero Tafur*, ed. López Estrada, 181; trans. Letts, 146: 'aunque non tanto quanto devían, por ser gente muy viçiosa é embuelta en pecados' (my emphasis).

schismatics, Pero Tafur is quite uninterested in religious differences, despite making the effort to visit the council of Florence, where he caught up with the Byzantine court once again.[69] For Pero Tafur sin was sexual. He has a story which implies that sodomy was rife in Constantinople, while rumour had it that the Byzantine empress was unhealthily involved with her brother.[70] It sounds as though Pero Tafur had picked up on the gossip he heard during his stay in the imperial entourage at Constantinople and then used it to condemn the Greeks.

This lack of sympathy for Byzantium is all the more surprising because Bertandron de la Broquière and Pero Tafur visited Constantinople when negotiations over the Union of Churches were under way. However, the former did not approve; the latter was not interested. The circumstances which had produced a degree of warmth for Byzantium in the courts of Europe were coming to an end. Western sympathy had had its roots in that bout of self-examination induced by the 'Babylonish Captivity' of the papacy at Avignon and the Great Schism that ensued. Western self-confidence had then begun to seem misplaced. The schism with the Greek Church could no longer be blamed entirely on the Greeks, even Philip de Mézières was agreed on this. The emphasis shifted to ways to bring help to the stricken Byzantine empire. Given the disarray of the papacy this was seen by a crusade propagandist, like Philip de Mézières, as the particular responsibility of the chivalry of western Christendom. The belief that Byzantium and the Levant were an arena for chivalric deeds is exemplified in the adventures of Boucicaut and Lannoy. It was an idea that put down deep roots and explains why Philip the Good, duke of Burgundy, remained wedded to the crusade even after the fall of Constantinople in 1453. It was still powerful enough among an older generation at the Burgundian court to stifle the discouraging assessment of the Byzantines brought back to Philip the Good by Bertrandon de la Broquière. The latter's views on the Byzantines were the product of personal experience. Unlike other western travellers who were the guests of the Byzantine court, Bertrandon was exposed to the hostility of ordinary Greeks. This evoked dispassionate and objective comment in the fashion of much late medieval western travel writing. But his sullen reception by the Greeks contrasted with the hospitality and companionship which Bertrandon had known among the Turks; and the Greeks suffered by comparison.

---

[69] *Pero Tafur*, ed. López Estrada, 289, 292; trans. Letts, 225, 227.
[70] *Pero Tafur*, ed. López Estrada, 159, 176; trans. Letts, 130, 142.

Reception at court meant that Pero Tafur was protected during his stay in Constantinople from popular dislike of Latins, but he is in his way even harsher in his comments about the Greeks of Constantinople than Bertrandon de la Broquière. He reflected the self-criticism that was rife in a society that was teetering on the abyss. The Byzantine court and intelligentsia blamed the failings of their people — largely sexual — for their reduced circumstances. Ever since the reign of Justinian it was normal for sodomy to be trotted out as an explanation for disasters; always remembering the fate of the cities of the plain. The denunciations directed by Joseph Bryennios in the early fifteenth century against Greek sexual proclivities only follow — if more luridly — a traditional pattern.

Bryennios was one of Constantinople's leading churchmen under Manuel II Palaiologos (1391-1425), a great preacher and controversialist, whose opinion counted.[71] He was bitterly opposed to negotiations over the Union of Churches. He was convinced that the Latins were using them as a cover for their own ambitions against Constantinople. His concern over Latin intentions reflected the new purpose that the papacy brought to the question of the reunion of churches in the aftermath of the Great Schism. It was felt that the return of the church of Constantinople to Rome would do much to restore the prestige of the papacy. The reunion of churches was a topic that was of little interest to 'knights errant', such as Bertrandon de la Broquière and Pero Tafur. It was of much greater interest to the humanists of Italy, who had begun to discover ancient Greece. For them talks about the Union of Churches provided opportunities to further their work of rediscovering antiquity by bringing them into contact with Byzantine scholars. This seems to be one of the lessons that can be culled from the career of the greatest antiquarian traveller of the time, Ciriaco of Ancona (c. 1391-1455): he helped to persuade the Byzantine platonist George Gemistos Plethon to attend the council of Florence.[72] A vogue for classical antiquity was a new factor in the way westerners regarded the Greeks. It led some Renaissance scholars and travellers to regard Constantinople as the guardian of the classical heritage.

The attitudes of the antiquarian travellers were different from those of the 'knights errant', such as De la Broquière and Tafur. They were not informed by the same chivalric values. Their outlook was none

---

[71] L. Oeconomos, 'L'état intellectuel et moral des Byzantins vers le milieu du XIVe siècle d'après une page de Joseph Bryennios', in *Mélanges Charles Diehl* (Paris, 1930), 225-233; D. M. Nicol, *Church and Society in the last centuries of Byzantium* (Cambridge, 1979), 99-100.

[72] See C. M. Woodhouse, *Gemistos Plethon. The Last of the Hellenes* (Oxford, 1986), 130.

the less distinctively western. The difference was that it was still in the process of being worked out. The observations made by western antiquarians during their travels in the Greek lands would make their own significant contribution. It produced a shift of interest from Constantinople to Greece.[73] The antiquarians were not very sympathetic to Byzantium, which seemed to have betrayed its allotted role as the guardian of classical antiquity. For the moment it is enough to note a surprising contradiction at the heart of their attitude to Byzantium. They were generally critical of the moral condition of the Greeks of their time, but they were admiring of the monastic life pursued on Mount Athos.

This is especially evident in the work of the Florentine Cristoforo Buondelmonti.[74] Cristoforo's two works — *Descriptio insulae Cretae* [75] and *Liber insularum Archipelagi*[76] — enjoyed immense success. He was born in the late fourteenth century into a patrician family of Florence. He had an aunt who was married to Leonardo I Tocco, count of Cephalonia. Family connections of this kind gave Cristoforo great advantages when it came to exploring Greece and Constantinople. He was also closely connected with the humanist circle at Florence which centred on Niccolò Niccoli. Cristoforo's *Description of Crete* was dedicated to Niccolò, so it is possible that his initial decision made around 1414 to go to Rhodes in order to study Greek was done under Niccolò's auspices. His passion for antiquity is apparent in his efforts to re-erect a colossal statue of Apollo on the island of Delos. They were unsuccessful. When Ciriaco of Ancona visited the island twenty-five years later, he saw the colossus broken in two.[77] This interest in classical antiquity did not preclude a visit to Mount Athos. Cristoforo has left the first extended description of the Holy Mountain by a western traveller.[78] He reckoned that there were about 30 monasteries on the mountain. In some, he had counted 100 monks; in others, as many as 500. His description becomes a eulogy of their way of life. 'The place where they live is so to say a palace of angels; there reigns the

---

[73] R. Weiss, *The Renaissance Discovery of Classical Antiquity* (Oxford, 1969), 131-144.

[74] R. Weiss, 'Un umanista antiquario: Cristoforo Buondelmonti', *Lettere italiane* 16 (1964), 105-116.

[75] Cristoforo Buondelmonti, *Descriptio Insule Crete*, ed. M.-A. van Spitael (Heraklion, 1981).

[76] *Description des Iles de l'Archipel par Christophe Buondelmonti*, ed. E. Legrand (Paris, 1897).

[77] E. W. Bodnar, 'A visit to Delos in April, 1445', *Archaeology* 25 (1972), 210-215.

[78] *Description des Iles de l'Archipel par Christophe Buondelmonti*, ed. E. Legrand (Paris, 1897), 92-94. See R. Gothóni, *Tales and Truth: Pilgrimage on Mount Athos* (Helsinki, 1994), 24-25.

odour of sancity and a spiritual fervour; modesty characterises their way of life.'[79]

This estimate of the quality of monastic life on Athos was echoed some twenty-five years later by Ciriaco of Ancona, but what caught the latter's eye was the richness of the monastic libraries, not only in the church fathers but in the classics too. The highpoint was a visit to the monastery of Iveron. The abbot happened to be away and Ciriaco was able to acquire *magna voluptate* a copy of Plutarch's *Moralia* from the monastic library. The monasteries of Mount Athos therefore fulfilled a useful function in Ciriaco's eyes: they had preserved the heritage of classical antiquity.[80]

Buondelmonti's enthusiastic response to the monasteries of Athos contrasts with his description of the 'ill-starred city of Constantinople' as he calls it.[81] He visited Constantinople in 1422. He has not left us a detailed description of the city, although his view of Constantinople is vivid testimony to the dilapidated state of the city.[82] He lists the still magnificent churches, but fails to provide any description. What interested him were the monuments surviving from late antiquity, such as the columns, the cisterns and the monuments in the hippodrome. Good antiquarian that he was, he copied the inscription on the obelisk in the hippodrome.[83] He observed correctly that the reliefs on the columns of Theodosius and Arcadius depicted the events of their reigns and did not foretell future disasters, which was the popular belief.[84] Buondelmonti noted too the pedestals on which the horses taken away to Venice were supposed to have stood.[85] This is reminiscent of Manuel Chrysoloras's description of Constantinople in his comparison of the old and new Romes.[86] You could tell what a great city Constantinople had been because 'many other statues used to be in the city as shown by their remaining pedestals and the inscriptions on them'. Chrysolaras penned his description of Constantinople in a letter that he despatched from Rome in 1411 to the future Emperor John VIII Palaiologos. However, it was much discussed in humanist circles once Chrysoloras had sent a

---

[79] *Description des Iles*, ed. Legrand, 94.53-56.

[80] *Cyriacus of Ancona's Journeys in the Propontis and the Northern Aegean 1444-1445*, ed. E. W. Bodnar and C. Mitchell (Philadelphia, 1976), 50-56, 66 n. 119.

[81] *Description des Iles*, ed. Legrand, 84.2-4.

[82] G. Gerola, 'Le vedute di Costantinopoli di Cristoforo Buondelmonti', *Studi bizantini e neoellenici* 3 (1931), 252-261.

[83] *Description des Iles*, ed. Legrand,87.90-93.

[84] *Description des Iles*, ed. Legrand, 88.113-115; cf. R. Macrides, 'Constantinople: the crusaders' gaze', in this volume.

[85] *Description des Iles*, ed. Legrand, 88.108-113.

[86] C. Mango, *The Art of the Byzantine Empire 312-1453* (Toronto, 1986), 250-252.

copy to his former student Guarino.[87] Buondelmonti was therefore likely to have been aware of Chrysoloras's description of Constantinople before he set out for the east around 1414. Chrysoloras was dead by the time that Buondelmonti visited Constantinople, but his brother John was there. Among the latter's pupils was the young Italian humanist Francesco Filelfo who was likely to have made contact with Buondelmonti and to have introduced him to Byzantine intellectual circles.[88]

This helps to explain his surprising hostility towards the Greeks of the city. They had become degenerate: 'Today forgetting their ancient glory and becoming gross, the Greeks only seek to satisfy their appetites.'[89] He noted the colossal amounts of food the citizens of Constantinople ate. That explained, he thought, why a quarter of them suffered from epilepsy.[90] They were not worthy of the Greek fathers of the church, such as Chrysostom and John of Damascus.[91] These comments sound like second-hand opinions rather than direct observations. It is more than likely that Buondelmonti was picking up on the despair felt by Byzantine churchmen and intellectuals, such as Joseph Bryennios.

Buondelmonti seems never to have met Ciriaco of Ancona, though it is surmised that the latter had a copy of the *Liber Insularum*.[92] Ciriaco came from a merchant family of Ancona. By the age of 16 he was already in charge of one of the family's shops and soon after that he was *en route* to Alexandria. His contact with Italian humanism began in 1420 when he worked for the future Pope Eugenius IV on the harbour installations at Ancona. Thereafter, he travelled indefatigably around the Levant recording classical sites and copying inscriptions. Of all fifteenth-century western travellers Ciriaco is the one that is likely to have been best acquainted with Constantinople in its last days. He visited it at least six times between 1418 and 1447.[93] He wrote about

---

[87] H. Homeyer, 'Zur *Synkrisis* des Manuel Chrysoloras, einem Vergleich zwischen Rom und Konstantinopel', *Klio* 62 (1980), 533.

[88] There is only a presumption that Filelfo and Buondelmonti met at Constantinople, but the former's friendship with Ciriaco is documented: Francesco Scalamonti, *Vita viri clarissimi et famosissimi Kyriaci Anconitani*, ed. and trans. C. Mitchell and E. W. Bodnar (Philadelphia, 1996), App. III, 191-95.

[89] *Description des Iles*, ed. Legrand, 89.158-161.

[90] *Description des Iles*, ed. Legrand, 89.163-164.

[91] *Description des Iles*, ed. Legrand, 89.164-167.

[92] C. Mitchell, 'Ex libris Kiriaci Anaconitani', *Italia medioevale e umanistica* 5 (1962), 283-299.

[93] Scalamonti, *Vita* (as in n. 88), 13-18; J. Colin, *Cyriaque d'Ancône. Le voyageur, le marchand, l'humaniste* (Paris, 1981), 13-64.

the city, copied inscriptions and sketched its main buildings and monuments. Sadly, his notebooks, his *Commentaria* in five volumes, almost certainly perished in a fire which destroyed the Sforza Library at Pesaro in 1514. All that survives of his work on Constantinople are copies of a sequence of seven drawings of St. Sophia[94] which are none the less impressive for being well known. Ciriaco also took the trouble to copy one inscription from the north tympanum of St. Sophia. It reads, 'Time threatens to destroy this inimitable work. This we prevent through our efforts. But, o most high king, open to us a mansion which time does not reach.'[95]

This neatly signposts Ciriaco's work as an antiquarian. The preservation of the past was his laudable aim, but the past that interested him was the classical past, not Byzantium which was beyond hope. Whereas it is mostly an educated guess that Buondelmonti was influenced in his attitudes by contacts with Byzantine intellectuals, in Ciriaco's case it can be shown with some certainty that his attitudes to the classical past owed much to those Byzantine neoplatonic circles connected with Gemistos Plethon. They were obsessed with the belief that it was possible to resuscitate the moribund corpse of Byzantium by a return to classical virtue. Plethon fell foul of the Orthodox church in Constantinople and went into a comfortable exile at Mistra in the Peloponnese.[96] It was there that Ciriaco fell under his spell. Quite fortuitously, there has survived Ciriaco's notebook for 1447-48, the year he spent at Mistra in the company of Gemistos Plethon.[97] From Mistra he made a journey southwards into the Mani. It has an intrinsic value as the first detailed western description of the region. But for our purposes it shows how Ciriaco had absorbed the values of Plethon's circle. His account is written in Latin, but his innermost thoughts are given in Italian. He laments the passing of the glory that was Greece:

> Today's inhabitants of Laconia and the Spartan range of Taygetus and the town of Mistra — the ancient having been abandoned — exercise servile arts and certain vile mysteries and are dominated by barbarians and foreigners .... However, the nature of the place

---

[94] C. Smith, 'Cyriacus of Ancona's seven drawings of Hagia Sophia', *Art Bulletin* 69 (1987), 16-32.
[95] Smith, 'Cyriacus of Ancona's seven drawings of Hagia Sophia', 22.
[96] See Woodhouse, *Gemistos Plethon* (as in n. 72), 17-31, 83-86.
[97] R. Sabbadini, 'Ciriaco d'Ancona e la sua descrizione autografa del Peloponneso trasmessa da Leonardo Botta', in A. Ratti, ed., *Nel iii centenarios della Biblioteca Ambrosiana, 1609-1909. Miscellanea Ceriani* (Milan, 1910), 203-232.

cannot be completely denied, since from it come forth men who are upright by nature and disposed to virtue.[98]

He provides examples of local people he had met who were exemplars of the Spartan spirit.[99] He was heartened by the way that in the Mani the people seemed to have kept alight the Olympic torch. They still had a stadium for footraces and prizes were allotted to the victors.[100]

The fall of Constantinople to the Turks sparked off conflicting reactions in the west. The surge of emotion it produced had little to do with the Greeks. It had much more to do with Constantinople as a symbol. There was a sense of failure: the west had not been able to save Constantinople. It exposed the futility of chivalric ideas that emphasised the responsibility of western knighthood for the security of Constantinople. It equally revealed the emptiness of humanist rhetoric which proclaimed Byzantium's role as the treasure house of classical antiquity. This sentimental response soon evaporated. It was replaced by a feeling that the Greeks were not worthy of their past greatness; that they themselves were responsible for their downfall. Ironically, this was a reflection of ideas that had circulated among the Byzantine elite, as its members desperately tried to come to terms with the rapid decline of the Byzantine empire from the middle of the fourteenth century. It was a time-honoured way of searching for solutions to their plight. Byzantine self-criticism was picked up by western travellers and fed into their assessment of Byzantium.[101]

The importance of travel literature is that it is part of that process whereby one society or civilisation assesses another. Medieval travel literature confirmed preconceptions and strengthened an existing self-image. But towards the end of the middle ages there occurred, as Joan-Pau Rubiés has recently demonstrated, a radical shift in western travel literature which produced something approaching a systematic evaluation of other societies. This helped to provide a new perspective on the outside world.[102]

The injection of greater objectivity into western travel literature came at a time when Byzantium was failing — a fact confirmed by a succession of western travellers, some of whom found the Turks a more congenial subject. Others turned their gaze to the past, to classical

---

[98] Sabbadini, 'Ciriaco d'Ancona', 221-222.
[99] E.g. George Choirodontes: Sabbadini, 'Ciriaco d'Ancona', 222.
[100] Sabbadini, 'Ciriaco d'Ancona', 218.
[101] See I. Ševčenko, 'The decline of Byzantium seen through the eyes of its intellectuals', *DOP* 15 (1961), 169-186.
[102] J.-P. Rubiés, *Travel and Ethnology in the Renaissance* (as in n. 1), 136-147, 388-398.

antiquity. These 'antiquarian' travellers considered among other things that Byzantium had failed in its allotted task of preserving or even properly appreciating the material remains of its classical past. Their views built on Byzantine self-criticism, but in a way that allowed western humanists to appropriate ancient Greece as part of their claim to be the guardians of classical antiquity. This was only confirmed by the ignorance displayed by the Greeks of their classical heritage which became a stock theme of later western visitors to Greece.

It was not only Byzantine self-criticism that was relayed to the west by travellers. While Byzantium may have ceased to count as a political power, Mount Athos retained all its prestige as a great and powerful monastic centre. It was a spiritual beacon, which proclaimed the continuing strength of Orthodoxy. The Ottomans early recognised its importance. The Byzantine elite continued to look to Mount Athos as a source of hope. There was also pride in its spiritual achievements. This was another side to the Byzantine reaction to decline, one that was picked up in western travel accounts and conveyed to the west. Respect for the Athonite way of life remained part of the repertoire of western travel accounts; so too was a taste for the holdings of Athonite libraries.[103]

To conclude, later medieval travel accounts played an important part in fixing a western view of Byzantium that held good well into the eighteenth century. But first of all an older and in many ways more sympathetic view of Byzantium had to be discarded. The reports coming back to the west on the eve of the fall of Constantinople had a part to play in this. They suggested that the Greeks did not appreciate the aid that the west was willing to offer. Not only were they ungrateful, they were also morally corrupt. In the aftermath of 1453 it was possible to assess Byzantium afresh, building on the work of antiquarians, for whom medieval Byzantium was not exactly an irrelevance, but had failed in the duty allotted to it after the event: to preserve the classical heritage against the barbarian.

---

[103] Gothóni, *Tales and Truth* (as in n. 78), 29-66, 96-106.

Section IV
Going over it — representations of travel and space

15. The conquest of space*

L. Brubaker

Travel, the subject of the symposium that generated this volume, involves transient movement; images, the subject of this chapter, are static. What they share is the ability to encompass multiple points of view and multiple locations. The sixth-century Madaba mosaic map (Fig. 15.1), for example, allows viewers to move from site to site with their eyes in a manner analogous to — if with infinitely less effort — the way that travellers move from site to site with their feet. As this analogy brings forcibly to mind, there are, of course, considerable differences between looking at an image of a landscape and moving through the landscape itself. One of these differences is control. Travellers on the ground must be prepared for the unexpected, a requirement not demanded of viewers of the Madaba map, whose experience of the topography of the lands around Jerusalem is calmly circumscribed. The Madaba mosaic map presents one way to control space; one way to encapsulate the experience of distance, which involves movement over space and time, into a single package. To show that movement itself is something else again. Images of travel must capture a moment of a sequential narrative and make it stand in for the whole journey. In a miniature from the *Christian Topography* (Fig. 15.2), for example, the journey of Saul from Jerusalem to Damascus, during which he was blinded by the light, found Christ, and took on the new name of Paul, is all condensed into a single frame.

The Madaba map and the narrative of Paul's journey each suppose a different set of relationships between an image and its viewers, and with their lived experience of actual travel, but the mosaic and the miniature do have something in common. Maps and images of travel are

---

* I thank the other participants in the symposium for helpful discussion after the paper, and Chris Wickham for comments on an earlier draft of the chapter.

From *Travel in the Byzantine World*, ed. Ruth Macrides. Copyright © 2002 by the Society for the Promotion of Byzantine Studies. Published by Ashgate Publishing Ltd, Gower House, Croft Road, Aldershot, Hampshire, GU11 3HR, Great Britain.

both ways to visualise the conquest of space. This chapter is about some ways that this concept was worked out in Byzantium.

The Madaba mosaic map was laid in the middle of the sixth century. It was apparently always the pavement of a church, and was once considerably larger than it now is: the roughly 30 square metres that survive are less than a third of its original extent, which was nearly 16 metres (c. 50 feet) long and 6 metres (c. 20 feet) wide.[1] The original church is long since gone; and while the present church was rebuilt on the old foundations, so that we know that the orientation of the mosaic vis-à-vis the apse remains the same as it was, the elevation of the early Byzantine church is irretrievably lost. From its original dimensions, we can guess that the mosaic originally showed Syria, Palestine and Egypt in considerable detail; what is now best preserved are the banks of the Jordan, the Dead Sea, the Negev, and the Nile delta. The decision to put this elaborate representation on the floor of the church at Madaba was presumably prompted by various symbolic interpretations of church interiors that were composed in the sixth, seventh and eighth centuries, which interpreted the spaces within a church as emblems of the cosmos.[2] Often, as for example in the writings of Maximus the Confessor (580-662), the apse was equated with heaven while the nave was equated with the earth.[3] It seems likely that some

---

[1] See, most recently, M. Piccirillo and E. Alliata, eds., *The Madaba map centenary 1897-1997*, Studium biblicum franciscanum, collectio maior 40 (Jerusalem, 1999), with full bibliography. The map is also conveniently reproduced in M. Piccirillo, *The mosaics of Jordan* (Amman, 1992), fold-out plate between 80 and 81, figs 62-77 (hereafter Piccirillo, *Mosaics*). A detailed description appeared in H. Donner, *The mosaic map of Madaba*, Palaestina antiqua 7 (Kampen, 1992); a good discussion in P. Donceel-Voûte, 'La carte de Madaba: cosmographie, anachronisme et propagande', *Revue biblique* 95 (1988), 519-542.

[2] See A. Grabar, 'Le témoignage d'une hymne syriaque sur l'architecture de la cathédrale d'Edesse au VIe siècle et sur la symbolique de l'édifice chrétien', *Cahiers archéologiques* 2 (1947), 41-67; P. Donceel-Voûte, *Les pavements des églises byzantines de Syrie et du Libnan. Décor, archéologie et liturgie*, 2 vols. (Louvain-la-Neuve, 1988), I, 485-488; K. E. McVey, 'The domed church as microcosm: literary roots of an architectural symbol', *DOP* 37 (1983), 91-121; *eadem*, 'The Sogitha on the church of Edessa in the context of other early Greek and Syriac hymns for the consecration of church buildings', *Aram* 5, A Festschrift for Dr Sebastian P. Brock (1993), 329-370; and, more generally, M.-T. Olszewski, 'L'image et sa fonction dans la mosaïque byzantine des premières basiliques en Orient: L'iconographie chrétienne expliquée par Cyrille de Jérusalem (314-387)', *Cahiers archéologiques* 43 (1995), 9-34.

[3] PG 91.672. See Grabar (as in n. 2); H. Maguire, *Earth and ocean: the terrestrial world in early Byzantine art* (University Park, Pa., 1987), 24-28, esp. 26; and the brief remarks in P. Donceel-Voûte, 'From Madaba to Mallorca: the iconographical programme of the church building and the image in its context', *Frühes Christentum zwischen Rom und Konstantinopel*,

understanding along these lines inspired the floor we see now, though other ideas are also worked out on the floor. Symbolic appropriation of the landscape — control by representation — is certainly one facet of the image; but it is evident from the care with which the topography of the map and the physical space of the church itself have been coordinated that other goals were equally important.

Near the centre of the original composition was Jerusalem, identified in the red cubes reserved for the most important inscriptions as 'the holy city of Jerusalem' (Fig. 15.3).[4] It was aligned with the apse, and its cardinal points were coordinated with those of the church: standing at the western edge of the mosaic, which the inscriptions indicate to be the preferred point from which to view the ensemble, east is at the top, toward the apse, north is to the left, south to the right, and west towards the entrance to the church. Directional alignment — both axial and cardinal — was, clearly, important to the mosaicist. The city is surrounded by a wall punctuated with towers, and is bisected by a colonnaded street that runs from St. Stephen's gate (now known as the Damascus gate) to the Sion gate, beyond which is the area of southern Jerusalem enclosed by an extension of the old wall that had been commissioned by the Empress Eudokia in the 440s. Except for the Sion gate, the colonnaded street, the church of Caiaphas (?),[5] and the church of the Holy Sepulchre with its baptistery, in the middle of that street, the city is arranged to be seen from the west: so we are shown the outside of the western wall, and the inside of the eastern one, with its own major gate of the Sheep Pool, where Christ healed the paralytic.[6] From this point of view, the Holy Sepulchre is upside down, but it too has had the coordinates of the Madaba church imposed upon it: the represented space has been arranged to conform with real space, and follows the east/west axis of the Madaba church itself; the entrance to

---

Resümees, 14 Weltkongress für christliche Archäologie (Vienna, 1999). I thank Hans Buchwald for this reference.

[4] As first noted by Donceel-Voûte, 'La carte de Madaba' (as in n.1), 522-523, Madaba was probably once represented in the area that no longer survives between Jerusalem and the apse, thus indulging in civic promotion of a type familiar from other churches in the region. See also E. Alliata, 'The pilgrimage routes during the Byzantine period in Transjordan', in Piccirillo and Alliata, eds., *The Madaba map centenary*, 121-124; and P.-L. Gatier, 'L'idéologie de la cité et la carte de Madaba', in Piccirillo and Alliata, eds., *The Madaba map centenary* (as in n. 1), 235-238.

[5] For this identification, see Donnor, *Mosaic map* (as in n. 1), 92.

[6] This is now, confusingly, known as the gate of St. Stephen. For more on the representation of Jerusalem, see W. Pullan, 'The representation of the late antique city in the Madaba map: the meaning of the cardo in the Jerusalem vignette', and A. Ovadiah, 'The churches of Jerusalem on the Madaba mosaic map', both in Piccirillo and Alliata, eds., *The Madaba map centenary*, 164-171 and 252-254.

the Holy Sepulchre was at the east end of the complex, with the Rotunda of the Anastasis at the west end, exactly as it appears on the mosaic. As a result of this precision, though Jerusalem as a whole is portrayed to be viewed from the west, the Holy Sepulchre itself is most comprehensible from an eastern vantage point — that is, from the apse.[7]

The representation of Jerusalem tells us that to the armchair travellers who commissioned and made the Madaba mosaic map, there were two critical principles that governed topographical representation, and by which space was ordered and controlled. The first was the coordination of real and represented space: that is, the cardinal alignment of the church was imposed on the view of Jerusalem, and the location of the city in the centre of the mosaic was determined by the plan of the church. The second was the sacrifice of consistent perspective to the interests of symbolism: that is, the Holy Sepulchre was manipulated (turned upside down) not only to align the mosaic representation with actual east and actual west, but also to make the most holy site in Jerusalem coherent from the most holy site in the church, the apse. At Madaba, the image of the cityscape was fixed and controlled by its context, which means that the virtual traveller whose eyes wander over the mosaic cityscape of Jerusalem is forced to accept a set itinerary.

In fact, the visual strategy mapped out on the Madaba floor insists upon a particular type of travel across the entire landscape. Colour, scale and text work together to impose a hierarchical structure on the topography, and it is a distinctly Christian hierarchy.[8] Three features of this visual hierarchy are particularly relevant to this chapter.

First of all, as we have already seen, Jerusalem is in the centre of the map. This is because it was the most important Christian city in the Holy Land, and was believed by some Christian authors to be the geographical centre or navel of the earth (*omphalos*).[9] Jerusalem also takes up the most room of any settlement represented, thereby displacing the smaller villages around it: the hierarchy of religious geography takes precedence over actual geographical relationships.

---

[7] Like the Sion gate of the Jerusalem portrait, buildings at the east and west extremities of other cities are sometimes placed at right angles to the major western point of view and thus appear to be lying on their sides (see, e.g., Gaza: Piccirillo, *Mosaics*, fig. 69), but only Jerusalem shows fully inverted buildings.

[8] On this point, see M. Avi-Yonah, *The Madaba mosaic map* (Jerusalem, 1954); and, for a parallel in pilgrimage rhetoric, J. Elsner, 'The *Itinerarium Burdigalense*: politics and salvation in the geography of Constantine's empire', *JRSt* 90 (2000), 181-195.

[9] See J. Wilkinson, *Jerusalem pilgrims before the Crusades* (Warminster, 1977), 28; S. MacCormack, 'Loca sancta: the organisation of sacred topography in late antiquity', in R. Ousterhout, ed., *The Blessings of Pilgrimage* (Urbana, 1990), 27.

The location of the Nile is a second striking geographical feature imposed by a Christian understanding of topography. Although the Nile in fact runs from south to north, on the Madaba mosaic map, it flows from the east to empty into the Mediterranean: Fig. 15.4 shows the Nile delta, with fragments of the Mediterranean at the bottom of the reproduction. The various branches of the delta are meticulously and accurately labelled, closely following the description in Herodotos's *History*, and it seems very unlikely that whoever planned this pavement did not know — either from Herodotos or from personal experience — that the course of the Nile was not as it has been represented on the mosaic.[10] Long before the Madaba pavement was laid, however, Christian writers had identified the Nile as Geon, one of the four rivers of Paradise described in Genesis (2.8-14), which also located Paradise to the east of the earth.[11] A Christian cartography had, then, to bring the waters of the Nile in from the east, exactly as they appear on the Madaba map.

Finally, nearly all of the sites included on the map are identified by inscription — with, as mentioned earlier, the most important of them highlighted in red — and most of the names, locations and descriptive tags attached to the sites were taken from the Bible or from something similar to the *Onomastikon of biblical place names*, a geographical lexicon of the Bible compiled by Eusebios around 320.[12] One site, for example, is identified as 'the wilderness of Sin where the manna and quails were sent down',[13] a description that refers to Exodus 16 and Numbers 11. This reliance on the Bible and a biblical lexicon imposes Christian nomenclature on the landscape, and (obviously) privileges biblical sites, whether or not they still existed as settlements when the Madaba map was made.

This symbolic Christian topography coexists, however, with features that have a more practical than signative value. We are shown, for example, a watchtower on the west bank of the Jordan, near a ferry that was pulled along a rope across the river. The fourth and the

---

[10] See Donner, *Mosaic map*, 67-68, 79-81.

[11] For both, see the *Christian Topography*, Book IV, 7: W. Wolska-Conus, ed. and comm., *Cosmas Indicopleustès, Topographie chrétienne* I, Sources chrétiennes 141 (Paris, 1968), 544-545. See further H. Maguire, 'The Nile and the rivers of paradise', in Piccirillo and Alliata, eds., *The Madaba map centenary*, 178-184.

[12] See L. Di Segni, 'The Onomasticon of Eusebius and the Madaba map', in Piccirillo and Alliata, eds., *The Madaba map centenary*, 114-120; Di Segni, 'The legends of the Madaba map', in the same volume, 47-101; and for discussion R. Markus, 'How on earth could places become holy? Origins of the Christian idea of holy places', *Journal of early Christian studies* 2 (1994), 257-271.

[13] Di Segni, 'The legends of the Madaba map', 95; Donner, *Mosaic map*, 69-70.

ninth milestones on the route between Jerusalem and the Mediterranean are identified (Fig. 15.3 = TO TETAPON and TO ENNA below Jerusalem to the left);[14] and the mosaicist has carefully included the villages and stations (none of which has any biblical significance) along the route between Palestine and Egypt: Gaza, Thauatha, Betylion, 'the border between Egypt and Palestine' (in red), Rinokoroura, etc.[15] Details such as these reinforce the message conveyed by the basic cartographic accuracy of the map as a whole (and it is worth stressing that the Madaba mosaic provides the most accurate plan of the region known to have been produced before the nineteenth century)[16]: which is that the pavement should not be viewed *only* on the symbolic level. Pragmatic and symbolic, secular and sacred: historical biblical sites that had long since disappeared by the sixth century and modern settlements that had only recently been developed are not set in opposition on the map but rub shoulders companionably within the stable framework of the floor. It is not a particularly equitable coexistence — the visual hierarchy is ideologically firmly Christian — but secular sites are not negated by omission. It *is* hegemonic: the Christian topography represented by the Madaba map has totally and seamlessly assimilated all facets of the *oikoumene* (the inhabited world).[17]

The original Madaba building is associated with a group of about a dozen other churches in the area of what is now modern Jordan that also show cityscapes on their floors and that range in date from 531 to 718-9, a period that covers nearly two centuries, and extends well into the Umayyad era.[18] These chart a changing conception of what was important to capture of the spatial ambient of a city or town,[19] and

---

[14] Di Segni, 'The legends of the Madaba map', 71; Donner, *Mosaic map*, 53.

[15] Di Segni, 'The legends of the Madaba map', 91-93; Donner, *Mosaic map*, 74-75, 77; Piccirillo, *Mosaics*, fig. 69.

[16] Donner, *Mosaic map*, 80

[17] The omission of monasteries is sometimes noted (e.g. Donner, *Mosaic map*, 31), but, since churches are only depicted as parts of cityscapes, and are not individually labelled, the lack of named monasteries does not seem exceptional.

[18] Cityscapes also appear in neighbouring regions: see, e.g., A. Zaqzuq, 'Nuovi mosaici pavimenti nella regione di Hama', Atti del convegno: Arte sacra e profana a Bisanzio, *Milion* 3 (1995), 237-256.

[19] On cityscapes in general see, e.g., J. Deckers, 'Tradition und Adaptation. Bemerkungen zur Darstellung der christlichen Stadt', *Mitteilungen des deutschen archaeologischen Instituts, Römische Abteilung* 95 (1988), 303-382; G. Wataghin Cantino, 'Veduta dall'alto e scena a volo d'uccello. Schemi compositivi dall'ellenismo alla tarda antichità', *Rivista dell'Istituto nazionale di archeologia e storia dell'arte*, n.s. 16 (1969), 30-107; and C. Bertelli, 'Visual images of the town in late antiquity and the early middle ages', in G. P. Brogiolo and B. Ward-Perkins, eds., *The idea and ideal of the town between late antiquity and the early Middle Ages*, Transformation of the Roman world 4 (Leiden, 1999), 127-146.

provide a very visible record of how the conquest of space changed between the sixth and the eighth century. The Jordanian city portraits show us that east Roman ideas of how best to visualise urban experience changed between the end of late antiquity and the beginning of Byzantium.[20] A run of monuments that exposes this shift follows.

- St. John the Baptist, Jerash, mosaic dated by inscription to 531.[21]
- SS. Peter and Paul, also at Jerash and probably dating to the 540s.[22]
- SS. Lot and Prokopios, Khirbat al-Mukhayyat, dated by inscription to 557, with a generic cityscape flanked by a boatman transporting amphorae and a fisherman with a wicker basket.[23]
- Church of the Lions, Umm al-Rasas, with an indiction inscription that dates either to 574 or to 589, with a portrait of the settlement, then known as Kastron Mefaa (Fig. 15.5), in the north colonnade.[24]
- Church of the priest Wa'il, Umm al-Rasas, dated by inscription to 586, with generic cityscapes inserted between personifications of the seasons (later defaced).[25]
- Church of bishop Sergios, Umm al-Rasas, dated to 587-8, which shows what appears to be a church with an outbuilding.[26]
- St. John, Khirbat al-Samra (near Bostra), dated 634, with a cityscape with two domed churches.[27]

---

[20] See N. Duval, 'Essai sur la signification des vignettes topographiques', in Piccirillo and Alliata, eds., *The Madaba map centenary*, 134-146; Duval, 'Le rappresentazioni architettoniche' in M. Piccirillo and E. Alliata, eds., *Umm al-Rasas/Mayfa'ah I, Gli scavi complesso di Santo Stefano*, Studium biblicum franciscorum, Collectio major 28 (Jerusalem 1994), 165-230; G. Canuti, 'Mosaici di Giordania con raffigurazione di città: itinerary di pellegrinaggio?', *Jahrbuch für Antike und Christentum* 20/2, Akten des XII. Internationalen Krongresses für christliche Archäologie 2 (1995), 617-629; R. Farioli Campanati, 'I luoghi santi della Palestina secondo la documentazione musiva e gli oggetti devozionali', in *Dalla terra alle genti, Catalogo della mostra, Rimini 1996* (Milan, 1996), 122-132.
[21] J. W. Crowfoot, *Churches at Jerash, a preliminary report of the joint Yale-British School expeditions at Jerash*, British School of Archaeology in Jerusalem, supplementary papers 3 (London, 1931), 24, pl. 7.
[22] Crowfoot, *Churches at Jerash*, 29, pl. 12.
[23] Piccirillo, *Mosaics*, fig. 209.
[24] Piccirillo, *Mosaics*, fig. 337.
[25] Piccirillo, *Mosaics*, fig. 397.
[26] Piccirillo, *Mosaics*, fig. 370.
[27] Piccirillo, *Mosaics*, fig. 592.

- Lower church, al-Quwaysmah (near Amman), dated 717-8, with churches and shrines used as infill in a pattern of interlaced ovals and squares.[28]
- St. Stephen's, Umm al-Rasas, main pavement, dated 718. The inner frame shows ten cities from the Nile delta; while the outer frame shows fifteen cities from the banks of the Jordan (Figs. 15.6-15.7), with eight sites from the west bank on the north, and seven cities from the east bank on the south. The cardinal coordination of Madaba is not quite achieved here, but the basic idea that church topography and physical topography could be made to coincide has been retained.[29]
- Church on the acropolis at Ma'in, dated 718-9, also with cities from the banks of the Jordan arranged in geographical coordination.[30]

The *changes* evident from this fleeting scan of topographical portraits can be encapsulated and pinned down by a comparison of two images of one settlement, Kastron Mefaa (Umm al-Rasas), that were represented there in mosaics laid about 150 years apart, one (Fig. 15.5) from the Church of the Lions (574 or 589), the other (Fig. 15.6) from St. Stephen's (718). When deciding what was most important to record, the sixth-century mosaicist and the eighth-century one fixed on some of the same things: the similarities in shape and focus — with two fortified areas linked by a large open space focused on a column on steps — are obvious. The differences are, too. The later mosaicist had little interest in creating a sense of space, but was very concerned to identify the building placed in the foreground: its three prominent hanging lamps could have left its viewers in no doubt that this was a church.

Jerusalem from the mid-sixth-century Madaba map (Fig. 15.3) and Jerusalem from the 718 floor at St. Stephen's at Umm al-Rasas (Fig. 15.7) reveal the same changes. Both the sixth- and the eighth-century cityscapes focus on the dome of the Holy Sepulchre, but there are obvious differences: at Madaba the building is clearly an important site indicator, but it is not the only one, while at Umm al-Rasas the rest of the city has been largely subsumed into this one particularised detail. By 718 at Umm al-Rasas, memories of sites visited were visualised almost exclusively as churches; urban topography was commemorated,

---

[28] Piccirillo, *Mosaics*, fig. 454.
[29] Duval, 'Le rappresentazioni architettoniche' (as in n. 20), 165-230.
[30] Piccirillo, *Mosaics*, figs. 296-299, 303, 305-306, 308-310.

much more than before, as Christian topography — and this was in Umayyad Palestine.

The change in the way urban memories were visualised was not primarily an issue of style. This can be shown by a simple comparison. At more or less the same time as the mosaics at Umm al-Rasas were set, the famous so-called Barada panels at the Great Mosque in Damascus were installed (Fig. 15.8): these too show buildings, and technical details suggest that they may have been set by artisans from Constantinople.[31] Be that as it may, the differences between the mosaics at Umm al-Rasas and Damascus, which are not in fact very far from each other (120 miles, a four-day journey in the eighth century), plot different conceptions of topography that have little to do with artisanal training and everything to do with what architectural landscapes meant to different audiences. Both rely on idealised landscapes, and both could be interpreted as metaphorical depictions of paradise.[32] But memories of places seen, evocations of places visited, idealised views of one's home town are, in the mosque at Damascus, represented by urban villas set along the Barada river; in the church at Umm al-Rasas, they are represented as churches. The church mosaics show churches, usually as part of, but dominating, larger settlements; the mosque mosaics portray domestic structures equitably strung along the waterfront. If Umm al-Rasas shows the ultimate development of the Roman cityscape, the Great Mosque reveals a new twist on the late antique Nilotic landscape. Neither shows a fundamental shift in approach to how to visualise a settled landscape, though the Christian pavement does reveal a shift in emphasis within a traditional formula.

The most significant difference between the two programmes has to do with audience rather than with image. The Christian users and viewers of the church at Umm al-Rasas lived under an Umayyad government. Around the second quarter of the eighth century, Christians themselves removed many figures from earlier church

---

[31] Technical details — the materials used for tesserae, colour combinations, setting bed, and underdrawing techniques — show so many similarities that the somewhat problematic documentary evidence pointing in this direction (on which see H. A. R. Gibb, 'Arab-Byzantine relations under the Umayyad caliphate', *DOP* 12 [1958], 221-233, esp. 225) may be correct.

[32] For this interpretation of the mosque mosaics, see B. Finster, 'Die Mosaiken der Omayyadenmoschee von Damaskus', *Kunst des Orients* 7 (1970/1), 83-141, esp. 117-121; K. Brisch, 'Observations on the iconography of the mosaics in the Great Mosque at Damascus', in P. Soucek, ed., *Content and context of visual arts in the Islamic world* (Papers from a Colloquium in memory of Richard Ettinghausen) (University Park, Pa., 1988), 13-23; R. Förtsch, 'Die Architekturdarstellungen der Umaiyadenmoschee', *Damaszener Mitteilungen* 7 (1993), 177-212.

mosaics and carefully replaced them with scrambled cubes to make abstract patterns.[33] This had nothing to do with Byzantine Iconoclasm, which was roundly condemned by the eastern patriarchs;[34] it had everything to do with social pressure from Muslim neighbours. As Theodore Abu Qurrah (c. 745-c. 820) makes clear, Islamic arguments against images were often persuasive. Less than half a century earlier, John of Damascus had defended image veneration against the iconoclast policies of Constantinople; Abu Qurrah, in contrast, wrote a tract about the value of Christian images not to condemn Byzantine Iconoclasm, but to convince his local Christian audience, swayed by the beliefs of their Islamic friends, that icons were not idols.[35] The desire to deflect criticism on a very local and intimate level provides the most compelling context for the apparent change in taste witnessed by the floor mosaics of mid-eighth-century churches in Palestine.[36] In these circumstances, it is arguable that the focus on ecclesiastical architecture at Umm al-Rasas — and the increasing emphasis on church representation as emblematic of settlement throughout Palestine — was, at least in part, a preservative reaction to the newly-dominant Islamic culture.

The Christian topography memorialised by the mosaics of Palestine affected other media as well. At about the same time as the Madaba map was installed, Constantine of Antioch, a pepper merchant, wrote a long treatise that he entitled a 'Christian Topography'.[37] It was profusely illustrated from the start, and three later copies survive — these often go under the name of Kosmas Indikopleustes, a nom de plume

---

[33] See esp. R. Schick, *The Christian communities of Palestine, from Byzantine to Islamic rule: a historical and archaeological study* (Princeton, 1995), 189-200; and S. Ognibene, 'The iconophobic dossier', in M. Piccirillo and E. Alliata, eds., *Mount Nebo: new archaeological excavations 1967-1997*, Studium biblicum franciscorum, Collectio major 27 (Jerusalem, 1998), 373-389. For more general comments, R. Schick, 'Palestine in the early Islamic period: luxuriant legacy', *Near Eastern Archaeology* 61/2 (1998), 74-108; and A. Linder, 'Christian communities in Jerusalem', in J. Prawer and H. Ben-Shammai, eds., *The history of Jerusalem. The early Muslim period 638-1099* (Jerusalem, 1996), 121-162.

[34] Discussion in Schick, *Christian communities of Palestine*, 210-211.

[35] See S. Griffith, 'What has Constantinople to do with Jerusalem? Palestine in the ninth century: Byzantine orthodoxy in the world of Islam', in L. Brubaker, ed., *Byzantium in the ninth century: dead or alive?* (Aldershot, 1998), 181-194, esp. 189-190.

[36] See further Schick, *Christian communities of Palestine*, 218-219; L. Brubaker and J. F. Haldon, *Byzantium in the iconoclast era, ca 680-850: the sources* (Aldershot, 2001), 35-36.

[37] W. Wolska, *La Topographie chrétienne de Cosmas Indicopleustès: théologie et science au VIe siècle* (Paris, 1962); for the text, with translation and commentary, W. Wolska-Conus, *Cosmas Indicopleustès, Topographie chrétienne*, 3 vols, Sources chrétiennes 141, 159, 197 (Paris, 1968-1973).

invented in the eleventh century.[38] Constantine's main thesis was that the world had been created in the shape of the ark of the covenant. In figure 15.9, the inhabited world is in the foreground, the great mountain behind which the sun slid at night is in the background, and Christ is in heaven at the top. A close-up view of the inhabited world is also provided. Because the miniaturist (unlike the Madaba mosaicist) was not constrained by the orientation of a church, it is to our right, with north at the top in the configuration with which the modern world is most familiar. The four rivers of Paradise, which include the Nile, flow from Paradise (to the east) to water the earth. The waters which surround the earth contain medallions of the four winds, and the earth itself is punctuated by the Mediterranean Sea (called the 'Roman Gulf' as it was on the Madaba map as well) and several other smaller bodies of water.[39]

The *Christian Topography* is, perhaps, an extreme example of the impact of religious beliefs on one's view of the world, and it expressed a point of view that was not universally accepted in Byzantium.[40] The narrative images in the manuscript — the ones that show travel itself rather than the lands travelled — do, however, follow widely accepted Byzantine conventions.

The conversion of Paul, with which this chapter opened (Fig. 15.2), shows Paul's route from Jerusalem (in the upper left) to Damascus (in the upper right). Here, Jerusalem is virtually indistinguishable from Damascus, and neither city reveals any feature that one might be tempted to interpret as Christian. This is not unusual. In fact, narratives of travel rarely christianise the landscape. When the topography itself is not the focus of the image, it tends to remain ideologically neutral. In the miniature of Paul's conversion, what interests the miniaturist is how to visualise the narrative of travel. The point of origin and the destination are clearly indicated, and the journey moves — as is almost always the case in Byzantine images of travel — from left to right. The physical journey is, however,

---

[38] Vat.gr.699 (ninth century): C. Stornajolo, *Le miniature della Topografia Cristiana di Cosma Indicopleuste. Codice Vaticano Greco 699* (Milan, 1908); Sinai.gr.1186 (eleventh century): partially reproduced in K. Weitzmann and G. Galavaris, *The Monastery of Saint Catherine at Mount Sinai, The illuminated Greek manuscripts* I: *from the ninth to the twelfth century* (Princeton, 1990), 52-65, figs 123-183, pls IX-XIII; Florence, Laur.plut.9.28 (eleventh century).

[39] See further K. Kitamura, 'Cosmas Indicopleustès et la figure de la terre', in A. Desreumaux and F. Schmidt, eds., *Moïse géographe. Recherches sur les representations juives et chrétiennes de l'espace* (Paris, 1988), 79-98.

[40] See, e.g., the ninth-century review in Photios' *Bibliotheke*: ed. R. Henry, *Bibliothèque*, I (Paris, 1959), 21.

unmarked by topographical indicators: there is not even a groundline. Not all Byzantine images of travel, however, are so obstacle free.

Even a handful of travel images show that the narrative of travel had a particular set of codes in Byzantine imagery. Though some of these changed over time, the experience of vicarious armchair travel, or of 'going over it' through viewing images of travel and re-thinking one's own journeys, followed a predictable route, certain features of which remained remarkably stable.

On a page from the sixth-century Vienna Genesis, the miniaturist has painted Rebecca, waterjug slung over her shoulder, walking along a colonnaded street that leads from the city of Nahor toward a spring, represented by a personification (Fig. 15.10). Although we are not shown the gesture, we know that Rebecca must have filled her jug at the spring, for at her second appearance she is giving Eliezer a drink.

A ninth-century image of travel shares many features with the sixth-century one. On a page from the Paris Gregory, the miniaturist has painted Joseph leaving his father and youngest brother, walking to meet his brothers (Fig. 15.11).[41] After various other adventures, Joseph is sold to merchants, and they all journey together to Egypt, where Joseph is purchased by Potiphar.

In both of these miniatures, painted three centuries apart, travel involves leaving an urban environment, and the divide between urban and rural is marked — by a river nymph and a change in direction in the Vienna Genesis, by a pillar in the Paris Gregory.[42] In both miniatures, the accoutrements of civilisation (walls, buildings, columns) end when the rural environment is entered, and rocky mounds take their place.

Despite this similarity, one notable difference between the two miniatures is the visual attitude toward the rural and, by extension, toward travel through it. In the Vienna Genesis, the rural landscape is not threatening; in the Paris Gregory, bad things happen to Joseph for the entire three-and-a-half registers that he is in the country. This is true of many rural images in the Paris manuscript. In the story of the Good Samaritan (Fig. 15.12), for example, the traveller leaves Jerusalem for Jericho — the outer limits of both cities marked, as in the

---

[41] See my *Vision and meaning in ninth-century Byzantium: image as exegesis in the Homilies of Gregory of Nazianzus* (Cambridge, 1999), 173-179, 316-328.

[42] Reminiscent of the boundary markers discussed by Rosemary Morris in '"Beating the bounds": the establishment of a boundary in Byzantium', abstract of paper in *Bulletin of British Byzantine Studies* 26 (2000), 66. Markers similar to those in the Homilies miniature also appear in the middle Byzantine Octateuchs: see K. Weitzmann and M. Bernabò, *The Byzantine Octateuchs*, Illustrations in the Manuscripts of the Septuagint 2 (Princeton, 1999), 157, 262, 265, figs. 656-659, 1346-1349, 1360-1363.

Joseph miniature, by piers — and once out of the urban precinct (neatly defined by a gorge) he is attacked, stripped, and left for dead in a rocky and desolate landscape. His rescuer, the Good Samaritan (here envisioned as Christ), is separated from the rural desert by another change in level, this one aligned with the pier signalling a return to civilisation. Images of travel in both the sixth-century Vienna Genesis and the ninth-century Paris Gregory mark the transition from urban and rural, and associate the clutter of civilisation with the urban environment while leaving the rural landscape rocky and barren, but the dangers of travel are expressed far more explicitly in the later book.

Sea travel is slightly different, though equally hazardous, as any standard Jonah sequence reveals.[43] Jonah leaves the safety of the city (Tarsus) and steps into a boat. He is promptly thrown overboard and swallowed by a sea-monster, before being regurgitated and re-entering civilisation, represented by the city of Nineveh. For Jonah, being at sea was not a bundle of laughs. But other images of sea travel are less overt.

Figure 15.13 shows Gregory of Nazianzus travelling by boat to an unspecified destination. He is pictured twice, once departing (we see him stepping into the stationary boat, with its furled sail), and once arriving.[44] The miniaturist has emphasised the shift in narrative movement by changing the pattern of the waves midway across the register. The figures receiving Gregory at his final destination are unclear, but those sending him off are well preserved, and are identifiable from other miniatures in the manuscript as Gregory's entire immediate family (his parents, brother, and sister). The miniature introduces Gregory's *Life*, and Gregory's journey is joined by two other significant moments in his life: his ordination (presumably as patriarch of Constantinople) in the middle, and his funeral at the bottom. When we turn to the text of the *Life* to find out what journey it can possibly be at the top of the page that compares in importance to Gregory's consecration and death, we find nothing. Gregory did not, ever, take a trip by boat from his family to anywhere. What we see here is travel as metaphor: braving the dangers of travel, Gregory leaves the safety and stability of his family, thereby demonstrating his moral strength and physical and intellectual courage. It is no accident that travel by sea is specified: Byzantine sea journeys were hazardous, and the fear that they induced is a familiar *topos* of Byzantine literature.[45] That Gregory's moral and intellectual fibre was

---

[43] See B. Narkiss, 'The sign of Jonah', *Gesta* 18 (1979), 63-76.
[44] Brubaker, *Vision and meaning* (as in n. 41), 134-137.
[45] A. Kazhdan and G. Constable, *People and power in Byzantium. An introduction to modern Byzantine studies* (Washington, D.C., 1982), 42-43; C. Galatariotou, 'Travel and

metaphorically represented by his willingness to travel surely tells us something about attitudes toward the actual physical conquest of space in the Byzantine world, just as the importance of travel in this visual encapsulation of the great moments of Gregory's life tells us that images of that conquest could have multiple meanings.

The Madaba mosaic map and the cityscapes of Palestine are topographic references that did not, apparently, depend on maps in the modern sense of the term, but — to the extent that they borrowed from any established tradition — nodded to pictographs of towns and significant landscape features that were made as *ad hoc* and temporary commemorations of particular landscapes.[46] But the conquest of space that they represent has little to do with any generalised mapping of the known world in any cartographic sense.

It is sometimes assumed that pictures such as the Madaba mosaic map served as guides to pilgrims to the Holy Land, but how could they? People might have walked the map in some sort of symbolic appropriation of the holy sites; people who had travelled to those sites already might have used the Madaba as a way to retrieve their memories of them; but no one could have used the mosaic as a real map: save for one very short section leading out of Jerusalem (Fig. 15.3, on the left),[47] it has no roads or footpaths or even river beds (wadis) on it. The Madaba map, and the Palestinian cityscapes, are evocative, not diagrammatic. Space is not defined, it is familiarised. The intention of the artisans who set the Palestinian mosaics was not to convey the reality of real movement by real people over real time, it was to

---

perception in Byzantium', *DOP* 47 (1993), 221-241, esp. 226; G. Dennis, 'Perils of the deep', in C. Sode and S. Takács, eds., *Novum millennium: Studies on Byzantine history and culture dedicated to Paul Speck* (Aldershot, 2001), 81-88; and also M. Mullett's chapter in this volume.

[46] See G. Bowersock, *Roman Arabia* (Cambridge, 1983), 164-186; B. Isaac, *The limits of empire: the Roman army in the east*, rev. edn. (Oxford, 1992), 401-408, 447-448; idem, 'Eusebius and the geography of the Roman provinces', in D. L. Kennedy, ed., *The Roman army in the East* (Ann Arbor, 1996), 153-167. More generally, see C. Delano Smith, 'Geography or Christianity? Maps of the Holy Land before AD 1000', *Journal of theological studies*, n.s. 42 (1991), 143-152; D. R. French, 'Mapping sacred centres: pilgrimage and the creation of Christian topographies in Roman Palestine', *Jahrbuch für Antike und Christentum* 20/2, Akten des XII. Internationalen Kongresses für christliche Archäologie 2 (1995), 792-797. For a different point of view, Y. Tsafrir, 'The maps used by Theodosius: on the pilgrim maps of the Holy Land and Jerusalem in the sixth century CE', *DOP* 40 (1986), 129-145, esp. 136-140; and compare the chapters by H. Donner, E. Weber, P. D. A. Harvey, and I. Roll in Piccirillo and Alliata, eds., *The Madaba map centenary*.

[47] This is the beginning of the road between Jerusalem and Neapolis, represented in white cubes: Donner, *Mosaic map*, 25.

encapsulate known space (or space imagined to be known) for a captive audience.

If the Madaba map is not about the broadening experience of travel, even less so are the images of actual journeys in the Byzantine world. The Vienna Genesis was neutral, but by the ninth century, at least in the Paris Gregory, representations of travel involve formulaic oppositions between the safety of urban life and the dangers of forays into the country. While the mosaic cityscapes evolve into churchscapes, images of travel come to celebrate the virtues of staying at home.

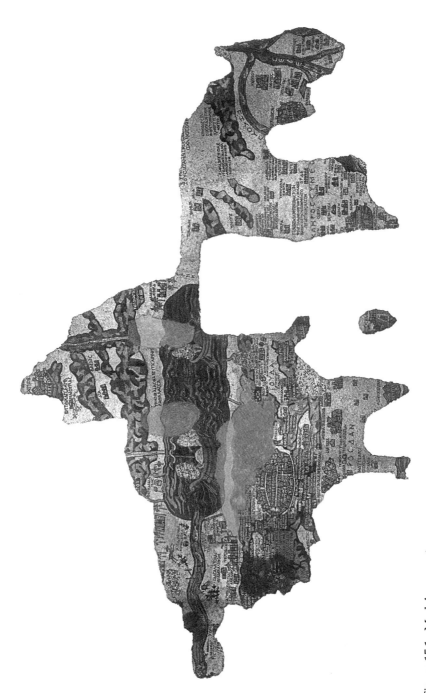

Figure 15.1 Madaba, mosaic map

Figure 15.2 *Christian Topography*, the journey of Saul from Jerusalem to Damascus (Sinai. gr. 1186, f. 126v)

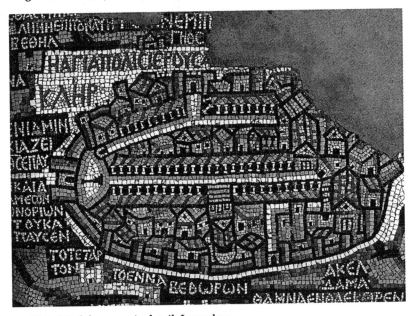

Figure 15.3 Madaba, mosaic detail: Jerusalem

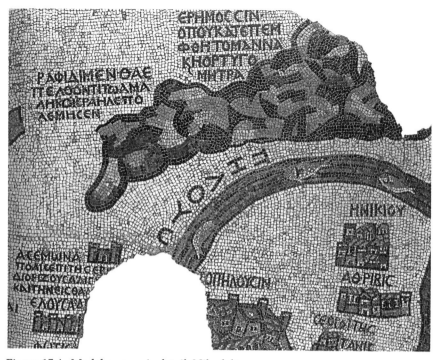

Figure 15.4 Madaba, mosaic detail: Nile delta

Figure 15.5 Umm al-Rasas, Church of the Lions, mosaic detail: Kastron Mefaa

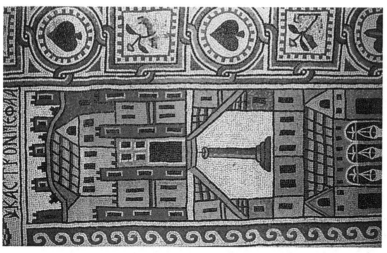

Figure 15.6 Umm al-Rasas, St. Stephen, mosaic detail: Kastron Mefaa

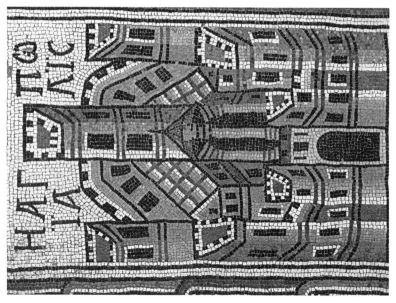

Figure 15.8 Damascus, Great Mosque, mosaic detail: Barada landscape

Figure 15.7 Umm al-Rasas, St. Stephen, mosaic detail: Jerusalem

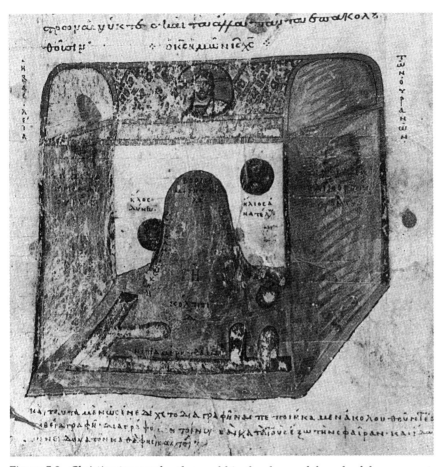

Figure 5.9 *Christian topography*: the world in the shape of the ark of the covenant (Sinai. gr. 1186, f. 69r)

Figure 15.10 Vienna Genesis: Rebecca and Eliezer (Vienna, Nationalbibliothek, cod. theol. gr. 31, pict. 13)

Figure 15.11 Paris Gregory: scenes from the life of Joseph (Paris. gr. 510, f. 69v)

THE CONQUEST OF SPACE 257

Figure 15.12 Paris Gregory: detail, parable of the Good Samaritan (Paris. gr. 510, f. 143v)

Figure 15.13 Paris Gregory: detail, Gregory leaving his family (Paris. gr. 510, f. 452r)

16. In peril on the sea: travel genres and the unexpected

M. E. Mullett

O eternal God, who knowest the hidden things, who has understood everything before creation, Lord Jesus Christ, hear me the sinner, and give us in thy name a favourable wind, so that we may cross the open sea, and glorify thy name for ever.[1]

We can have no doubt that Byzantines were aware of the dangers of death by drowning[2] for anyone who indulged in maritime travel. We may also believe with Catia Galatariotou that the Byzantines, both on a personal and on a cultural level, loathed travel.[3] What I want to suggest in this paper is that, on a textual level, shipwreck, adverse winds, calms, and pirate raids were expectedly unexpected — and essential to some travel genres as well as to the world view of Byzantium.

I shall use this term 'travel genres' in two senses: one is the technical rhetorical sense meaning the genres declaimed before or after travel; the other is the more commonly accepted sense of literary genres with

---

[1] Βίος καὶ πολιτεία τοῦ ἐν ἁγίοις πατρὸς ἡμῶν Νικολάου ἀρχιμανδρίτου γενομένου, 8, ed. and trans. I. Ševčenko and N. P. Ševčenko, *The Life of St Nicholas of Sion* (Brookline, Mass., 1984), 29.

[2] See for example representations of the crossing of the Red Sea, and, far more graphically, and redolent of scenes from *Titanic*, of the human detritus of the Deluge. For the crossing of the Red Sea see Vat. gr. 747 fol. 89v, Smyrna, EvSchool A.1, fol. 81v, Topkapi gr. 8, fol. 197v, Vat. gr. 746, fol. 192v, Paris gr. 139, fol. 419r, Vat. reg. gr. 1, fol. 46r, in J. Lowden, *The Octateuchs: a study in Byzantine manuscript illumination* (University Park, Pa., 1992), figs. 133-138. For the Deluge, Cod.Vindob. theol. graec. 31, fol. II, 3, in E. Wellesz, *The Vienna Genesis* (London, 1960), plate 1; Ashburnham Pentateuch, fol. 9r, see K. Weitzmann, *Late Antique and Early Christian Book Illumination* (London, 1977), plate 45.

[3] C. Galatariotou, 'Travel and perception in Byzantium', *DOP* 47 (1993), 221-241.

From *Travel in the Byzantine World*, ed. Ruth Macrides. Copyright © 2002 by the Society for the Promotion of Byzantine Studies. Published by Ashgate Publishing Ltd, Gower House, Croft Road, Aldershot, Hampshire, GU11 3HR, Great Britain.

examples which include, or comprise, narratives of travel. And though I shall range fairly widely in Byzantine literature, I shall end up in or very close to the Byzantine twelfth century.

There are five rhetorical travel genres: the *propemptikon*, which 'speeds its subject on his journey with commendation', the *syntaktikon*, which is the farewell of the departing traveller, the *prosphonetikon*, which is an address to someone arriving, and there is the *epibaterion*, the speech a traveller makes on arrival.[4] Each could follow the generic prescriptions, or invert them by keeping the order of *topoi* but showing the opposite emotions and functions; each can include another (that is take on the resident *topoi* of another genre).[5] In Byzantium these genres do not pertain only in strictly epideictic rhetoric or indeed to high-style literature; examples can be found in all the interactive and some narrative genres and forms: for a *propemptikon* see middle Byzantine saints' lives when the abbot and community gather to send the conspicuous young ascetic on his way;[6] for a paired *syntaktikon* and *epibaterion* see John Mauropous's poems 47 and 48, on leaving and returning to his house in Constantinople,[7] for *prosphonetikon* see the *eiseterioi* for Agnes de France,[8] for *epibaterion* Prodromos's poem XL in the voice of Isaac Sebastokrator returning to Constantinople after many adventures,[9] and for *syntaktikon* his own reactions on leaving Constantinople on the occasion of his journey to Trebizond with his friend Stephen Skylitzes.[10]

---

[4] For the prescriptions for *propemptikon, syntaktikon, prosphonetikon and epibaterion*, see Menander Rhetor, Περὶ ἐπιδεικτικόν, ed. D. A. Russell and N. G. Wilson, *Menander Rhetor* (Oxford, 1981), V, XV, X, III, 126-134, 194-200, 164-171, 94-115.

[5] F. Cairns, *Generic composition in Greek and Roman poetry* (Edinburgh, 1972) is still the most sophisticated as well as ground-breaking treatment; A. Fowler, *Kinds of literature. An introduction to the theory of genres and modes* (Oxford, 1982) is particularly helpful on modulation, 191-212; M. Mullett, 'The madness of genre', *DOP* 46 (1992), 233-243, draws some lessons for Byzantium.

[6] E.g. Βίος καὶ πολιτεία καὶ μερικὴ θαυμάτων διήγησις τοῦ ἁγίου καὶ θαυματουργοῦ Νίκωνος μυροβλύτου τοῦ Μετανοεῖτε, ed. D. Sullivan, *The Life of Saint Nikon* (Brookline, Mass., 1987), 12-14, 58-66.

[7] John Mauropous, poems 47-48, ed. P. de Lagarde, 'Johannis Euchaitorum metropolitae quae in cod. Vat. gr. 676 supersunt', *Abhandlungen der königlichen Gesellschaft der Wissenschaften zu Göttingen, phil.-hist. Klasse* 28 (1881), 88.

[8] J. Strzygowski, 'Das Epithalamion des Päaologen Andronikos II', *BZ* 10 (1901), 546-567; M. J. Jeffreys, 'The vernacular eiseterioi for Agnes de France', in E. Jeffreys and A. Moffatt, eds., *Byzantine Papers* (Canberra, 1981), 101-115.

[9] Theodore Prodromos, XL, ed. W. Hörandner, *Theodoros Prodromos, Historische Gedichte*, WBS 11 (Vienna, 1974), 391-393.

[10] Theodore Prodromos, LXXIX, ed. Hörandner, 550-552.

The fifth rhetorical travel genre is *hodoiporikon*, a traveller's account of a whole journey. This genre was not highlighted in the Menandrian treatises, and Francis Cairns's classic treatment of genre in classical literature contains only one example, Rutilius Namatianus's *De reditu suo* — though a more liberal interpretation of voice might include both *Odyssey* and *Aeneid*.[11] In that it calls for extended autobiographical treatment, it is found only in restricted contexts until the twelfth century: an obvious exception is in pilgrims' accounts.[12] And some of the best are pigeon-holed under other genres. For example, the text we know as the *Pratum spirituale*, or the *Leimonarion*, of John Moschos was thought of by the Byzantines as an example of the *paradeisos* genre — though there is more both of desert and sea than there is of meadow about it. But it did not take a William Dalrymple to see that it is (with whatever padding from his experiences at Deir Dosi and the monastery of the Aeliots on Mt. Sinai) a wonderful collection of stories in the frame of a journey with Sophronios around the monasteries of the eastern Mediterranean: Palestine to Antioch, to Cilicia, to Cyprus, to Alexandria and Sinai, to Samos and Rome. Compared with the authors of other frame story collections like Chaucer and Boccaccio, Moschos keeps the frame to a minimum: a 'when we were in Alexandria' or a 'the *gerontes* of that monastery told us' suffices.[13]

By the twelfth century other personal accounts of travels are making their way through like other kinds of autobiographical writing:[14] a communication at the symposium focused on a fourteenth-century account by Libadenos. The one text normally known as *hodoiporikon* is the four-book poem written by Constantine Manasses, but the title appears in no contemporary manuscript: one manuscript has no lemma, the other calls it Constantine Manasses on his *apodemia* (absence, exile) in Jerusalem. It is to Leo Allatius's identification of the poem with an *hodoiporikon*

---

[11] Cairns, *Generic composition* (as in n. 5), 284.

[12] In general terms see K. N. Ciggaar, *Western travellers to Constantinople: the west and Byzantium, 962-1204, cultural and political relations*, The Medieval Mediterranean 10 (Leiden, 1996).

[13] John Moschos, Λειμών, PG 87.3. 2847-3116 (hereafter Moschos, *PS*), trans. J. Wortley, *The Spiritual Meadow of John Moschos*, Cistercian Studies 139 (Kalamazoo, 1992), the inspiration for W. Dalrymple, *From the Holy Mountain*. (We still await the critical text of Philip Pattenden.)

[14] For autobiographical writing see M. Hinterberger, *Autobiographische Traditionen in Byzanz*, WBS 22 (Vienna, 1999); M. Angold, 'The autobiographical impulse in Byzantium', *DOP* 52 (1998), 52-73.

that we owe the current title.[15] Exile is certainly what that text is about: it is the story of an embassy to Jerusalem in 1177 to try to arrange a marriage between Manuel I and Melisende: it is written with magnetic concentration on Constantinople, apostrophised by Manasses at the end of the first three books:[16] the poem ends with thanksgiving for his safe return.[17] The emphasis on absence, the comic characterisation of natives encountered, the grumbles about climate and food place it in the very familiar context of lawyer exiles of the eleventh and episcopal exiles of the twelfth century whose letters are clearly written to flatter and amuse a metropolitan readership, the most serious difference in Constantine's case being that he had actually achieved the longed-for goal of return to Constantinople.[18] Later examples might even include the Latin epic poem of Ubertino Pusculo, whose account of the Fall of Constantinople in four books has only traces of the full travel account he gave in a speech in Brescia of his journey home which included capture and slavery by the Turks, ransom by the Venetians, capture by pirates and abduction to Rhodes, escape, crossing rough seas and desert islands to Crete and so probably via Venice to Brescia.[19]

Hodoiporikon fundamentally involves first person narrative, and in this way it overlaps with the second category of texts which can be described as travel genres. These are the major literary forms of hagiography, the novel, and letters, and it is useful to see in what ways they deal with travel and its difficulties. Saints' lives, as Nancy Ševčenko taught us long ago,[20] take to the water with ease. Saints travel, often frequently and early on to various holy places; their icons of course make independent voyages. They travel on missions, or flee from Constantinople to Emesa to escape pursuing husbands, and return, with all the girls, because they were missing their spiritual father.

---

[15] Constantine Manasses, Τοῦ Μανασσῆ κυροῦ Κωνσταντίνου εἰς τὴν κατὰ τὰ Ἱεροσόλυμα ἀποδημίαν αὐτοῦ, ed. K. Horna, 'Das Hodoiporikon des Konstantin Manasses', BZ 13 (1904), 313-355.

[16] Ed. Horna, book I, ll. 331-336, pp. 334-335; II, ll. 153-158, p. 339; III, ll. 102-106, p. 342.

[17] Ed. Horna, book IV, ll. 187-194, p. 347.

[18] For the exile discourse of the twelfth century see M. E. Mullett, 'Originality in the Byzantine letter: the case of exile', in A. R. Littlewood, ed., *Originality in Byzantine literature, art and music* (Oxford, 1995), 39-58.

[19] See the forthcoming edition and facing translation by M. J. McGann and E. A. M. Haan, BBTT 5.1 (Belfast).

[20] N. P. Ševčenko, 'The final voyage: scenes of the translations of relics', *XVIII International Congress of Byzanine Studies, Moscow 1991*, II, *Résumés des communications* (Shepherdstown, Pa., 1996), 1018-1019.

(Fortunately 'they reached the imperial city after an unexpectedly calm passage'.[21]) They live on deserted islands, or on the sea-shore[22] and meet frequently with seafaring folk, or are moved on by Arab pirates.[23] Monasteries keep boats and set out on embassy to the emperor,[24] on trading expeditions,[25] or to borrow books.[26] There is a strong sense of confidence in travel in saints' lives, certainly if you travel with a holy man, though this cannot have always been so, to judge from miffed complaints that a holy man died at sea and so his relics were not recoverable:

> It happened by the judgement which only God knows that this very holy man, who was dedicated to God, after boarding a ship and sailing to the royal megalopolis was drowned in the waves of the sea along with his fellow passengers. Thus were we deprived of his holy body and do not have in reliquaries his sacred and blessed remains which would benefit us very much. For as long as he survived in the flesh, he enriched all of us in the activity of his healings, and after his death he could have provided much more healing power to pilgrims through contact with his relics.[27]

There are sometimes dangers in travelling with sinners — though not always. Contrast the chilling story in Moschos about the Mary who killed her child in order to clinch a second marriage, with Mary of Egypt's cavalier attitude to fornicating her way to the Holy Land.[28]

---

[21] Βίος καὶ πολιτεία τῆς ὁσίας Ματρόνης ch. 11, 28, AASS, Nov.III (Brussels, 1910), 796, 803, trans. J. Featherstone in *Holy Women of Byzantium: ten saints' lives in English translation*, ed. A.-M. Talbot (Washington, D.C., 1996), 30-31, 44-45.

[22] Βίος καὶ πολιτεία καὶ μερικὴ θαυμάτων διήγησις τοῦ ὁσίου πατρὸς ἡμῶν καὶ θαυματουργοῦ Λουκᾶ τοῦ νέου τοῦ ἐν Ἑλλάδι κειμένου, ed. C. L. Connor and W. R. Connor (Brookline, 1994), 51, 83.

[23] Βίος καὶ πολιτεία τῆς ὁσίας μητρὸς ἡμῶν Θεοδώρας τῆς Θεσσαλονίκης, ed. S. A. Paschalides (Thessalonike, 1991), 77.

[24] R. Morris, 'Divine diplomacy in the eleventh century', *BMGS* 16 (1992), 147-156.

[25] R. Morris, *Monks and laymen in Byzantium, 843-1118* (Cambridge, 1995), 220.

[26] On monastic book-borrowing see J. Waring, 'Literacies of lists', in C. Holmes and J. Waring, eds., *Education, literacy and manuscript transmission in Byzantium and the neighbouring worlds*, The Medieval Mediterranean (Leiden, forthcoming).

[27] Βίος καὶ πολιτεία τῆς ὁσίας μητρὸς ἡμῶν Ἀθανασίας καὶ μερικὴ τῶν αὐτῆς θαυμάτων διήγησις, 9, ed. L. Carras, 'The Life of St Athanasia of Aegina', in A. Moffatt, ed., *Maistor* (Canberra, 1984), 199-224, here at 214; trans. L. Sherry, in A.-M. Talbot, ed., *Holy women*, 149.

[28] Moschos, *PS* 76, *PG* 87.3. 2927-2930; trans. Wortley, 7-59; cf. Sophronios, Βίος Μαρίας Αἰγυπτίας, 21, *PG* 87.3. 3697-3726, here at 3712, trans. M. Kouli, in A.-M. Talbot, ed., *Holy women*, 81.

> One summer day I saw a huge crowd of Libyan and Egyptian men running towards the sea. I asked someone who happened to be next to me, 'Where are these men running?,' and he answered, 'Everybody is going to Jerusalem for <the feast of> the Exaltation of the Holy Cross .... Then I said to him, 'Would they take me with them if I wanted to go along?' He replied, 'If you have the money for your passage and expenses, no one will prevent you.' ... So ... I threw away the distaff I was holding ... and ran towards the sea where I saw the other people running. And I saw some young men standing at the seashore, about ten or more, vigorous in their bodies as well as in their movements, who seemed to me fit for what I sought .... I rushed shamelessly into their midst, as was my habit. 'Take me where you are going,' I said, 'Surely you will not find me useless' .... How can I possibly describe to you what followed? What tongue can declare, or what ears can bear to hear what happened on the boat and on the journey and the acts into which I forced these men against their will? There is no kind of licentiousness speakable or unspeakable that I did not teach those miserable men. I am truly surprised, my father, how the sea endured my profligacy ...[29]
>
> One day I was sailing along with passengers on board, both men and women. We came out on to the high sea and all the other ships were sailing well, some to Constantinople, some to Alexandria, others elsewhere. The wind stood well for each of them, but we alone could make no headway. We remained stuck in the same place for fifteen days, not moving at all from where we lay. We were in great distress and despair, not knowing why this should be. As I was the master of the vessel, responsible both for the boat and also for all who sailed in her, I began to pray to God about the matter. One day there came to me a voice of no visible origin saying: 'throw Mary out and you will make good way.'[30]

The voice comes again, the master tricks her into telling her story, and then because he 'still did not want to throw her into the sea just like that', he gets into a dinghy to see if it is his sins that are holding back the ship and nothing happens, then

> he came back on board and said to the woman: 'You get down into the dinghy.' She did; and as soon as she set foot in the dinghy, it turned round about five times and then sank to the bottom of the

---

[29] Sophronios, *VMary*, 21, PG 87.3. 3712, trans. Kouli, 80-81.
[30] Moschos, *PS*, 76, PG 87.3. 2928, trans. Wortley, 57-58.

deep. Then the ship sailed on and in three and a half days we completed a journey which should have taken fifteen.[31]

Moschos has several groups of maritime stories: the off-hand treatment of one of the three blind men who told their stories at the Tetrapylon in Alexandria shows the privations of life at sea: 'as a young man I was a sailor. We set sail from Africa, and on the high sea I developed ophthalmia. As I could not go and get treatment, white spots appeared on my eyes and I lost my sight.'[32] Or the merchant of Askalon who set sail and lost all his goods and everything else he was carrying at sea.[33] There are the wonderful surreal Red Sea stories from Rhaitou and Sinai: the story told by fishermen of how a heavy sea held them up for ninety days and they found three dead anchorites and then were able to sail on;[34] the story of the two anchorites who lived on a waterless island and whose boat capsized leaving them to die of thirst, in sequence, tidily, with a tortoiseshell to tell the tale: 'Abba Gregory of Pharan died after going twenty-eight days without drinking water; but I have gone thirty-seven days without a drink.'[35] They found both the corpses intact; they took them back and buried them at Rhaitou. And the equally surreal account of the two anchorites who turned up for the liturgy naked and refused to take with them the only monk who realised they were naked: 'they offered a prayer and then, before my very eyes, they went on to the water of the Red Sea on foot and departed across the sea.'[36] There are perils here, no fun, but no fear. 'If anyone does not believe this, it is no burdensome journey to Lycia, where he can inform himself of the truth.'[37]

Laymen do have problems: there is the minimally edifying story of the gem-engraver whose ship's boy overheard the crew plotting to throw him overboard and for the sake of his stock-in-trade; he took pre-emptive action by emptying his samples into the sea instead: the sailors were amazed and their conspiracy was frustrated.[38] And the shipowner at Lepte Akra in Cilicia whose 35,000 *modioi* ship was held up with 300 workmen for two weeks trying to launch her, until a holy man turned up, distracted the shipowner, made three prostrations and

---

[31] Moschos, PS, 76, PG 87.3. 2929, trans. Wortley, 59.
[32] Moschos, PS, 77, PG 87.3. 2932, trans. Wortley, 59.
[33] Moschos, PS, 189, PG 87.3. 3068, trans. Wortley, 162.
[34] Moschos, PS, 120, PG 87.3. 2984, trans. Wortley, 98-99.
[35] Moschos, PS, 121, PG 87.3. 2983-2984, trans. Wortley, 99.
[36] Moschos, PS, 122, PG 87.3. 2983-2986, trans. Wortley, 99-100.
[37] Moschos, PS, 215, PG 87.3. 3108, trans. Wortley, 192.
[38] Moschos, PS, 203, PG 87.3. 3093, trans. Wortley, 182.

made three signs of the cross and told the magnate, go now and launch your vessel. 'Putting his trust in the elder, the ship-owner went with a very few men and as soon as they took the strain, the ship was found to be in the sea. And everyone glorified God'.[39] And there is a pair of stories with different solutions to the same problem:

> There was an anchorite in the area of the holy Jordan, Theodore by name, who was a eunuch. He was obliged for some reason or other to go to Constantinople so he boarded a ship. The vessel was delayed so long on the high sea that they ran out of water. Sailors and passengers alike were greatly afflicted by anxiety and despair. The anchorite stood up and stretched out his hands to heaven, to the God who saves our souls from death. He offered a prayer and sealed the sea with the sign of the cross. Then he said to the sailors, 'Blessed be the Lord! Draw as much water as you need.' They filled every receptacle with fresh water out of the sea and everybody glorified God.[40]

> Abba Gregory the anchorite told us: I was returning to Byzantium by ship and a scribe came aboard with his wife; he had to go and pray at the Holy City. The ship-master was a very devout man given to fasting. As we sailed along, the scribe's attendants were prodigal in their use of water. When we came in the midst of the high sea, we ran out of water and we were in great distress. It was a pitiful sight: women and children and infants perishing from thirst, lying there like corpses. We were in this distressing condition for three days and abandoned hope of survival.[41]

Gregory dissuades the scribe from killing the master and the crew and

> the scribe quietened down, and on the fourth day, about the sixth hour, the ship-master got up and cried in a loud voice, 'Glory to thee, Christ our God!' and that in such a way that we were all astonished at his cry. And he said to the sailors, 'Stretch out the skins', and whilst they were unfolding them, look! a cloud came over the ship and it rained enough water to satisfy all our needs. It was a great and fearful wonder, for as the ship was borne along by the wind, the cloud followed us, but it did not rain beyond the ship.[42]

---

[39] Moschos, *PS*, 83, *PG* 87.3. 2940, trans. Wortley, 66-67
[40] Moschos, *PS*, 173, *PG* 87.3. 3041, trans. Wortley, 142.
[41] Moschos, *PS*, 174, *PG* 87.3. 3041, trans. Wortley, 143.
[42] Moschos, *PS*, 174, *PG* 87.3. 3041, trans. Wortley, 143.

For the full range of what a holy man can do for the traveller, when storms arise,[43] when ships cannot leave the harbour[44] or change course and put in,[45] the life of St Nicholas of Sion is the classic locus. But it also gives us a sense of the ritual of travel, the preparation for a journey,[46] the prayers, 'O Lord, do not afflict us in the open sea but help us',[47] the visions,[48] the negotiations 'and the sailors received us with joy and the Lord gave us a favourable wind',[49] the saintly foreknowledge that 'we are about to face great danger at sea'.[50]

> And that night a great storm arose at sea, and the ship was about to be engulfed by the waves. When the sailors saw that they were in jeopardy, they fell down before the servant of God, pleading and saying to him: 'Lord Father, rise and pray for us, since we are in danger. For the wind and the waves are against us. And the servant of God Nicholas said: The Lord hath a long arm and will take care of his servants. Let us but have faith in Him, that if God wishes, He can save us.' And bending his knee once again, the servant of God Nicholas prayed for long hours. And at the end of the prayer they all responded to him with the 'Amen'. And the wind and waves stilled, and there was great calm at sea.[51]

In other saints' lives, the sense is more of what the travel can do for the saint. It takes three kinds of journey (the military expedition of Himerios and Niketas Magistros, the expedition of the Euboian hunters, and abduction by pirates from Lesbos) nesting inside one another, to bring the story of St. Theoktiste to her devoted audience[52] — no, actually four, since we are never told what brought the anchorite Symeon to the uninhabited island of Samos, presumably *xeniteia*. He proves his credentials as holy man by giving a shipping forecast:

> You will sail across to Naxos, and after lying in harbour there for one day, you will sail away on the second day and reach Crete on

---

[43] VNich, 30, ed. and trans. Ševčenko and Ševčenko, 54.
[44] VNich, 36, ed. and trans. Ševčenko and Ševčenko, 62.
[45] VNich, 37, ed. and trans. Ševčenko and Ševčenko, 64.
[46] VNich, 27, ed. and trans. Ševčenko and Ševčenko, 50.
[47] VNich, 37, ed. and trans. Ševčenko and Ševčenko, 64.
[48] VNich, 28, ed. and trans. Ševčenko and Ševčenko, 52.
[49] VNich, 27, ed. and trans. Ševčenko and Ševčenko, 50.
[50] VNich, 28, ed. and trans. Ševčenko and Ševčenko, 52.
[51] VNich, 30, ed. and trans. Ševčenko and Ševčenko, 54.
[52] Niketas Magistros, Βίος τῆς ὁσίας μητρὸς ἡμῶν Θεοκτίστης, AASS Nov.IV (Brussels, 1925), 224-233, trans. A. Hero, in A.-M. Talbot, *Holy women*, 101-116; the *Life* is found in a stunning twenty-seven manuscripts.

> the third without having to fear any hardship. You will carry out your mission in accordance with your wish and the emperor's order, and when you return home you will be well received by him who sent you.[53]

He then makes his pitch: Niketas is to write down the story of Theoktiste. After the tale is told, the adverse winds calm. 'With these instructions and gentle admonitions the great man sent us on our way. And since the winds were fair we reached the island of Dia the next day.'[54] The head wind which brought them to Paros made the tale possible, just as Theoktiste's sanctity is proved by the miracle of the Euboian hunter:

> Late that evening, we put out from the land, set sail, and were on our way. Since favourable breezes were blowing, we were flying, so to speak, before a fair wind, and expected to reach Euboia by morning. But at daybreak we found ourselves back in the same harbour as if the ship were held fast by an anchor or a sea monster. Fear and terror seized us all, and we looked at one another trembling as we sought to determine the cause of this delay.[55]

The hunter sneaks back to the church and they try again

> When we were far out at sea, for the ship was flying like a bird, with the sail bellying out with wind, on a straight and unimpeded course I told my companions what had happened, how I had found the blessed one and she had recounted the story of her life and about the holy communion and her death. I also told them that I had boarded the ship the previous evening with the saint's hand in my possession and for that reason perhaps we were held back although we expected to sail away. And that now we were rightly proceeding on a straight course because I had put the relic back.[56]

The hunters insist on going back to the church, find her body has disappeared:

> Dismay and terror seized us all and we ran hither and thither, looking round about carefully lest she had been moved or come back to life. We ran round the entire forest and the groves seeking to discover if that divine treasure was perhaps hiding somewhere.

---

[53] NikMag, *VTheoktiste*, 13, AASS, 227, trans. Hero, 107-108.
[54] NikMag, *VTheoktiste*, 23, AASS, 232, trans. Hero, 115
[55] NikMag, *VTheoktiste*, 21, AASS, 231, trans. Hero, 113-114
[56] NikMag, *VTheoktiste*, 21, AASS, 230-231, trans. Hero, 113-114.

So ... having failed to find the remains of the blessed woman, we went back to the ship, weighed anchor and went home, glorifying and praising God Who works wonders and miracles always.[57]

In this *Life* the winds and the waves are major actors in a plot which ensures the telling of the tale.

In its exploitation of Mediterranean travel it inevitably recalls the second genre which deals with travel, the ancient novel.[58] This was revived again in the Byzantine twelfth century, but through direct mimesis of ancient texts,[59] and more subtly in the process which Bakhtin called novelisation,[60] influenced narrative in the period when, as far as we know, novels were not written.[61] Few ancient novels managed a plot in which the perils of the sea did not figure.[62] Chariton's *Chaireas and Kallirhoe* (mid-first century A.D.) has the heroine in Syracuse taken for dead and then grave-robbed by the pirate Theron who carries her off to Miletos where he fails to sell her as a slave, and so contemplates dropping her overboard, but finds a buyer before he succeeds in doing so. Meanwhile, the hero Chaireas mounts a sea-search, tracks down the pirate and sets off to Miletos, but on the way his trireme is attacked, and he is taken prisoner and sold as a slave in neighbouring Karia.[63]

The *Ephesiaka* of Xenophon (mid-second century) moves its lovers, Anthia and Habrokomes, from Ephesos to Rhodes and then they are becalmed at sea, the ship is attacked by Phoenician pirates and then the couple is taken to Tyre. Anthia is taken to Syria, married to a goatherd, sold to merchants, suffers shipwreck, and is captured by a brigand, tries to kill herself, is taken for dead, buried, tomb-robbed and

---

[57] NikMag, *VTheoktiste*, 22, AASS, 231, trans. Hero, 114
[58] For convenient reference see B. P. Reardon, *Collected ancient Greek novels* (Berkeley, 1989); for a classic encapsulation, E. L. Bowie, 'The Greek novel', in P. E. Easterling and B. M. W.Knox, *Cambridge History of Classical Literature* (Cambridge, 1985), I, 683-699.
[59] R. Beaton, *The medieval Greek romance*, 2nd edn. (London, 1996), esp. 54-57. There is direct evidence in monastic inventories for the availability of the ancient texts, for example *Leukippe and Klitophon* in both Boilas's Theotokos Salem and in Michael Attaleiates's foundation. This is supported by indirect evidence; for example it is quoted in the *Life* of Theoktiste.
[60] On novelisation, see M. M. Bakhtin, 'Epic and novel', trans. C. Emerson and M. Holquist, *The dialogic imagination*, University of Texas Press, Slavic Series 1 (Austin, Texas, 1981), 5-8.
[61] For a discussion, ultimately unsatisfactory, of this process, see S. McAlister, *Dreams and suicides. The Greek novel from Antiquity to the Byzantine empire* (London, 1996), 84-114.
[62] Even psKallisthenes has Alexander's diving bell. See though psLucian's *The Ass* and *A Babylonian Story* which are both land-locked.
[63] Chariton, *Chaireas and Kallirhoe*, ed. G. Molinié (Paris, 1979).

taken to Alexandria. Habrokomes searches for her body, also goes to Egypt, but is captured, sold as a slave, falsely accused of murder, tried and sentenced to death. Anthia is carried off to Egypt, Habrokomes' search for her takes him to Italy, but before he finds her she leaves for Rhodes. Habrokomes departing for Ephesos stops in Rhodes where they finally meet and return to Ephesos and live happily ever after.[64]

Achilles Tatios's *Leukippe and Klitophon* (late second century), in a first-person narrative, starts in Tyre where the lovers decide to elope and take ship bound for Alexandria. They are shipwrecked at the beginning of book 3 and washed ashore at Pelousion. After many adventures they take ship for Alexandria but Leukippe is abducted, apparently beheaded on the pirate ship and taken to Ephesos where Kleitophon, unknowingly comes with a widow he has married. The lovers are reunited and after many adventures go to be married in Byzantion.[65]

In Heliodoros's *Aithiopika*, (third or late fourth century), the novel to end all novels, the lovers Theagenes and Charikleia are shown in tableau at the mouth of the Nile and the story is told of how they were brought from Delphi where they met. Heading for Egypt but pausing at Zakynthos they learned of pirates waiting in ambush for their ship and sail secretly at night; they are attacked by pirates and Charikleia is lost to the pirates. By the time the story so far has been told, at the end of book 5, Chariklea has been rescued but Theagenes lost, she sets off to find him, discovers him at Memphis, and after they have been taken to Ethiopia in book 10 and after many adventures, are married.[66] Even Longos's *Daphnis and Chloe* (200 A.D.) which, compared with the flashy sensationalism of Heliodoros, depends on the pastoral depiction of closely observed adolescent love, season by season, separates the couple by the device of abduction from the sea.[67]

The revived twelfth-century novels no less than the ancient ones depend on calms, storms, shipwrecks and pirates to separate the couple or to blow them off course and make their later separation more possible. Only Niketas Eugeneianos has Drosilla carried off by land rather than sea;[68] both Theodore Prodromos's *Rhodanthe and Dosikles*

---

[64] Xenophon of Ephesus, *Ephesiacorum libri V*, ed. A. D. Papanikolaou (Leipzig, 1978).

[65] Achilles Tatius, *Leukippe and Klitophon*, ed. S. Gaselee (London and Cambridge, Mass., 1917, rev. ed. 1969).

[66] Heliodorus, *Ethiopika*, ed. R. M. Rattenbury and T. W. Lumb, trans. J. Maillon, 3 vols (Paris, 1935-43).

[67] Longos, *Daphnis and Chloe*, ed. O. Schönberger (Berlin, 1960, 2nd edn. 1983).

[68] Niketas Eugeneianos, *Drosilla and Charikles*, ed. F. Conca, *Il romanzo bizantino del XII secolo* (Turin, 1994), 306-496.

and Eustathios Makrembolites's *Hysmine and Hysminias* make full use of marine plotting. *Rhodanthe and Dosikles* begins with a pirate attack on Rhodes which puts hero, heroine and a chance acquaintance called Kratandros into prison, where the story is told of how hero and heroine arrived in Rhodes and the hero tells how they came there from Abydos: after a whirlwind courtship he had in fact abducted her. Their adventures continue in the pirates' homeland and they are caught up in a war between the pirates and Bryaxis the king of Pissa, and in book 6 a naval battle, complete with frogmen, is described. The lovers are captured by the king of Pissa, but put in separate ships (in book 6), and Rhodanthe's ship is forced on to a rock and she is rescued by a passing merchant ship on its way to Cyprus. Meanwhile Dosikles tries to drown himself, but reaches Pissa. Rhodanthe's master in Cyprus turns out to be Kratandros's father and after she tells her story, the father sets out for Pissa to find him and rescues his son and Dosikles. After an attempted poisoning in Cyprus, the parents of the lovers appear and they all go home to Abydos for the wedding.[69]

In *Hysmine and Hysminias* the lovers meet when Hysminias goes on embassy from Eurykomis to Aulikomis; they elope from Aulikomis, but the ship runs into a storm and Hysmine is thrown overboard to placate the gods; the grieving Hysminias is regarded as a bad omen and is marooned where he is captured by Ethiopian pirates and carried off to Daphnipolis. He goes on embassy to Artykomis — where he discovers Hysmine rescued from the sea by a dolphin. After adventures they are reunited, their parents turn up and they go back to Aulikomis for the wedding. Here the essential separation in the plot is economically engineered by the shipwreck in book 7. Without shipwrecks and pirates it is hard to see how these intrepid lovers could have been separated — and then there would have been no story.[70]

Interestingly most of the later romances do manage to do without shipwrecks and pirates; but Belthandros and Chrysantza flee during a storm, are separated crossing a river, believe each other to be dead, but they find each other, stagger to the sea, hail a passing ship which turns out to belong to the hero's father's navy, and they sail happily home to Constantinople to be married.[71] All this is very tame after the baroque complexities of Heliodoros. And the *Tale of Troy* has Paris

---

[69] Theodore Prodromos, *Rhodanthe and Dosikles*, ed. M. Markovich (Stuttgart, 1992); ed. Conca, *Il romanzo*, 64-302.

[70] Eustathios Makrembolites, *Hysmine and Hysminias*, ed. I. Hillberg (Vienna, 1876); ed. Conca, *Il romanzo*, 500-686.

[71] *Belthandros and Chrysantza*, ed. E. Kriaras, Βυζαντινὰ Ἱππoτικὰ Μυθιστoρήματα, Basike Bibliotheke 2 (Athens, 1955).

shipwrecked and taken in by some monks on an island; Helen is living on another island, they meet, love, she gets pregnant so they flee together by sea to Troy. So the ancient and twelfth-century plot of lovers separated by shipwreck is inverted here: the lovers meet by shipwreck and their elopement is ended only by the Trojan War.[72]

So shipwreck, high seas, adverse winds, pirate attacks are inscribed into the ancient and twelfth-century novels in an even more crucial way than in the saints' *Lives* we examined. In a different way, these facts of travelling life are also inscribed into the last genre I wish to examine, the letter. Unlike the novel and saints' lives, letters were not normally a narrative genre:[73] the major exception to this rule is in set-piece descriptions of journeys. Here in first-person narratives, the excitements of dangers overcome are written up for the fearful exhilaration of the reader, who knows that since the horrendous journey described another successful one has taken place — or else he would not be reading the letter at all. Separation is a structural feature of epistolary discourse, and plays on absence and presence exploited in its vocabulary. 'Your letter consoles us for separation by the gulf of sea and the mountain. Would that I could hurl it into the sea so that it would be transformed into a continent.'[74] Presence/absence, far/near, separation/unity, distance and exile are fundamental features of the Byzantine letter.[75] Anxiety about travel and complaints about the difficulties of travel make the precious letters when they do arrive all the more precious:

> We have had great difficulty in obtaining a carrier for our letter to your reverence because in our land people shudder so at the winter that they cannot bring themselves even to put their heads out of their chambers for a moment.[76]

---

[72] The *Tale of Troy*, ed. L. Nørgaard and O. Smith, *A Byzantine Iliad; the text of Par.Suppl.Gr 926 edited with apparatus, introduction and indexes*, Museum Tusculanum: opuscula graecolatina 5 (Copenhagen, 1975).

[73] See M. Mullett, *Theophylact of Ochrid: reading the letters of a Byzantine archbishop* BBOM 2 (Aldershot, 1997), 18ff. for a full explanation of the interactive and monoaxial nature of the Byzantine letter. For letter-collections as narrative however, see 283-288.

[74] Hierotheos monachos, ep. 27, see J. Darrouzès, 'Un recueil épistolaire du XIIe siècle: Acad.roum.cod.gr.508', *REB* 30 (1972), 210.

[75] On these oppositions see M. Mullett, 'The classical tradition in the Byzantine letter', in M. Mullett and R. Scott, *Byzantium and the classical tradition* (Birmingham, 1981), 80ff.

[76] Basil of Caesarea, ep. 48 to Eusebius bishop of Samosata, ed. R. J. Deferrari, *St Basil, the letters*, 4 vols (London and Cambridge, Mass., 1930), I, 314.

> I should like to travel to Keos, but, fearful by nature, I content myself with hungry eyes in that direction. I am a land creature; I fear the sea and the bands of pirates who lurk around there.[77]

The most famous of all is Synesios's letter 5 to his brother Euoptios.

> We straightway started at dawn with a wind that blew from the stern all that day and the following one, but towards the end of the second day the wind left us and we were in despair. However only too soon should we be longing for a calm. It is the thirteenth day of the waning moon, and a great danger was now impending, so at the very moment when we should have stayed in harbour, we so far forgot ourselves as to run out to sea. The storm opened with north winds and with heavy rain during the moonless night, presently the winds raged without measure, and the sea became deeply churned up ... first the sail-yard began to crack, and we thought of tightening up the vessel, then it broke in the middle and very nearly killed us all. It seems that this very accident, failing to destroy us, was the means of our salvation ... we were carried along during a day and a night, and at the second birdsong, before we knew it, behold we were on a sharp reef which ran out from the land like a short peninsula. Then a shout went up, for someone passed the word that we were close to the shore itself. There was much shouting and very little agreement. The sailors were terrified, whereas we through inexperience clapped our hands and embraced each other. We could not sufficiently express our great joy. And yet this was accounted the most formidable of the disasters that had beset us. Now when day appeared a man in rustic garb signalled and pointed out which were the places of danger and those that we might approach in safety. Finally he came out to us in a boat with two oars and this he made fast to our vessel. Then he took over the helm, and our Syrian gladly relinquished to him the conduct of the ship. So after proceeding not more than fifty stadia he brought her to anchor in a delightful harbour the name of which I believe is Azarion, and there disembarked us on the beach. We acclaimed him as our saviour and good angel ....
>
> ... As for you, may you never trust yourself to the sea, or if you really must do so, let it not be at the end of a month. [78]

---

[77] Euthymios Tornikes, ep. 2, to Michael Choniates: see Darrouzès, 'Un recueil' (as in n. 74), 210.

[78] Synesios, ep. 5, to his brother Euoptios, ed. A. Garzya, *Synesii Cyrenensis epistulae* (Rome, 1979), 11-26, trans. A. Fitzgerald, *The letters of Synesios of Cyrene translated into English with introduction and notes* (London, 1926), 80-91.

Jacqueline Long has drawn attention to the liveliness of the narrative, the agile pacing and deft modulation of tone, high drama and human exasperation, excitement and humour.[79]

There are two equally rich letters of the twelfth century, or at least one at the end of the eleventh, probably 1095, and the other at the beginning of the thirteenth, probably 1208.[80] To put the first in context, the collection of Theophylact of Ochrid has one delayed *syntaktikon*,[81] six *prosphonetika*,[82] three inverted *epibateria*,[83] a *propemptikon*[84] and two *hodoiporika*. One of these is very late in the collection, G120, which tells of his journey back from Constantinople (fraught with seasickness) by sea to Thessalonike and then on by land to Ochrid at the time of the second Norman War.[85] The other, probably dating to the emperor's time at Nikomedeia in 1095,[86] serves both as an inverted *syntaktikon* (normal for the exile discourse of his contemporaries[87]) and as an apology for a failed *epibaterion*.

> Holy mistress, from the time I journeyed to the Queen of Cities from Ochrid, my many sins have nailed me fast with many griefs. But I have not suffered anything like this present ill, of not being able to render the last and final obeisance to your Majesty ... and may your Majesty know this, that as I was returning from Nikomedeia, for it is there that the waves of my misfortunes had carried me, again and again I urged the sailors to turn the oars and direct the sails towards the island of Prinkipo, which has the honour of harbouring your Majesty, and to reduce the sail. Alas, they did not seem to hear my shouts, because their ears were deafened by the roaring of the north wind, of which a powerful gust, coming from Panteichion, made the crossing impossible unless we preferred to put in at Apollonias and afterwards safely reach the Great City. We made it, just scraping the land with the oars and thus far did we escape the

---

[79] J. Long, 'On an ill-fated Sunday Synesius set sail', BSC 17 (1991), 45-46.

[80] Theophylact, ep. G4, to the ex-basilissa Maria, ed. P. Gautier, *Théophylacte d'Achrida, lettres*, CFHB 16.2 (Thessalonike, 1986), 137-141; Nicholas Mesarites, to the monks of Evergetis, ed. A. Heisenberg, 'Neue Quellen zur Geschichte des lateinischen Kaisertums und der Kirchenunion', *Sitzungsberichte der bayerischen Akademie der Wissenschaften, phil.-hist. Klasse* (1923), 35-46.

[81] Theophylact, ep. G4, ed. Gautier, II, 17-141.

[82] Theophylact, epp. G10, 13, 32, 68, 69, 86, 118, ed. Gautier, II, 161, 171-173, 237-239, 373-377, 453-455, 549.

[83] Theophylact, ep. G5, G6, G7, ed Gautier, II, 143-151.

[84] G41, ed. Gautier, II, 269.

[85] Theophylact, epp. G4, G120, ed. Gautier, II, 137-141; 553-557.

[86] Anna Komnene, *Alexiad*, X.v.1-3, ed. B. Leib, 3 vols (1938-1945), II, 205-206.

[87] On inversion see Cairns, *Generic composition* (as in n. 5), 127-137.

sea. I constantly wanted to satisfy my desire and rush to my only support after God. But the murderous south wind struck as if by agreement with the north wind so that each with its immense blasts should hurt us in turn. What happened then? The possibility of escape was offered by Him to whom is entrusted the safeguard and reform of our fortunes, but the sebastos and praitor of Dyrrachion thwarted my desire. It goes without saying that the desire of the sinner will perish, saith the Lord.[88]

The letter is addressed to the despoina kyra Maria, begins with his disappointment in not seeing her before he left for Ochrid (who will comfort the depth of his suffering? Who will load upon his feebleness bearable burdens? No one, except that, knowing her goodness, she will receive his letter in exactly the same way that she would have received him if he had managed to visit her in person.[89]) He goes on to press his letter on her, to ask for her protection for himself and for his brother Demetrios. After the included *hodoiporikon* he then turns to inverted *syntaktikon*. Since he has been in Ochrid, where he has been for such a long time, all his possessions have rotted and stunk, even those which are normally pleasant and sweet-smelling. That is why he goes down among Bulgars, he 'a real Constantinopolitan, and — strange to say — a Bulgarian exuding the smell of sheepskin and worse, which makes people think you have felt sick in front of me, you to whom my stink would have had the scented effect of a strong and very pleasant perfume'.[90] He proceeds with this imagery, so much so as to suggest a gift of perfume,[91] and ends with an elaborate prayer. This letter, longer than most, has been taken out of its normal chronological sequence and placed at the head of three major manuscripts,[92] making it a kind of signature cover which could have marked a presentation copy. What is interesting about it is the way in which the relationship with his patroness Maria of Alania[93] plays on the travel account: he is not simply concocting an elaborate excuse for not visiting his patroness, nor offering her the gift of a highly decorated account; he is commemorating in his description the forces which kept them apart and constrained him to carry out *proskynesis* by letter. While reinforcement

---

[88] Theophylact ep. G4, ed. Gautier, II, 137-139.
[89] Theophylact, ep. 4, ed. Gautier, II, 137.
[90] Theophylact, ep. 4, ed. Gautier, II, 141.
[91] 141.61: εὐωδιάσθη; 141.67: quoting Song of Solomon 5.13; 141.74: εὐωδίας Χριστοῦ; 141.75-77: θυμιατήριον, θυμιάσῃς, θυμίαμα.
[92] Vat.gr.89, Vat.gr.432, Berolin.Phil 1417.
[93] On which see M. E. Mullett, 'The "disgrace" of the ex-basilissa Maria', *BSl*, 45 (1984), 202-210, here 209-210.

of the patronage relationship is paramount here, there is also a concern with his own identity: he records his double identity as Constantinopolitan and Bulgarian, a rare explicit recognition that what all these twelfth-century literati feared most had happened, he had 'turned into a barbarian living for years in Ochrid'; the worst barbarians, the worst *agroikia*, the worst deserts were inside.[94] In some kind of way the travel had taken him out of himself and allowed him to reevaluate the relationship with Maria as well as catch himself for once unawares.

The last travel letter is another *hodoiporikon*, of a journey in the opposite direction, from Constantinople to Pylai and then on by land to Nikomedeia, Neakome and Nicaea. It is an extended letter from Nicholas Mesarites to the abbot and community of the monastery of Evergetis, just outside the walls of Constantinople,[95] a community which in its *typikon* was forbidden to receive private letters.[96] Only the first four chapters deal with the sea-voyage, which are handled with all of Synesios's comic spirit, some ludicrously baroque images and considerable brio. It is offered in the spirit of a gift, as a (late) thank-you letter for his stay in the monastery and some impressively cooked and presented meals;[97] Paul, the homonym of the Great Paul, is specifically thanked.[98] Three episodes, of dangerous currents, of an encounter with pirates, and an accidental near-drowning, put a comic gloss on what is in Theophylact an elegiac experience of frustrated reunion, what in hagiography would be played for the opportunities for the holy man, and in the novels are played for sensation, pace and plot.

> Just about the beginning of the day, having changed course after the acropolis, and encountered the barbaric, wild, fearful, rushing downpour of waters which I would say is well named, and those who have crossed before describe it as a violent attack of barbarians.[99]

---

[94] On all this see M. Mullett, 'The Other in Byzantium', *Strangers to themselves; the Byzantine Outsider*, ed. D. C. Smythe, SPBS 8 (Aldershot, 2000), 1-22.

[95] For Evergetis see M. Mullett and A. Kirby, *The Theotokos Evergetis and eleventh-century monasticism*, BBTT 6.1 (Belfast, 1994); *Work and worship at the Theotokos Evergetis*, BBTT, 6.2 (Belfast, 1997).

[96] EvHyp, 22, ed. P. Gautier, 'Le typikon de la Théotokos Evergétis', *REB* 40 (1982), 65-67.

[97] Mesarites, *Gramma* (as in n. 80), 1, ed. Heisenberg, 36.

[98] Mesarites, *Gramma*, 1, ed. Heisenberg, 36. The Great Paul is either the apostle or the founder of Evergetis (or both).

[99] Mesarites, *Gramma*, 2, ed. Heisenberg, 36.

He then falls among pirates:

> I unexpectedly saw a galley with oars like a centipede and this ship leaps out from those heavy rocks which lay beside the harbour, they are called vain rocks, and rushed over the surface of the sea like the fatal strike of a murderous snake or like a flash of lightning sifting through the clouds and burning up everything it meets. And fear and panic seized everyone, and no one was able to speak to his neighbour. For all were terrified by this. For that vessel not only carried strong oarsmen, glaring like Gorgons, but also swordsmen, and spearsmen and guards bearing bows, not any old bows. (here follows an ekphrasis) ... but the kind of thing a barbarian mind breathing slaughter has devised ....[100]
>
> What do you think I thought, holy Nazarenes, when such sharks surrounded us? It was not possible to get in a corner or hide in the hold of the ship or to pray for some wild wave to be stirred up against the ship so as to sink us, or that the seas should gape widely and swallow us in our fear rather than falling into the hands of the pirates. You might describe this as a kataphatic story rather than an apophatic one. So when those bloodthirsty and accursed men unexpectedly fell upon us we were searched vigorously. When our possessions appeared to be other than they had expected — for neither silver nor gold had been stored in our wallets — they turned to a second examination. They groped after our buttocks and rumps and calves and the reproductive parts of the body, and having poked around us they also investigated the boat itself, and we came out from that experience without travelling shoes or tunics. And when they were again unsuccessful in what they wanted, they stared grimly at all of us, as having exerted themselves in vain, and those piratical countenances gave us to understand that they wanted to make some profit out of us. For sometimes the state of their faces was like a smile, other times it was full of harshness and disgust. When we detected this we cast aside cowardice and hastened to speak in a peaceful fashion. They were delighted and gave us their right hands and more vigorously gazed at our hands in the hope of catching sight of any trace of silver or gold. When they saw what they wanted — for the feast was improvised sooner than they thought — those who a little while before were rough and had scowling faces immediately became cheerful and pleasant and ordered us quickly to clamber up on their ship and they commanded the captain of the ship to set sail.[101]

---

[100] Mesarites, *Gramma*, 2, ed. Heisenberg, 37.
[101] Mesarites, *Gramma*, 3, ed. Heisenberg, 37-38.

All was not over.

> One of those climbing up to the pirate ship, who had dirty hair, and the poorest of clothes, a vagabond by profession, who had a wallet over his shoulder and breast but in general was like a snail, hurrying before the others and seizing the way up first on to the pirate ship, for he wished safely to seat himself on the bench before the others, on account of the barbaric nature of his language and his talkative and jocose nature, twitting us for losing our possessions, he got tangled up with another vagabond 'for a vagabond begrudges a vagabond as a beggar begrudges a beggar': he slips head first into the sea. And the wretch would have perished swallowing a lot of seawater if one of those with us had not swum like a madman. For he was dressed only in a linen chiton and, throwing himself into the sea, he saved the wretch from danger. And when he was brought up we placed him in the bows and he spewed out a lot of sea water he had ingested and vomited it forth from seasickness.
> So he vomited a lot of seawater and we with a fair wind put in at Pylai. It is the fruit of Asia, an entrancing polichnion ....[102]

This account, which now moves on to the disadvantages of land travel, exploits the literary potential of maritime disaster in a way that other twelfth-century texts do not. The vivid images, the detailed observation, are lacking in the novels: after all the pleas and curses Hysmine is stripped and dropped overboard in less than a hundred words,[103] compared with the loving care devoted here to street scum who simply slipped and had to be rescued — or to Moschos's Mary; Hysminias's marooning is dealt with in fewer,[104] and Dosikles watches Rhodanthe's ship sink in eight lines;[105] the greatest marine enthusiasm is reserved for the frogmen in the sea-battle in book 5.[106]

And the twelfth-century saints' *Lives* also take maritime travel very much for granted: Leontios of Jerusalem,[107] like all the Patmos texts, assumes the normality of difficult and dangerous Dodecanese journeys: of course whole monastic communities moved on in their small boats, complete with their builders, when the chance of greater

---

[102] Mesarites, *Gramma*, 4-5, ed. Heisenberg, 38-39.
[103] Eustathios Makrembolites, *Hysmine and Hysminias*, VII.15, ed. Conca, 611.
[104] Eustathios Makrembolites, *Hysmine and Hysminias*, VI.17, ed. Conca, 615.
[105] Theodore Prodromos, *Rhodanthe and Dosikles*, VI.39-51, ed. Conca, 198.
[106] Theodore Prodromos, *Rhodanthe and Dosikles*, VI.8, ed. Conca, 198. H. Hunger, 'Byzantinische "Froschmänner"?', *Antidosis. Festschrift für Walter Kraus zum 70. Geburtstag*, Wiener Studien, Beiheft 5 (Vienna, 1972), 183-187.
[107] See D. Tsougarakis, *The Life of Leontios of Jerusalem. Text, translation, commentary* (Leiden, 1993).

monastic hesychia presented itself — or the wrangles of the community became too great. Answering the imperial call to turn up at Constantinople or Euripos, maintaining *metochia* on other islands, keeping in touch with the secular authority on Samos, borrowing and lending books — all had to be achieved by sea,[108] but they do not stand out from the text as did the earlier hagiography and psychophelitic tales we looked at earlier; they impress by their low-key, everyday background presence.

We need to go to the letters of the period, to Hierotheos monachos, in a monastic community up the Bosphoros and in touch with other monasteries and nunneries of the time, for a sense of the harshness of the maritime environment and the fragility of communication: the sea is foregrounded in this collection: Darrouzès even identifies as authentic a letter which talks of calm at sea, because of the mention of the sea.[109] In the two lives of Meletios, the only maritime episode is Meletios's management of the timing of John Doukas's reconquest expedition: he advised that immediate circumstances were not propitious, John should write to Karykes on the subject of peace and wait at Euripos for the reply.[110]

In contrast to these lives of course Mesarites is at an advantage in that he is dealing with a first person account: but that is also available to Nicholas Kataskepenos in the life of Cyril Phileotes where there is an extended naval episode during the time that Cyril worked for three years on a Black Sea pilot.[111] Perversely, and surely in conscious subversion of the expectations of the receivers of hagiography, Nicholas does not present dangers at sea as an opportunity for the saint to show foreknowledge, or to triumph over the forces of the elements, or to walk on water, or any of the skills of earlier saints: Nicholas uses Cyril's time at sea to show how modestly and strictly he kept to his diet even when fruit and vegetables were in short supply and were hogged by the carnivorous sailors. He nipped off at every landfall not to gather his quota of water[112] but to carry out his private programme of genuflexions and flagellation in private. The opening, 'one day we were sailing on business to the Danube forts, we had carried it out and were

---

[108] For the texts associated with Christodoulos of Patmos see E. Vranousse, Τὰ ἁγιολογικά κείμενα τοῦ ὁσίου Χριστόδουλου ἱδρυτοῦ τῆς ἐν τῷ Πάτμῳ μονῆς (Athens, 1966).

[109] Darrouzès, 'Un recueil', 226; we look forward to the edition of Michael Grünbart.

[110] Nicholas of Methone, *VMel*, 16 (27), ed. C. Papadopoulou (Athens, 1968), 61-62.

[111] Nicholas Kataskepenos, *VCyril Phileotes*, ed. and trans. E. Sargologos, *La vie de saint Cyrille le Philéote, moine byzantin († 1110)*, Subsidia Hagiographica 39 (Brussels, 1964), 57-65.

[112] Cf J. H. Pryor, 'Types of ships and their performance capabilities', above, 33-58.

returning home,'[113] seems to promise a naval episode, but it is more about the difficulties of maintaining *askesis* on a boat. But then in terms of Cyril's somewhat eccentric formation the function of his three years at sea in the lack of any ordinary coenobitic experience is to demonstrate his *hypakoe*; 'this is why he lent himself to navigation under a pilot. Life was executing the orders of the pilot and those with him. Think of the ship as a monastery and the pilot as the abbot.'[114] The episode where he is too exhausted by fasting and too cold to climb to the mast and the crew fall at his feet in awe, saying 'keep away from us for we are sinners', might have been a recognition scene of the power of the saint: in fact it is his weakness, his failure to carry out *hypakoe* at the skipper's order to which they react in compassion and charity.[115]

This is not to say that maritime adventures had lost their appeal for writers and readers of the twelfth century, simply that variatio and experiment could take for granted certain expectations of the function of perils at sea. There was not much more the twelfth-century novel could do with sea stories after Achilles Tatios's shipwrecks or Longos's raiding-attack, though they remain in position as a crucial hinge in plotting. And as saints' lives seek to demonstrate the usefulness of holy men in the twelfth century's colder climate,[116] saints for whom the sea represents not so much an elemental force to be conquered with God's help as business as usual, an opportunity to demonstrate centrality to the fortunes of the state or simply how not to make a holy show of yourself have adapted to changed political circumstances.[117]

If we want to see developments in the twelfth century in the literary exploitation of the dangers of travel it is not in the novel or in saints' lives but in epistolography that we should look. It is no accident that Galatariotou's five examples include the Bulgarian letters of Antiochos as well as our Mesarites text, and there are ways in which Mouzalon and Manasses also take on characteristics of the letter.[118] These

---

[113] *VCyril*, 5.9, ed. Sargologos, 63.

[114] *VCyril*, 5.2, ed. Sargologos, 58.

[115] *VCyril*, 5.11, ed. Sargologos, 64-65.

[116] P. Magdalino, 'The Byzantine holy man in the twelfth century', *The Byzantine saint*, ed. S. Hackel, Studies Supplementary to Sobornost 5 (London, 1981), 53-66.

[117] On the embarrassment factor, ways in which monks could let one another down in public estimation, which included lack of stability, excessive self-mortification or economic boom, see M. E. Mullett, *Death of the holy man, death of a genre* (Brill, forthcoming).

[118] For these texts, chosen for 'the multiple levels of the perception of reality', S. Doanidou, ' Ἡ παραίτησις Νικολάου τοῦ Μουζάλωνος ἀπὸ τῆς Ἀρχιεπισκοπῆς Κύπρου· Ἀνέκδοτον ἀπολογητικὸν ποίημα', *Hell* 7 (1934), 109-150; J. Darrouzès, 'Deux lettres de Grégoire Antiochos écrites de Bulgarie vers 1173', *BSl*, 23 (1962), 276-284; *BSl* 24 (1963), 65-86.

personal first person accounts focus less on cosmic adventure or on battles with the supernatural than on small scale, personally observed, almost trivial, less than catastrophic, episodes exploited for entertainment, shared relief, a development of the comic, but always with an emphasis on the reinforcement of the relationship between writer and recipient, the primary axis of correspondence. Theophylact's relationship with his major patron leads him to embellish an apology for delayed *syntaktikon* with an exciting *hodoiporikon* passage; Mesarites's relationship with his Evergetis hosts requires a highly vigorous and outrageously embellished *hodoiporikon* in return for their hospitality, complete with monastic jokes. This is not new in the twelfth century, as we saw with the Synesios account, which is addressed to his brother, who is implicated in the averted disaster and in an explicitly confessed mixture of tragic and comic elements.[119] He is able to use the detail and excitement of Acts 27 with the first-person immediacy of Achilles Tatios. And though there is no direct borrowing, Synesios is a writer available to the intertextuality of eleventh- and twelfth-century authorship.[120] His use of the experience of the fragility of communication, the relief in relationships not broken by catastrophe, the inclusion of the addressee, may well lie behind Theophylact's reinforcing courtliness. The comedy of Synesios's villainous cast of characters, the Syrian Jew, the crew each with a different disability, 'the lame, the ruptured, the left-handed, the goggle-eyed', the big breasts of the women in the ethnographic section (so much more welcoming than a viper on Malta), the self-mockery,[121] may lie somewhere behind Mesarites's account.

Conclusion: the expected and the unexpected

We have looked in this paper at saints' lives, at the novel and at epistolography, and we have seen that each engages in a different way with the possibilities of the unexpected at sea. The novel, as Bakhtin saw so clearly, for adventure time to work, requires 'space and plenty of it.'[122] The quest to overcome spatial distance is at the heart of the plotting of the novels: separation and reunion, enforced movement

---

[119] Synesios, ep. 4, ed. Garzya, 11.

[120] There are, for example, two allusions in Theophylact's letters to Synesios, in G32, ed. Gautier, II, 237 and G75, ed Gautier, II, 461. See E. Papaioannou, 'Michael Psellos's rhetorical gender', *BMGS* 24 (2000), 133-146.

[121] All in ep. 4, ed. Garzya, 11-26.

[122] M. M. Bakhtin, 'Forms of time and of the chronotope in the novel', trans. Holquist, *Dialogic imagination* (as in n. 60), 99.

through space are the essentials of the genre, and in this sense the unexpected is not only expected but also required on a vast canvas of undifferentiated ocean: for a shipwreck you must have a sea, but which particular sea makes no difference at all. The adventure space of a saint's life bears some similarities as a result of novelisation, and is also in its own right a triumphalist demonstration of the empire-wide operations of the holy. Holy men are not, with very few exceptions, limited to a single community; even if they are on a column the world comes to them. Like the heroes of the novel the heroes of hagiography submit to travel, and triumph through its adversities: the thematic of escape, abduction, pursuit, search is mirrored by the rhythms of monastic *xeniteia*.[123] In some ways hagiography resembles Bakhtin's model for the chivalric romance rather than the ancient novel: the unexpected and only the unexpected is expected[124] — ships turn round in the night and arrive back where they started.[125] In the letter, the travel may revert to a human scale (the Marmara not the Mediterranean[126]) and concentrate on ethnographic coherence rather than the abstraction of an alien world, but it shares an optimistic view of the fundamental importance of communication to Byzantine society. And the broad Mediterranean canvas of the late Byzantine letter-writers in their journeys from Cyprus to Crete to Italy to Trebizond, getting ahead of the post, doubling back, catching up with correspondents,[127] equals the breadth of vision of the ancient novel.

All share the adventure-space of trial: in the novel, however bad it looks, however much the ship seems to have gone down with all hands or the heroine executed on the pirate ship, all trials are survived, and the fundamental trial of separation engineered by peril at sea is resolved in conclusion; in the saint's life, all trials must be survived, by the saint, and others saved by him from perishing; in the letter for it to have arrived at all means not only that the journey described has concluded successfully but also a subsequent letter-bearing expedition has united the separated correspondents again. The simple fact of communication is its own triumph. So this experience of trial through travel is fundamentally an optimistic one, reinforcing relationships,

---

[123] The patterns of Middle Byzantine hybrid monasticism which involve moving through space in a monastic life have been mapped out by D. Papachryssanthou, 'La vie monastique dans les campagnes byzantins du VIIIe au XIe siècles', *REB* 43 (1973), 158-182; R. Morris, *Monks and laymen in Byzantium 843-1118* (Cambridge, 1995).

[124] Bakhtin, *Dialogic imagination*, 152.
[125] *VTheoktiste*, 21, AASS, Nov IV, 230.
[126] As in both the *hodoiporika* of Theophylact and Mesarites.
[127] Mullett, 'Classical Tradition' (as in n. 75), 88-89.

enhancing reputations, enabling narrative. And to meet expectations of the unexpected, generic requirements can be subordinated or elaborated: the most vivid narratives have the common feature of generic inclusion: the letter includes narrative; the saint's life or novel includes first person narrative of the traveller in direct speech.[128]

In spatial terms, the marine event is crucial in different kinds of journey: in the letter a storm or shipwreck throws off-course the fundamental and bindingly important journey between the two recipients; in the novel shipwreck or capture by pirates separates the adventures of the lovers who have left home together, meet up again at a different point and return together to the home city to live happily ever after; the goal of hagiographies is not tidy resolution and a return to the home city — it is a journeying on, calling no place home,[129] until the saint reaches at the end of his voyage the true bourne of Paradise.

It will be clear by now that my approach to the engagement of these texts with marine peril is not altogether close to that of Catia Galatariotou. In her paper at the symposium on Diplomacy later published in *Dumbarton Oaks Papers*, she privileges the personal level of reality in five travel writers of the twelfth century and argues for a generalised abhorrence of travel in writers of the period as well as highly developed individual differences and consciously personal reactions.[130] Her approach supports and complements Alexander Kazhdan's comparison of the use of the image of a ship on a tempestuous sea in Niketas Choniates and Nikephoros Gregoras which he develops to reveal the underlying attitudes of the historians to life, the universe and everything: 'for Gregoras the course of events fluctuates unpredictably and inexplicably, often for the worse but also for the better': 'for Choniates events change constantly for the worse'; 'caught in the stormy sea of life, Choniates expected no harbours, but only rocks'.[131]

In using narratives of travel to psychoanalyse the dead what is left out of the equation by both Galatariotou and Kazhdan is the literary

---

[128] On inclusion see Bakhtin, 'Discourse in the novel', *Dialogic imagination*, 320-321. Examples: narrative in the letter is required by hodoiporika; in hagiography, Cyril's account of the Danubian voyage; for travelogue in the novel see the exchange of stories by Dosikles and Kratandros, *Rhodanthe and Dosikles*, I-III; the account of Charikles to Kleandros is the equivalent in *Drosilla and Charikles*.

[129] Moschos, PS, 12, PG 87.3. 2861: συνεχῶς λέγε, ὅτι Ξένος εἰμί.

[130] Galatariotou, 'Travel and perception' (as in n. 3), 225-226, for abhorrence of travel; 230-240, for personal reactions.

[131] A. Kazhdan, 'Ships in storms: on imagery and historical interpretations', A. Kazhdan and S. Franklin, *Studies on Byzantine literature of the eleventh and twelfth centuries* (Cambridge, 1984), 264-278; at 271, 278.

context, generic discourse and the horizon of expectations of the textual community. Galatariotou says 'a discussion of the genre of each text falls outside the scope of this paper. Such a discussion would not, as far as I am aware, prejudice in any significant way the findings of this study'.[132] In contrast, I hope that I have in this response suggested significant ways in which a concentration not on the levels of factual, cultural or personal reality but on textual reality, and specifically on genre, allow us to see that whatever the personal response of individuals to travel experiences, their accounts are phrased for a metropolitan audience accustomed to different models of adventure-space in which travel fundamentally broadens the mind.

---

[132] Galatariotou, 'Travel and perception', 221, n. 1.

Index

Numbers in bold refer to Tables.

Abu Mina, 154
Abu'l-Fida, 179
Abu'l-Kasim, emir, 208
Abydos, 45-46, 61, 114, 271
Achilles Tatios, 270, 280-281
Achinos, lake, 89
Acre, **50**
Adrianople, 74,79, 81, 82, 84, 85
Adriatic, 11, 69, 79, 82
adventurers, 165
adventures, 85, 183, 225, 246, 260, 270, 271, 280, 283
Aegean Sea, 4, 5, 6n, 10, 33, 46, 47, 109, 157
Aegean, islands of the, 61
Aegyptus, diocese of, 109
Aeliots, monastery of the, 261
Aeneid, 261
Africa, 12, 14, **49**, 105, 265
African War, **48**
Agathias, *Cycle*, 92n
Agay, 123
agelodromion 86
Agios potamoi, **48**
Agnes de France, princess, 173, 260
Agrigento, 8, 9n
Agyos Pelagos, 69
Aigyptos, *see* Cairo
Akkon, harbour of, 157
Albanians, 218
Alexander of Cappadocia, 152
Alexander the Great, 176, 269n
Alexandretta, 61, 68
Alexandria, 8, **24**, 33, 34, **49**, 100,102, 103, 157, 158n, 160, 189, 229, 261, 264, 270
Alexandria crusade, 217
Alexandria, lighthouse of, 190
Alexios I Komnenos, emperor, 46, 207n, 208
Alexios II Komnenos, emperor, 173

Alexios IV, emperor, 198, 199
Alexios V Mourtzouphlos, emperor, 199n, 203, 204, 209n
Algeria, 105
Alps, 18
— Julian, 95
Amalfitans, 211
Amalric, king, 208
ambassadors, 150, 156, 166
Ambrosiana library, 39
Amman, 242
Amneia, **24**
Amorion, **24**
Amphipolis, 84
Anastasius I, emperor, 76n
Anastasius II, emperor, 120
Anastasios, monk, 78
Anastasis, 160
Anastasius Bibliothecarius, 78
Anatolia, 122n, 125, 145
Anchialos (Pomorie), 77
anchorites, 265
Ancona, 226, 227, 229
Andrew Libadenos, 156, 158, 261
Andrew, apostle, 151n
Andriake, port, 104
Andronikos II, emperor, 83, 85, 188, 189
Andronikos III, emperor, 85, 186, 189
Andronikos Zaridas, 83n, 84n
Anemodoulion, 183
Ankara, battle of, 219
Anna Komnene, 208
Anna, daughter of Michael VIII, 82n
Anonymous Allatii, 160
Antaiopolis, 103
Antakya, 125
Anthemios of Tralles, 184
Anthia, 269, 270
Anthony of Novgorod, 193n
Antioch, 104, 157, 159, 244, 261

Antiochos, 280
antiquarians, 226, 227, 232
Antonios, monk, 188
Apameia, 104
aphthartodocetism, 216
apodemia, 261
apokreas, 111
Apollo, statue of, 227
Apollonia, 73, *see also* Aulona
Apollonias, 274
Apollonios of Tyre, 207
Aponiana (Favignana), **49**
Appian, *The Civil Wars*, **48**, **49**
Apsyrtos 92, 94, 95
Apulia, 68, 79n
aqueduct of Valens, 183, 221
Arab writers, 179, 182, 184, 185
Arabic, 54n, 97n, 165
Arabs, 6n, 18n, 161
Aragon, king of, 63
Arcadius, column of, 228
Archipelago, 61, 64, 68, 67, 71
Arculf, pilgrim, 158
Arethas, 202n
Argonauts, 53
Aristotle, 216
ark of the covenant, 245
Arkadioupolis, 78
Armenia, 64
Arras, 196
Artykomis, 271
Asaf, 187
ascetics, 160
Asia Minor, 6, 12, 14, **24**, 25n, 37, 61, 67-69, 82, 87, 100, 104, 114, 152n
    shrines of, 23
Asia, 103, 278
Askalon, **36**, 37, 100, 101, 265
askesis, 280
askia, 118
Asparuch, 76n, 77n
Astilyanos, 184, 185, *see also* Stylianos
astronomy, maritime, 62, *see also computus*
Athanasios I, patriarch of Constantinople, 113n
Athanasios, correspondent of Nikephoros Gregoras, 83n
Athena, statue of, 200n, 206
Athens, **24**
Atlantic Ocean, descriptions of, 60

Attica, 152n
Aubry of Three Fountains, 209n
Aulikomis, 271
Aulona, 26n, 73
Austria, 79
Auxerre manuscript, 173, 174
Auxerre, 175-178
Auxerre, municipal library of, 173
Avars, 74
Avignon Papacy, 225
Avranches, 173, 175, 176
Avranches, municipal library of, 172
Avşa, island (Türkeli adası), 129
Axios, valley of, 83
Aya Thekla, 22
Azarion, 273

'Babylonish Captivity,' 225
Baghdad, 195
Balkan coast, 61
— corridor, 25
— migrations, 27n
— peninsula, 74, 80, 82
— roads/routes, 26, 80
Balkans, 4, 25, 26, 27n, 28n, 67, 77, 80, 82, 109, 176, 222
Baltic, 221
Bamberg, 170
bankers, 206
Barada panels, 243
Barada, river, 243
Barakhya, 187
Barbery, 64
Barcelona, 63
Bari, 4, 5, 79
barile, 55
Basil I, emperor, 78
Basil, merchant and monk, 6n
Basil, *patrikios* and *parakoimomenos*, 39, 40, *see also Naval Warfare*
Basilika, 115
basilike hodos (*hodos basileios*)/ *basiliakai hodoi*, 83, 87-90
Bataiguier, 123
Bayezid I, Ottoman ruler, 218
Beaufort scale, 45, 46n, 47, 52
Beaufort, Sir Francis, 45n
Bebrycians, spring of the, 53
Belgrade, 74, 79, 80, 81n, 222
Belisarios, **50**
Bellerophontes, 202n

Belthandros, 271
Benjamin of Tudela, 193n, 195
Benno II of Osnabrück, king, 169
Bergamo, 67n
Beroe (Stara Zagora), 77, 81
Berroia, 82n
Berzé, 176
Beta-thalassemia, 20
Bethany, 160
Bethlehem, 149, 154, 160
Betomolachon, 101
Bible, 153, 239
Biblical sites, 239, 240
bigae, 80
Bithynia, 20, 103
Bizye (Vizye), 85
Blachernai, 62
Blachernai, church, 211, 220
Blachernai palace, 196, 199, 220
Black Death, 20, 21
Black Sea, 13, 14, 23, 61, 63, 64, 66, 69, 109, 113, 132, 145, 279
blessings, 10, *see also eulogia*
Bocca d'Avedo, 61, *see also* Abydos and Dardanelles
Boccaccio, 261
Bodrum, 123
— Archaeological museum, 142n
— Museum of Underwater Archaeology, 137
Boilas, 269n
Boldensele, William, 214, 215
Bon, cape, **49**
Bonaparte, Napoleon, 34
Boniface of Montferrat, 198, 209
Book of Deeds, 214, 218, 219, *see also* Boucicaut, Marshal
Book of the Eparch, 111-113, 115n, 117n, 118n
Bordeaux pilgrim, 156, 159
Bosnians, 218
Bosphoros, 112, 219, 279
Bostra, 241
Boucicaut, Marshal, 214, 217-221, 223, 225, *see also Book of Deeds*
Boukoleon, palace, 199, *see also* Great Palace
Bouleron, region of, 78
Bourbon, duke of, 220
bouttia, 118
Bozburun, 35

Braco, port of, 62
Brescia, 262
Breve chronicon de rebus siculis, **48**, **50**
Brindisi, 8n, **49**, **50**, 79
Britain, 20
British Mediterranean Fleet, 34
Bromosyrta, 89
Broquière, Bertrandon de la, 221-226
Brussels, 190
Bryai, 89
Bryaxis, king, 271
Brysis (Pınarhisar), 84, 85
Bubonic plague, 20
Bulgaria, 28, 79, 80, 139, 141, 186
Bulgars (Bulgarians), 25, 74, 76, 78, 80, 218, 275
— invasion of, 82
Buondelmonti, Cristoforo, 202n, 227-230
Burgundy, 218, 225
— court of, 215
Butrinto, 68
Byzantion, 270
Byzantium, 3-6, 8, 10, 14, 18, 19, 20, 22, 28, 54, 77, 86, 109, 117, 155, 161, 169, 171-175, 185, 188, 207, 213, 214, 216-219, 220, 221, 223, 225, 227, 230-232, 236, 241, 245, 259, 260, 266
— /the Empire, court of, 166, 169, 198, 223-226

Caesarea (Palestine), **36**, 142n
Caesarea Philippi, 159
Caffaro, *De liberatione civitatum Orientis liber*, **48**, **50**
Cagliari, **50**, 70
Caiaphas, church of, 237
Cairo Geniza, 54, 143n
Cairo, 158, 160
Calabria, **24**
Caliphate, **24**
Çamaltı Burnu, *see* shipwrecks
Cana, 159
Canterbury Tales, 214, *see also* Chaucer
Capernaum, 159
Cappadocia, 103, 152
caput Turkiae, 68
Caputvada (Ras Kaboudia), **50**
Caramela, 69
Carnuntum, 95
Cartagena, **49**
Casilik, 114, *see also* Kazıklıköy

Cassiopia, 68
Castile, court of, 220, 221
Catalans, 85
— invasion of, 82
Catalonia, 172
Catenae, 92n
Catherine of Alexandria, saint, 160
Caumont, Nompar de, 71
Cephalonia, 227
Cerigo, island of, 70
Chaireas and Kallirhoe, 269
Chalke Gate, 180
Chalkidike, 86, 88, 89, 113
Chalkis, 37
Chandax (Iraklion), 51
Change, the, 206, *see also* Forum of Constantine
Charikles, 283n
charitable institutions, 170, *see also* religious institutions
Chariton, author, 269
Chariton, saint, 154
Charlemagne, 19n, 22, 169
chart(s), 65, 69
— maritime, 59, 60, 66, *see also* portulans
Chatillon, 176
Chaucer, 214, 261, *see also Canterbury Tales*
chelandion/chelandia, 39, 53
— *ousiaka*, 53n
— *pamphyla*, 53n
Chelidonia, cape, 37
Chios, 13, 14, 37, 46, 114, 118, 123
Christ, 13, 144, 152, 154, 160, 188, 217, 235, 237, 245, 247, 259, 266
— tomb of, 160
Christendom, Latin, 218, 219
Christian cartography, 239
Christian Topography, 235, 244, 245, *see also* Kosmas Indikopleustes
Christian topography, 239, 240, 243, 244
Christianity, 150, 152, 188, 219
Christodoulos of Patmos, saint, 154
Christoupolis (Kavala), 78, 84n, 88
Chrysantza, 271
chrysinos (aureus), 115n
Church fathers, 154, 229
Church of the Lions, 241, 242
Church of the priest Wa'il, 241
chylos, 112

Cicero, 74
Cilicia, 103, 261, 265
Ciriaco of Ancona, 226-230, *Commentaria*, 230
Cista Ficoronica, 53
Claudius Balbillus, prefect, 34
clausurae (clusae), 81
Clavijo, Ruy Gonzales de, 207, 220, 221, 223
Clazomenai, 94n
coaster, 37, *see also* ships
coins, 11, 12, 17, 28, 143, 144, 147
colic, 92
colloquia Monacensia, 170
commerce, maritime, 13n, 129, 140, 147
communications, 3-7, 9-14, 16-21, 23, 25-28
compassus orbis, 69
computus (astronomy), 62, *see also* astronomy, maritime
Conpasso de navegare, 60-63, 65, 66, 69, 70
Conrad III, king, 80
Conrad of Montferrat, 198
Constantia, half-sister of Constantine I, 95
Constantine Akropolites, 88
Constantine I, emperor, 95, 115n, 153, 182, 185, 196, 201, 202n, 206
Constantine IV, emperor, 27n, 77n
Constantine VII Porphyrogennetos, emperor, 40, 181n
— obelisk of, 181
Constantine Manasses, 156, 261, 262, 280
Constantine of Antioch, 244, 245
Constantinople, 4, 5, 6n, 8, 10, 11-14, 21, 23, **24**, 25, 26, 27n, 28, 33, **36**, 37, 38, 45-47, **50**, 61, 62, 63n, 68, 69, 73, 74, 76-79, 82-85, 88, 99, 100, 102-105, 109, 110, 112n, 113-116, 118, 119, 122, 128, 129, 133, 137, 139, 140, 150, 151, 152n, 153, 156, 161, 166-169, 173, 177, 179-182, 184, 186-191, 193-199, 201-206, 208, 210-212, 214-223, 224-232, 243, 244, 247, 260, 262, 264, 266, 271, 274, 276, 279, *see also* Byzantium
— Arab siege of, 120
— bakeries of, 110n
— council of (869-870), 78
— inhabitants of, 110, 196, 212
— Latin conquest of, 168
— 'Patriarchal School' of, 168

— people of, 204
— visitors to, 204
Constantinopolitan coin circulation, 12n
Constantinopolitan topography, 193, 205, 237-240, 242
Constantinopolitans, 25, 197, 201, 205, 207, *see also* homo constantinopolitanus
Constantius II, emperor, 151n
Contarina, 124
Corfu, **49**, 68, 70
Corinth, 4, 26, 27, 141
Cornelius Scipio, **49**
couriers, 96
Crete, **50**, 51, 57, 63n, 69, 70, 118, 152n, 157, 227, 262, 267, 282
Crotone, 8
Crusade
— First, 26, 69, 80, 193, 210n
— Second, 80, 193, 194, 196
— Third, 68, 81
— Fourth, 22n, 82, 193, 197, 203, 206, 209n, 212
Crusaders, 69, 70, 79-82, 143, 157, 165, 166, 167, 173, 174, 176, 193-195, 197n, 198-200, 206, 211, 218, 219
crusades, 65, 67, 73n, 79n, 81, 109, 156
crusading expeditions, 71, 195
Cutty Sark, 34
Cyclades, 157
Cyprus, 17, 45, 46, **50**, 64, 69, 70, 113n, 157, 217, 261, 271, 282
Cyril of Scythopolis, saint, 104, 150, 153
Cyril Phileotes, 279, 280

Dalmatia, **24**
Dalrymple, William, 261
Damascus, 16n, 35, 159, 189, 229, 235, 237, 243-245
Damietta, 157
Danes, 19
Daniel of Ephesos, 156, 158, 161
Danube, **24**, 73, 76n, 94, 95, 279
Daphnipolis, 271
Daphnis and Chloe, 270
Dardanelles, 33, 46, 61, 81n, 82
Datius, bishop of Milan, 26n
De cerimoniis, 40
De divisione orbis terrarum, 69
De viis maris, 65
Dead Sea, 159, 160, 236
Deir Dosi, 261

Delos, 227
Delphi, 270
Deluge, 259n
Demetrias, 6n
Demetrios, brother of Theophylact of Ochrid, 275
Demetrios, saint, 114, 209, 210
demosiai (demosiakai) hodoi / demosia hodos, 81, 87, 89, 90
Derbyshire, 19
Descriptio insulae Cretae, 227, *see also* Buondelmonti, Cristoforo
Dia, island of, 268
Diaz, Bernal, 197
Diegesis peri tes Hagias Sophias, 184, 185
Digest, 92n
al-Dimashqi, 189
Diocletian, emperor, 95n, 103n
Dionysiou, monastery of (Mount Athos), 18
Dioscorides, 92n
DNA, 19, 20n, 21, 22, 28
Dodecanese, 157, 278
Dorestad, 18
Doria, Hilario, 220
Dormition, 111
Dosikles, 270, 271, 278, 283n
dromon(s), 5, 10n, 33, 39, 40-43, 45-47, **50**, 51, 54, 57
— battle *dromons*, 43
— *bireme*, 39, 44, 52-55
— *galeai*, 39
— trireme (*triereis*), 40n 41, 42, **49**, 55, 202
dromos, 86
Drosilla and Charikles, 283n
Drosilla, 270
Dyrrachion, 4, 73, 79, 275
dysury, 94

East Midlands, 19
Easter, 16n, 84, 111
Eboda, 101
Ebro, **49**
Ecloga, 111n
Ecumenical Council, Third (Constantinople), 27n
Ecumenical patriarchate, 22
Edessa, 209n
Edirne, *see* Adrianople
Egeria, 155

Egnatian Way, *see* Via Egnatia
Egypt, 34, 65, 96n, 100, 101, 149, 150, 153, 155n, 157-160, 236, 240, 246, 263, 270
Egyptian obelisk, 181, 190n, 228
Eirene, widow of John Palaiologos, 83, 84
Eirene, wife of Constantine VI, 77
Eirenopolis (Isauria), **24**
Ekinlik island, 129
Elias of Enna, saint, 154
Eliezer, 246
elite(s), Byzantine, 8, 9, 23, 24, 231, 232
Emesa, 154, 262
Emmaus, 159
encomia, 210
England, 221
envoys, 25n, 26n
Ephesiaka, *see* Xenophon
Ephesos, 6n, 22, 84, 100, 103, 104, 156, 158, 161, 269, 270
epibaterion, 260, 274
epidosis, 84
Epiphaneia, 104
Epiphanios Hagiopolites, 150, 155, 157
Epiros, 76
epistolography, 154, 280, 281
Epistre lamentable et consolotaire, 218, see also Mézières, Philip de
epitaphs, 100-102, 105, 106,
Ergene, *see* Regina
Ethiopia, 270
Euboia, 268
Euboian hunter(s), 267, 268
Euchaita, 22
Eudokia [Athenais], empress, 153, 237
Eugenius IV, pope, 229
eulogia, 154
Euoptios, 273
euporista, 92n
Euripos, **48**, 279
Europe, 3, 6, 11, 19, 23, **24-26**, **48**, 65, 73, 76, 79, 143, 165, 166, 169, 173, 195, 210, 221, 225
— courts of, 225
Europeans, 166
Eurykomis, 271
Eusebios, *Onomastikon*, 239
Eustathios Makrembolites, 271
Evagrius, 104
Evergetis, monastery of, 276, 281

Exaltation of the Holy Cross, feast of the, 264
Exodus, 239
expeditions, 40, 53, 71, 195, 224, 263

Farmer's Law (*Nomos Georgikos*), 110, 111, 118
fever, 92
Fibonacci, Leonardo, 65
Ficoroni, Francesco, 53n
Filelfo, Francesco, 229
Finigha (Finike), 46, 69
Flanders, 195, 196, 211n, 221
fleet(s)
— Byzantine, 53, 57, 109
— English, 68
— galley fleets, **48**, 51
— Genoese, 219-220
— grain fleet, 103
— of the crusaders, 69, 50
Florence, 222-227
— council of, 222, 224, 226
Florimont, 175, 176
Forum of Arcadius, 204, *see also* Xerolophos
Forum of Constantine, 183, 200n, 206
Forum Tauri, 204, *see also* Forum of Theodosius; Tauros
France, 11, 22n, 79, 123, 173, 195, 197, 211n, 218, 219, 221
Franks, 173, 211
Frederick I Barbarossa, emperor, 81
Frederick II, emperor, **50**
French (language), 168n, 196, 202, 203, 207, 209
Fulcher of Chartres, 193-197

Gabala, 159
Gainas, 204
Gaius Galerius, prefect, 34
Gaius, 171
Galata, 103, 105, 187, *see also* Pera
galeai, 39
Galilee, 14, 17, 155n, 159
galleys, 39, 40-43, 45, 47, **48**, 51-55, 277
Gallipoli, 177, 217, *see also* Kallipolis
Games, the (hippodrome), 183, 206, 207
games, board, 147
Gate of the Golden Mantle, 199, *see also* Tetrapylon
Gaza, 12, **36**, 38, 100-103, 159, 240

INDEX

Gaziköy, 125, 128
Genesis, 239, *see also* Vienna Genesis
Genoa, **50**, 54, 145, 156, 219
Genoese, **50**, 56, 63, 145, 219, 220
gente di mare, 67
Geoffrey of Bouillon, 80
geographical commentaries, 156
geographical treatises, 179
Geon, 239, *see also* Nile
Geoponika, 110
George Akropolites, 118n
George Gemistos Plethon, 226, 230
George Oinaiotes, 85
George, emperor, 188, 189
George, *kandidatos/protokankellarios*, 78
George, saint, 159, 176
Georgia, **24**
Gerasimos, saint, 154
Germans, 211
Germany, 79, 169
Gesta Regis Ricardi, 67, *see also* Roger of Howden
Gethsemane, 160
al-Ghazari, 189, 191
Gibraltar, strait of, 61
Gizeh, 153, 161
Glass Wreck, 133, 134, 137, 148, *see also* shipwreck(s)
glass/glassware, 18, 124, 140-144, 148, 190
glassmakers, 141
glossaries, 169, 170
Golden Gate, 25, 62, 180, 199, 223
Golden Horn, 221, 222
Gomatou, 89
Good Samaritan, 246, 247
gorgons, 277
Gospels, 144
gradientes nautarum, *see* portulan(s)
Graecia, **24**
graffiti, 10n
grammar school, 170
granaries, 116, 117
Grand Turk, 223
Great Britain, 7n
Great Church, 189, 217, *see also* Hagia Sophia
Great Interpreter, 166n
Great Mosque, 243
Great Palace, 180, 182, 196, 199, *see also* Boukoleon, palace

Great Schism, 218, 225, 226
Greece, 7, **24**, 26, 28n, 68, 73, 226, 227, 230, 232
Greek Church, 225
Greek (language), 5, 13, 65, 165, 166, 168-177, 202, 208, 211, 222
Greeks, 82, 167, 168, 200-204, 206, 207n, 208-212, 215-218, 221-227, 229, 231, 232
Gregory I, pope, 18n
Gregory of Burtscheid, 170
Gregory of Dekapolis, saint, 78
Gregory of Nazianzus, 35, 41, 247
— Sermons of Gregory of Nazianzus, Paris manuscript of the, 35, 41, 246, 247, 249
Gregory of Pharan, abba, 265, 266
Gregory the Great, pope, 26
Guarino, student, 229
guesthouses, 155
guidebooks, *see proskynetaria*
guides, 7, 64, 81, 84-86, 166, 172, 181, 189, 208, 248
Gunther of Pairis, 168, 193, 197,199, 200n, 203-205, 208n, 211, *see also* *Hystoria Constantinopolitana*
Gytheion, 219

Habrokomes, 269, 270
Hadrian II, pope, 78
Hadrian, emperor, 157
Hagios Mamas, church of, 89
Hagia Sophia, church of, 37, 181n, 182, 183-185, 187, 188, 190, 191, 196, 199-201, 211, 215, 220, 230, *see also* Great Church; Holy Trinity, church of
hagiography/hagiographies, 7, 8n, 14, 154, 155, 262, 276, 279, 282, 283
Hagios Paulos, 88n, 89
Hajji 'Abd Allah, 189, 190
al-Hakim, 143
halmaia, 112
hamaxegos, 86
hamsa, 145
al-Harawi, 179, 181, 184, 201
Harald of Norway, 174
Harun Ibn Yahya, 181n, 183-185, 188
Hawrān, 104
Hebrew, 54n, 165
Hebros, 73n

292   INDEX

'Heerstrasse', 26, *see also* military road; *via militaris*
Helen of Troy, 272
Helena, empress, 152, 153
Heliodoros, 270, 271
Hellenika, *see* Xenophon
Hellespont, 177
Henry II, king, 170
Henry the Lion, 81
Henry the Navigator, 214
Heraclius, emperor, 11, 14
— statue of (actually Justinian I), 200, 201
Herakleia, 45
Herodotos, *History*, **48**, 239
Hierissos, 89
Hierokles, 94n
Hierotheos, 279
Hilarion the Georgian, saint, 154
Himerios, 51, 267
Hippiatrika, 92, 94n, 97
hippodrome, 180, 181-183, 184, 190, 199, 200, 206, 207, 228, *see also* Games
Historia de expeditione Friderici, 81
historical geography, 59
hodoiporikon / hodoiporika, 156, 261, 262, 274-276, 281, 282n
hodos, 86
Holy (True) Cross, 215, 264
Holy Apostles, church of, 182, 191, 199, 200, 202, 211, *see also* Seven Apostles, church of
Holy Bush, 160
Holy Land, 70, 79, 149, 150, 152n, 153, 155, 156, 161, 187, 248, 263, *see also terra sancta*
Holy Mountain, 88, *see also* Mount Athos
Holy Sepulchre, 152, 238
Holy Sepulchre, church of, 159, 218, 237, 238, 242
Holy Trinity, church of, 202 (actually Hagia Sophia)
homo byzantinus, 161
homo constantinopolitanus, 110, 116, *see also* Constantinopolitans
hoof-dressing, 95
Horeb, 160
horse-doctor(s), 91, 92n, 94, 95n, 96
hospitality, 79, 225, 281
Hoşköy (Chora), 128
Hula, lake of, 159

humanists, 232
Hungarians, 79
Hungary, 79, 80
Huns, 26
hypakoe, 280
Hysmine and Hysminias, 271
Hysmine, 271, 278
Hystoria Constantinopolitana, 168, *see also* Gunther of Pairis

Ibn Battuta, 183, 185-189
Ibn Khurradadhbih, 179, 180
Ibn Rusta, 183
Iconium, 68, 103
Iconium, sultan of, 68
Iconoclasm, 244
icons, 160, 200, 208, 209, 211, 244, 262
Idrisi, 179, 180
Ignatios the Deacon, 10n
Ignatios, architect, 184, 185
Ilias Ambrosiana, 41
Illyricum, 28n
imperial roads, *see basilike hodos/basilike hodoi*
innkeepers, 85
Inscriptiones Christianae Urbis Romae, 105
Institute of Nautical Archaeology (INA), 128, 129, 131, 137
insulae minores, 69
intellectuals, Byzantine, 229, 230
interpreter(s), 166, 169, 187
interscalmium, 40, 55
Ioannis, 140
Ios, 51
ippiatroi, *see* horse doctors
Isaac II, emperor, 199
Isaac, *sebastokrator*, 260
Isidoros of Miletos, 184
Iskandil Burnu, 123
Istabrin, 183, *see also* Staurion
Istanbul Naval Museum, 142n
Istanbul, 45n, 180
Italian humanism, 229
Italian patois, 168n
Italian, 61, 230
Italians, 20
Italo-byzantines, 20
Italy, 7n, 14, 17, 20, 24, 26, 73, 76, 79, 95, 105, 226, 270, 282
Itinerarium Antonini, 103
Itinerarium Antonii Placentini, 155

INDEX

Itinerarium Burdigalense, 155, 156
Itinerarium peregrinorum, 48, **50**
itinerary/itineraries, 8, 175, 200, 211
— maritime, 64, 65n, 68, *see also periploi*
Iveron, monastery of (Mount Athos), 228
Izmir, archaeological museum of, 142n
Izmit, gulf of, 114, *see also* Nikomedeia, gulf of

Jacobus of Verona, monk, 70
Jaffa, 37, 157, 159
Jakobos Meloites, 150/151, 156, 158n
Jason, argonaut, 53
Jerash, 241
Jericho, 157, 160, 246
Jerusalem, 14, 16, 22, **24**, 149-151, 153-155, 157-159, 187, 194n, 208, 213, 221, 235, 237, 238, 240, 242, 245, 246, 248, 261, 262, 264, 278, *see also* New Jerusalem
Jews, 189
Johanitsa, 209, 210
John I Tzimiskes, emperor, 18n
John I, pope, 26n
John Chrysoloras, 229
John Chrysostom, 152, 229
John Doukas, 279
John Mauropous, 260
John Moschos, 38, 261, 263, 265, 278
John of Damascus, saint, 35, 229, 244
John of Ephesos, 100, 101, 103
John of Lyda, 102
John Palaiologos, 83
John Philagathos, 170
John Phokas, 156, 157, 159
John the Fearless, 218
John the Vlach, *see* Johanitsa
John Tzetzes, 167, 168, *Theogony*, 167
John V Palaiologos, emperor, 217, 223
John VI Kantakouzenos, emperor, 215n, 216
John VII Palaiologos, emperor, 219, 220
John VIII Palaiologos, emperor, 224, 228
John XXII, pope, 215, 216
Jonah, 247
Jordan, river, 17, 149, 154, 155n, 160, 236, 239, 242, 266
Joseph, 153, 161, 246, 247
Joseph Bryennios, 226, 229
Joshua, 202n
Judaea, 17

Judaeo-Arabic, 54n
Julius Caesar, **49**
Justin I, emperor, 76n
Justinian I, emperor, 14, 102, 104, 115n, 160, 182, 184, 185, 190, 200, 201, 226
— column of, 182, 184, 185, 190
— edict of, 103
— statue of, 201, 215
Justinian II, emperor, 27n, 76, 77
Justinianic plague (contagion/pestilence), 20, 21, 99, 109, *see also* Bubonic plague

kados/kadoi, 53, 55, 57
Kallipolis, 82, *see also* Gallipoli
kapelos, 85
Karakilise, 91n
Karbaioi, 89
Karia, 269
Karyes, 88n
Karykes, 279
Kassandra, 88, 89
Kastamonitou, monastery of (Mount Athos), 88n
Kastron Mefaa (Umm al Rasas), 241, 242
Katakale, 89
Kaukana, **50**
Kavala, *see* Christoupolis
Kaxeti, **24**
Kazıklıköy, 114n *see also* Casilik
Kefar Hananya, 16n, 17
Keos, 273
Kephallenia, **49**
Keşan, *see* Rossa
khatun, 186
Khirbat al-Mukhayyat, 241
Khirbat al-Samra, 241
Khludov Psalter, 35
Kibyrrhaiots, theme of the, 138
Kidron valley, 160
Kleandros, 283n
kleisoura, 76, 77
Kometopouloi, 79
Korone, 34
Kos, 46, 138
Kosmas Indikopleustes, 244, *see also Christian Topography*
Kratandros, 271, 283n
Krum, khan, 76, 77
Kuber, king, 76n, 77n
Kumtepe, 129

Köçük Çekemece, 85
Kypsela, 73n
Kythera, 71
Kyzikos, **24**

Le Songe du vieil Pelerin, 214, 217, *see also* Mézières, Philip de
lachana oma, 112
Laconia, 230
Laiazzo (Yumurtalık), 69
Lakedaimon, **48**
lameness, 92, 94
laminitis, 94
Lampsakos, **48**
Lannoy, Ghillebert de, 221, 222, 223, 225
Laodiceia, 159
Laon glossary, 170
Latin empire, 198, 199
Latin, 5, 65, 150, 155, 165-167, 169-174, 230
Latins, 167, 168, 207n, 211, 216, 226
Laudes Constantinopolitanae, 153
Laura of St. Sabbas, 160
law, maritime, 145
Lazaros Galesiotes, saint, 154
Leimonarion, 261, *see also* Pratum Spirituale; John Moschos
lemboi, **49**
Lenten fare, 111
Lenten period, 117
Leo Allatius, 261
Leo of Catania, saint, 8
Leo VI, emperor, 39, 40n, 43
Leon, 139
Leontios of Jerusalem, 278
Leontius of Damascus, 16n
leophoros, 81, 87
Lepte Akra, 265
Lesbos, 51, 267, 251, *see also* Mitylene
letter(s), 5, 27, 28, 54, 67, 73n, 83-85, 88, 90, 94, 96n, 111, 113n, 118n, 122n, 144, 152, 156, 203, 204, 206, 221, 228, 262, 272-276, 279, 280, 282, 283
— of credit, 144
— letter collections, 11
— travel letter(s), 82, 85, 276
Leukippe and Klitophon, 269n, 270
Levant, 27n, 218, 219, 225, 229
— Arab, 21
Liber de existencia riveriarum et forma maris nostri Mediterranei, 66

Liber insularum Archipelagi, 227, 229, *see also* Buondelmonti, Cristoforo
Liber secretorum fidelium crucis, 69, *see also* Sanudo, Marino
libre de navegar, 63
Libya, 123
Licinius, emperor, 95
Life of St. Abraamios of Emesa, 154
Life of St. Athanasia of Aegina, 174n
Life of St. Chariton, 154
Life of St. Christodoulos of Patmos, 154
Life of St. Cyriacus, 104
Life of St. Elias of Enna, 154
Life of St. Gerasimos, 154
Life of St. Gregory Dekapolites, 78
Life of St. Gregory of Nazianzus, 247
Life of St. Hilarion the Georgian, 154
Life of St. John of Hephaistopolis, 104
Life of St. Lazaros Galesiotes, 154
Life of St. Nicholas of Sion, 154
Life of St. Nicholas, 104
Life of St. Porphyrios of Gaza, 35
Life of St. Symeon the New Theologian, 209n
Life of St. Theodore of Sykeon, 105, 154
Life of St. Theoktiste of Lesbos, **48**, **50**, 51, 269
Lignidus (Lychnidus), 26n
Lilybaion (Marsala), **49**
Limassol, **50**
literature, 214, 149n, 3
— Byzantine, 247, 260
— classical, 261
— Latin, 65n
— medical, 92n
— patriographical, 207, 208
— pilgrimage, 161
— western, 213
Liudprand of Cremona 7, 202n
Livy, *From the foundation of the city*, **48**, **49**
logothetes tou dromou, 87
London 34, 68
Longos (Sykia), 88n, 270, 280
Lot and Prokopios, saints, church of, 241
Louis II, king, 78
Louis VII, king, 194
Louis VIII, king, 80
Louis, saint (Louis IX), king of France, 70
Louvre Exhibition (1992-93), 209
Lucan, *The Civil War*, **48**, **49**
Lucius Aemilius Paulus, **49**

Lucius, 171
Lüleburgaz, see Arkadioupolis
Lycia, 157, 265
Lydda-Diospolis, 159
Lyons, 216
Lyons II, council of, 216

Ma'in, church at, 242
Macedonia, 73, 76, 82, 90
Madaba church, 236, 237
Madaba mosaic map, 235-240, 242, 244, 245, 248, 249
Madaba, 238, 242
Magyars, 28
Makri, gulf of, 69, see also Fethiye
malaria, 20
Malea, cape, 61, 64, 68, 70
Malta, **50**
Mandeville, Sir John, 213-217, *Travels*, 213, 214, 216
Mangana, Cape, 62
Mani, 230, 231
mannekenpis, 190
mansiones, 91
Manuel Chrysoloras, 218, 228, 229
Manuel I Komnenos, emperor, 194, 196, 198, 202n, 208, 262
Manuel II Palaiologos, emperor, 219, 220, 226
Marcellinus Comes, 105
Marco Polo, 213
mare apertum, 122
mare clausum, 120n
Mangana, cape, 62
Maria of Alania, 275, 276
Maritsa, 81, 177n, 176
Mark the Deacon, 35, 36, 38
Marmara island, 119n, 122n, 132-134, see also Prokonnesos
Marmara islands, 128, 129
Marmara region, 282
Marmara Sea, 13, 14, 45, 112, 113, 125, 128, 129, 131, 133, 134, 139, 282, *see also* Propontis
Marmaris, 124
Maroneia, 4, 78
marriages, mixed, 166
Marsa Lucch, 123
Marsala (Lilybaion), **49**, 124
Marseille, 12
Martin I, pope, 27n

Martin of Pairis, 168, 193
al-Marwazi, 179, 180n
Mary of Egypt, saint, 263, 264
al-Mas'udi, 179
Matthew, bishop of Ephesos, 84, 85
Maurice, emperor, 33
Maximus the Confessor, saint, 236
maydan, 181
medicines, 92n
Mediterranean Pilot, 7
Mediterranean, 5, 6, 20, 25, 61, 65, 66, 70, 71, 100, 105, 106, 109, 122, 127, 118n, 132, 138, 139, 141, 145, 157, 159, 239, 240, 245, 261, 269, 282
— portulans of the, 65, 71
— shipping, 27
— shipping networks, 21
Meles, river, 94n
Melito of Sardes, 152
Meletios, saint, 279
Melisende, 262
Melos, 61
meltemi, 37, 47
Memphis, 270
Menandrian treatises, 261
mercenaries, 6, 174, 175, 178, 222
merchant mariner, 11, *see also* ships
merchant shipping, 109
— travellers, 6
— voyages/trips, 5, 6
merchants, 5, 69, 71, 74, 109, 122, 125, 143n, 144, 166, 174, 222, 246, 269
Mesopotamia, 103
Messina, 34, **50**, 68
metochia, 279
Mexico, 197
Mézières, Philip de, 217, 218, 225, *see also* Le Songe du vieil Pelerin
Michael VIII Palaiologos, emperor, 82, 113
— column of, 191
Michael Attaleiates, 122, 269n
Michael, captain, 142, 143
Middle English, 213n
migrations, 26
— of European and Amerindian populations, 19
— of Slavs and Bulgars, 25
Milan, 95
Miletos, 184, 269

military road, 73, 74, 79-81, 86, 90, *see also* Heerstrasse and *via militaris*
millennium, Byzantine, 28
Milutin, Uroš II, 82n, 83
Miracles of St. Demetrios (*Miracula S. Demetrii*), 77n, 114
miraculum, 34
Miroslav, 140
Mistra, 219, 230
Mitylene, 46, 220, *see also* Lesbos
Modon, 70n
Moesia, 24
monasteries, 22n, 86, 87, 88, 128, 134, 138, 160, 174-176, 188, 208, 211, 220, 221, 228, 240n, 261, 263, 279
monastic libraries, 228
— schools, 170
— *typika*, 110, 111, 117
monasticism, 153n, 282n
— western, 169n
Mongols, 84, 186
— nvasion of, 82
monopation, 87
Mont Saint Michel, 172
Morocco, 38, 186, 261
Moses, 160
Mount Athos (Holy Mountain), 17, 73n, 74, 86, 88, 89, 127, 216, 227, 228, 232
— libraries, 232
— monasteries, 87, 88, 128
— relics of, 22
Mount Carmel, 159
Mount Ganos, 13, 14, 85, 119, 121, 127-129, 132-134
Mount Golgotha, 159
Mount Katrina, 160
Mount of Olives, 160
Mount Olympos, 127
Mount Sinai, 16n, 149, 154, 155n, 157, 159-161, 261
Mount Sion, 160
Mount Tabor, 159
mulomedici, 191n
Murad I, Ottoman emir, 214
Muslims, 182, 183, 186, 188, 189, 191
Myra (Stamiris), 69, 104
Myron, 140
Mysia, 103

Nahor, 246
Naples, 6n, 13

Narbonne, 11
naukleros, 38
Naval warfare, 39, *see also* Basil, *patrikios* and *parakoimomenos*
Naxos, **50**, 51, 267
Nazarenes, 277
Nazareth, 159
Nea church, 183, 202n
Neakome, 276
Neapolis, 248n
Negev, 100, 101, 104, 236
Neocaesarea, 185
Nessana, 14, 100, 101, 102
Nestos valley, 84n
New Jerusalem, 153
New Testament, 150, 156
— places, 159
Nicaea, 276
— council of, 77
Niccoli, Niccolò, 227
Nicholas Kataskepenos, 279
Nicholas Mesarites, 276, 279-281, 282n
Nicholas Mouzalon, 46, 280
Nicholas of Sion, saint, 154, 267
Nicolas of Stamiris, saint, 69
Nicolaus of Martoni, 70
Nikephoros Gregoras, 9n, 83, 84, 88, 89, 283, *Roman History*, 83, 84n
Nikephoros I, patriarch of Constantinople, 25
Nikephoros II Phokas, emperor, 40, 181n
Nikephoros Ouranos, 39, 57, 58n
Niketas Choniates, 9n, 168, 200n, 206, 207, 211, 283
Niketas Eugeneianos, 270
Niketas Magistros, **48**, **50**, 51, 267, 268
Niketas, doux, 80
Nikolaos, 139
Nikomedeia, 91n, 94n, 274, 276
— gulf of, *see also* Izmit, gulf of
Nikon of Naples, saint, 13, 14, 28
Nikopolis crusade, 218
Nikopolis, 218, 219
Nile, 99, 157, 158n, 161, 236, 239, 245, 270
Nineveh, 247
Niš, 79-81
Nišava, 80
nomisma, 174
Nomos Georgikos, *see Farmer's Law*
Nomos Rhodion Nautikos (Rhodian Sea Law), 115, 117

INDEX

Noricum, 95
Norman War, 274
Norse sagas, 207n
nosochomium, 170
Notitita urbis Constantinopolitanae, 110n
Novara, Campano da, 65

Ochrid, 82n, 274-276
Odo of Deuil, 80, 167, 1193, 194, 196, 197
Odo, son of Stigand, 175
Odyssey, 261
oinos enchorios, 112
Old French, 213n
Old Norse, 19
Old Testament, 150, 152, 154, 156, 161
olocotinon/olocotina/olokotina (lacotina), 174
Olympias II, 40-42, 43n, 52
ophthalmia, 265
Oribasios, *Synagogai iatrikai*, 92n
Oriens, diocese of, 109
Orthodox church, 230
Orthodoxy, 232
Otranto, 8, 17n, 79
Otto III, emperor, 170, 171
Ottoman Turks, 218
Ottomans, 179, 191, 219, 221
ousia, 40, 53

packhorses, 80
Paisios Hagiopolites, 150, 156-158, 161
Palaiologan period, 120, 189
palaios dromos (hodos/strata), 87
palaiostraton, 87
Palestina II, 17n
Palestine, 79n, 100, 103, 104, 119, 123, 149, 150, 152-154, 157-159, 236, 240, 243, 244, 248, 261
Palestrina (Praeneste), 53n
Palm Sunday, 158
Pamphylia, 157
Panagia ritual, 10n
Pannonia, 95
Panteichion, 274
papacy, 218
papal correspondence, 27
papal legates, 27n, 76n, 78
Paphos, 37, 45, 46
Parastaseis Syntomai Chronikai, 204, 205, 208
parexeiresiai, 41
Paris, 23, 125, 213n, 272

Paros, 51, 268
Passion of Jesus Christ, crusading order, 217
Passion, relics of, 215
— Crown of Thorns, 215
— Lancehead, 215
— Nail, 215
— Sponge, 215
— True Cross, 215, 264
— Tunic, 215
Patara, 37, 46
Patmos, 154, 278
Patras, 26n
Patria, 205, 207
patriarchal registers, 10
Paul (Saul), 235, 245
Paul of Aegina, 92n
Paul, apostle, 276
Paul, monk, 276
pedestrians, 87
Pegasos, 202n
pelagion, 61
Pelagonius, 94n
Pelagos, 124
Peloponnese, 70, 219, 230
Pelusium, 99, 103
pepaliomene hodos, 87n
Pera, 221, *see also* Galata
Perdikas of Ephesos, 156
Peregrinatio ad loca sancta, 155, *see also* Egeria
Pergamon, 17n
Peribleptos, monastery, 220
Periegesis, 158
periploi, 59n, 64, 65, *see also* itineraries-maritime
Pero Tafur, 201, 223-226
Persians, 104
Pesaro, 230
Peter and Paul, saints, 144
— church of, 241
— feast of, 111
Peter the Hermit, 79, 80
Peter the Patrician, 26n
Peter, king of Cyprus, 217
Peter Thomas, papal legate, 217
Phaleron, **48**
Pharaoh Chefren, pyramid of, 161
pharaohs, 161
Pharan, oasis of, 160
Philadelphia, 217

Philip Augustus (Philip II of France), king, 68, **50**
Philip the Good, 225
Philip V (the Great), **49**, 176
Philippi, 159
Philippopolis (Plovdiv), 26, 77, 79, 81, 176
Philopation, palace, 196
phlebotomy, 94
Phoenicia, 17n
Phokas, emperor, 33
Photios, patriarch of Constantinople, 11, 115, 185
Picardy, 196, 198
pileggi, 61, 66
pilgrim(s), 6, 70, 71, 79, 80, 125, 150, 152-161, 165, 166, 169, 194, 199, 248, 263
— Russian, 210, 193
— narrative(s), 213, 214
— ships, 156
— souvenirs, 16
— writings, 160
'Pilgrim's Road', 79
pilgrimage(s), 16, 37, 69, 70, 79n, 125, 127, 149, 150-153, 155, 156, 158, 159, 161, 194n, 214
— literature, 161
Pilgrimage, 214, *see also* Boldensele, William
pilot books *see* portulans
Pinarhisar *see* Brysis
piracy, 145
pirate raids/attacks, 145, 259, 272
— ship, 270, 278, 282
pirates, 68, 78, 262, 267, 270, 271, 273, 276, 277, 283
— Arab, 78, 263
— Phoenician, 269
Pisa, 65
Pisan chart, 66
Pisans, 211
Pissa, 271
pistrinae, 110n
pithos / pithoi, 37, 38, 118
plakotos (plakote)/ plakotoi 86n, 87
Pliny the Elder, 34
ploion, 46
Plovdiv *see* Philippopolis
Plutarch, *Moralia*, 228
polichnion, 278
Polybios, 73n, *The Histories*, **48**, **49**

Pomorie *see* Anchialos
Pompeians, 19n
Pompeii, 18
poroi, 88
Porphyrios of Gaza, 36, 38
portolano, 59n
portulan chart, 59, 68, 69
portulan(s) (pilot books), 59, 63, 64
— Greek, 63, 64
— Italian, 63
— Mediterranean, 71
— partial, 65
— Venetian, 60
Potiphar, 246
Pozzuoli, 34
Pratum Spirituale (Spiritual Meadow), 38, 261, *see also* Leimonarion; John Moschos
Preslav, 141
Prinkipo, 274
Procopius, *The Persian Wars*, 99, 101, 103
— *The Vandal War*, **48**, **50**,
Prodromos in Petra, church of, 220
Prokonnesos, 45, 62, 129, 133, *see also* Marmara island
Prokopios, anchorite, 38
Prokopios, saint, 247
prooimion, 92
propemptikon, 260, 274
Propontis, 129n, 156, *see also* Marmara Sea
proskynesis, 275
Proskynetarion de situ terrae sanctae, 155, see Theodosios, archdeacon
proskynetarion/proskynetaria, 150, 152n, 154, 155, 159-161,
prosphonetikon/prosphonetika, 260, 274
prota, 174
Prota, 85
protosebastos, 177n
Prousa, 94n
provisions, 43, 110n, 116n, 120,
pseudo-Dionysos, 100n
pseudo-Kallisthenes, 269n
pseudo-Lucian, 269n
Ptochoprodromos 110, 112, 117, 118
Ptolemais, harbour, 157
public roads, *see demosiai hodoi*
Purgatory, 216
Pusculo, Ubertino, 262
Pylai, 276, 278

— port of, 91n

Qalat Seman, 154
al-Qazwini, 179
quadrigae, 80
quadrireme, **49**
quartarolo, 55
quinquireme, **49**
al-Quwaysmah, 242

Radolibos, 87n
Ras Kaboudia *see* Caputvada
Rebecca, 246
recipes
— Lenten, 117
— Levantine, 119
Red Sea, 158, 160, 259n, 265
Reggio, 8, **24**
Regina, river, 78
Rehovot, 101
relics, 5, 8n, 22, 23, 28, 150, 151n, 153, 160, 168, 197, 199, 200, 208n, 209n, 211, 215, 221, 223, 224, 263, *see also* reliquaries
— catalogue of, 208n
religious institutions, 175, *see also* charitable institutions
reliquaries, 22n, 154, 263, *see also* relics
Renaissance scholars, 226
Renaissance travellers, 226
renovatio imperii, 171
Rhaidestos (Tekirdağ), 37, 45, 46, 85, 116n, 139
Rhaitou, 158, 160, 265
Rhine, 18
Rhodanthe and Dosikles, 270, 271
Rhodanthe, 278
Rhodes, 33, 35, **36**, 37, 38, 45-47, 61, 68, 69, 70n, 104, 123, 137, **138**, 157, 219, 220, 227, 262, 269-271
Rhodian Sea Law, 117
Rhodope mountains, 139
Richard Coeur de Lion (the Lionheart), **50**
Rinokoroura, 240
Ripoll, 171
robbers, 78, 82n, 85
Robert, son of Stigand, 175
Robert of Clari, 193, 195, 197-212
Roger of Howden, 68, *Chronica*, 67-68
— *Gesta Regis Ricardi*, 67-68

roman courtois, 172
Romania, 61, 68, 142n
Roman Vergil, 41
Romans, 180
Rome, 6n, 8, 11, 18n, **24**, 27, 53n, 76, 78, 105, 106, 183, 195, 217, 218, 226, 228, 261
Rome, church of, 222
Rossa (Rusköy-Keşan), 82
Rotunda of the Anastasis, 238, *see also* Christ, tomb of; Holy Sepulchre
Royal Navy, 7
Rustichello of Pisa, 213
Rutilius Namatianus, *De reditu suo*, 261

Sabbas, saint, 160
Sacra Parallela, 35, 41
Saewulf, 37
sailing capability, 37
— directions, 59n, 64, 65n, 68
— season, 27n
sailors, 10n, 47, 69, 70, 265
St. Anna, church of, 160
St. Catherine, monastery, 158, 160
St. Gall, 170
St. George of Mangana, church/monastery, 220
Saint Gervais, 123
St. John Stoudios in Petra, church of, 220
St. John Stoudios, church of, 220
— monastery of, 10
St. John the Baptist, church of, 241
St. John the Forerunner, monastery of, 160
St. John, church of, 241
St. Mark, relics of, 8n
St. Michael, monastery of, 170
SS. Peter and Paul, church of, 241
Saint Pierre le Vif, monastery, 173
St. Polyeuktos, church of, 12n
St. Sabbas, monastery, 155
St. Stephen, church of, 242
St. Stephen's gate (Damascus gate), 237
St. Symeon, harbour of, 157
St. Theodosios Koinobiarches, monastery, 160
Saint-Vincent, cape of, 61
St. Vincent, Lord, 34
saints' lives, 260, 263, 267, 272, 278, 280, 281
saldamarios, 118n

salt-pits, 113
Samareia, 157
Samarkand, 220
Samos, 46, 118, 261, 267, 279
Sampson, hospital, 182
Sancta sanctorum, 22
Santa Quaranta, 68
Santes Creus, monastery, 210
Santorini, *see* Thera
Sanudo, Marino, 69
Saracens, 214, 221
Saraçhane, 119
Saraylar, 132-134
Sarmatians, 94
Sarti, 88n
Saso (Sazan), island, **49**
Saul, *see* Paul
Sava, river, 80
Savoy, count of, 217
Sbeitla, *see* Sufetula
scala de Romania, 61
Scampae, 26n
Scalambri, cape, **50**
scholia, 92n
scola Greca, 168
seals, 11, 144, 166n, 175n
— lead seals, 12, 17, 28, 144
seasickness, 278
Sebastopol, 69
Selimiye (Bozburun) Wreck, 131
Selymbria, 78, 85
Sens, 173
Serbia, court of, 83
Serbs, 218
— invasion of, 82
Serçe Limanı, *see* shipwrecks
Serdica, *see* Sofia
Sergios (bishop), church of, 241
serpent column, 207
Serres, 88
Setvill, 71
Seven Apostles, church of, 200, 202, (actually Holy Apostles, church of)
Sheep Pool, gate of, 237
ship movements, African, 9n
— Italian 9n
shipping notices, 51
shipping route(s), 13, 158n
ships, *see also chelandia, dromons, galeai*
— merchant ship (merchant mariner), 11, 137, 147, 271

— sailing ships, 33, 38
— warship, 9n
shipwreck(s), 13, 28, 119-121, 123, 125, 129, 141, 259, 269, 270, 271, 280, *see also* Glass Wreck
— Çamaltı Burnu I, 131
— Serçe Limanı, 13, 35, 124, 131, 132, 137, 138, 141, 143n, 144
— Tekmezar (I), 129, 131
— Yassı Ada (I), 34, 35, 37, 120n, 123, 129, 131
Sibyl, prophesies of, 203
Sicily, 11, **24**, **50**
— kingdom of, 42
sightseeing, 159, 179
Silivri, *see* Selymbria
silva Bulgariae, 81
silversmiths, 206
Simonis, daughter of Andronikos II, 83
Sinai, 22, 158, 160, 265
Sinope, 69
Sion gate, 237, 238n,
Sion, monastery, 104
Skopje, 83, 84, 88
skortzidia, 119
skyllein, 9
Skyths (Mongols), 84
Slavonic, 150
Slavs, 25, 74
snakes, 9
Sofia (Serdica), 74, 79, 81
Solomon, 187
Sophronios, 261
Souda, 94n
Sounion, cape, 61
Spain, 171
spatharocandidatus, 78
spina, 181, 207
Spiritual Meadow, *see Pratum Spirituale; Leimonarion;* John Moschos
Sporades, 46, 123, 124
Stadiasmos of the Great Sea, 64, *see also periploi*
stadiodromikon, 63n
Stagira, 216
Stamiris (Myra), 69
Stara Zagora, *see* Beroe
Stephen of Byzantium, 161
Stephen of Novgorod, 195
Stephen Skylitzes, 260

INDEX

Stigand of Mézidon, 175, *see also* Odo, son of Stigand; Robert, son of Stigand
stoicheiosis, 207
Strabo, 73n, 127
Straliz, *see* Sofia
strategos/strategoi, 57, 58
— of Thessalonike, 78
Strobilos, 37
Stroumitsa, 84, 88
Strymon 77, 78, 84, 86, 88, 89
Stylianos Mappa, archbishop of Neocaesarea, 185
Suez, 160
Sufetula (Sbeitla), 105, 106
supplies, 38, 70, 81
— food, 79, 83, 114, 120
— water, 37, 38, 52, 55, 57, 112n
Sydney, 34
Sykeon, 105
Symeon, anchorite/hermit, 51, 267
Symeon, tsar, 79
Symi, 138
Synada, 24
Synesios, 273, 276, 281
syntaktikon, 260, 274, 275, 281
Syracuse, 34, 269
Syria, 13n, 69, 100, 103,119, 140, 141, 144, 149, 150, 153, 155, 157, 159, 183, 222, 236, 269,
Syriac, 165
Syrianos Magistros, 57, 58n
Syros, island, 10n

Tabula imperii byzantini, 4
tagmatophylax, 175n
Taktika, 40n, 43, *see also* Leo VI
Tale of Troy, 271
Tamburlane, 219, 220
Taormina, 13n
Tarragon, 210
Tarsus, 247
Tauros, 183, 206, *see also* Forum Tauri; Theodosius, column of
Taygetus, 230
Tekirdağ, 85, 125, 128, 129, *see also* Rhaidestos
Tel Anafa, 17n
Tel Dan, 17n
Tenedos, 46, 117

terra sancta, 151, 153, 154, 156, 158, 159, *see also* Holy Land
Tetrapylon (in Alexandria), 265
Tetrapylon, 183, *see also* the Gate of the Golden Mantle
thalamepoulos, 175n
Thasos, 17
Thauatha, 240
Theodora, empress, wife of Theophilos, 46
Theagenes, 270
Theodore Abu Qurrah, 244
Theodore Metochites, 83, 87, *Presbeutikos*, 83
Theodore of Sykeon, saint, 154, 156
Theodore Stoudites, 6, 7, 9, 11
Theodore, anchorite and eunuch, 266
Theodore, anchorite, 38
Theodoros II Laskaris, emperor, 118n
Theodoros Prodromos, 260, 270
Theodosian Code, 91n
Theodosius I, emperor, column of, 182, 183, 228, *see also* Egyptian obelisk
Theodosius II, emperor, 153
Theodosios Zygomalas, 156
Theodosios, archdeacon, 155
Theodosios, *spatharios*, 79
Theoktiste, saint, 267, 268, *see also Life* of,
Theomnestos, 92, 95, 97
Theophanes the Confessor, 25, 33n, *Chronographia*, 48, 50
Theophano, empress, 170
Theophylact of Ochrid 274, 276, 281
Theophylaktos Simokattes, 33, 34
Theotokos Salem, 269n
Theotokos, 154, *see also* Virgin Mary
Theotokos, house of the, 160
Thera (Santorini), 51, 61
Theron, pirate, 269
Thessalonike, 4, 6, 24, 36, 37, 73n, 74, 76-78, 82, 83, 84, 88, 89,114, 209, 210, 274
Thessaly, 152n
Thrace, 20, 73, 77, 78, 81, 82, 84, 90, 112, 118, 119
Tiberias, 159
Tiberius, emperor, 34
Titanic, 259n
Topağaç, 132, 133, 134
tourists, 166
Tower of Babel, 165
Trabzon, 125, *see also* Trebizond

trachanas, 112
trade, 6, 12, 113, 133
— stock-in-trade, 265
— wine trade, 14
— maritime, 109, 147
trademarks, 14
Tralles, 104
transport, 3, 4, 12, 16, 18
travel
— dangers of, 247, 280
— descriptions of, 10
— genres, 259, 260, 262
— images of, 9, 235, 245-247, 249
— intermediate, 5
— land/overland, 4, 28, 278
— long-distance, 5, 26
— maritime/sea, 4n, 25/26, 76, 122n, 147, 247, 259, 278
— mixed, 4n
— narrative(s) of, 214, 220, 245
— ritual of, 267
travellers, 7, 10, 13, 25, 26, 70, 71, 74, 78, 85, 94, 125, 150, 153, 155-158, 160, 161, 165, 167, 172, 173, 177-179, 196, 223, 226, 232, 235
— antiquarian, 226
— Byzantine, 23, 24, 161
— eastern, 24
— Greek, 155, 156
— merchant, 6
— Russian, 202n
— secular, 158
— western, 62, 179, 184, 188, 191, 193n, 194n, 210, 213, 223, 225,
Travels of the Infante Pedro, 214
Trebizond, 69, 260, 282, *see also*, Trabzon
trireme (triereis), *see dromon(s)*
Tripolis, 159
Trojan War, 272
Troy, **49**, 129
Tunisia, **50**
Turkey, 68, 142n
Turkish, 179
Turks, 85, 187, 214, 219, 222-225, 231, 262
— invasion of, 82
Tyre, 157, 269, 270
tyrine, 111
Tzazon, **50**

Umm al Rasas, 241, 243, 244, *see also* Sergios, bishop, church of; Church of the Lions; Church of the priest Wa'il
Union of Churches, 216, 221, 222, 226
urban topography, 242
Urban V, pope, 217
Uroš II Milutin, king, 83
Utrecht, 18
Uzbak, 187

Valerius Marianus (Marinus), senator, 34
Vardar, *see* Axios
Varennes, Aimon de, 175-177
Varna, 118, 142n
Varos, Bishop, 104
Vatican register, 62 216
Venetians, 6n, 18n, 209, 211, 222, 262
Veneto, the, 11
Venice, 6, 8, 11, 64, 67n, 70, 76, 140, 156, 172n, 228, 262,
Vergil, 41
Veronica's Cloth, 209n
veterinary handbooks, 92
Via Egnatia, 4, 25-27, 73, 74, 76, 78, 79, 82-85, 88, 90,
via militaris, 74n, 82, *see also* military road; 'Heerstrasse'
via regia, 87
Vienna Genesis, 246, 247, 249
Villehardoin, Geoffrey de, 110, 193, 195, 197-199, 203-205, 208n, 210, 211
Virgin Mary, 201, *see also* Theotokos
— image of, 200, 209
— miracles of, 210
Vize, *see* Bizye
Vlachs, 218

Walther, Paul, 70
al-Wardi, 179
WHO, 116
Widukind, 19n
William of Tyre, 193, 208
William of Tyre, Continuator of, 199n
Wolfger of Prufening, 170, 171

xeniteia, 267
Xantheia (Xanthi), 84n
xenodochium, 170
Xenophon, **48**, 269
Xenophontos, monastery, 89
Xerolophos, 204
xerophagia, 111

xylophorikon/xylophoron hodos, 86

Yaqut, 179
Yassıada, *see* Yassı Ada
Yassı Ada, *see* shipwrecks

Yersinia pestis, 21
York, 65
Zakynthos, 270
Zora, 104
zygophlaskia, 118